D0900341

# THE TALIBAN AT WAR, 2001-2018

ANTONIO GIUSTOZZI

# The Taliban at War

## *2001–2018*

# OXFORD

UNIVERSITY PRESS

Oxford University Press is a department of the
University of Oxford. It furthers the University's objective
of excellence in research, scholarship, and education
by publishing worldwide.

Oxford New York

Auckland    Cape Town    Dar es Salaam    Hong Kong    Karachi
Kuala Lumpur    Madrid    Melbourne    Mexico City    Nairobi
New Delhi    Shanghai    Taipei    Toronto

With offices in

Argentina    Austria    Brazil    Chile    Czech Republic    France    Greece
Guatemala    Hungary    Italy    Japan    Poland    Portugal    Singapore
South Korea    Switzerland    Thailand    Turkey    Ukraine    Vietnam

Oxford is a registered trade mark of Oxford University Press
in the UK and certain other countries.

Published in the United States of America by
Oxford University Press
198 Madison Avenue, New York, NY 10016

Library of Congress Cataloging-in-Publication Data is available

ISBN: 9780190092399

Printed in India

# CONTENTS

# ACKNOWLEDGEMENTS

This book is the result of a research project carried out with King's College London (KCL) and funded by the Economic and Social Sciences Research Council (or ESRC, with the project entitled 'The Taliban's War: The Other Side of the Afghan Conflict, 2001–2015', ESRC Grant ES/L008041/1). Thanks to the ESRC's support, it was possible to carry out extensive fieldwork. The project was carried out with the support of Professor Theo Farrell, then Head of the War Studies Department at KCL (he has since moved on), whose help was invaluable in preparing the proposal to the ESRC and who then steered the research effort towards its timely and successful completion. Professor Farrell also contributed to the processing of the interview transcripts, played a key role in quality control and enforced ethical and safety standards. Finally, he commented extensively on the first version of the manuscript.

The book has also benefited from work completed for related projects, covering specific aspects of the Taliban's activities and organisation. This includes another project carried out with Professor Farrell on the Taliban in Helmand, which provided the model for this book, and important work carried out with Claudio Franco in 2011–14 on the Taliban's Peshawar Shura.

The author thanks all those involved, especially the Afghan researchers, who for safety reasons will remain unnamed, as well as all those in KCL's administration who supported the research effort. Many thanks also to all who commented on the text, in particular Professor Thomas H. Johnson at the Naval Postgraduate School and other anonymous reviewers. The author also wishes to thank Michael Dwyer and everybody else at Hurst Publishers.

# ACKNOWLEDGEMENTS

The author furthermore thanks all those who contributed to the development of his ideas and views on the subject in countless meetings, workshops and conferences. They are far too numerous to be individually mentioned here.

Naturally, the author assumes all responsibility for the analysis contained in this text, and any errors remain his own.

# INTRODUCTION

The Taliban Emirate, established in 1996, was in 2001 overthrown relatively easily by a coalition of US forces and various Afghan anti-Taliban groups. Few at the end of 2001 expected to hear again from the Taliban, except in the annals of history. Even as signs emerged in 2003 of a Taliban comeback, in the shape of an insurgency against the post-2001 Afghan government and its international sponsors, many did not take it seriously. It was hard to imagine that the Taliban would be able to mount a resilient challenge to a large-scale commitment of forces by the US and its allies.

## How the Taliban re-emerged

> It's not easy being in the Taliban. It's like wearing a jacket of fire. You have to leave your family and live with the knowledge that you can be killed at any time. The Americans can capture you and put you in dog cages in Bagram and Guantánamo. You can't expect any quick medical treatment if you're wounded. You don't have any money. Yet when I tell new recruits what they are facing they still freely put on this jacket of fire. All this builds my confidence that we will never lose this war.[1]

During 2009–13 the Taliban stood against a much larger force, with the US contribution to the coalition amounting at one point to over 100,000 men. With US funds, the Afghan security forces increased to over 300,000 men by 2014, and US allies contributed tens of thousands of additional combat troops. The Taliban's enemies, particularly the Americans, had immense superiority in terms of technology and firepower; airpower in particular inflicted heavy

1

casualties on the Taliban. The Taliban mostly relied upon military technology from the 1950s, and had little or no anti-aircraft defences except heavy machine guns. During 2002–14 Taliban combat groups often took casualties averaging between 10–20 per cent yearly. By 2014, few of those who had entered the insurgency in the early years were still alive to tell the tale. Almost all still in the ranks, particularly in the elite mobile units, would have seen many of their comrades in arms blown to pieces. Whatever one might think of the Taliban and their cause, their resilience should not be in doubt.[2]

As coalition combat forces mostly withdrew in 2014, though the Taliban could not claim to have yet won the war, they had achieved a lot by not losing it. As of 2019 the war continues, but the survival and growth of the Taliban during 2002–13 (after which they could profit from the reduction of coalition troop levels) is a question deserving an explanation, which this book seeks to provide.

The Taliban claim that their moral righteousness, in serving the cause of Islam, has allowed them to surmount all these challenges. Though high morale has undoubtedly been a factor, this book investigates other explanations as well. It looks at the way the Taliban organised militarily and how that organisation evolved. It looks at how and whom the Taliban recruited. It looks at their tactics, including the innovation and adaptation that took place and how that was managed by the leadership.

This is not, however, a book of pure military history. It is also a political history of this group, and in particular of how they transformed organisationally. As will become clear, for the Taliban (perhaps even more than for most other organisations) organisational adaptation was a painful process, with major political implications. The group's different components viewed organisational adaptation through different lenses, depending on the particular set of interests they were defending. The outcome of this organisational adaptation, in other words, cannot be simply explained as a reactive adaptation to external challenges. It was a deeply political debate that shaped the the peculiars of how the Taliban adapted, making it sub-optimal from a purely military-technocratic point of view. In this sense the point of departure is that adopted by Weinstein in his *Inside Rebellion*,[3] where he argues that the environment faced by insurgents shapes their violence, though this work expands the argument to include the Taliban's internal debates as a key component of the story.

This volume has benefited from a body of published literature. The relationship with Al-Qaida, the Taliban's most important external link, is dealt with in an extensive study by Alex Strick van Linschoten and Felix Kuehn.[4] Anand Gopal's work on the Taliban in the south of Afghanistan also proved very useful, although most of it was still unpublished at the time of writing.[5] Van Linschoten and Gopal also co-authored a very useful study of the Taliban's ideological evolution.[6] Mike Martin produced a detailed study of Helmand, which includes a wealth of material on the Taliban's local politics.[7] Some aspects of the Taliban's politics are discussed at length in Thomas Ruttig's Afghanistan Analysts Network (AAN) reports.[8] The Taliban's code of conduct has been the subject of much interest, with a full volume dedicated to it in addition to several articles.[9] Among the Taliban's various components, the Haqqani network is the only one to have attracted significant separate attention.[10]

This work has also relied upon existing discussions of external support for the Taliban, though these are few; the most detailed treatment remains Matt Waldman's 2010 article.[11] While researching the Taliban's finances, Gretchen Peters's work on the groups relationship with the narcotics trade and David Mansfield's work on opium taxation provided useful support.[12]

Accounts of western military engagements with the Taliban proved useful in understanding the group's operations, the foremost example being Theo Farrell's *Unwinnable*.[13] Some memoirs and discussions of personal experiences in Afghanistan helped to provide background for this study, in particular Carter Malkasian's *War Comes to Garmser*.[14] Reports by journalists in the field also provided very useful material, first and foremost Sean Rayment's *Bomb Hunters*.[15] The author has previously published work on the Taliban's military adaptation, and this book can be regarded a distant offspring of these earlier writings.[16] The author has also produced or co-produced studies of the Taliban in Helmand and in the north, as well as of the Taliban's Peshawar Shura, of the Taliban's organisational character and of their intelligence operations.[17]

## Why focus on the military organisation?

The extreme complexity of the Taliban's organisational apparatus is the reason for the focus on a sole field of activity, arguably the most important for an insurgency: the military. Inevitably it was not possible, and it would have been misleading, to completely insulate the military aspect from the surrounding politics, and from other organisational aspects such as finance. The focus, however, is primarily on the military and its adaptation. Despite this limiting of this study's scope, one should not forget that the Taliban invested considerable human and financial resources in non-military activities, most notably their judiciary, but also in education, propaganda and various governance activities. Occasional refence is made throughout the book to these, though space does not permit a detailed discussion.

## A polycentric organisation

Certainly in comparison with the most well-studied insurgent movements, the Taliban are peculiar insofar as they have been markedly polycentric in their organisation, particularly after their transformation into an insurgency in 2002.[18] It is important to point out that the Taliban's polycentrism was a largely internal development, differing from polycentric insurgencies that fragmented into multiple rival organisations and parties. The Taliban developed their internal polycentrism in part at least because of the way the insurgency progressed: separate groups of Taliban joined together initially for self-defence purposes, or under the leadership of a local charismatic mullah, and then were gradually pulled into regional or national organisational structures. Because scholars of insurgencies have long focused on those influenced by Leninism and Maoism, this organisational strategy has puzzled many observers, not least in Western militaries. Movements organised in a polycentric and horizontal fashion, like the Taliban, are particularly difficult to analyse, not only as a result of the scholarship's tendency to look for evidence of centralisation, but also because the lack of centralised organisation inevitably forces the analyst to explore the movement at the granular level, and understand each component on its own terms. This is arduous and time consuming, and also further complicates the task of explaining the Taliban's evolving organisational methods to the reader.

This polycentric character also has implications for any analysis of the conflict. Within and outside the Taliban, debate continues as to whether such a structure is an advantage or a liability. Has the polycentrism of the Taliban strengthened their resilience? It could be argued that compared to a centralised, single chain of command insurgencies, the multiple, disparate chains of command of the multiple centres of power rendered it impossible, or at least more difficult, for NATO forces to gain the upper hand through targeting the insurgents' leadership. Killing one 'key' leader would only disable a comparatively small segment of the Taliban's fighting force: the particular network built around that leader. Tens of other networks would continue operating unaffected.

It can also be argued that the polycentrism of the Taliban, while perhaps useful when fighting the 'war of the flea' (in Robert Taber's words) against forces equipped with immensely superior firepower and technology, became a liability when the Taliban had to come up with a coherent strategy for assuming power and capitalising on their successful resistance effort. The book explores both arguments in detail.

## What the Taliban set out to defend: The old social order

The way in which the Taliban emerged and in particular the way they set up their insurgent organisation was in part the result of a force of circumstance (the American-led campaign to topple their government, which scattered their forces around Afghanistan and Pakistan), and in part a consequence of their worldview. In a sense the original Taliban insurgents can be described as eponymous 'anti-Leninists': they rejected the idea of centralisation of power and authority as an evil import from the West or from the (Marxist-Leninist) East. Contrary to their Muslim Brotherhood rivals, the Taliban did not originally try to selectively co-opt Leninist concepts, even in a disguised form. While Brotherhood parties were often as centralised as the leftist groups they opposed, the Taliban were genuinely polycentric at all levels.

While the former hoped to 'Islamise' modernity, the original Taliban sought to reject modernity itself. The roots of the Taliban were in the conservative clerical opposition to the modernising Afghan state, from the 1920s onwards.[19] The social order they defended featured decentralisation and a small state apparatus primarily tasked with defending against external threats and guaranteeing a social order centered around customs and religion. State education, sciences, Western languages and ideas were rejected altogether in favour of 'traditionalist' Islam.[20] As this book will discuss, this rigidly conservative-traditionalist approach did not prove conducive to developing effective martial skills. Modern science, and hence modern education, has something useful to teach insurgents who want to use mortars, employ advanced communications equipment, or manufacture mines. Computing technology is invaluable for organisational purposes, helping to store files and records much more efficiently. Centralised organisation and tight chains of command are relevant to the task of organising coordinated offensives with the aim of taking power. As such, the Taliban, initially without even realising it, started mutating into something different, bearing a greater resemblence to their rivals of the Muslim Brotherhood. This mutation affected multiple arenas of activity, but this volume focuses on the military aspect in particular.

## A movement more than a party, but gradually institutionalising

The Taliban insurgents were originally more of a movement than a 'party' in any meaningful sense. Even when faced with the need to develop a more sophisticated and hierarchical organisation to more effectively fight the war, they opted to set up a decentralised shadow state structure, rather than a hierarchically organised party. The movement maintained its horizontal, decentralised structures and in fact continued developing and expanding them according to the same model. By creating shadow state structures, in a sense the Taliban were (among other concerns) also trying to preserve their ideological purity.

However, even long before the withdrawal of the bulk of foreign troops in 2014, many among the Taliban realised that a polycentric military strategy would not deliver their war aims. A series of debates began on how to increase their ability to shift the military effort between different regions of Afghanistan, while concentrating forces tactically when required. Ideas for reform clashed with conservative attitudes, leading to confrontations that sometimes became violent. Partially successful reforms led to an increasingly complicated system, where the old military organisation of the Taliban survived alongside more centralised systems. This book traces these reforms and counter-reforms, the debates, the implementation and the impact on the Taliban's combat effectiveness.

## The role of external support

A particularly controversial aspect of any attempt to study the Taliban is locating their external sources of support. The Afghan government has always accused the Pakistani authorities of having provided safe haven and financial and logistical support to the Taliban, but one of the key discoveries of the research conducted for this book was that the level of external support to the Taliban throughout the years, and particularly from 2008 onwards, has been grossly underestimated. Pakistan was far from alone in supporting the Taliban, according to Taliban sources and outsiders.[21] In interviews, Taliban members, intelligence operatives, and diplomatic and military sources confirmed that support, or part thereof, also accrued in large quantities from the Arab Gulf countries and Iran for several years. Evidence for the alleged support provided by some other countries is scanter, but the overall picture as portrayed by Taliban sources (quite contrary to their own interests) is that of a movement increasingly dependent on external support, with internal sources of revenue playing an ever more marginal role. This in a sense should not be surprising as it mirrors the fate of the post-2001 Afghan government, largely reliant on external handouts and consuming resources at a rate far exceeding what could be paid for through state coffers. Financial dependency tends to result in control exercised by donors, a theme that will emerge frequently throughout this study.

Inevitably, reliance on external support had multiple effects on the Taliban. This volume deals only with the impact on their military. Here three different types of external support (financial, logistical and advisory) have all been important and certainly contributed decisively to shaping the evolution of the Taliban's armed wing. This is not, however, to say that the Taliban were simply a product of this external support. In fact, the Taliban's military organisation has always been quite peculiar and convoluted, in all likelihood because of contrasting external and internal pressures.

## Tomorrow's model insurgency?

As Western militaries were leaving Afghanistan in 2014, their commanding officers breathed a sigh of relief: that very peculiar military environment was no longer their concern. Whatever lessons might have been learned and whatever adaptation these militaries had to go through during their thirteen years in Afghanistan could be finally dispensed with, or so they assumed. However, although the Afghan military environment is indeed peculiar, the conclusion that little of long-term value could be gleaned from the experience of fighting in Afghanistan is mistaken.

'Polycentric' is not to be confused with 'fragmented'. There is little in common between the anti-colonial resistance met by European armies in much of Africa and Asia in the seventeenth and eighteenth centuries, and the Taliban's polycentrism. The Taliban were the first polycentric insurgency that Western militaries encountered, but they are unlikely to be the last. Much will depend on decisions made at the political level, but similar insurgencies are already active at the time of writing in places such as Syria and Pakistan.

Polycentrism implies multiple chains of command, where fragmentation implies competing chains of command. Decentralisation in turn implies a weakness in this command structure, where centralisation demands a single, strong chain of command. Among insurgents of various leanings the debate over each philosophy's relative merits continues. It certainly cannot be asserted that decentralisers and polycentrists have won the debate: the Islamic State embodies an extreme version of centralised insurgency. But decentralisers and polycentrists have something to sell: their modus operandi is more resilient in the face of counter-insurgency efforts driven by modern technologies. Maintaining a centralised command and control structure in the face of drones, signal intelligence and guided bombs tends to result in a very high casualty rate at the top of the centralised structure, something which many insurgent leaderships wish to avoid.

Although the Taliban might not have developed their structure simply because of their superior wisdom, they have become an example and a source of inspiration for other insurgents, many of whom fought alongside the Taliban after 2001 and had direct experience of the Afghan war.[22]

## Methodology

The majority of this research is based on oral sources, of which three types are specified in the references. The first (referred to as 'source'/'sources') are short conversations, mostly via telephone, in which a very limited number of questions were asked. A second type are the formal interviews, typically ranging between 20–30 questions and conducted specifically for the ESRC project, of which this book is the primary output. This second type is identified by the type of interviewee ('leadership', 'commander', 'cadre', etc.), followed by a number. The third type consist of interviews conducted for other projects, mostly but not exclusively before the ESRC project took place. These are identified by the same system as for the ESRC interviews, except that the number is preceded by the acronym 'OP'.

All interviews were carried out by two teams of researchers, each led by a research manager. The researchers were mostly Afghans, with a minority from Pakistan. The researchers had all taken part in previous projects and were therefore experienced with the demanding task of interviewing insurgents. Almost all researchers had a background in journalism and were originally chosen for their contacts and access. Because they had already extensive experience in interviewing members of the Taliban (including the Helmand pilot which preceded this project, see below) they did not need to be trained, but were briefed about the specific requirements of this project:

a. to inform the interviewees about the purpose and uses of the interview (producing a book about the history of the Taliban);
b. to categorise by interest area each interview or series of interviews;
c. to ensure anonymity of sources;
d. to take precautions to avoid any tracking by third parties;
e. to securely handle transcripts and original notes, and to destroy these after delivery.

During the briefings the author and two research managers reviewed potential interviewees based on the contacts they had available; after every wave of interviews a new briefing session was held to discuss achievements and problems, identify gaps in information and identify possible new interviewees on the basis of new contacts accrued during the research.

The interviewees were selected in order to secure a balanced output, covering all components of the Taliban's organisation, geographical areas of activity, ethnicities, tribes and ranks. The researchers followed a snowball sampling approach, using personal and kinship networks to gain access to interview subjects and to get recommendations for further interviews. The initial group of interviewees were approached through personal and kin channels, in order to increase the likelihood of their agreeing to be interviewed. These channels also helped ensure the safety of the interviewers. After the first wave of interviews, interviewees were used (where available) as new contacts to facilitate the next wave. Interviews were carried out only when safe locations for both interviewers and interviewees could be agreed.

Interviewees were told that the interviews were either feeding into a book (those carried out specifically for the ESRC project) or into 'articles' (those carried out for other projects). The interviews were always carried out in 'waves' in which a first wave of a few interviews was used to obtain details and names, which were then used to develop more precise questionnaires. By demonstrating in the interviews a high level of accumulated knowledge already, the interviewers became more adept at eliciting cooperation from interviewers, and thus obtaining more detailed answers.

The interviews were carried out in mutually convenient places in Afghanistan, Pakistan, Iran and occasionally the Arab Gulf. When safe locations could not be agreed, the interviews did not take place. The author took himself part in fifteen test interviews.

No ESRC interview was recorded, as interviews usually objected to this. The research team felt that while many might have been convinced to speak on record, they would not have been as candid. Instead notes were taken in the language of the interviews (usually Pashto or Dari), and then transcribed and translated by a dedicated member of the research team. Of course, this introduced a limitation in our study, in that the words and phrases in the transcripts are those mediated through the researchers' notes and the translator's words.[23]

This project adhered to principles of ethical field research.[24] Strict compliance with these protocols was ensured, including by informing interview subjects about the project and safeguarding their identities.[25] The author triangulated data from different interviews, and where possible different researchers, to improve the reliability of the findings.

The main ESRC project, 'The Taliban at War', was piloted in Helmand in 2011–12. The pilot sought to reconstruct and document the Taliban campaign in the province based on interviews with Taliban members and local elders. In all, fifty-three members were interviewed and fifty-eight elders. Some of the interviews were with small groups and some were conducted one-to-one. The research findings were reported in a paper co-authored with Theo Farrell and published in July 2013.[26] A major benefit from the Helmand study was the ability to interview senior Taliban figures for this project. This is significant because our Taliban interviewees in Helmand gave us a limited insight into the higher-level politics of the insurgency, such as details regarding power struggles between leaders in Quetta and Peshawar, and the differing perspectives of the political and military wings of the movement. Building on the success of the pilot project, the researchers were able to conduct over forty interviews with senior Taliban members in Pakistan, including members of the commissions and the Rahbari Shura, and leaders of various fronts.

Finally compared to Helmand the research team was able to add new categories of interviewees:

a. Former Taliban members, who could discuss particularly sensitive issues that active members might be reluctant to confront: abuses, arbitrary violence or power struggles;

b. External collaborators such as informal bankers and smugglers;

c. Foreign advisers providing training to the Taliban, including Iranian Revolutionary Guards, Pakistani officers and a single Saudi adviser.

The Helmand pilot was also a source of useful lessons for improving the output of the follow-up project, as well a test for field interviewers (as were other previous episodes of field research). One researcher's involvement was ended during the Helmand pilot project after it was found that he had been manipulating the transcripts. Compared to the Helmand interviews, the author also decided to constantly review and adapt questionnaires in order to maximise the ability of the research team to follow up on interviews and extract information from the sources. In contrast to Helmand, each wave was further subdivided into mini-waves, allowing the author to revise and adapt questionnaires every 2–3 interviews.

Table 1 lists the number of Taliban members interviewed specifically for the ESRC project in each of the four categories (former Taliban, Taliban fighters and commanders, Taliban cadre, and senior Taliban leaders), and the location of the interviewees. The identities of the senior leaders were largely known already, while the commanders were identified through known Taliban contacts, to make sure they represented different regions and different Taliban constituencies. A commander is defined here as in command of a group (25–30 men) or a team (10 men); the large majority of those interviewed were commanders of groups. The project team also interviewed 8 non-Taliban smugglers and advisers based in Pakistan, 6 women activists based in Kabul, and 79 local elders from 10 provinces. Table 2 lists another 191 interviews utilised for this book, but carried out for other projects, including the Helmand pilot study. Among the interviewees were 14 Taliban leaders and 88 cadres.

Since the late 2000s, Afghans in rural communities have been repeatedly interviewed by civilian aid advisors, Western military patrols, and Afghan researchers working for ISAF, typically to ascertain their views on all manner of things related to the stability and security of their locality. Thus, they were very familiar with the practice at the time the field research was conducted. More puzzling, perhaps, is the many Taliban members who agreed to be interviewed. Some of these clearly saw an opportunity through the interviews to spread propaganda. Thus, a member of the Taliban provincial council for Helmand presented a misleading picture of the Taliban being in complete control of Garmser district: he claimed that Taliban governors 'inquire about the problems of every resident', and that armed Taliban 'roam freely and openly'; he asserted that government soldiers were convinced that 'bothering Taliban is tantamount to knocking at death's door.'[27] Such bluster was fairly common in the project interviews, as was a general narrative of Taliban popularity; all Taliban interviewees reported that the Taliban in their area had the support of the common people. However, many interviewees were also remarkably open. For example, a fighter from Ghazni admitted to the limitations of Taliban combat medicine: 'we don't have fixed clinics, we have mobile doctors, and most of the time we send our wounded fighters to Pakistan for treatment.'[28] More noteworthy is the fact that, as will be obvious throughout the book, interviewees often expressed sharp criticism of the Taliban, and provided ample detail about internal divisions and struggles.

Although oral sources should always be treated with caution, much of the content of the interviews was therefore far from mere propaganda. In addition, the interviews reveal the perspectives of those who were interviewed – Taliban cadres, commanders, fighters, activists, local elders, women activists, and so forth. The interview transcripts help understanding how these individuals experienced, remembered and viewed the war. They also reveal the motives of those Afghans who joined the insurgency. Second, the interviews provide insight into the politics of the insurgency, both at the local level between rival warlords, communities and insurgent commanders, and at the senior level within the Taliban leadership. Third, the interview transcripts provide factual information about the conduct of the insurgency, including tactics and training, the organisation and command of fighting units, the use of foreign fighters, and the functioning of Taliban courts and the shadow government. In using the interview transcripts to reveal perspectives, politics and facts, the author has been sensitive to the background of the interviewee, including tribal and familial networks and life experience. For this reason, each interview started with the interviewee providing an oral autobiography (something which is in any case common in Afghan social interactions), to enable us to situate their subsequent answers. Thus informed, the author was also able to exercise due caution regarding our interpretations of the answers. By interviewing so many in different places and at different times, with two different research teams, the project minimised the possibility of interviewees colluding to mislead.

One area requires caution nonetheless. It concerns the use of numbers by Taliban and local elders, including when discussing financial data. Simply put, our interviewees would often cite numbers that were wildly inaccurate. For example, one Taliban member told us that 'according to my estimates, there must be 4–5,000 Taliban' in Garmser district in 2012.[29] Such an estimate would suggest that there were tens of thousands of insurgents in Helmand alone, which was obviously not the case. Western officers would sometimes dismissively refer to 'Afghan maths', meaning that when an Afghan local elder referred to numbers, be they numbers of Taliban attackers or numbers of civilians killed and injured in western operations, these should be divided by ten. The assumption, not wholly unreasonable, was that locals would exaggerate for political purposes when needed. However, there is also a cultural dimension at play. Social life is regimented in the West by precise measures of time, distance, and volume, and those brought up in such an environment are trained from a young age to think fairly precisely in numerical terms. But for rural communities in many less developed parts of the world, including Afghanistan, where education is more rudimentary and many are illiterate, units of measurement are less precise. Most people don't have watches and so time is measured by the sun. Distance is measured by fields and valleys. Agricultural produce provides the natural measures of volume. With the exception of commercial transactions, rural Afghans have little need to count in large numbers. Thus, many of our interviewees were not in the habit of numerical thinking and this is reflected in how they used figures, often not to provide a precise estimate of size but to convey the impression of scale. Thus, for example, if a Taliban commander tells us that there are 400 foreign fighters in his district, what we could infer from this statement is that there is a large number.

There are two exceptions to this treatment of numbers. Where the numbers are small and concern those in the interviewees' immediate fighting group (or family for a civilian interviewee) who have been killed or injured, the author tended to take them at face value. For example, 28 of the Taliban members interviewed in Helmand in 2012–13 were prepared to disclose the size of their respective fighting groups and how many of their fighters had been martyred over the previous year. Fighting groups typically numbered between 20 and 40, and the numbers killed as reported by interviewees varied from 2 to 17. Of course, the author remains alert to interviewees who would have intentionally sought to mislead. In the case above, the variance in fighters killed across districts in Helmand, as claimed by the interviewees, was consistent with where ISAF focused operations in the province in 2010.

The other exception was when numbers where provided by qualified Taliban cadres serving in the relevant structure (such as a military commission or logistics), and the numbers were confirmed by at least one additional source. So in the case of overall membership numbers we found that the figures provided in interviews were quite close to estimates by the Taliban's security services (NDS), to which the author had access, and therefore these figures were treated as substantially reliable (having allowed for the inevitable 'fog of war' which makes it difficult for any organisation to collect accurate statistics). The case of Taliban funding data presents further difficulties for the researcher – abundant data was provided, but collectively leads to funding estimates well over the dominant assessment by other analysts. The author has decided to use most of this data for three main reasons. The first is that if we accept Taliban/NDS numbers, then even a rough calculation of what it would cost to run the structure leads to numbers much higher than usual estimates. The second reason is that estimates by other organisations, such as the UN, roughly match those provided by the sources in matters of Taliban tax revenue. The UN does not discuss the Taliban's foreign funding in detail, particularly that from state actors, for understandable reasons. The third reason is that some of the intelligence and military analysts the author came in contact with while researching this book privately agreed that official figures of around $500 million/year in 2014–16 appeared far too low.[30]

## Some terminology

As the reader will see, the Taliban have developed their own peculiar terminology (in part inspired by the 1980s jihad against the Soviet Union) to signify concepts specific to the organisation. The term *shura* (council) is used for all kinds of representative structures, including at the top level (these being the repositories of political authority, at least in theory), but also confusingly at the regional, local, provincial and district level. The terms *komisiun* (commission) and *daftar* (office) are instead used for executive organs; the *komisiun* ranks higher than the *daftar*. In the military structure common terms include *mahaz* (front), *loy mahaz* (large front), *grup* (group) and *dilghay* (team). The *mahaz*es were organised on a local basis and could rely upon a few hundred members, while the *loy mahaz*es needed to be 'licensed' by the top level shuras and would normally have thousands of members. The groups were the original basic combat unit, roughly equivalent to a platoon. Later the *dilghay* was introduced, similar to the group except in name – the difference was that the *dilghay*s were under a different chain of command (the Military Commission's, as will be explained). The term *wali* (governor) is translated throughout the book as it is the exact equivalent of the term used by the Afghan government. Vice versa, the term *nizami massul* (pl. *massuleen*) is not translated throughout the text, because the subtle implications it carries are difficult to convey through a literal translation ('military representative').

## Outline

The book is organised into seven chapters and a conclusion. The first chapter discusses the collapse of the Taliban's Emirate in 2001, its impact on the group and the first (unsuccessful) efforts to re-organise into an insurgency in 2002–4.

The second chapter looks at the emergence of a serious Taliban insurgency under the leadership of the so-called Rahbari Shura in 2005–9. This was the golden era of the original Taliban, with the group in the ascendancy and full of confidence. This positive trend was broken by four main developments. One was the US surge in southern Afghanistan, which started seriously impacting the Taliban from 2010 onwards. Another was a crisis in the relationship between the Quetta Shura and its external sponsors, which negatively affected funding streams. The third was a growing crisis in the legitimacy of the Quetta Shura as the group's overall leadership, resulting in alternative and competing centres of power emerging. This process is mostly discussed in Chapter 3, focusing on the episodes concerning the Haqqanis and the Peshawar Shura. The fourth development was the emergence of dissent within the Quetta Shura itself, over strategy and organisation.

Chapter 4 discusses the crisis of the Quetta Shura, with particular reference to the effects of the 'surge' and internal dissent. The crisis prompted a major effort by the Taliban to adapt to changing circumstances, which is discussed in great detail in Chapters 5 and 6, respectively dedicated to tactical and organisational adaptation.

Chapter 7 completes the volume by discussing the comeback of the Quetta Shura, thanks to the weakening of most competing centres of power and resurgent interest from the Taliban's foreign sponsors. The comeback did not however lead to a full consolidation of the Quetta Shura's control over the rest of the Taliban.

The conclusion discusses the transformation of the Taliban during 2002–15 through different perspectives. As the Taliban professionalised, their original ethos came under question. Although their adaptation was in many regards successful, as Western intervention was withdrawing in 2014 there was still a clear sense that the Taliban had not fully matured into an insurgent organisation which could seize power.

# 1

## THE COLLAPSE OF THE EMIRATE AND THE EARLY REGROUPING, 2002–4

The incipient polycentrism of the Taliban insurgency was evident from its early days (2002–4), when the Taliban started parallel re-organising efforts in different locations. The strength of these efforts varied from mere tens of men to several thousand, and initially these operations were largely independent of each other, to the extent that the Taliban insurgency might well have become completely fragmented if no overall command system had been established. Several centres of Taliban re-mobilisation in fact never linked up to the others. Even when links began to be forged in earnest in 2003–4, the emerging Taliban leadership in Quetta was a coalition of commanders, each with his own personal following, who then mostly co-opted other lesser or local leaders, each bringing his own constituency and maintaining control over it.

### 1.1 Disarray 2001–2

The fall of the Taliban was swift and brutal. Following 11 September 2001, Taliban forces were obliterated in a lightning war prosecuted by American special forces and their Afghan allies, supported by an armada of warplanes. Mullah Cable, a Taliban commander renowned for his toughness, recalls what it was like to be under US bombardment early in the war: 'My teeth shook, my bones shook, everything inside me shook.' After witnessing his comrades being decimated by the bombing, Cable gathered the rest of his men and told them to go home, before himself deserting.[1] In total, the US Air Force and

17

Navy dropped 18,000 bombs in their air campaign, of which 10,000 were precision munitions. Nobody knows the exact numbers of Taliban killed but according one estimate between 8,000 and 12,000 perished.[2] By this count, up to 20 per cent of Taliban fighters had been eliminated by early 2002, the Taliban Emirate had ceased to exist as a physical entity, and its leader, Mullah Mohammed Omar, had fled to Pakistan.

Although there were claims in 2001–2 that the Taliban had staged a tactical retreat in the face of Operation Enduring Freedom and were waiting to strike back at the first opportunity, it is now clear beyond any doubt that the Taliban had indeed been completely routed by November 2001. Two members of the Taliban recalled their feelings at that time when interviewed by Pakistani journalist Sami Yousufzai:

> Realizing the danger, I immediately sent my wife and children to Pakistan. The entire government started to fall apart. I never thought the Taliban would collapse so quickly and cruelly under U.S. bombs. Everyone began trying to save themselves and their families. When the bombing began, I changed out of my usual white mullah's garb, put on an old brown shalwar kameez, and headed for Pakistan. I crossed the mountains on foot, and at the top I turned around and said: 'God bless you, Afghanistan. I'll never come back to you under our Islamic regime.'[3]
>
> When the bombing started, I was commanding some 400 fighters on the front lines near Mazar-e Sharif. The bombs cut down our men like a reaper harvesting wheat. Bodies were dismembered. Dazed fighters were bleeding from the ears and nose from the bombs' concussions. We couldn't bury the dead. Our reinforcements died in their trenches. I couldn't bring myself to surrender, so I retreated with a few of my men in the confusion. [...] Our Islamic Emirate had collapsed with less than 40 days of resistance—I couldn't accept that. Allah would let us rise again, I thought, because of all the blood we had spilled for Islam.[4]

The 'tactical retreat' narrative was propagated by the Taliban themselves, who in 2002 were issuing communiques from Mullah Omar announcing the imminent return of the Islamic Emirate. Many in the Afghan security forces endorsed this narrative ('the Taliban are lurking out there') in order to legitimise their own wars of revenge. The narrative was actually supported by some lingering fighting in 2002–3, involving Taliban remnants, while some violent incidents that took place throughout 2002 or early 2003 were also attributed to the Taliban, with little evidence. In reality the Taliban were dispersed and in complete disarray. Even in areas where there had been no fighting during the American-led onslaught on the Emirate, Taliban leaders fled to Pakistan after negotiations with local elders.[5]

It was midway through 2002 before they started reconnecting with each other in their Pakistani exile. One source, who would become one the Taliban's main leaders after 2002, explained:

> After the Taliban's defeat, we did not see each other till 2002. Some of our leaders when to Karachi, some went to Quetta and some went to Waziristan. In 2003 we started sending messages to each other and visiting each other. [...] From 2001 till 2002 I did not have any positions, I was talking with others about politics. We were separated, we were not together. We were writing to one another, we did not call because the situation was not good that time.[6]

The Taliban were considered a spent force even by their former patrons. Until 2003 the Pakistani security services at best ignored the Taliban, and in some cases even handed them over to the Americans, as in the case of Mullah Zaeef. According to one of the leaders:

> The main problem we were facing was that there were restrictions [imposed] on us by the Pakistanis. We were afraid at that time; we thought that if we got caught, we would be given to the Americans. Indeed, they arrested some at that time and handed them over to the Americans. We were not able to start the jihad against the Americans – if we organised any meeting and went out, we would be arrested.[7]

Living underground and dispersed around Pakistan made it very difficult for the Taliban to even start planning a comeback, let alone implement it. The leaders lacked any experience in working underground – even the jihad of the 1980s had not really been an 'underground' movement for those who had been involved. Re-mobilising old members and recruiting new volunteers was difficult in the absence of a visible, 'over-the-ground' presence. They needed safe meeting places for their leaders to meet, discuss, plan and manage, and these were lacking.

Most importantly, there were very few funding sources at this point, and no supplies were being delivered. The first fundraising efforts by the dispersed leadership in 2002 and early 2003 only managed to attract very modest amounts from some sympathetic Afghan businessmen and a few Arab donors. Efforts to raise Islamic taxes – Zakat and Ushr – also produced little. In addition, tribal elders were almost unanimously opposed to any notion of the Taliban starting a new war and denied them support and facilitation.[8]

The weak prospects of a Taliban resurgence reportedly pushed some of the leaders (or even all according to one source) to consider trying to join the political process in Kabul, meeting in November 2002 in Pakistan to discuss this possibility, with follow up meetings reportedly taking place until 2004. Opposition from within the movement and indifference in Kabul prevented this initiative from taking off.[9] One of the lessons the Taliban seem to have learnt from this experience is that negotiating from a position of weakness would lead nowhere. But how were they going to gather the strength they needed?

## 1.2 The Taliban regroup 2002–7: The local Taliban fronts

### Early activities in the south

From 2002 onwards, various Taliban groups deeper inside Afghanistan started low-scale underground operations, independently of any input from the leaders hiding in Pakistan. Usually these early insurgents organised themselves in groups and *mahazes* ('fronts', see 'The early military system' below and 'Some terminology' in the Introduction), gathering numbers between tens and a few hundred. The early Taliban insurgents in the south relied on local facilitators and sympathisers, mostly mullahs, to gather intelligence and recruit more supporters.[10]

> We would meet every week with the mullah. We would talk about the situation, especially about the government and the foreign forces. We had long discussions and the mullah would try to convince us to fight against these people.[11]

In Pakistan, a number of Taliban leaders would try to mobilise their personal contacts within the remnants of the movement, both in Pakistan and in Afghanistan.[12]

> In 2003-4 we were visiting and arranging some meetings but we were very fearful.[13]
>
> 'Gul Agha [a senior Taliban figure] called me one day,' recalled one former Taliban commander. 'He told me that this is the time to do jihad. He invited me to Quetta so that we could discuss our options.'[14]

Initially the response was muted and the ranks of the Taliban were thin. Mostly these first few underground groups were involved in propaganda and recruitment activities. Their initial activites were focused on re-organising, recruiting and securing funding and supplies. It was not without risk because provocateurs from the Afghan security services were also actively posing as recruiters and trying to enlist disgruntled Taliban. The most visible element of Taliban activities, by 2003 were the targeted assassinations, particularly against pro-government clerics, and the campaign of intimidation through night letters, urging people not to collaborate with the 'invaders'.[15]

> My father's former student returned as promised a week later. I decided to join him. I helped assassinate those people who had continued their contacts with the government and the Americans. I didn't want to kill, but I was determined to bring back our Islamic regime and get rid of the Americans and the traitors allied with them.[16]

The main hub of Taliban activities in Kandahar province was in the rugged and remote district of Shah Wali Kot.[17] In Kandahar and neighbouring Helmand province several Taliban networks operated from the beginning, organised around a number of prominent Taliban leaders. Mullah Faruq, for example, commanded one of the largest networks in the south and started his first operations against the Americans from Maruf District. During that time he was reportedly in command of 1,200 people in Kandahar province, including non-combatants.[18] In other parts of the south, different Taliban leaders were mobilising their own forces. According to a local elder in the Nahr-i Seraj district of Helmand:

> at the beginning when the Taliban came we didn't know to which 'party' or 'network' they belonged, because they would appear at the night threatening government staff. Then after two or three months when they appeared during the day and we saw them, we learned that they belonged to Akhtar Mansur.[19]

The local groups of Taliban often started coalescing together into 'fronts'; coalitions of groups under the leadership of some relatively senior Taliban figure, who would use his experience to teach them how to fight, mobilise some resources on the basis of his personal contacts, and perhaps link up with other groups of Taliban active in the region and beyond. These low-level activities started in various pockets throughout the south, including Ghazni province (which the Taliban consider to be part of the south). Before the arrival of the Quetta Shura, the jihad in Ghazni was led by three local commanders: Mullah Fulad, active in Qarabagh and Muqur, Commander Daud, active in Jaghatu, and Mawlavi Wassiq, active in Gilan and Nawa; each reportedly had 80–140 men.[20] In Ghazni the pattern was dissimilar to Helmand and Kandahar in one respect: the large Taliban networks already taking shape in the south (such as Faruq's and Mansur's mentioned above) in 2002–3 did not have any local equivalent.[21]

What local villagers at that time referred to as 'major Taliban operations' look today quite minor considering what happened afterwards. One of the first such 'major operations' in the south was the capture of Nishan village in Kandahar province. There was no government presence there, and the whole operation was focused upon interrogating the inhabitants to find government collaborators:

> I remember, I was going to my cousin's wedding. I was in market of a village named Nishan, and I realized that Taliban had taken the whole village. I have seen around 400 Taliban walking around. Taliban were checking the people if they were the government's employee or not. They caught some people in this way. Some of them were killed or taken by Taliban. On the night of the wedding, they took two people with them. After three days, we found the bodies of these two people. One was an old man and the other a young person.[22]

## Early activities in eastern Afghanistan

In the east, sporadic Taliban activity began as local initiatives of some Taliban commanders, groups of foreign jihadists often linked to Al-Qaida, and pro-Taliban networks in the FATA and NWFP. Nangarhar province was the first epicentre of Taliban activity within eastern Afghanistan. Three autonomous fronts inspired by the Taliban emirate, but initially not connected to the southern Taliban, sprang up in Nangarhar in 2002–3. The first to appear was the Spin Ghar Mahaz, a small front that operated in remote areas of the province (Dare-ye Noor, Momand Dara) and recruited Pashais, Sharis and Nuristanis in 2002–4; it had about 400 men organised into groups of 50. Other prominent leaders were relatively low rank Taliban officials like Qari Hamza, who had been a district head in Jalalabad city, and Mullah Agha Ahmadi, formerly a custom house official. Led by Mawlavi Bilal Sediq Shari, a former Emirate official (who had been the governor of Kamdesh district), the group was never well funded and was hampered by weak logistics. In 2004 it rallied to the Quetta Shura, merging with the forces of Mawlavi Kabir in 2005 after its leader, Bilal Sediq, was killed.[23]

The second autonomous front was known as the Ijraya Shura, formed in May 2002 by a group of former mid-rank Emirate officials, led by Qari Khalid and Ishaq Faryabi. Unlike to the previous two, this front was active not just in Nangarhar, but also in the other eastern provinces of Nuristan, Kunar and Laghman, with a claimed peak strength in 2005 of about 1,300 men (combatants and otherwise), as well as in Kapisa and some parts of the north (Faryab, Baghlan), with another 800–900 men. The Ijraya Shura also had a mobile *mahaz* based in Pakistan, with another 2,000 men on its books, of whom probably only a minority were mobilised at any given time.[24] The Ijraya Shura also differed from the other networks of the time in that it structured itself as a small party, rather than as the personal retinue of a charismatic warrior mullah. Understandably, notwithstanding its centralised character, it was initially perceived by the majority of the lower ranks as just another network: differently organised perhaps, but nothing more than an eastern *mahaz*.[25] In reality, as its name suggests, the Ijraya Shura had from its beginning the ambition of evolving into something more. It wanted to establish a more sophisticated command, control and logistical centre, but during 2002–4 the Shura did not have the resources necessary to set up such a structure.

The third autonomous front to appear was the Tora Bora Mahaz, which from 2003–4 mainly recruited Pashtuns in the Shinwari and Khogyani areas near the Pakistani border (Bati Kot, Achin, Dur Baba, Pachir wa Agam, Shirzad, Momand Dara, Chaparhar and Hissarak). Formed by the son of one of the *mujahidin* leaders of the 1980s, Yunis Khalis, Anwar ul Haq Mujahid, it included among its leadership the prominent commander Sajjad. Better funded than the Spin Ghar Mahaz, this front reportedly managed to mobilise 1,400–500 men.[26]

The absence of a major logistical hub in the region held back activities in the east, where until 2005 there was nothing comparable to the Quetta Shura, which could dispense money and supplies.[27] Taken together, the visible activities of these three fronts were modest in 2002–4, even compared to the south. Most Taliban attacks were cross-border raids from Pakistan. In Bati Kot district, for example, they could initially only carry out raids from Pakistan territory.[28] Only in the Khogyani districts (western Nangarhar) had the Taliban already infiltrated to a significant scale by 2004, establishing a pattern similar to that discussed above for the south.[29] Mullahs sympathetic to Taliban were asked to start preaching in favour of jihad and an assassination campaign started targeting elders deemed hostile to the group.[30]

Outside Nangarhar another major eastern hub of jihadist activity emerged in 2004 around Dost Mohammed in Nuristan and Kunar; mountainous areas where fighting a guerrilla campaign was comparatively easy.[31] Dost Mohammad was not a former Taliban member; he was in Bajaur teaching in a madrasa when the Taliban emirate collapsed in 2001. He only started his activities in Nuristan in 2004, with some support from the Quetta Shura and from Al-Qaida, linking up small groups through his chain of command and logistics structure.[32]

*Early activities around Kabul and the north-east*

The Kabul region resembled provinces like Ghazni, where early Taliban operations were heavily fragmented and even the big fronts almost absent, not to mention the *shuras*. One exception was the presence of the Ijraya Shura in Kapisa, as mentioned above.

In Wardak, local Taliban networks activated themselves in 2005, led by four commanders from the are who each led a front of 100–300 men:

- Mawlavi Zalmai, in Nerkh;
- Mullah Ghaus, in Chak;
- Mullah Nurullah, in Jalrez;
- Mullah Mustafa, in Sayedabad.[33]

These networks remained poorly supplied and resourced until they came in contact with the larger *shuras* from 2006 onwards.[34]

The situation was similar in Logar, where groups of local Taliban started activating in 2004–5, mostly in Baraki Barak, Kharwar and Charkh.[35]

The largest local front to emerge in the north-east was the Khalid bin Walid Mahaz (from the name of a madrasa), which operated in Baghlan from November 2003 until September 2007, when it dissolved into the Peshawar Shura following the killing of his founder and leader, Mawlavi Rahmatullah Baghlani. According to former members, the front had about 400 fighters in 2004, rising to about 900 at the time of its dissolution. This front was officially recognised by the Quetta Shura and incorporated into it in 2006 only, even if its activities had been encouraged by Quetta from the start; before that it supported itself through local taxation. In 2007, shortly before its dissolution, it transferred its loyalty to a new Shura rising in Peshawar (see further discussion in Chapter 3).[36]

*Drivers of re-mobilisation*

The large majority of Taliban interviewees ritually mentioned freeing the country from the control of the infidels as their main reason for joining the jihad. While expected, such claims should not be dismissed as mere propaganda.[37] Clearly, however, there were less subjective reasons for the Taliban's old members to remobilise.

Almost universally, interviewees indicated that crucial in allowing the leadership to re-establish itself at the head of an insurgent force was the arbitrary and abusive treatment of many former Taliban, as well as of others even very loosely linked to the Taliban regime. According to an elder in Daman, 'they had no choice'.[38] According to a commander from Shahid Hassas, 'You had to choose the Taliban or Afghan government'.[39] A senior source in the Gardi Jangal Shura claimed that during the first few months of the Karzai regime it was already becoming clear that the Americans were persecuting former Taliban and religious scholars and violating Pashtun customs.[40] In Helmand, for example, six months after the fall of the Taliban, a range of local strongmen linked to the coalition in power in Kabul consolidated their power. The situation soon started deteriorating. One former member of the original provisional district council of Nad Ali recounted:

> When the official police chief and district chief arrived... they had no experience of how to behave with the villagers, and so day by day the situation got worse... There was lots of extortion and stealing, and people were killed, and someone was even burned in their car by these government people, and day by day people got fed up with the government and welcomed the Taliban back into their districts.[41]

Soon there began the harassment and targeting of former Taliban, who were trying to stay in their villages away from trouble after the demoralising defeat of 2001. Many were then pushed into the insurgency as a result.[42] The government began to be perceived as corrupt and ineffective; the Taliban started sensing their opportunity:

> For two years the people waited and watched the government, and they realised it was a weak government, and not at all like what they had thought at the beginning. They realised they could defend themselves against it and started jihad.[43]

The cases of Helmand and Kandahar are particularly well studied,[44] but examples of this abound everywhere.[45] Abuses by the authorities and US units drove some villagers towards supporting the Taliban:

> At the end of 2002 the Afghan police raided our mosque. They grabbed my father and hauled him in front of the villagers, accusing him of being with the Taliban. They demanded to know where the Taliban's weapons were stored. They personally insulted him and then threw him in jail. He was 70. The faithful at our mosque went to the police and complained. People who a few months before seemed to have turned against my father now supported him. They said it was a disgrace for the police to have entered the mosque wearing their shoes, and to have arrested an old, crippled imam. In early 2003 he died. I was a just a kid, but the police arrested me too, twice – once from my house, once from the mosque. They interrogated me, asking stupid questions like: 'Where are the Taliban?' or

'Where are the weapons hidden?' My family sold our motorbike to raise the money to free me. The police also arrested my brother, who was a schoolteacher. The police even arrested, insulted, and manhandled a 90-year-old mullah in our district. People's attitudes were changing; they were becoming angry at the police and the local officials for the disrespect they were showing toward mosques and mullahs.[46]

At the same time former members of the Taliban were being harassed and driven towards taking up arms:

Once when I went to my aunt's home, the foreigners with a couple of Afghan soldiers arrived at my house in order to arrest me. As they didn't find me there, they persecuted my family, taking my wife's gold and one-hundred thousand rupees from my home. When I returned to my home, I found my family in tears, and my house ransacked. It made me very nervous, I didn't know where I should go, or to whom I should petition. There was no one. I decided to consult with the elders. They told me there was no one I could appeal to – there was no sense in petitioning because I would not receive any positive result. On that day, I decided to make jihad, to fight against the government and the foreigners till my death. If I were to die, it would be my duty as a man, if I stayed alive, I would keep fighting against them.[47]

Among those who were forced to flee to Pakistan was future Taliban leader Akhtar Mohammad Mansur, who in early 2002 was living in a village in Maywand, hoping to be forgotten.[48] When pushed, even a senior member of the reputedly 'hard-line jihadist' Haqqani network admit that harassment by government forces was a factor in re-mobilisation.[49]

Taliban veterans often have fond memories of those early days of the post-2001 insurgency, when they were fighting with little no foreign support:

At the beginning when we joined, they were doing good [...]. They were not closing the schools, they were trying not to kill Afghans, and they were targeting Americans. Simply, I want to say: the Taliban were not acting against the villagers – Taliban did not allow thieves, and fought the warlords. They kept the villagers happy.[50]

In reality it is questionable how much support the early Taliban insurgents could find. At this stage attempts by the Taliban to infiltrate Afghanistan were often unsuccessful, as in an episode in Garmser in 2004, when five Taliban fighters trying to infiltrate the district were easily flushed out.[51]

## 1.3 The first attempts to set up command and control systems

### The South: The short-lived Gardi Jangal Shura

The first attempt to bring some organisation to the disparate groups of Taliban fighting inside Afghanistan occurred as early as 2002 in the south of the country. A group of Taliban leaders and cadres set up camp in Gardi Jangal, a traditional smugglers' base near the Pakistan–Helmand border, where an Afghan refugee camp was also located. This group started organising in April 2002 and started operations on 4 May, becoming known among its members as the Gardi Jangal Shura. The main figures in Gardi Jangal were mid-level former officials of the Emirate, such as Mullah Mohammad Hussain (the Taliban's governor of Kandahar at the time of the American attack), Mullah Abdul Jalil Akhwandzada (former deputy minister of foreign affairs), and Mullah Ahmad Jan Akhundzada (who had been governor of Zabul and Uruzgan).[52]

The area of operations of the Gardi Jangal Shura was the four core southern provinces (Kandahar, Helmand, Zabul and Uruzgan). According to a Taliban cadre close to Mullah Hussain, it was in fact groups of fighters who had remained mobilised after the defeat that approached the leaders in Pakistan and asked for support. The leaders in turn contacted their colleagues and cadres who had also taken refuge in Pakistan, and asked them to get involved.[53]

The fighters affiliated with the Gardi Jangal Shura relied on weapons and ammunition stockpiles left over by the Emirate inside Afghanistan. The Shura sent a representative to each province, who was given authority over all the groups affiliated with Gardi Jangal. Typically these were experienced cadres who knew the local fighters and commanders. The basic military organisation of the Shura consisted of 23 groups of around 50 men each, for a total of 1,100–1,200 men, according to former members. The Gardi Jangal Shura never had the resources to establish any shadow governance apparatus, support structures, or an intelligence apparatus of any kind, nor did it ever pay salaries to its fighters. The command structure was very lean: the Shura, the provincial representatives and the commanders. The group commanders had to handle their own logistics, taking delivery of supplies in Pakistan and carrying them into Afghanistan, or buying what they needed themselves on the black market. While not uncommon in the Afghan insurgencies of the 1980s onwards, this dramatically reduced the time dedicated to actually waging war.[54]

The Gardi Jangal Shura was primarily self-funded through religious taxes, with some contributions by sympathetic 'businessmen' and smugglers; in total this did not amount to much and was only viable because weapons and ammunition stocks were available in Afghanistan. Some tribal *shura*s like the Ishaqzais Shura (mostly influential in Helmand) also lent some support.[55]

All the Gardi Jangal Shura sources contacted claimed that they were not receiving any support from Pakistan and were entering Pakistani territory clandestinely. Recruitment was only carried out inside Afghanistan and never in Pakistan, not even in madrasas.[56]

Still, despite its very limited resources the Gardi Jangal Shura was a step ahead of the fronts that conducted Taliban activities elsewhere at that time. It was in fact a network of fronts – the first manifestation of the 'network of networks' that became a Taliban trademark. The Gardi Jangal Shura never acquired much notoriety due to its relatively small-scale operations and its brief existence. In June 2003 it shut down under pressure from the newly formed Rahbari (Leadership) Shura (based in the Pakistani city of Quetta, see below), which was trying to monopolise control over all Taliban groups. Most of the members and fighters of the Gardi Jangal Shura refused to accept the authority of the new Shura in Quetta and simply dispersed. Mullah Hussain did not get along with Mullah Baradar, one of the key figures in the emerging Quetta Shura, and retired, later to be killed in North Waziristan. Of the leaders, only Abdul Jalil Akhwandzada agreed to join the Quetta Shura, bringing with him 200 fighters.[57]

Although the existence of the Gardi Jangal went unnoticed by the outside world, it accounted for much of the low-level fighting in the south in the year of its existence. One of its senior cadres indicated that 265 of its fighters were killed in 13 months, suggesting a yearly casualty rate of over 20 per cent.[58]

### The emergence of the Miran Shah Shura in the south-east

Around the same time, efforts to improve the organisation of the incipient insurgency were taking place in North Waziristan, where former Taliban commander and Minister of Tribal Affairs Jalaluddin Haqqani and his entourage had taken refuge in 2001. They started re-organising almost immediately. According to one member of the Haqqani network:

> We went to Miran Shah, North Waziristan and South Waziristan, but the Pakistani government behaved amicably with us compared to other Taliban groups. The other Taliban were afraid and mostly escaped to the Arab countries; they were in a

bad situation up until 2005. Instead we had all the facilities; we had no financial problems or logistical problems and we always had a safe haven. This was the reason we started operations against the Americans and Westerners in Afghanistan as early as 2002–3.[59]

This account of proceedings may be a rather rose-tinted view. During the second half of 2002 Haqqani armed groups appeared in Paktia and Khost, but the level of activity was 'very weak', as one member of the Miran Shah Shura admitted.[60] American estimates in early 2002 were of a maximum of 1,400 men the Haqqani network could call upon.[61] The group was known and continues to identify itself as the Haqqani Shabaka (Haqqani Network); fighters entering the villages would identify as Taliban first and Haqqani Shabaka second.[62]

As former fighters heard that the Haqqanis were re-organising, they came forward to volunteer. This was not always straightforward. One recalls:

I needed to make amends for not having joined the fight. I started asking around if the mujahedin were still active, but no one could give me a real answer. Then one day I heard about a young Afghan named Azizullah who had been in the resistance – he's in jail now in Afghanistan. I went to his house, and told him I wanted to help the resistance against the Americans if it was forming. He lied, saying he was only a poor man and had nothing to do with jihad. Then one day I saw him walking to the mosque. I joined him. He was still hesitant, but finally he said he could help. He gave me directions to a militant camp in Waziristan and a letter of introduction.[63]

Dispersed members of the Haqqani Shabaka in North Waziristan, South Waziristan and Hango started reforming and the leaders started interacting. The Haqqanis' men were supplemented by Al-Qaida and other volunteers, including significant numbers from the FATA. According to a commander of the Haqqanis in the south-east:

At first I didn't hear any Afghans talking about going back to fight. But the Arabs did, and they encouraged the Afghans and the local tribal people not to give up. Nothing much happened for the first year or so, but then the Arabs started organising some training camps. [...] They moved openly on the main roads and in the towns and villages, showing no concern about security. I decided to leave my studies and join their resistance. [...] After two months of hard training, we graduated. There were 200 of us: about 160 local tribals, a few Punjabis, and about 40 Afghans like me. We were divided up into 10 groups. Each had two or three Arabs assigned to it as commanders and instructors.[64]

As this shows, at the outset foreign fighters accounted for a large portion of the Haqqanis' fighting strength. Arabs aside, particularly important were the networks of sympathisers in Pakistan, largely based in the north-west:

> ... the commander called me back that March. He told me he was working with [Pakistani pro-Taliban commander] Nek Mohammad to arrange for one of the first cross-border attacks against American forces in Afghanistan. Even with Nek Mohammad's help, we only had usable weapons for 50 of the roughly 200 mujahedin who had been trained. But 50 of us – a couple of dozen Arabs, three or four Afghans like myself, and some Waziri and Mehsud tribals – were armed and ready to go.[65]

This early re-mobilisation was limited not only by scarce resources. These isolated, small insurgent groups were fighting against the odds and faced huge risks; they did not enjoy widespread support among the villagers. The same commander quoted above remembered the first raid into Afghanistan:

> It was very dangerous back then. We had to run quickly and stay out of sight. We didn't want villagers to see us. At that time they weren't very supportive, and there were spies looking for us. We wanted to reach the cover of ravines, rocks, and trees before the sun rose.[66]

Another commander recounts a similar experience:

> One night in April [2003], we crossed the border in five pickups and one larger truck. Once we were safely across, we sent the vehicles back to wait for us on the Pakistan side. Our target was a US base just across the border at Machda, in Paktika province. We attacked at dawn. I think we really surprised them. We shelled them with 122mm rockets and mortars for about 30 minutes. But we didn't get close enough to fire our Kalashnikovs; before we could move in, American helicopters came, raining rockets and bullets on us. Terrified, I crawled and ran to escape death. Amid the noise and explosions, dust and smoke, I remember seeing six of us cut down and killed: two Arabs, three tribals, and an Afghan.[67]

Recruitment of individuals not previously linked to Al-Qaida or to the Taliban was rare at this stage; the small groups of insurgents were very worried about infiltration and even letters of introduction by senior Taliban would not spare recruits being carefully vetted.[68]

These early forays were militarily insignificant, but were meant to show to the mass of hesitent members that the movement was active and fighting back.

> We showed our resolve by fighting, by taking a stand. We knew we'd be back. We carried the stiff and bloodied bodies of our martyrs back to Wana. Thousands of

locals attended their funerals, saying it was an honour to witness the burial of these martyrs. People brought flowers, ribbons, colored cloth and flags to decorate their graves. As the news traveled, many former Taliban began returning to Wana to join us.[69]

Only once the Haqqanis and their allies managed to demonstrate some capacity to fight, support from the Pakistani authorities started flowing in significant amounts. One of the Haqqani network recalls:

> When they saw our capabilities, they also started supporting us. They supported us financially and logistically; this was the reason that we could commence large-scale operations against the Americans and foreign forces. Pakistan promised us that any time we conducted operations in Afghanistan, they would provide us refuge in North Waziristan, South Waziristan, Quetta, Bajaur and Peshawar. After any operations we would cross back to those areas in Pakistan. This was the reason we could commence operations after [Afghan President Hamid] Karzai came to power.[70]

According to a senior member of the Miran Shah Shura, it helped that regional geopolitics were shifting at the same time:

> ...when Pakistan recognised that America was not serving their interests and the Indians were also strengthening their influence in Afghanistan, they started supporting the Taliban.[71]

During the second half of 2002 and early 2003, Jalaluddin Haqqani and his closest collaborators also entered into negotiations with the Pakistani authorities over the prospect of starting the jihad in south-eastern Afghanistan. Pakistan reportedly endorsed the notion, encouraging the Haqqanis to fight back.[72] These discussions eventually led to the establishment of the Miran Shah Shura on 14 February 2003. At this early stage the elderly Jalaluddin was still the head of the network and presided over the Miran Shah Shura, which derived its name from the location of its HQ, in the Waziristani town of Miran Shah. Jalaluddin's main collaborators were his sons Serajuddin and Yahya, and his brother Khalil Rahman. At the provincial level the main commanders were:

- Qari Rauf Zakir (Khost province);
- Mawlavi Sangin (Paktia Province);
- Qari Aziz Haqqani (Paktika Province);
- Mawlavi Sabur (Logar Province).

Pakistani support was reportedly explicit:

*The opening ceremony was attended by many senior Pakistani government officials and politicians such as General Hamid Gul, General Abdullah and Moulana Fazal Rahman.*[73]

The Miran Shah Shura had the aim of uniting the disorganised efforts of the local fronts and groups described above and establishing a formal chain of command, systematising and expanding recruitment, and strengthening logistics. According to one of the Haqqanis' leaders:

We collected our friends; we collected people from the madrasa and gave them weapons to fight again. We travelled in Afghanistan and Pakistan and convinced people to fight against the Americans and the Afghan government.[74]

During 2003 the Miran Shah Shura started managing military activities in Paktia and Khost, extending then its area of operations to Paktika and Logar from 2004 onwards.[75] In 2003 the Shura appointed its Representatives (*Massuleen*) to 46 districts and four provinces, a development which gave it a relatively centralised command and control structure on the ground long before the main leadership *shura* in Quetta started developing its own.[76]

Unlike the Gardi Jangal Shura, the Miran Shah Shura was there to stay. It turned into one of a growing number of Taliban command and control centres, maintaining an uneasy relationship with the others, particularly those in the south.

## *The Quetta Shura emerges*

The top political leaders of the Taliban in the south were slower to coalesce, but by early 2003 they were better able to operate as restrictions on their movements were gradually lifted. Signs of local Taliban groups re-mobilising against the new government in Kabul and its Western allies were multiplying, putting the leaders under pressure to capitalise on these developments. Finally, more funding started becoming available from a variety of sources. This is how the Rahbari Shura (Leadership Council) came into being.[77] The Rahbari Shura is often referred to as the Quetta Shura by the Taliban and external observers alike. Technically, there is no such thing as the Quetta Shura, but in this book the term will be used from now on to indicate the complex organisation that gradually evolved around the Rahbari Shura: commissions, sub-*shura*s, offices, fronts and so forth.[78]

Formally established on 14 March 2003, its existence was only announced to the world about three months later, in June.[79] The founding members were all senior Taliban figures, and among them stood out Mullah Abdul Ghani Baradar (former deputy minister of defence), Mullah Dadullah (one of the foremost military commanders of the Emirate), Mullah Faruq (another military commander), Mawlavi Akhtar Mohammad Mansur (former minister of civil aviation) and Mullah Gul Agha Ishaqzai (a close collaborator of Mullah Omar).[80]

According to one of its members, the original aim of the Rahbari Shura was not to overthrow the Karzai administration, as this was considered unrealistic. The intent was instead to exercise pressure on the Americans and on Kabul, hoping to force them to seek some accommodation with the Taliban. In other words, they aimed to strengthen their negotiating position.[81] It is not clear whether this should be regarded as merely the member's personal opinion or a shared and openly agreed-upon aim of the Rahbari Shura as a whole.

Mullah Omar did not attend the launch of the Rahbari Shura, but later endorsed it. The very fact that a legitimate leadership of the movement had resurfaced allowed for more systematic and successful fundraising, for the elaboration of plans and a strategy, and also presented the dispersed southern Taliban with a more attractive option to the isolated groups active until then.[82]

The Quetta Shura brought the first semblance of large-scale organisation to the insurgency in the south.[83] One of the first decisions of the newly established Rahbari Shura was to put the provincial and district governors it was appointing in charge of all groups operating in its areas. In turn the governors responded to the Rahbari Shura. The first shadow governor was appointed to Kandahar as early as 2003, followed by the governor of Helmand in 2004 and then by governors in the other provinces of the south and surroundings in 2005. Wardak, Ghazni and Baghlan received governors only in 2007.[84] Because the situation was heretofore chaotic and clearly disadvantageous to the Taliban, with groups and fronts barely communicating or collaborating with each other, the introduction of the new system was a welcome development.[85]

Support from Pakistan was still very modest in 2003–4 and initially the Taliban were only allowed to cross the Kandahar–Helmand portion of the Pakistani border without hindrance. Taliban sources estimated external financial support in 2003–4 at $20 million per year.[86] This level of foreign funding, though modest, allowed the Taliban to boost their still-primitive procurement and logistics.[87] Foreign support was also a morale booster: 'After 2004, when Pakistan and some of the Arab countries started sending funds, we felt happy; we could tell ourselves that some nations were supporting us.'[88] However it was not until 2005 that the Pakistani security services openly told the Taliban that their presence in Pakistan would be completely tolerated and that they would even be sheltered.[89]

In early 2003 activities were limited to Kandahar and Helmand, but by the end of 2004 the Taliban were operating in Kandahar, Helmand, Zabul, Uruzgan, Ghazni, Paktia and Paktika.[90] During the second half of 2003 and throughout 2004 operations intensified considerably, as a future commander recalled:

> By the middle of 2004, we were hearing rumours that the Taliban were operating once again in Ghazni. Friends and relatives in other rural districts were saying that armed men were beginning to show up in villages at night on motorbikes. Within a few months, signs of them began appearing everywhere. At first we saw shabnama ['night letters'] that the Taliban would leave in shops, mosques, and other public places, warning people not to cooperate with [Afghan President Hamid] Karzai and the Americans. By the beginning of 2005 the Taliban began targeted killings of police officers, government officials, spies and elders who were working with the Americans.[91]

Various sources recounted a similar pattern of gradual organised infiltration: first a few Taliban emissaries would contact former members of the movement and other trusted people. Little by little they would widen the circle of people they would meet. The next step was organising some general meetings, where they would call people to support the jihad against 'the cruelty of the government, the killing and beating of innocent people for no reason, Jews jailing innocent Muslims for no reason' and for 'the defence of Islam and the spreading of jihad', warning people not to work for or collaborate with the government.[92] The general meetings usually involved the attendance of the elders. At this point the presence of the Taliban in a specific area would become obvious, with the reaction of the villagers usually mixed. In Panjwai, for example, 'Some of the elders were in favour of the Taliban while some were against'.[93] Taliban teams would cover their faces when in the open and their first activities were kidnappings and assassinations of presumed government spies and collaborators, in addition to burning down government clinics and schools.[94] Out of fear, government officials started to leave the villages where they were living.[95]

Occasionally, small groups of fighters would turn up at a mosque with some mullah and preach in favour of jihad, hoping to win over the villagers. Village and tribal elders were approached not for recruitment, but for logistical support and permission to enter their villages. Similarly, businessmen were approached for funding.[96] Gradually the Taliban started visiting the villages systematically (where possible) to talk to the elders and villagers, conveying their own vision of events and criticising the activities of the government, foreign forces and anybody else they considered hostile.[97] The Taliban mostly used mosques to deliver their views to the villagers, telling them that 'the international forces are fighting against Islam and it is [every Muslim's] holy obligation to stand up for jihad'.[98]

Some aspects of village-level Taliban propaganda are not likely to have been managed or at least planned centrally, but rather to be the result of spontaneous efforts by the Taliban themselves and sympathisers. However, the Taliban propaganda machine might have encouraged and even actively promoted their spread. An example of this was the pro-Taliban ballads (*taranas*), which have become very common in parts of Afghanistan.[99] Here the role of the more advanced organisation centered around the Rahbari Shura has been evident.

## The Miran Shah Shura bows to the Rahbari Shura

The claimed status of the Quetta Shura as the leadership of the Taliban was greatly enhanced when the Miran Shah Shura recognised it. As discussed above, the Miran Shah Shura had started operations first. The Quetta Shura invited Miran Shah to align with it when it was formally established in 2003. The Haqqanis agreed and two of their representatives sat on the Rahbari Shura until 2007. The Quetta Shura funded the Miran Shah Shura, at least in part, and in exchange the latter agreed to accept the former's authority. The Rahbari Shura would need to authorise any operations, which would also take place under the auspices of commanders recognised by the Shura. Provincial and district governors would be appointed by the Rahbari Shura and *ushr* and *zakat* taxes were to accrue to it.[100]

Despite the alignment with Quetta, the Miran Shah Shura remained largely autonomous and maintained a field organisational apparatus, which differed from Quetta's. Unlike the Quetta Shura, the Miran Shah Shura was always composed of a single network.[101] This allowed Miran Shah to decide matters faster than Quetta and made centralisation much less controversial.

The agreement with Quetta, however, implied that the Haqqanis could no longer claim a monopoly over the provinces in which they were operating. The Quetta Shura already had a presence in Paktika, but following the agreement in 2005 armed groups loyal to Quetta started appearing in the other three provinces the Miran Shah Shura considered its turf: Khost, Paktia and Logar. The Quetta Shura had some success in establishing a foothold in parts of Paktia, where the local Taliban network, independent of the Haqqanis and led by Nasrullah Mansur, was centered around Zurmat district.[102]

As the finances of the Quetta Shura improved, the link with Miran Shah strengthened. Quetta started transferring funds and supplies to Miran Shah and providing 'advice'.[103] The strengthening relationship was symbolised by the fact that once Quetta started appointing provincial and district governors, it did so for the four provinces under Miran Shah. The Haqqanis did not have governors, but just provincial- and district-level military commanders, who would co-exist with the governors.

## 1.4 The early military system of the Quetta Shura

### The combat groups

The early insurgents organised themselves at the tactical level around local Taliban leaders of some repute, who became commanders of the fighting groups. Since they were emerging largely spontaneously and autonomously, they varied in size and organisation. During the early years of the post-2001 insurgency, an individual wanting to join the jihad would not join the Taliban as an organisation, but would rather seek personal allegiance to a commander. This relationship was often defined by personal, familial or tribal ties, as expressed by the term *andiwal* ('friend', also variously translated as 'comrade', 'brother-in-arms'), used to describe this relationship of men personally linked to their commander.[104] The approach of the early days was informal and ad-hoc, as described by one commander: 'Anyone who could find 10 fighters could set up a unit; he would then collect *zakat* within the area and buy weapons locally.'[105]

As the Quetta Shura started establishing its grip on these fighting groups, it tried to systematise their functioning and organisation. In order to facilitate management and supplies, a mandatory fixed strength of 25 men was imposed upon each group, labelled a *sar group*. In practice, since it was not always possible to rapidly replace fallen fighters, and some combatants would take leave, the actual number was often below that. The majority of these groups were local in character and usually operated near their villages, but some were mobile and able to deploy around their province (see below).[106] Often, a particularly popular Taliban commander or local leader would gather several groups around himself, launching a 'front', often dedicated to a Taliban martyr or a particular madrasa.

The Quetta Shura also tried to enforce a chain of command, which had the provincial governors at the top, district governors as intermediate leaders and group commanders at the bottom. The governors were given the authority to sack group commanders in case of wrongdoing.[107] Typically groups were ethnically and tribally homogeneous in composition.[108] The networks and fronts that had been forming autonomously even before the Quetta Shura turned up were integrated into the structure, probably with the long-term intent of merging them into it altogether. But at this early stage it was common practice for a front commander to become district governor or, for the more powerful, even provincial governor. Their men would stay with them, and some loose local groups or groups belonging to other fronts would also be placed under their command. At the same time some of the front commanders' groups, operating outside the district, would be placed under the orders of another governor. The trade off was meant to create a territorially unified chain of command, although the links between front commander and his men (*andiwal*) in other districts were not severed.

Although the Taliban used generic denominations like 'group' regardless of the specialisation, in fact different specialisations gradually developed. While the majority of groups were in fact guerrilla units, others specialised in mine-laying, in intelligence, in special operations, heavy weapons, sniping, tax collection and so forth. The Taliban would avoid associating the specialisation of these groups with their names, aware that their communications were being scrutinised by their enemies.[109]

### *The military leaders and the beginning of an organised insurgency*

As the Quetta Shura started organising, a few relatively large networks centered around the most prestigious military leaders were already informally developing. These were charismatic commanders such as Dadullah, Faruq, Ibrahim, Dr. Wasi and Baradar (to be discussed more extentively below), who had their own following for whom they were solely responsible. Typically, formations of 300–350 men would deploy for operations throughout the south and neighbouring provinces such as Farah, Nimruz and Ghazni.[110] In Kandahar in particular, Mullah Dadullah and Mullah Faruq were the first military leaders of importance to appear in 2003, operating mainly in the districts of Maruf, Arghistan, Daman, Shah Wali Kot, Nish and Panjwai (and Garmser in Helmand). Mullah Baradar, Ihsanullah Rahimi and Dr. Wasi joined them in 2004–5.[111]

Among other prominent early insurgent commanders, the best known was Mullah Obeidullah, who had been defence minister during the Emirate. Often the main distinction of these commanders was that they were brave or ruthless enough to take a command when the average fighter was still terrified by the awesome display of American power during Operation Enduring Freedom.[112] Dadullah was the most powerful of them all and gathered around himself in Chaman and Quetta about 2,000 Taliban veterans between the second half of 2002 and early 2003, waiting to start operations against the Western 'invaders'.[113] Dadullah was in fact the first Taliban commander to launch an operation in the south. On 4 February 2003 his man carried out an attack in Sangin district in Helmand. At that time the leaders (Dadullah among them) were still busy trying to launch the Rahbari Shura.[114]

Despite, or perhaps because of his brutal reputation, Dadullah was very popular among the ranks of the Taliban.[115] One Taliban leader noted:

> He was the strongest commander in the Quetta Shura from 2003 until his killing, because he was was really cruel and did show not mercy to anyone. If you see from 2003 till 2007 that the Taliban gained so much ground, it was because of him. […] After his killing there was no longer as strong a commander in the Taliban as he.[116]

Similarly, another recalled:

> When he was alive, half of Helmand was in our hands, as well as many districts of Kandahar province. He was a very cruel person; all the people were afraid of him. No one would ever dare to wrong him. He would tell people that either they captured an area or they were not to return to him.[117]

Apart from being the single most powerful military commander the Quetta Shura had under its direct control, Dadullah was rapidly appointed by the Shura to lead all Taliban operations in the southern provinces. All the other senior commanders had to bow to him, including Mullah Baradar, Faruq and Ibrahim. 'They were afraid of him', said a former member of the Rahbari Shura.[118]

In a sense, Dadullah's primary value to the Taliban was that he was able to unify them on the battlefield, due to his coercive approach and the absence of an adequate organisation to achieve the same. However, not everybody appreciated Dadullah's role; some members of the Rahbari Shura, like Akhtar Mohammad Mansur and Abdul Majid, considered him a liability because of his brutality.[119]

One major limitation of the governors-based system introduced in 2003 by the Rahbari Shura was that these big military leaders were not given roles proportionate to their influence. This limitation was quickly acknowledged; indeed it was probably in an attempt to recognise his widespread influence that Dadullah was appointed general commander. It is worth noting that a much less charismatic figure, Mawlavi Hafiz, had been initially appointed to the job.[120]

## 1.5 Overall impact of early Taliban efforts

During 2002–4 the focus was largely on reconnecting and remobilising the old Taliban. There was little effort to recruit beyond their existing constituencies.[121]

> We did not send representatives to talk with the elders because we did not need to talk with them. We sent emissaries to other Taliban forces in Afghanistan, visiting mosques to deliver them weapons to fight.[122]

It was Taliban leaders and cadres who travelled through Pakistan first, and then increasingly Afghanistan as well, inviting former members and others in their family to reactivate and join the insurgency:

> ... suddenly the Taliban's defense minister, Mullah Obaidullah, came to see me – the first senior Taliban leader I had seen since our collapse. He was travelling around Pakistan to rally our dispersed forces. Half of the leadership were back in touch with each other, he said, and they were determined to start a resistance movement to expel the Americans.[...] Obaidullah told me: 'We don't need you as a deputy minister or bureaucrat. We want you to bring as many fighters as you can into the field.'[123]
>
> It was decided that each commander should set about finding his former soldiers and prepare to return to Afghanistan to fight. I was sent to Quetta, where survivors from my unit had settled. There had been 400 fighters under my command. In Quetta I found 15 of them. They embraced me and were eager to return to free our land of the American invaders.[124]

While the remobilisation of a significant portion of former Taliban members might be considered a modest achievement, it may well have been enough for the group to establish their initial credibility as a viable insurgency.

So far in this early period (2002–4) three distinct organisational strategies can be identified, which developed in parallel. The first was the loose growth of groups and network, without any superstructure to manage them. It is worth pointing out at this point that although in gradual decline after 2004, this mode of organisation, which can be termed 'polycentric-fragmented', never fully disappeared. In 2017 there were still independent groups operating, including the Free (Azadi) Taliban and a few small splinter groups.[125]

A second mode of organisation was that promoted by the Quetta Shura: polycentric with multiple chains of command. This will be further explored below. The third mode was the Haqqanis', which is interesting because of its patrimonial-centralised character. One question which arises and is worth discussing further is why the Haqqanis managed to centralise around a strong personality, and the Quetta Shura did not.

The first nationwide test of the Taliban's capabilities came with the 2004 presidential elections. Washington and other Western capitals identified the elections as important benchmarks of progress and success in Afghanistan, and accordingly the Taliban saw them as necessary and opportune targets: both very visible and very vulnerable.

The Taliban's operational capacity to actually attack and intimidate voters was limited mainly to Kandahar, Zabul, Uruzgan, Helmand and Ghazni, the latter still being outside the organisational umbrella of the Quetta Shura. According to the Taliban themselves, 20 districts were prevented from voting entirely, as well as 200 villages spread around other districts.[126]

Overall, even taking these Taliban claims at face value, the campaign against the elections achieved modest results. There were also reports of tensions within the leadership over the failure to sabotage the elections.[127] Clearly, despite progress in setting up a more sophisticated organisation, the Taliban still had a long way to go to make a serious impact. A Taliban leader interviewed acknowledged that, with the insurgency not yet being supported very generously by neighbouring countries, they lacked the resources for a widespread campaign in 2004.[128]

Reportedly, US President Bush warned Pakistani President Musharraf that he needed orderly elections in Afghanistan, and Musharraf complied by restricting movement across Pakistan's border.[129] According to a single source, the only support the Taliban received for the cause of foiling the 2004 elections (as well as ever since) was from the Saudis, who might have had their own reasons for not wanting to see shining electoral process in Afghanistan.[130] What is certain is that in any case, the Taliban had few resources available at that time and the campaign against the elections wrought little damage.

# 2

# THE APOGEUM OF THE QUETTA SHURA, 2005–9

By the second half of 2003 the Taliban could already be described as a polycentric insurgency, as they had two centres of power (Miran Shah and Quetta). In addition, both the Quetta Shura and the Gardi Jangal Shura structured themselves as 'networks of networks'; in other words, they were polycentric structures at all levels.

As funding levels increased, from 2005 onwards the Rahbari Shura started creating a range of structures under its authority, to improve its ability to organise the insurgency. These were primarily 'commissions' – executive organs tasked with implementing policies decided by the Rahbari Shura – and 'councils' (the *shura*s), which had a more representative role. Of the former, the first to be created were the military commission, initially led by Dadullah, and then after his death by Akhtar Mohammad Mansur, and the Tolana (Society) Commission, dealing with issues related to education, health and so on. The Masherano Shura was also established to make appointments in the provinces (of governors and commanders), taking into account the interests of the different networks.[1] Several other commissions would follow gradually over the years, including the Political Commission, the Health Commission, the Finance Commission and the Recruitment Commission.[2]

Naturally, the military apparatus was the focus of the bulk of organisational efforts. While the Quetta Shura was taking shape, it was also focusing on expansion, with mixed results. Underpinning all these developments was an increase in the funding directed towards the Quetta Shura.

## 2.1 The Quetta Shura expands its influence

*The Taliban's breakthrough in the south, 2005–6*

There is near-universal consensus among the Taliban that 2005 represented a turning point for the insurgency. At this point they started reaching out beyond the old circles for those who had been directly involved with the Emirate, approaching mullahs and village and tribal elders to invite them to join the jihad against foreign troops in Afghanistan.[3]

In Kandahar Province, Taliban activites started to reach new districts in 2005–8, including Daman, Arghandab, Maywand and Panjwai. An elder from Zhirai indicated that the Taliban reached their peak strength in his district in 2007–8.[4] Even in parts of Kandahar close to the city, like the district of Daman, where the Taliban had never had a solid base, the weakness of the government created a space for them. By 2005 the Taliban's district governor and his 200 fighters were becoming the dominant local force, despite operating underground and having no stronghold within the district.[5] By 2009 they operated in all sixteen districts of the province and were beginning to threaten the city of Kandahar itself, which they continued to penetrate.[6]

> We talked with shuras, elders and the ulema in the mosques. We would tell mullahs to convince people to join the Taliban; we would tell village elders to give shelter to us in our fight with foreign forces. In those days we needed to seek support because we were not very strong. We needed shelter, weapons, food, money and the rest.[7]
>
> Things became easier in 2005 because we started receiving foreign support, in addition to support from the villages, the shura and the tribes. We captured more areas. Our numbers swelled to 10000, 15000 – many had arrived from other areas.[8]

In Helmand small-scale armed activities began in mid-2005, as the Taliban started moving towards the more central and heavily populated districts from their strongholds in Baghran in the north and Garmser in the south.[9]

The parliamentary elections of 2005 provided another test to measure the growing capabilities of the insurgency. The ability of the Taliban to disrupt these elections was significantly greater than it had been during the 2004 presidential contest. According to Taliban sources, 30–40 districts (approximately 10 per cent of the countryside) were prevented from voting. In part, the increase in violence was the result of more external aid becoming available, with the Pakistani ISI's Directorate S for the first time committing itself to the effort.[10] One senior Taliban source reported that the ISI paid the group $30 million in 2005 to be used in efforts to stop the elections.[11]

However, even with a large infusion of external funding and greater consequent reach, the disruptive impact of the 2005 campaign was still modest. Elders interviewed confirmed that the Taliban were more active that year, but to limited effect. Each stated that their individual districts had been affected (even in the north), but the majority of anti-election activity consisted of sermons in mosques warning against participation, and the distribution of threatening night letters. Violence was sparse, even in a Taliban stronghold like Daychopan (in Zabul).[12]

In sum, the insurgency was stronger in 2005 than in 2004, but it still lacked the widespread military power and coordination to cause large-scale disruption. A few areas already had a strong Taliban presence, like Zabul Province, but otherwise the group were still in the early organisational stages. As one commander noted with regards to Ghazni Province, the insurgency was too busy organising itself and managing its own expansion, and so did not prioritise targeting the election.[13]

After 2005, however, the insurgency accelerated considerably. One commander described how he found the country in 2007, having been away for years:

I visited the south and spoke to Taliban units, to elders and villagers, and sought new recruits. [...] I travelled to eight provinces in 20 days. The unpopularity of the Karzai regime helped us immensely. In 2005 some Afghans thought Karzai would bring positive change, but now most Afghans believe the Taliban to be the future. The resistance was getting stronger day by day.[14]

One senior member of the Rahbari Shura estimated that on the eve of the American surge of 2009–12, much of Helmand and Kandahar were under their control (see also Annex I):

Until 2009 some areas of Kandahar and Helmand remained under our control. In Helmand we had Dishu, Reg, Khaneshin, Garmser, Nad Ali, Marja, Sangeen, Kajaki and Musa Qala – about 70 per cent of the province. In Kandahar we controlled the districts of Registan, Shubarak, Maruf, Daman, Panjwayi and Arghandab. 40 per cent of the province was under our control.[15]

After 2004, one of the main campaigns of the newly confident Taliban was against state education. Attacks on schools were occuring on a small scale by 2002 and were mostly attributed to the Taliban, but a coordinated campaign against state education only started in 2006. It was at this time that the Quetta Shura established an Education Commission, which took charge of managing the campaign in the field.[16] In December the Taliban leadership included in its *layeha*, the code of conduct issued to field commanders, instructions to attack schools that did not abide by the rules established by the leadership; these included the bans on the post-2001 curriculum, on the new textbooks gradually being adopted, and on girls' education. Allegedly, the Taliban leadership took the decision after a major discussion during the previous months.[17] The incorporation of that decision in the *layeha* meant all girls' and boys' schools that used post-2001 textbooks and syllabi were liable to be attacked. However, the real innovation of the *layeha* was to lay out a clear procedure by which attacks on schools could be authorised: first a warning had to be administered, then a physical beating and eventually (in case of non-compliance) the killing of teaching staff and the burning of the school.[18] The actual increase in the pace of attacks against schools was already noticeable in the course of 2006. ISAF (International Security Assistance Force) sources estimated that attacks against schools increased by 65 per cent in that year.[19]

## *The Quetta Shura expands beyond the south*

Under great pressure in the south, by 2006–7 the Taliban was focusing efforts (with some success) on transferring military and political cadres to areas where the insurgency was underdeveloped or non-existent, typically trying to re-establish old connections with people who had worked with them in the 1990s. Successful cadres would be rewarded with promotions, often becoming the local leadership in provinces and districts newly acquired by the insurgency. The central leadership had to operate by consensus and had little power to enforce decisions on individual networks; in fact the chain of command operated through the networks: the field commanders would receive orders through the network representative in the province. In other words, in 2005–8 the organisation did develop in comparison to what had existed before, but it did not turn into an effective 'real time' command and control management system; it was aptly described in a UNAMA report as serving to enable other activities, and perform conflict resolution.[20]

The Taliban's formal entry into an area would be preceded by an organised propaganda effort to lay the ground for an active insurgency. Mullahs were sent to preach in the mosques from 2006 onwards, while an organised effort was made to target for recruitment students from western Afghanistan in Pakistani madrasas. As outlined, the first signs of Taliban activity involved intimidation and occasional attacks on 'collaborators', threats to schools and so forth.[21]

The northwest was infiltrated through Ghormach and Jawand (districts in Badghis Province) or areas in Ghor Province.[22] In the northeast, a long supply line came from Nuristan through the provinces of Laghman, Kapisa, Panjshir and Baghlan, supported by a Gujar commander,[23] Ghafoor Khan, whose men knew the mountain tracks of the region well.[24] These Pashto-speaking nomads are well-acquainted with the mountainous topography of the region and despite being few in number, they hold disproportionate importance within Taliban ranks.

In these areas, where the group was expanding, the Taliban planned more carefully than in the south. Political agents and preachers spearheaded the armed groups, trying to convince individuals and groups to join the movement. They – as well as fighters – mainly came from the embattled provinces in the south as well as from Pakistan. The insurgents first operated in groups of four to five fighters, mainly doing 'armed propaganda', that is, offering their services as mobile courts, collecting taxes and intimidating those who were unsympathetic. They would visit particular villages on occasion, never staying for more than one or two nights. Among other instructions, they would tell families not to send their sons to serve in the Afghan security forces. Kinship ties and local hospitality were exploited for the initial foray, after which individuals and communities drew gradually closer to the Taliban. Criminal groups would be hired to destabilise the area,[25] and once the Taliban launched their intimidation campaign, threats to pro-government elements increased and, most importantly, started being carried through. Next, they gradually expanded the size of their armed forces through local recruitment and merging groups. At this point they would start escalating military activities. In Faryab, for example, this phase began in the second half of 2009,[26] while in Kunduz it was already underway in early 2008.

This expansion usually meant absorbing existing resistance fronts, which may or may not have initially been Taliban-inspired. In Baghlan, for example, the Khalid Beni Walid Mahaz, mentioned in Chapter 1, was absorbed in 2006.[27] In Ghazni the local fronts mentioned in Chapter 1 had limited impact, lacking supplies and funding as they did, until Quetta and other Shuras turned up:

> 2006 and 2007 were our worst time, because we were faced with financial and logistical problems while we still lacked medicine and facilities to treat wounded fighters or transfer them to other countries. 2008 was much better because all of these problems were solved: we found doctors and we received financial and logistical support.[28]

As such, the arrival of Quetta-based forces was welcomed. The local Taliban, strengthened by these reinforcements and better supplies and funding, started making dramatic inroads. In 2007 the Taliban attacked Jaghatu district and were able to occupy it for a few hours. Local elders report how the Taliban enjoyed widespread popular support among the Pashtun population of several districts at this time.[29] By 2008 the jihad in Ghazni was spreading to Tajiks as well. In 2008, Tajik commander Mustafa joined the fight in Deh Yak with 140 men, followed by Qari Mohammad Ahmadi in Jaghatu and then several others.[30] Similarly, it was 2007 before the Quetta Shura could spread to Wardak.[31] It was a slow start for the Taliban's insurgency; it would take until 2009 before they started enjoying widespread support.[32]

### The co-optation of non-Taliban networks begins

In several provinces, the autonomous local fronts that existed before the Quetta Shura or other Taliban formations arrived had nothing to do with the group. This was the case, for example, in Herat. Under the Emirate, the Taliban did not have much community support in Herat and did not recruit extensively in the area. This made kickstarting an insurgency there difficult. Western Afghanistan was remote from the Taliban's supply lines to Pakistan and the ground one had to cross to reach the region was mostly flat and open, heightening the risk of interception.[33] Despite these obstacles, Herat served as an early example of the group's attempts to reach out to new constituencies and to co-opt them to join the jihad.

By 2005 an endogenous insurgent movement was developing in Herat, with disgruntled jihadi commanders – most with no previous connection to the Taliban – seizing the initiative and decamping to the mountains, including Amanullah, Abdullah Zekria and Mullah Sahib Zada. These insurgent leaders tended to be former commanders of Jamiat-i Islami and Hizb-i Islami, who were operating independently of the Taliban and had very limited resources at their disposal; one of the Taliban's future leaders in the west described this phase of jihad in Herat as 'not serious'.[34]

From February 2007 onwards these commanders were gradually co-opted into the Taliban, or asked to join in exchange for support. This was the case with Amanullah, who went to Quetta to negotiate with the Rahbari Shura. Some of these early insurgents were already recruiting in madrasas before linking up with the Taliban, suggesting that they were somewhat ideologically motivated.[35] It appears that the Iranian Revolutionary Guards brokered the agreement between the Taliban and local insurgents in the west, supporting the groups financially, presumably in order to establish some client groups within the Taliban.[36] In total, perhaps 1,000 local insurgents in the west joined the Taliban during 2007.[37] The leaders were given the right to choose the appointees to senior Taliban positions in the districts where they were most active.[38]

How genuine were these conversions to the Taliban's creed? Clearly some were opportunists, for whom the Taliban were just a vehicle:

> I had my own group that had about sixty or seventy Taliban members. In truth, I was against the ideology of the Peshawar Shura, Quetta Shura or Mashhad office. I was only [interested in] jihad against the foreigners – it was my only goal.[39]

However, during 2007 the Quetta Shura commenced efforts to leave a stronger imprint upon the Herati insurgency by sending senior cadres, Shohabuddin Delawar and Abdul Raziq, to manage affairs, with the latter being appointed as the first shadow governor in July 2007. The formerly independent local insurgent commanders became even more incorporated into the broader structure; they started sending their members to study in Pakistani madrasas, apparently accepting that they and their men should be gradually assimilated into the Taliban. These strongmen helped the Taliban establish a direct presence by making their bases and local support networks available.[40]

Aside from co-opting local insurgents, from the start of their activities in Herat the Taliban set out to do grassroots recruitment of their own, as usual targeting their former members.[41] But genuine Taliban who hailed originally from Herat were a rare find in the early days of the insurgency; there were just two or three such commanders in Pashtun Zarghoun, for example.[42] The same was true in Obeh district.[43] However, together with cadres, the Taliban also sent fighters and commanders from the south, to protect their cadres and strengthen their hand. Shahbuddin Delawar, for example, arrived with 150 men.[44] The newly co-opted local insurgents started acting as scouts for the Taliban.[45]

> The Taliban's first problems were that they did not understand the language and were not familiar with the geography of this province. The local people did not support them, and were not behaving well with them. They were faced with problems of money, logistics and supplies. With time, these problems were solved, because the local people became satisfied with them.[46]

With local help, the Taliban started finding their feet relatively soon in Herat. The first pockets of community support emerged in Shindand, due to a conflict between some Pashtun clans on one side and the Tajik strongman of Herat, Ismail Khan, on the other. The Taliban offered support to the clans against Khan, thereby winning support.[47] They also found support in a number of other Pashtun enclaves in the region.[48]

The big turning point in Herat was in 2008, when the Iranian Pasdaran started providing supplies on a significant level, after having already initiated small scale support in 2007. The supply lines from Iran were far shorter and safer than those from the south, and the Taliban in the west no longer had to compete with the south for the allocation of resources. The Iranians also started pushing many of their contacts and allies among local communities towards the Taliban, increasing their support base and facilitating local recruitment.[49]

Gradually the original local insurgents were completely absorbed into the Taliban, with no trace left of their former identity. The process of absorption was aided by the killing of almost all the original leaders by security forces, ISAF and local rivals.[50]

As with elsewhere, even the north witnessed the two converging paths of Taliban mobilisation. Local Taliban networks and dissatisfied commanders of other parties started mobilising with little or no external support, while infiltrators also started arriving from outside, firstly from Pakistan, later from southern Afghanistan also, some of them returnees. Already by October 2009 a German military intelligence officer confirmed the presence of Helmandis in Chahar Dara,[51] while sources in the south confirmed that Helmandis had been dispatched northward.[52]

Similarly, in Faryab the first armed insurgents were not Taliban, but disgruntled members of other groups and parties. Lacking resources, they were not very active, carrying out just 1–2 attacks a month, and focused instead on controlling some remote villages.[53] These local strongmen were from the anti-Taliban protagonists of the 1990s civil wars, such as Jamiat-i Islami (originally an moderate Muslim Brotherhood-type group), Hizb-i Islami (a similar Islamist grouping) and Junbesh-i Milli (a secular organisation with roots in the 1980s leftist regime's militias).[54]

During 2007, militants from Ghormach District in neighbouring Badghis Province started infiltrating Faryab. These efforts were still limited in scale and quite amateurish in execution, but the insurgents became more adept during 2008. By 2009, the Taliban coming from Badghis Province had gained a foothold and initiated a programme of local taxation, which has been expanding since then.[55] It took some time to set up functioning logistics because of the long distance from Pakistan, but by 2009 this problem was resolved.[56] The *shuras* (both Quetta and Peshawar, see Chapter 3 for the Peshawar Shura) primarily established a foothold by co-opting these strongmen and relying on their local knowledge. Reportedly it was Qari Ziauddin, and a couple of other commanders not yet linked to the Taliban, who travelled to Quetta and requested support.[57] The Quetta Shura used their strongholds of Ghormach and Bala Murghab in neighbouring Badghis to infiltrate Faryab.[58] Contrary to the situation in Herat, from the early days in Faryab the local insurgent forces were quickly merged into the Taliban.[59]

Baghlan was peculiar in that its first active Taliban unit post-2001 consisted mostly of Tajiks, despite the province having a large Pashtun population. The most prominent was Mawlawi Dad-e Khoda who, Taliban sources claimed, had 300 men under his command; in 2008 the Afghan security services estimated the group's strength at 200 armed fighters. Among Pashtuns, discrete support for the Taliban continued during 2007–8, with little evidence for the preparation of armed activities at this time. Religious figures were known to act on behalf of the Taliban among Pashtun communities in the northern parts of Baghlan.[60]

*Failure in the east*

The historic leadership of the Taliban having been based in the south or south-east (in the case of the Haqqanis), there were few Taliban leaders in the east who could command a sizeable following comparable to that of the southern networks (as discussed in Chapter 1): there was no eastern Dadullah.[61] Quetta nevertheless made several attempts to establish a foothold in the east, first by dispatching Mullah Kabir, a senior Taliban leader who had been minister of foreign affairs under the Emirate. Perhaps chosen because he was not a southerner, hailing instead from the south-east, Kabir nonetheless achieved little.[62] Kabir deployed to eastern Afghanistan in 2003, with a few senior cadres and funds allocated to expand the influence of the Rahbari Shura there. Kabir started operations in the districts of Hesarak, Shirzad, Khugyani, Durbaba and Bati Kot.[63]

Due to the group's weak roots in eastern Afghanistan, Kabir could mobilise only about 600 men between Nangarhar, Laghman and Kunar. He was also allocated only modest funds by Quetta, rendering his forces uncompetitive; the Rahbari Shura was still prioritising the south at that time. Only the small Spin Ghar Mahaz agreed to support him, while the Tora Bora Mahaz of

Anwar ul Haq Mujahid, Dost Mohammed and the Ijraya Shura colluded with Hizb-i Islami insurgents, who did not even consider themselves Taliban, in resisting the attempted take-over by the Quetta Shura. In particular they prevented efforts by the Quetta Shura to recruit locally.[64] By 2004 the Tora Bora Mahaz had 1,500 men and was able to keep Kabir's recruiters out of its areas of influence. Kabir approached the various tribal *shura*s of the east but met with near wholesale rejection of this outsider leading a assortment of mostly southern Taliban cadres and assuming to lead the easterners in jihad. Only the Shinwari Shura allowed him to recruit in its areas, and few Shinwari showed interest in joining anyway. Unable to recruit inside Afghanistan, he resorted to focusing his efforts in Pakistani madrasas. Then, in 2005, a group of eastern Taliban and former Hizb-i Islami cadres set up the Peshawar Shura, discussed in detail in Chapter 3. The Peshawar Shura was also opposed to the Quetta take-over and started putting pressure on Kabir and his men. Eventually, as the Peshawar Shura started gaining access to substantial funding, they forced Mullah Baradar in Quetta to recall Kabir in 2007, in order to avoid an open clash. Kabir's men either followed him back to Quetta, stayed with the shadow governors (which Peshawar allowed to operate even if they still answered to Quetta), joined the ranks of the Peshawar Shura or simply left the struggle.[65]

A measure of Kabir's failure was the fact that even before the Peshawar Shura was launched, new local fronts were forming outside the Quetta Shura's sphere of influence. The Tor Ghar Jabha, for example, was established in 2006 by Qari Mawin from a mix of local fighters, mostly from the Naser tribe, but also Sherzad and Khogyani, and Pakistani Taliban members. This small front rejected Kabir's leadership and in 2007 was absorbed into the Peshawar Shura.[66]

Relying on southern cadres and madrasa recruits from the east, the Quetta Shura could not expand its influence eastwards more than marginally between 2004–7.[67] They could not compete with the Taliban networks that had roots in the east and a more mixed social composition (including significant numbers of state-school educated members).[68] Eastern Taliban sources pointed to the lack of local and tribal roots among Kabir and his men:

> He was implementing the rules of Quetta here [...]. The local people did not want him either and the local Taliban did not want to take orders from the Quetta Shura.[69]
>
> Kabir had relationship with [southern] Durrani [tribes] and he wanted to bring Durrani here. The local Taliban did not want their leaders to be from Kandahar.[70]

Mawlavi Kabir eventually disappeared in 2012, either killed or arrested by the Pakistanis, and even his closest collaborators are not sure of his fate.[71]

## Drivers of increased support for the Taliban

Why was 2005 a turning point? A key factor was a change in Pakistan's attitude, as two senior Taliban leaders explained very clearly:

> Pakistan removed all the restrictions and we told all Taliban members that Pakistan does not want to arrest us, they want to support us.[72]
>
> In 2005 Pakistan ended their restrictions upon us, and they and the Arab countries started supporting us. We opened offices and *shura*s there.[73]

By 2007 at the latest, even the Iranian Pasdaran were supporting groups of Taliban in Helmand among other areas (including the west, as discussed above).[74]

The shift was also underpinned by the belief that the foreign supporters upon whom Kabul and its local allies were relying would not stay forever. Carter Malkasian tells of Garmser's district governor's attempts to bring a pro-Taliban *'alim* to work with him, only to be told that '[the Americans] will leave you! You will be alone'.[75]

An elder from Dand had his own way of explaining the shift:

> People here understand that whoever can govern by night is stronger. The government could control our area during the day, while the Taliban would govern here during the night. Therefore, people started supporting the Taliban.[76]

The Afghan government started being perceived as weak and ineffective, and its foreign supporters as lacking determination. In Garmser, by the end of 2005, village elders sensed the shift and started working with the Taliban.[77] In Baramchah, the Baluchi private militia – tasked by Sher Mohammed Akhundzada with controlling the area – also cut a deal with the Taliban.[78] In Nahr-i Seraj the members of the 93rd division in Nahr-i Seraj joined the Taliban after being demobilised.[79] At the same time the Taliban were emboldened by the perceived weakness of their opponents:

> When we saw in 2005 that they did not have the strength to fight us, we decided to capture provinces like Kandahar and Helmand.[80]

The other main driver of Taliban expansion was the persistence of the abusive attitude of the local Afghan authorities. Abuses by the security forces of the new regime and their local allies started driving a significant portion of the population towards any opposition movement which could protect them, or take revenge. In response to the first signs of Taliban re-mobilisation, the evermore frequent American raids and the humiliation of local elders created a base of support for the insurgency.[81]

In Garmser and Nad Ali, police abuse appears to have been a factor favouring Taliban re-mobilisation.[82] Ghazni was no exception:

> By the end of 2005 the Taliban's ranks in Ghazni were expanding. [...] The Americans and their Afghan allies made mistakes after mistake, killing and arresting innocent people. There was one village in Dayak district near Ghazni City where the people had communist backgrounds, from the days of the Russians, and had never supported us. But the police raided the village, beat the elders at a mosque and arrested them, accusing them of being Taliban. They were freed after heavy bribes were paid. After that incident the whole village sent us a message asking forgiveness for the abuses of the communist era.[83]

In the north also, former Taliban and clerics suspected of sympathising with the Taliban were often persecuted by powerbrokers and local authorities.[84] Abuses by local figures like the Andarabi commanders and Amir Gul in Baghlan Jadid drove Taliban re-mobilisation in the area.[85]

> Villagers had no other way to survive the crimes of Amir Gul and commander Kameen, other than seeking Taliban protection. People had to join the Taliban in order to stand against Amir Gul and commander Kameen.[86]

The Afghan security forces in certain areas would round up suspects at the first sign of Taliban activity, and in some cases drove them into the hands of the insurgents. This seems to be how Mullah Nadir, the first significant Taliban commander to emerge in the north-west (on the border between Sar-e Pol and Jowzjan), gained his influence.[87]

As a result, the Taliban were able to 'position themselves as protectors of the population against the police.'[88] The Taliban kept abreast of developments and 'targeted those areas where locals were most disaffected'; in some case the local population itself approached the Taliban for protection.[89] In Helmand, for example, Abdul Rahman Jan, the province's chief of police until 2006, and his appointees in the districts were particularly notorious for robbing and abusing the local populace and carrying out extra-judicial murders.[90]

Most interviewees, whether Taliban or local elders, stressed the importance of how the group positioned themselves as avengers against an unjust order.[91]

The importance of airstrikes and special forces raids as a factor in mobilisation was confirmed by several elders.[92] The immense power displayed by the US air campaign started turning civilians against the Americans and their Afghan allies. An elder in Ghazni asked, 'Couldn't they use their new technology to differentiate between the criminals and innocents?'[93] He was not alone in feeling disconcertment:

> Once, at night, foreign troops conducted an operation in our district, I don't know why. They attacked a home, and as a result they also killed two kids and one woman. [...] What was their crime? It has driven me crazy as well as the other villagers. This disaster made everybody nervous; this is why some people decided to join with the Taliban and start fighting against the foreign troops, to take revenge against them.[94]

An elder in Wardak, now hostile to the Taliban, admitted to having sympathised with them for a period as a result of the indiscriminate house searches:

> ...every night there were American search operations in our district – they were looking for former Taliban commanders and arrested lots of people who had left the Taliban movement, but even so they were captured by the Americans, their houses were searched with dogs during the night and even their women were searched by American men. Lots of other innocent villagers who didn't have any link to the Taliban were also arrested or harrassed by the Americans and the local district authorities. Really even I, a normal villager, grew tried of the cruelties of the Americans and of the local authorities – I was happy for the return of the Taliban to our district...[95]

The new local elite, linked to the coalition government which had gained power as a result of US intervention, appears to have assumed the right to pursue their local rivals by labelling them as Taliban, as eloquently put by one of them:

> 'The Taliban are the enemy, [...] but they are local people, it is a house on house fight: the source of this war is the thirty years of fighting that has created *badal* on *badal* [revenge on revenge]'. 'If they are my [local] enemies and I work for the government, then they are Taliban [by definition – because the government's enemy is Taliban].'[96]

Taliban recruitment was greatly facilitated by this abusive behaviour, according to a member recruited during this period.[97] The Taliban started being seen as the only vehicle available for exacting revenge. According to one recruit (who became a commander):

I told the district governor that my brother was only a farmer and I wanted justice for him. My nephew was only 10 years old and now he is disabled, I wanted justice for him too. But the district governor told me that he could not do anything because my brother was killed by American special forces, and he had no knowledge of who those troops were and from whence they came to Jaghatu district.[98]

Conflicts among powerbrokers aligned with Kabul helped the Taliban's expansion.[99] Neglect by the authorities allowed the Taliban to operate relatively undisturbed in the early days of the insurgency, when they were vulnerable. The police would not react at the sight of Taliban fighters a few hundred meters away, even sometimes letting them carry out attacks under their noses.[100] One elder from Panjwai (Kandahar) recounted how he took part in a delegation that visited the provincial governor to warn him of a Taliban presence in Morgahn, an area within the district. The governor ignored the warning and then a wave of murders started, with targets including pro-government teachers, elders and mullahs.[101]

In some cases it was worse than neglect, with authorities tolerating the Taliban in the context of local power struggles among government officials. Cases like this were reported in Kunduz, Jowzjan and Faryab.[102]

While former Taliban were pushed into joining the insurgency and became its first generation of cadres, the Taliban as a movement regained credibility as the party that wanted to restore rule by Islamic law. Until 2005, however, this was only sufficient to allow the insurgency to slowly increase in size and momentum, until large-scale and open military activity commenced in 2006–7.[103] The timing of this upsurge suggests that British deployment was a key unleashing factor in Helmand. According to a commander from Nad Ali:

Before 2006 or 2007, people didn't want the Taliban in their villages, they didn't let the Taliban in... the Taliban were in Garmser. Then when the people became tired of the British troops and the Afghan government... they invited the Taliban in. They offered the Taliban food, rest and support, and welcomed them to the villages, supporting them when they fought.[104]

This is another point around which a vast consensus exists among the interviewees, in particular because of the concomitant destruction of opium fields. Programmes of opium eradication and the destruction of fields (whether real or perceived) naturally served to incentivise the population to invite the Taliban into their districts, and to join the fight against the government and the British:

In truth, the fighting started because of opium. They started destroying the opium fields of the people – that's why they became angry. The second reason is that they dropped lots of bombs [and carried out] airstrikes. Many people – [including] girls and women – were killed. People became very angry. But the fighting initially started because of the opium fields. [...] Opium was the food of the people. The rich had land and they grew opium, so it was good for them. For the poor, landless, farmers who worked the land, it was good, because they got 20 or 30 per cent of the opium, so it was a very lucrative job. When they started destroying the opium fields, the people – landowners, farmers, poor people – became angry, and they started fighting.[105]

The same could be said of other areas affected by the ISAF deployment to the south, such as Kandahar:

One good aspect of the Taliban was this – the Afghan government did not give permission for the cultivation of opium and cannabis, but the Taliban gave permission in our areas.[106]

Tribal rivalries were also aptly exploited by the Taliban. In Spin Boldak it was their rivalry with the Achakzais (who controlled the border police) that pushed the local Noorzai communities towards the Taliban.[107] Entire tribal sections, like the Alizai community in Garmser (a small portion of the whole Alizai tribe), started siding with the group.[108] An aspect of the flawed post-2001 set-up was the uneven distribution of government positions among the tribal communities, leaving some completely cut off and more likely to be attracted to the Taliban. As a rule, whole tribes would not join the Taliban in their entirety – except perhaps for the Ishaqzais, a major tribe only in Sangin and Nawzad districts. The divisions between pro- and anti-government were instead manifested at the sub-tribal level, for example, within the Alokozai tribe, the Khotezai sub-tribe was excluded from power and provided many recruits for the Taliban, while their traditional rivals the Bostanzai sub-tribe were well represented within the government.[109]

In areas of mixed ethnicity, ethnic friction also contributed to fill Taliban ranks. In Kapisa, alongside the usual house searches (this time by French troops), the perceived dominance of Jamiati Tajiks was a major factor in facilitating Taliban recruitment, with the support of Pashtun elders.[110]

In general, the Taliban seemed well-informed about local politics and manoeuvred accordingly to manipulate local conflicts and drive a wedge into existing fissures. The most obvious case is the ethnic conflict between Pashtuns and non-Pashtuns in Kunduz Province in 2009, where Pashtun communities in particular held grievances against local strongmen associated with the anti-Taliban alliance in 2001. But the same dynamics seem to have applied also within each ethnic group. Social and tribal fault lines have, for instance, been exploited by the Taliban among the Pashtuns of Baghlan, drawing the lower strata of society towards the insurgency. Some researchers have detected a pattern of Taliban exploitation of local rivalries among Uzbeks, too. The tendency of a weaker clan in a village to side with the Taliban repeats patterns of political alignment that were already present in the 1980s, and probably long before. The losers have a stronger incentive to support the outsiders: it is their only chance at 'making a revolution'.[111] Some night letters recovered in Kohistan District (Faryab) hint at how the Taliban exploited local rivalries for recruitment. In Kohistan, a long-standing rivalry existed between two halves of the district; the night letters invited villagers in one to pay tax to the Taliban in exchange for help in fighting the other half.[112]

Some social groups were already predisposed towards sympathising with the Taliban, having lost out in the post-2001 settlement. For example, in Garmser social groups such as squatters, who had earlier supported the Emirate, were forced off the land by the new powerbrokers and therefore turned to the Taliban.[113] As a result most Taliban supporters were lower class Baluchis and Ghilzais, from poor immigrant families.[114] In Baghlan, the Taliban recruited largely among the descendents of the third wave of Pashtun migrants from the south, who had wound up with humble jobs and little to no land, while Hizb-e Islami recruited mostly among the descendents of the second wave.[115]

In Helmand, some elders maintain that, for many, joining the Taliban promised not only an outlet for their rage and a chance for adventure or respect, but, ideology aside, represented the only realistic employment opportunity.

> They were jobless, the young. They didn't talk to the mullahs, they went straight to the Taliban. They saw it as employment.[116]

Others, however, deny the importance of economic reasons in recruitment.[117] In fact, the situation seems to have varied from district to district. Forced recruitment is mentioned by a small minority of interviewees – mostly elders unsympathetic to the Taliban along with a single group member, who alleged that his family was under heavy pressure to provide a fighter – but vehemently denied by others. The provision of logistical support did, however, operate through Taliban coercion.[118]

The Taliban are powerful. They come into a house, they say that we are fighting for you, fighting for God and to free you from these people – who is going to refuse them? Who can say no? People are forced to help them… People are tired of foreign troops, but they are also tired of the Taliban. One day people will go mad, take weapons and stand against the foreign troops.[119]

Finally, a significant driver of mobilisation was the widespread – and lasting – sympathy for the Taliban among the mullahs. The role of the clergy can not be underestimated: it retained a capillary distribution network in each village, and mullahs enjoyed the respect of the more conservative component of the village population. In some mosques inside Afghanistan, the Taliban and their sympathisers were already preaching in favour of jihad in 2002–4, but there was not yet a systematic effort by the incipient Taliban organisation to foster these types of activities.[120]

Even among the clergy in the north, support, or at least sympathy, for the aims of the Taliban seems to be quite extensive, particularly among the village mullahs. They are often afraid of losing their traditional unchallenged power to foreign influences, as a result of broader access to education, or even just due to a road being built to reach their village more easily. Sectors of the clergy were evidently openly preaching against the government and foreign presence well before a Taliban armed presence surfaced in the north, for example in Faryab in 2003–4 and in Takhar in 2005–6. Not every one of the many madrasas of the north (there is at least one per district) were involved in the insurgency, but some certainly were.[121] There was a constant flow of students back and forth between the villages of the Greater North and the madrasas of Pakistan, with a significant number returning fully indoctrinated as agitators for the Taliban.[122] According to local notables and clerics, 70 per cent of the mullahs in the north (of all ethnic backgrounds) – and perhaps an even greater percentage of madrasa teachers – were trained in Pakistan, which likely facilitated the spread of pro-Taliban sympathies. The actual appearance of the Taliban could only have encouraged a larger number of conservative mullahs to publicly state their sympathies, taking positions against the government and the foreign presence. Particularly where the Taliban did not enjoy extensive community support, the madrasas seemed to be the main source of grassroots recruitment.[123] [124]

As the Taliban's efforts started to become more thoroughly organised from 2005 onwards, in addition to employing techniques of persuasion and encouraging young, sympathetic mullahs to find employment in the villages, they proactively sought to replace mullahs with whom they were not politically compatible.[125] Mullahs were sent to the mosques to preach jihad in a systematic fashion, while existing imams were contacted and strongly encouraged to support the jihad.[126, 127, 128] The mosques were extentively used for recruitment purposes:

When the Taliban activated in our district, they collected the villagers into the mosques and encouraged them to join the jihad against the American colonisers...[129]

## 2.2 The military machine starts shaping up

As financial resources became more readily available, a more sophisticated structure developed around the Rahbari Shura. Over the years several commissions were established, of which the most important were Finance, Political (in charge of foreign affairs), Judicial, Health, Education, Agricultural, Recruitment, Logistics, Local, and of course the Military Commission. The Military, Logistics and Recruitment Commissions are discussed in Chapter 6. In addition to this, a plethora of offices, councils and departments were gradually established within the various commissions, or separately from them. These offices and departments dealt with a wide range of issues, ranging from propaganda to prisoners of war, from religious affairs to intelligence gathering.[130] Of these, we will here only be dealing with the most important structures, and particularly those related to the military effort. However, it is worth mentioning the Finance Commission, which first appeared in 2005 in the Quetta Shura. It was tasked with managing fundraising abroad, supervising local fundraising, and setting up funding targets and rates.[131] Later, more Finance Commissions were established in other *shura*s. The existence of dedicated, centralised financial structures also allowed the Taliban to save capital reserves for any rainy days ahead. The Peshawar Shura, for example, as of May 2015 reportedly had reserves amounting to $420 million.[132]

Every *shura* has financial reserves [...] This means that even if all the support stops [...], they have enough money that they can fight on for two years.[133]

One of the tasks of the Finance Commissions was investing the financial reserves of the Taliban in legal businesses and properties. The investments (under false names) were primarily located in Afghanistan, Pakistan and Dubai.[134]

As discussed in Chapter 1, appointments to Taliban governorships began in 2004, with appointees given formal command authority over all Taliban in their area of responsibility. The governors were supposed to supervise or perform all key activities, including those related to finance and logistics. Around them an increasingly sophisticated structure was built, described as follows in a Taliban publication:

> The Governor is directly responsible for the Supreme Command of that province and directs its military, civilian, financial and legal affairs. [...] Among his duties is the application of Shari'ah laws and statutes; supervision of directorate governors; execution of the war plan; supervision of financial resources and expenditures. Committees with appropriate authorities work with him on the provincial level, including the legal, military and financial committees; an education committee, etc.

In summary the tasks of different Taliban structures were thus described:

- Deputy governor: typically local, 'with experience in affairs of the region'.
- Military Commission: training, equipping, acting as a command group;
- Preaching and Guidance Commission: managing pro-Taliban clerics;
- Culture and Information Commission: managing the propaganda effort;
- Education Commission: managing Taliban-controlled madrasas and trying to influence state schools;
- Finance Commission: managing the funds allocated to the province;
- Health Commission: taking care of wounded members.[135]

However, the governors continued to struggle to assert their authority.[136] In fact, the organisation of the Taliban in 2005–9 very much rotated around a few key personalities, who could mobilise funding and support through their personal networks. Among them, until his death in 2007, Mullah Dadullah was the shining star:

> ...we lacked weapons and money. So I visited Mullah Dadullah. He had gone into Helmand province in early 2006 with 30 men. When he returned months later, he had organised 300 sub-commanders who each had dozens of troops. He had also signed up and was training hundreds of suicide-bomb volunteers. His return was like the arrival of rain after five years of drought. I gave him a list of our needs. [...] The next day he called me, took a page out of a notebook, wrote something on it, and gave it to me. The note gave the details of a man he said would help me. Back in Pakistan, I found the man. He kissed Dadullah's letter. After two weeks this man

had provided me with all the guns, weapons and supplies I had requested. Dadullah gave such letters to many people.[137]

Jalaluddin Haqqani was the other major fundraiser and organiser:

Jalaluddin Haqqani's tribal fighters actively came back to our side because the Americans and the Pakistanis had arrested his brother and other relatives. He appointed his son Sirajuddin to lead the resistance. That was a real turning point. Until then, villagers in Paktia, Paktika and Khost thought the Taliban were defeated and finished. They had started joining the militias formed by the Americans and local warlords, and were informing on us and working against us. But with the support of Haqqani's men we began capturing, sentencing and beheading some of those Afghans who had worked with the Americans and Karzai. Terrified, their families and relatives left the villages and moved to the towns, even as far as Kabul. Our control was slowly being restored.[138]

The need to more fully exploit these charismatic leaders as recruiters and mobilisers led to the formation of the *loy mahazes* in 2005. These had no upper limits on how many men they could mobilise, or on their area of deployment, and this suited the most prominent military leaders of the Taliban well. They also had the right to carry out their own fundraising, bypassing the Finance Commission.[139] Unlike local commanders, the *loy mahaz* leaders were even able to seek funding abroad.[140] Naim Mahaz, for example, in 2012 received most of its funding from Iran (70%), followed by Pakistan (15%) and through druglords (15%). It occasionally also received contributions from Arab countries and from China.[141] Some *loy mahaz*es were very poorly funded, such as Hussain Rahimi's, which in 2014 was receiving only $4 million per year from Quetta and subsisted largely on much more generous funds provided by Iran.[142] The creation of the *loy mahaz*es was also linked to the fact that some donors would only transfer funds to their protégés among the Taliban leaders.[143] It was not uncommon for donors to dictate where a *loy mahaz* should be active, and what it was to do.[144]

In order to establish a *loy mahaz*, a rule was imposed that a *loy mahaz* leader needed to be able to mobilise at least 1,750 men.[145] Later this was amended to 2,000 men.[146] Finally the minimum requirement for setting up a *loy mahaz* was increased, with a leader needing to demonstrate that he commanded the loyalty of at least 5,000 men (through collection of IDs).[147] Because the *loy mahaz* tended to offer more attractive conditions than the standard Quetta Shura recruitment package, they attracted commanders who volunteered to join:

It works like this... were I in Faryab province, say, I might have 20 or 40 men... I would contact [*loy mahaz* leader] Mullah Sattar and ask to fight for him, and he would then buy us weapons and send us money.[148]

Form the military point of view, the innovation of the *loy mahaz* compared to the governors' forces lay in how they were mostly composed of mobile forces, which could take the fight to wherever it was needed. Some *loy mahaz*es did not recruit any local Taliban. They had their own complex internal chains of command, connecting the *loy mahaz* leader to the fighting units, in an arrangement elsewhere described as a 'network of networks'.[149] It was, of course, some of the most prominent military leaders of the Taliban who started registering their *loy mahaz* with the Quetta Shura: the first *loy mahaz* leaders were Mullah Dadullah Lang, Mullah Baradar, Mullah Faruq and Mullah Ibrahim.[150]

Until 2007, only the four *loy mahaz*es mentioned above had been established: Dadullah's, Faruq's, Baradar's and Ibrahim's (in order of appearance), all formed in 2005–6. By 2005 the majority of the fighters of the Quetta Shura were already organised within these four *loy mahaz*es, whereas only 30–40 per cent were in groups directly subject to the orders of the provincial shadow governor. More importantly, the *loy mahaz*es were at that time the Quetta Shura's only mobile forces.[151]

Dadullah Lang was by far the most prominent of these *loy mahaz* leaders, with his role extending even further than this, as he occupied top positions in the Taliban's military structure. Dadullah was on bad terms with prominent Rahbari Shura figures such as Akhtar Mohammad Mansur, Mullah Osmani and Mullah Baradar throughout his career, as these leaders considered him too violent and cruel.[152]

Mullah Baradar was the best known of the Taliban political leaders and the de-facto head of the Quetta Shura; technically he was Mullah Omar's deputy, but Omar appeared only rarely at meetings and Baradar took almost all the key decisions.

Mullah Faruq hailed from the Alizai tribe and was a former classmate of Mullah Omar, joining the Taliban in 1996 and serving as district governor and adviser to Omar. Always close to the latter, he also entertained close relations with Dadullah Lang, Sirajuddin Haqqani and Abdul Majid. He had good connections in the Arab Gulf and was able to raise significant funding for his *loy mahaz*. Faruq had a reputation for cold relations with the Pakistani authorities: his *loy mahaz* had some Arab advisers, but never any Pakistani advisers. He was able to mobilise fighters across the southern tribes, despite being a rather senior Alizai tribesman.[153] In 2005 Faruq co-opted five large commanders linked to him, who together could muster over 1,000 fighters; on this initial base of support he started a recruitment campaign among former Taliban in the madrasas and refugee camps of Pakistan. He refused to appeal to the various sub-*shura*s of the Taliban for help, as they demanded funds to act as his recruiters, but he nonetheless did maintain relations with the Jangi Mangal sub-*shura*.[154]

Mullah Ibrahim was instead closely supported by the Ishaqzai sub-*shura*, which contributed about a third of its fighters. Like the others, he campaigned in the madrasas and in the villages for recruits, after gathering four senior Taliban commanders (Qari Ahmad Jan Akhwand, Mullah Sayed Rasool, commander Ziaurahman and Mullah Gul Rasool Ishaqzai) to form the core of the *loy mahaz*. Ibrahim received Pakistani support and his groups were advised by Pakistanis, unlike Faruq. He was close to Rahbari Shura members Abdul Majid, Ihsanullah Rahimi, Abdul Rauf and Abdul Kabir.[155]

The internal organisation of the *loy mahaz*es varied. All *loy mahaz*es needed to have district- and province-level representatives to coordinate with other Taliban, but apart from that they were free to organise themselves as they desired. Each *loy mahaz* tended to have a different tribal base, although recruitment was never exclusively tribal. For example, Baradar attracted many Popolzais to his *loy mahaz*, Ibrahim many Ishaqzais, and so forth.[156]

The personal loyalty of the *loy mahaz* members to the leader should however not be overestimated. Many cadres served in different *loy mahaz*es during their career. One from Uruzgan, for example, served with the Dadullah Mahaz in 2004–7 in Kandahar and Helmand; then with the Sattar Mahaz in 2007–9 in Herat and Farah; then with the Baradar Mahaz in 2010–11 in Zabul and Kandahar; and finally with the Zakir Mahaz in 2011 in Uruzgan. He left the Dadullah Mahaz when Dadullah Lang was killed, but then explained his repeated changes by saying that 'the other *mahaz*es were not conducting jihad correctly, and they were not acting justly. They were working for money. But Zakir's *mahaz* works for jihad and Islam.'[157] Another joined the Dadullah Mahaz in 2007, left in 2008 to work for the Ghazni shadow governor until 2010, when he joined the Mansur Mahaz, the *loy mahaz* of Akhtar Mohammad Mansur.[158] Quetta Shura rules allowed for such transfers, as long as the current and prospective *loy mahaz* leaders both agreed to the transfer.[159]

Already in 2005 a 'Council of Front Leaders' (*Mahaz Shura*), as mentioned in the Layeha of 2006, was established to solve disputes among insurgents.

The Mahaz Shura was meant to limit friction and improve organisational coherence. It operated by consensus but with a key input coming from Baradar's charismatic and well-respected leadership style.[160] In practice the rivalries among the *loy mahaz*es were so deeply entrenched that mere coordination among peers did not achieve much. Views about the importance of the Mahaz Shura varied widely, with some senior Taliban dismissing it as having always been of limited importance,[161] and others claiming that it was very important.[162]

In 2005–10 the Quetta Shura became increasingly dependent on the multiplication of *loy mahaz*es to maintain its fighting power. The system of double funding (the Rahbari Shura paid the *loy mahaz*es according to how many fighters they could muster, while the *loy mahaz*es were also allowed to raise funds independently) was supposed to link the fighting groups to the Rahbari Shura and give it influence over them, but also favoured the groups' expansion.[163]

The completion in fundraising among *loy mahaz*es could be bitter and lead to unreliable funding streams, with obvious consequences for the functioning of the Taliban's war machine. A good example of the vagaries of *loy mahaz* fundraising is provided by the Dadullah Mahaz. When it was relaunched in 2011, it initially received funding directly from the the Head of the Military Commission, Abdul Qayum Zakir, who wanted to reactivate a pool of aggressive commanders formerly loyal to Dadullah and thought the Dadullah Mahaz would support him against Baradar's supporters. The following year, however, Mansur enlisted help from Al-Qaida, the Iranians (who at that time were cooperating with Al-Qaida in Afghanistan) and the Haqqanis to fund the Dadullah Mahaz and lure it away from the influence of his rival Zakir. The Haqqanis saw the Dadullah Mahaz as an opportunity to expand their influence into southern Afghanistan. In sum, the Dadullah Mahaz was reportedly receiving direct funding amounting to $20 million yearly at this point, on top of what the Rahbari Shura was able to allocate.[164] The Dadullah Mahaz was led at that time by Mullah Dadullah's nephew, Qari Rahmanullah Yousafzai, who kept the front close to the hardline positions that characterised Dadullah Lang.[165] In January 2014 one of Dadullah's brothers, Mansur Dadullah, was released from a Pakistani jail and took the *loy mahaz* back under his control. He also enforced a 180 degree change in the policy prescribed up to that point, realigning with the 'moderates' within the Quetta Shura, at this point led by Akhtar Mohammad Mansur. The result was, however, the flight of funders like the Haqqanis, Pasdaran and Al-Qaida, which was then only partially replaced by Akhtar Mohammad Mansur's cash. Many hardline commanders from the Dadullah Mahaz defected to other *loy mahaz*es, established their own front as did Abdul Matin or Ihsan Rahimi, or even split from the Taliban altogether. In total, about 5,000 members of the Dadullah Mahaz are estimated to have left during this period.[166]

The competition for funding was bitter because an insufficiently funded *loy mahaz* would rapidly lose its manpower to other *loy mahaz*es, or see it disperse. Aside from the aforementioned case of the Dadullah Mahaz, other examples include the Sattar Mahaz, which in 2013 lost many commanders and about a quarter of its fighters to the Zakir Mahaz, as funding for Sattar from Pakistani sources was declining.[167]

As a result of this competition dramatic about turns in the foreign relations of the *loy mahaz*es were not uncommon, as Dadullah's case above shows. Another example is the Baradar Mahaz. Baradar's relationship with the ISI deteriorated in 2009 as he started working on a reconciliation deal with Kabul.[168] The Baradar Mahaz's funding came from Arab Gulf sources, through the Pakistani ISI. As this stopped, the Baradar Mahaz had to survive on some funding from Iran and from Akhtar Mohammad Mansur, while losing most of its fighters and commanders.[169] Some *loy mahaz* leaders turned to international jihadist organisations that were able to provide funding, even when their policies were not aligned. Taliban sources, for example, indicated that in 2013 the Mansur Mahaz was still receiving substantial funding from Al-Qaida, up to 20 per cent of its total budget.[170]

The development of the *loy mahaz* was instrumental in allowing the expansion of the Taliban in 2005–10 and beyond. In Herat the *loy mahaz*es of Mansur, Zakir and Naim played an important role,[171] as did the Baradar Mahaz in Faryab.[172] Often the *loy mahaz* deployments preceded the emergence of the Rahbari Shura's governors. In Ghazni, the Dadullah Mahaz appeared in February 2007 and rapidly expanded to the districts of Nawa, Gilan, Muqur, Qarabagh and Jaghatu. Local recruitment efforts with mosque imams, elders and tribal *shura*s started immediately. By 2008 the Dadullah Mahaz had reached Nawur, Zana Khan, Deh Yak and Andar and by 2009 the remaining districts with any significant Pashtun population were also affected: Giro, Ab Band, Malistan and Arjistan.[173] The Rahbari Shura arrived a few months later, appointing shadow governor Mullah Abdul Khaliq to recruit and lead locally.[174] In Wardak the Dadullah Mahaz arrived at about the same time as the governor's forces.[175] Mullah Janan and the Haqqanis appeared in Kunduz, Mullah Sattar in Baghlan, and so on.[176]

Then in 2007–8 as a result of the death of three out of four *loy mahaz* leaders, the Rahbari Shura started inviting all military leaders of some charisma to form their own *loy mahaz* and the proliferation of *loy mahaz*es started (see Figure 1 in the Annex):

> The Rahbari Shura would give money to *mahaz*es. Those who were in charge of one got a lot of money, so the number of *mahaz*es increased – everyone was trying to make a *mahaz*.[177]

The expansion in the number of *loy mahaz*es was also driven by power rivalries within the Quetta Shura. The Dadullah Mahaz and the Faruq Mahaz were recognised as the most active and warlike of the first generation, while the Baradar Mahaz was believed by some to not be sufficiently aggressive, and to instead have been created to counter-balance the other *loy mahaz*es and to attract funding:[178] 'Baradar is more moderate than others – his *mahaz* would always work to line their own pockets as well.'[179] Mullah Ibrahim's *mahaz* was considered the most moderate of the early *loy mahaz*es, but he also enjoyed the reputation of a leader who would often join his commanders on the battlefield.[180]

Whenever the Taliban needed to concentrate forces for large operations, the *loy mahaz*es would lead. A notable example was the battle of Pashmul, in September–October 2006, near Kandahar, where Mullah Dadullah managed to gather about 2,000 men and concentrate them in a relatively small area, in an attempt to take on foreign forces in a conventional, set-piece battle. Most, if not all, of the troops seem to have been provided by Dadullah's *loy mahaz*. During 2006, ISAF estimated that the Taliban brought 12,000 fighters from Pakistan into Afghanistan, 'emptying Quetta and other centres', although only some of these were sent to Pashmul.[181] In the event, the battle was a heavy tactical defeat for the Taliban, but Pashmul still represented a propaganda victory, as it conveyed the message that the insurgency was able, or at the very least willing, to take on the world's most powerful militaries in the open field, casualties notwithstanding.[182]

As well as driving home the point that the Taliban could not expect to take on international forces in conventional engagements, this rare example of a set-piece battle demonstrated the limitations of the *loy mahaz*-based system when it came to concentrating and coordinating military assets.[183] ISAF intelligence sources reported that in 2005–6 the Taliban believed they could escalate the level of confrontation to the 'conventional' stage in Kandahar; once that belief was proven misguided in Pashmul, it seemed clear that the Taliban needed an improvement upon the *loy mahaz* system to win the war.[184]

The *loy mahaz* internal chain of command and control was relatively strong, but was based on personal loyalties and not merit. In the absence of any kind of 'professional officer corps', in Pashmul even Dadullah's *loy mahaz* was forced to adopt a static defence posture, which could only lead to defeat when confronted with the firepower of western armies. The *loy mahaz*es were appointing cronies of their leaders as cadres, making them poor maneuver units. Moreover, it was difficult for these charismatic individuals to exercise control when their forces intermingled, as there was no real supra-*loy mahaz* command and control system. In such a situation, a larger Taliban operation could feature a number of commanders linked to different *loy mahaz*es, often imparting conflicting orders. The *loy mahaz*es' own chain of command duplicated that of the governors, creating a conflict between two or more (depending on how many *loy mahaz*es were present) chains of command. For example, in 2007 military intelligence sources intercepted a Taliban communication, showing that 400 Taliban in northern Helmand were refusing to join their comrades in Musa Qala to defend it from a major assault by British, American and Afghan army forces.[185]

The main vulnerability of the *loy mahaz*es was their dependency on the status of their leaders; any major development affecting them would have serious repercussions on the Taliban's capability to fight. After Dadullah's death on 8 May 2007, there were reports that Taliban operations were badly affected, as many Taliban commanders withdrew to Pakistan and about seven of his senior commanders even left the insurgency.[186] Others joined the new *loy mahaz* created in the wake of Dadullah's demise.[187]

Another drawback of the *loy mahaz* system was that it created new problems of discipline. Charisma aside, the first few *loy mahaz* leaders were among those cadres and commanders who had survived the Emirate; in particular, those who could rely on solid funding channels. Funds gathered abroad among Afghan and non-Afghan donors were sometimes gathered by the leadership and re-distributed, or distributed directly to the main *loy mahaz* leaders, apportioned on the basis of loyalty, recruitment, military potential or tribal following. Such direct funding further strengthened the *loy mahaz* leaders vis-à-vis the political leadership and the governors.[188] The bigger and better funded the *loy mahaz*, the more difficult to control it for the governors, particularly in the case of those which were less dependent on the funding provided by the Rahbari Shura, thanks to their own funding channels.[189] A veteran commander commented, 'At that time, all the *mahaz* commanders misused their positions – they behaved like kings.'[190]

Infighting became relatively common as a result, both between *loy mahazes* and governor groups, and among *loy mahazes*. Different *loy mahazes* could have very different allegiances. In Helmand some were close to Sher Mohammad Akhundzada, Karzai's governor and senator, and others were bitterly opposed to him. The Ibrahim Mahaz entertained particularly close relations with Sher Mohammed Akhundzada and even appointed a cousin of Sher Mohammed as senior commander for the south-west.[191] Then there was competition for territorial control:

> In fact the *mahaz* commanders are trying to gain more influence in Afghanistan and to have at least one representative in every province. The *mahaz* commander's first priority is to deploy their groups to those provinces or districs where they don't have any presence.[192]
>
> Everyone wants to become famous, become powerful, and get money from other countries. There is competition between the *mahazes*, they want to be stronger, bigger than the others. The bigger a *mahaz*, the more the Rahbari Shura relies on it and the more funding it gets from foreign countries.[193]

Dadullah Lang was considered extremely violent even by his Taliban colleagues, and was known for not even respecting the Shari'a. His men were the most reluctant to submit to the authority of the governors.[194] Only after his death did Baradar manage to bring Dadullah's men under the control of the governors, but by then the *loy mahaz* was disintegrating.[195] By contrast the Baradar Mahaz and the Ibrahim Mahaz were the most cooperative with the governors.[196]

The existence of different Taliban networks also contributed to problems for mobility:

> We don't accept Taliban even from Ghazni, or from other places. [...] We know the people in our area and they trust us. If Taliban come in from other regions, they may disturb the people; we don't know what they'll do during the night. They might destroy our reputation as well.[197]

What kept the Taliban military system somehow together was the personal role of Mullah Baradar, who doubled up as deputy of Mullah Omar and as leader of his own *loy mahaz*. In his first role, because of his personal charisma and the wide respect he enjoyed, Baradar was the reason the Taliban could bring some coordination to bear on the otherwise disjointed *loy mahaz* system. The description of the Taliban as a 'network of networks' was never more true than in this period, as the central leadership developed structures to enable a limited degree of strategic cooperation and coordination. In practice, it was Baradar himself had to intervene to resolve disputes and mediate among commanders and *loy mahaz*.

> Baradar operates like an old-fashioned Pashtun tribal head. He sits and talks not only with his senior military men and political officers, but also with low-ranking commanders and tribal elders. When he meets with civilians, whether they're local sheiks or members of the Taliban's political elite, the Quetta Shura, he exudes a relaxed, traditional, even deferential manner. Baradar even frequently takes notes at meetings, and he constantly refers to Mullah Omar and his pronouncements, Akhund says. The Helmand subcommander and other Taliban sources say Baradar adopts a sterner, more martial air with his military council, but even in those strategy sessions he tries to elicit opinions and bring everyone together in some kind of consensus.[198]

The limitations of this system were obvious, even when Baradar successfully managed to handle local crises. A disproportionate amount of time had to be spent in micromanagement and local tussles were often solved at the central level:

> Earlier this year, the Zabul province commander says, he mustered the nerve to seek Baradar's help. Three of his fellow Taliban commanders in the province had become more intent on feuding with each other than on killing Americans. They were quarreling about where each one's territory ended; about who could set up roadside checkpoints to extort money from travelers on which stretch of highway; and about women who had been so bold as to marry outside their tribes. Two of the rivals were even plotting to unseat the Taliban's provincial governor. The Zabul commander had never met Baradar before and hardly dared to hope his call would be taken seriously. But within three weeks he was summoned for a face-to-face meeting with Baradar in Quetta. He and Baradar talked for two hours. 'He listened attentively to my complaints and suggestions, asked some questions, and said he'd see what he could do.' The results were apparent within two weeks. Rather than keep the sitting governor or replace him with one of the competing commanders, Baradar brought in a tough new governor, Mawlavi Ishmael, from neighbouring Ghazni province. Baradar then clearly delineated which parts of the main highway would be under the control of which commander, and ordered them to share their income from roadside checkpoints more equitably. Finally, he flatly ordered the guerrillas to drop the dispute over the women.[199]

Baradar, a typical southern Taliban leader, did not conceive of a system based on anything other than personal leadership. In order to reduce the problems created by the competition among *loy mahaz*es, he tried to subsume his three competitors into his own *loy mahaz*. When Dadullah was killed, it was widely alleged among the Taliban that Baradar had a hand in it:

> Mullah Baradar and Dadullah were enemies. Dadullah was killed because there was a spy called Nawab giving reports to the Americans. He belonged to Baradar's group, and was even personally involved in killing Dadullah. The whole of the Kakar tribe then knew that Dadullah was dead, and passed reports on to the Pakistanis about Baradar, who was arrested.[200]

Whether or not there is any truth to this, certainly Baradar wanted to expand his control over the Taliban's mobile forces. When Faruq was killed, Baradar invited his senior commanders to join him, but they refused as they knew Faruq and Baradar had never been on good terms. One of Faruq's senior commanders, Shahpur, asserted his claim to the leadership of the *loy mahaz*, but was detained by Baradar for three months. About a quarter of Faruq's commanders and fighters joined the Dadullah Mahaz, while the majority went home.[201] Similarly, after the death of Mullah Ibrahim, Baradar tried to prevent the continuation of the Ibrahim Mahaz under the leadership of its second-in-command, Ahmad Jan Akhund, through cutting its Rahbari Shura funding, lobbying for the cutting of Pakistani support and offering jobs to Ibrahim's senior commanders. About half of Ibrahim's fighters joined the Baradar Mahaz, while the rest left the Taliban.[202]

Baradar's attempt to centralise power in his hands were only partially successful and they ended when he was arrested in Pakistan in 2010, with operations negatively affected as succession issues and reciprocal accusations split the Taliban. Soon, his *loy mahaz* started disintegrating, with groups splitting, joining other *loy mahaz*es, or simply giving up the fight.[203]

Despite its dysfunctional aspects, the *loy mahaz* system did not develop by mere chance. It reflected an important aspect of the Taliban's worldview: a kind of anti-Leninism. It was (and is) based on clerical organisational patterns present in Sunni Islam and particularly in the sub-continent, where the state has had relatively little impact in co-opting the clergy.[204] For this reason, internal debates over organisational issues, which will be discussed below, have been highly controversial and contentious.

## 2.3 The funding underpinning the expansion of the Quetta Shura

From the beginning of the post-2001 jihad, the Taliban have been trying to raise tax whenever possible. In practice this has only been practicable where the community elders were willing to collaborate. In areas where the Taliban have had little support, such attempts have been complicated:

> We can't move much in Deh Rawood district, so we cannot collect *zakat* from all the villages. Some Taliban collect *zakat* from those villages which are far from the district centre, where we can stay for at least one hour. But we don't collect it properly, even in those remote villages, we (not me, other Taliban) go over there for 30 or 45 minutes, take some food from the villagers and leave the area soon after.[205]

Where they were able to collect tax, it was mostly collected in kind and then sold at the bazaar to convert it into cash. After some attempts to force commanders to hand over tax revenue to the Finance Commission or the Military Commission, it was decided that graft would be impossible to prevent, and the Taliban leadership(s) authorised commanders in the field to spend any revenues on their group, simply reporting to the Quetta Shura the amount and how it was spent. The leadership ordered in 2008 that combat groups should account for all money and resources they received and collected, and provide proof of their activities. Thit was the point at which videoing Taliban attacks became standard practice.[206] The rationale behind centralising revenue collection was not just to stamp out the use of resources for personal benefit, but also to be able to distribute resources strategically, rather than leave them where they were collected. For a time the rules were implemented, but the system turned out to be too cumbersome as far as locally raised revenue was concerned:[207]

> Before, we gave the *zakat* to the Military Commission in the district and then they would supply the commanders for expenses related to weapons, ammunition, salaries and so on. But now the system has changed; we have orders to collect *zakat* and spend it on our own team or group. When we collect it we pay our fighters and buy weapons and ammunition – we spend the total amount on our own group.[208]

UN sources, monitoring the group's funding streams, also indicated that about 31% of Taliban revenue (estimated at US$400 million in 2011–12) did not accrue to the leadership but stayed in the hand of local commanders, whether authorised or not.[209] While exact figures cannot be confirmed, Taliban sources confirm that the taxation system was quite leaky. A source indicated that in 2012 only about $1 million in *zakat* (one of several taxes raised by the Taliban) accrued to the Peshawar Shura (see Chapter 3), and about $2.5 million accrued to the Quetta Shura.[210] In any case, the Quetta

Shura gradually accepted that it could not centralise tax collection. In 2013, all local taxation reportedly brought them $23 million, but a source estimated that 20% of all operational costs would be paid by local taxes, including money spent locally.[211] In 2014 two sources from the Kandahar Taliban gave estimates of 20% and 40% as to how much of their funding was locally sourced.[212] This suggests that there has been a growing acceptance of local taxes remaining with the area's Taliban. It should be noted that out-of-area mobile Taliban units would not benefit at all from local revenue; hence if local groups were raising 20–40% of the money they were spending, the average for the Taliban as a whole must have been considerably less.[213]

As the insurgency grew in size, these local taxes accounted for a declining portion of overall fundraising, until they became relatively marginal.[214] Since at least 2009, external support has become increasingly centralised in the hands of the Financial Commission(s), contrary to locally raised taxes.

> We can't sustain our jihad with the money that we collect from the local villagers' *zakat*. The villagers grow wheat and vegetables, so if we take 10% of [their earnings from] vegetables, how much we can earn? This money is good for emergency situations and for the daily needs of our fighters, but we get most of our fighting equipment from Pakistan – otherwise we could not sustain the jihad in Afghanistan.[215]

*Zakat* and *ushr* collection was controversial, and unpopular among villagers, who often argued that such taxes should be used for poverty relief in rural communities. While the Taliban either deny collecting *zakat* and *ushr* or assert that they employ a fair approach in collection,[216] sparing the poorer farmers,[217] the account provided by the large majority of elders interviewed is of people feeling coerced to give, and of poor farmers often (but not always) being forced to give.[218]

Of the 51 elders who were asked about *zakat* and *ushr*, three insisted the Taliban did not tax the poor, while three stated the contrary; the others did not comment on the issue. Local commanders and fighters may also have tended to bend the rules imposed by the leaders, raising unauthorised taxes. One elder in Wardak referred to this directly when he mentioned that villagers would pay *zakat* and *ushr* to madrasas and mosques, from where the Taliban could collect it; Taliban collecting tax from the villagers directly were assumed to be breaking the rules.[219]

However, the Taliban, even when bending the rules, would restrain themselves to collecting the stipulated 10 per cent rather than trying to squeeze more out of the villagers. Only four of the elders asked stated that the Taliban would take items from shops without paying.[220]

The issue of 'voluntary' contributions to the Taliban by local businessmen is also controversial; sometimes businesses contributed in kind, for example refuelling fighters' motorbikes for free. The Taliban naturally claim that such contributions are entirely voluntary,[221] but one did admit, as an example, that the mobile telephone companies were forced to pay protection money to save their mobile network rigs from being destroyed.[222]

The alternative view is that businessmen consider this protection money that they have to pay if they want to operate unhindered in insecure areas.[223] In the early days of the insurgency it was largely the local commanders who were left to secure the necessary funding; the leadership was only able to send weapons and some ammunition.[224] Over time the Taliban established a well-developed system for collecting contributions through the Companies Commission and its local branches, with educated cadres tasked with assessing the turnover of companies and the value of taxes owed.[225] The rule of thumb was that taxes and voluntary contributions would pay for salaries and some other expenses, while weapons and ammunition were mostly provided or paid for by the leadership.[226]

The taxation of ISAF supply convoys was particularly controversial. There is little doubt that it occurred, but the Taliban claim that deals over supply convoys were not allowed and all supplies should be targeted.[227] Still the taxation of the convoys occurred on such a large scale that it seems impossible the leadership would have been unaware of it.[228] Perhaps there was too much potential revenue for rules not to be bent. War booty was supposed to be transferred to the finance commission.[229] The convoys provided abundant resources to the Taliban in specific areas only, for example in Sayed Abad district in Wardak province:

> In Sayed Abad district there is plenty of money. We can earn lots of money from the highway [through] which ISAF logistics [convoys] pass. There are also lots of traders who pay so the Taliban do not attack their convoys [...]. But for the Taliban who are in other districts or villages, beside the *zakat* they collect they also receive money and weapons from Pakistan and Iran – they don't have the sources of income that we have here, so Pakistan supports them. The Taliban in Sayed Abad district receive very little support from Pakistan, because we [already] have a very good income here...[230]

Particularly where substantial amounts of money were made, the local Taliban networks were not at all keen on surrendering the cash to the Military

Commission. The dispute between Mullah Baz Mohammed, who ran his own networks in Farah, and Mawlawi Ismail of the Military Commission, even made it to the Western press. Mohammed was very successfully raising funds for his network in 2011, through his key ally Mawlawi Habibullah, and had caught Ismail's eye due to his failure to turn over the money to the Commission. Mohammed and Habibullah maintained that the money belonged to the Noorzai tribe and could not be handed over. The clash ended with arrests and kidnappings in retaliation, and damaged the relations between the Noorzais and the Taliban leadership.[231]

Aside from a few spots like Sayedabad, Taliban revenue collection inside Afghanistan only ever produced enough to fund a large-scale insurgency where and when the Taliban were largely in control of the main poppy-growing areas of Helmand and Kandahar. This trend has long been apparent to external observers. For example, in 2003–8, estimates of the Taliban's drug revenue reached as high as US$90–160 million/year, while in 2009 they peaked at an estimated US$155 million; while the UN maintained for 2011–12 an estimate of US$100 million, ISAF estimates were as low as US$40 million, both because of previous inaccuracy and to reflect the fact that the Taliban had been pushed out of many of the poppy growing areas of the south.[232] The DEA, conversely, at one point even estimated that 70 per cent of the Taliban's revenue was from drugs.[233] Taxation of the narco-economy takes different shapes. David Mansfield has convincingly demonstrated that Taliban taxation of the poppy harvest varies widely in scope, is often negotiated locally and is overall of relatively marginal importance to the group's war effort.[234]

In the early days of the insurgency, local taxation accounted for a larger share of the revenue, but gradually external donors became more generous, eventually rendering movement largely dependent on external funding. The complete dependence of the Taliban on foreign support in most areas of the country was so obvious by 2011–12 that few commanders would even try to deny the fact in interviews.[235] In principle, for the group's image it would have been more convenient for these Taliban members to claim that the movement was self-sustaining – a notion that Taliban propaganda does promote. The fact that interviewees admitted otherwise suggests two things. Firstly, it seems the claims might well be genuine, and secondly we may assume that within the Taliban this support was an open secret (by virtue of being so extensive). These considerations do not confirm the exact extent of this support, nor that the figures provided by the Taliban about external support are precise.

However, as explained in the introduction, Taliban data on local and external revenue tallies with high-end estimates by military/intelligence analysts and appears compatible with estimates of Taliban manpower (see Table 6 in the Annex). If we accept the figures provided by Taliban sources, the spike in external funding appears to date back to 2005, when funds provided or channelled through Pakistan jumped to $50 million, from $20 million in 2004. In 2006 another jump took them to $80 million, and by 2007 they had reached $105 million. This rise is in line with the trend in recorded levels of Taliban activity. According to the sources, the increase was made possible by the involvement of a growing number of foreign governments, all through the Pakistani ISI. In 2008 these sources paid $150 million to the Quetta Shura, with this level of support matched in 2009.[236]

## 2.4 Why the Quetta Shura's growth contained the seeds of later trouble

In 2005–10 the Quetta Shura invested major human and financial resources in building an overarching infrastructure, in an effort to be able to manage the combat groups it was establishing or co-opting. By 2006–7 it was even starting to attract groups that had no Taliban roots, and were instead linked to anti-Taliban parties and groups. While this could be described as a success, it was already starting to complicate the leadership's task, by stretching the spectrum of Taliban membership and making the group more diverse and less homogeneous. At the same time, the Taliban were increasingly relying on the *loy mahaz*es to conduct offensive operations. Similar in concept to a semi-feudal arrangement, where the regiment commander 'owned' the unit, the *loy mahaz*es expanded recruitment and enhanced fighting strength, but further compounded the management problems faced by the leadership. During this period, having mainly relied on the re-mobilisation of old Taliban, the Quetta Shura felt little need to set up intensive training and indoctrination programmes. It took the socialisation of any fresh recruits into the Taliban for granted. But while old cadres would take care of socialising new recruits into their groups, recent converts to the cause had less incentive and capacity to shape their fresh recruits according to the original Taliban model.

As the Quetta Shura Taliban were themselves becoming more diverse and polycentric, new autonomous centres of Taliban power were starting to emerge outside the Quetta Shura. None of them turned out to be fully in line with the Quetta model. This is the topic of the next chapter.

# 3

# THE EMERGENCE OF ALTERNATIVE CENTRES
# OF POWER TO QUETTA

By 2007–8 there was discord emerging among the Taliban in the south-east and the east. The Haqqanis has began their jihad even before the Quetta Shura, but their role had barely been recognised by their southern colleagues, and the Haqqanis' representation in Quetta was minimal. In the east, various Taliban and non-Taliban networks keen to join the jihad were also starting to coalesce into a larger structure. Again, resentment at political domination by the old-style, southern Taliban was a major driving factor. If the Taliban had been characterised by vertical polycentrism from the beginning, horizontal polycentrism was now about to impose itself too.

One of the most contentious issues between Quetta and the two emerging alternative centres of power was the model of authority and command adopted. One criticism shared by both new autonomous *shuras* (Miran Shah and Peshawar) was that the trademark Taliban polycentrism was inadequate. Paradoxically, the two new *shuras* imposed a much higher degree of horizontal polycentrism in order to protest against Quetta's vertical polycentrism (that is, what they considered its weak command system).

The two new *shuras* did not just undermine Quetta's claims to the leadership of the entire Taliban, but started directly competing with it. Peshawar in particular, at the peak of its power (2010–13), set itself up as the successor to the Quetta Shura for the leadership role.

## 3.1 The Haqqanis become an autonomous centre of power, 2007–

*The split from Quetta*

After their launch in 2002 (discussed in Chapter 1), the Taliban of the Miran Shah Shura gradually expanded beyond Loya Paktia. It only established a serious military presence in Logar from 2006 onwards, initially sending Zadran fighters in from Khost, Paktia and Paktika.[1] During 2006 much of Logar fell under Taliban control:

> All the suburban areas of Mohammad Agha District came under the control of the Taliban. In 2006, 70 per cent of areas were under their control. In 2005 the group was not very strong, and could only place mines by the side of the road and attack some convoys of American cars. In 2006 they became very strong, capturing police and army checkpoints and taking control of whole villages.[2]

In 2006 the Haqqanis started also sending combat groups to Wardak province, albeit on a limited scale, and opened front towards the city of Kabul.[3] Their entry into Wardak, however, created friction with the Quetta Shura and later with the Peshawar Shura as well (see Chapter 4), both of which had ambitions in Wardak, making coordinated Taliban activities impossible for years.[4] Later the Peshawar Shura asserted its authority more firmly, but the Miran Shah Shura forces never fully accepted this.[5]

Competition in Wardak was not the only source of tension with Quetta. Despite the quick development of a rather successful working arrangement during 2003–4 (see above), from the beginning there was friction between Quetta and Miran Shah, as the latter demanded to have representatives in each of the Quetta commissions, *shura*s and offices, while the Rahbari Shura and in particular Mullah Baradar were only ready to accept two representatives from Miran Shah (Ahmad Jan Wazir and Qari Idris Haqqani). In Quetta the Haqqanis were considered trusted military partners, but not seen as political partners.[6]

A key turning point in the relationship between the two Shuras was Jalaluddin Haqqani's withdrawal from active life in 2007 because of bad health. His son Serajuddin took over and immediately raised the issue of Miran Shah's representation in Quetta more aggressively. He had already emerged as a critic of the Quetta Shura in previous years. In a 2004 interview with *Asia Times* he stated:

> At present, the Taliban are powerful, but there is a problem in that we have lost our central command. We have many successful commanders, but as the central

command does not exist to give day-to-day decisions and policies, we have not been able to proceed very well so far with our strategies. Also, in the absence of such a central command, it is difficult to discuss all these proposals coming to us from the commanders.[7]

He also complained that Quetta was allocating only modest financial resources and supplies to Miran Shah in exchange for the latter's subordination. In addition, Serajuddin had reservations concerning the strategies of the Quetta Shura for confronting the international coalition formed to confront the Taliban, and about the domination by southern Pashtuns.[8] Serajuddin and others in the Miran Shah Shura had already since 2005 been lobbying the Quetta Shura to adopt guerrilla tactics and suicide bombing, but their ideas were rejected.[9]

Faced with continuing rejection by Quetta's heavyweights such as Baradar, Akhtar Mohammad Mansur and Ishan Rahimi, Serajuddin decided to declare the autonomy of the Miran Shah Shura on 7 August 2007. From that time onwards Miran Shah stopped taking orders from Quetta and claimed the status of a peer *shura*, rejecting subordination; among other actions it withdrew its recognition of Quetta-appointed governors.[10] In public, however, the Haqqanis continued to defer to the Taliban, for example by branding their videos in the 'Manba' al Jihad' series as products of the 'Islamic Emirate of Afghanistan'.[11] Elders in Logar said that when entering villages, Haqqani fighters always identified themselves as Taliban first and members of the Haqqani Network second.[12]

The declaration of autonomy was made possible by Serajuddin's ability to mobilise funding autonomously from Quetta. In 2008 Miran Shah was able to raise around $66 million, mostly from Pakistan and private donors in Saudi Arabia. It was not until 2010 that its funding really took off, coinciding with declining donor interest in the Quetta Shura, which was by then entering a state of deep crisis (see Figure 2 in the Annex).

External funding levels appear to have still fallen short of the Haqqanis' needs or ambitions. As it declared its autonomy, the Miran Shah Shura overruled the earlier decision of the Quetta Shura to leave *ushr* and *zakat* collection to the local Taliban commanders, and ordered instead for all revenue from these taxes to be transferred to its Finance Commission.[13] Perhaps the Haqqani leadership assumed that given its better organisational structure and greater cohesiveness, it would likely be able to collect taxes more effectively than Quetta. In reality, as some Haqqani interviewees acknowledged, local members of the network often cheated and under-reported the amounts collected, just as the Quetta Shura affiliates had been doing.[14] Interviewees mentioned at least one group commander who was punished for not having transferred revenue to the Finance Commission.[15] Another two interviewees admitted to cheating, hinting clearly at the complicity of the Miran Shah Shura representatives:

> The Miran Shah Shura told us that when we collect *zakat* and *ushr* we should give it to the District Representative and he will send it to the Shura, but we just give a little to him and we keep most of the [revenue] ourselves for our families. [We do this] because the salary we receive is not enough for our family's expenses.[16]
>
> Even when we want to send [tax revenue], we send very little: 20 or 30 per cent. The District Representative of the Miran Shah Shura in Kharwar District supports us [in this]; we also give some money to him. If he did not [acquiese], then we could not keep the funds.[17]

At the peak of Quetta's armed presence in Loya Paktia in 2007, there were 2,000 fighters in about 80 groups, of which 30 were assigned to Paktika, 20 were assigned to Paktia (where Zurmat district was a Taliban stronghold linked to Quetta thanks to the local network of Latif Mansur), 20 to Khost and 10 to Logar.[18] From that point onwards the local group experienced a steep decline. As the split took place, there were even efforts by the Miran Shah Shura to appoint its own governors, for a time leading to multiple governors existing in places like Logar and Paktika. The break between Quetta and Miran Shah led only temporarily to the Haqqanis attempting to prevent Quetta's access to what Miran Shah considered 'their' provinces. In practice the Haqqanis never had monopolistic control over all Loya Paktia and Logar; in Paktika the Quetta Shura still maintained a significant presence in 2015, while in Logar the Peshawar Shura had a presence. In Paktia and Khost, however, the presence of Quetta Shura forces gradually dried up.[19]

Eventually an agreement was reached, according to which Quetta would continue appointing the governors, but:

- The appointments would be made in consultation with the Haqqanis, who would retain a veto power on appointees;
- the governors would have only symbolic powers beyond the few armed groups under their direct control;
- the governor would be subject to the superior authority of the representatives of the Miran Shah Shura for each province.[20]

The new agreement also allowed Quetta Shura forces to operate in Paktika under the command of the Miran Shah Shura.[21] Similarly, after negotiating for some time a merger with the Peshawar Shura (see Chapter 4) in exchange for funds, Miran Shah decided to allow the Peshawar Shura to maintain a symbolic presence of a few hundred men in each of the Loya Paktia provinces and in Logar, led by their own commander, but under the superior authority of the Miran Shah Shura Massul (representative).[22]

The position of the Miran Shah Shura has always been that it desires friendly relationships, on a peer level, with the other Taliban *shuras*. It has also maintained that Quetta's leadership could be re-established if Miran Shah's demands were accepted.[23]

During 2007–15 the relationship between Miran Shah and Quetta was tumultuous. From time to time the Haqqanis would decide to participate in wider Taliban efforts to expand geographically. In 2008, for example, they sent combat groups to Kunduz and Baghlan, while in 2010 they send some to Takhar and Ghazni.[24] In 2013, relations warmed as Abdul Qayum Zakir's prevarication and arrogant assertion of his power at the head of the Military Commission pushed Serajuddin closer to Akhtar Mohammad Mansur, whose *loy mahaz* was allowed to expand its existing access to Loya Paktia.[25] In exchange for allowing the Quetta Shura, and later even the Peshawar Shura, access to some of 'its' provinces, Miran Shah sent large permanent deployments to Ghazni (in addition to the deployment of *fedayin* teams, see below) from March 2014.[26] As of late 2014, senior Taliban leaders were again describing the relationship between Quetta and Miran Shah as 'very bad'.[27]

## The Haqqanis' jihadism

The Haqqanis have been linked to Al-Qaida (AQ) throughout the post-Taliban regime period. They are in fact the only Taliban network that has been receiving uninterrupted support from AQ from 2002 until at least 2017. In 2017 the level of this support was estimated at $20 million by sources inside the Haqqani network. This is because, of all the Taliban networks engaged in support for global jihad, the Haqqanis are the most resilient and active. AQ expected facilitation from the Haqqani network for itself and its allies, which it has regularly received. Virtually all jihadist organisations linked to AQ have been on friendly terms with the Haqqanis, and have cooperated extensively with them.[28]

The Haqqani's horizons have nevertheless remained primarily limited to the region. Their ventures in Syria and Iraq in 2012–14 did open the door to the 'contamination' of the network by pro-IS ideas.[29] However, Syria excepted, the Haqqanis have not been directly involved in jihad outside Afghanistan/Pakistan, limiting themselves to hosting camps, training facilities, some direct training provision and the facilitation of movement within their areas of influence. Serajuddin is said to be very supportive of the idea of jihad in central Asia, and has offered protection and extensive support to central Asian and Chinese jihadists.[30]

A peculiarity of the Haqqani network within the Taliban has been the direct recruitment of Pakistani fighters into its ranks (as opposed as to the alliances formed by other Taliban *shuras* with independent jihadist groups). Vahid Brown and Don Rassler described it as 'able to provide value to local, regional and global actors while simultaneously incorporating inputs from each actor group into a combined system of violence.'[31] As of 2015, about 10 per cent of the Miran Shah Shura's manpower were Pakistanis, mostly coming from other jihadist groups such as Tehrik-e-Taliban Pakistan (TTP), Lashkar-e Taiba and Lashkar-e Jhangvi. As a result of this recruitment, the Haqqanis regularly send large numbers of Pakistani fighters into Afghanistan. In the summer of 2014, for example, they reportedly deployed 3,500 such fighters for three months, as part of a contingent of 9,500 madrasa volunteers; 310 of them were killed during the deployment.[32] In Logar in 2014, according to a source within the Haqqanis, 800 foreign fighters joined the group over the summer, including about 500 Pakistanis from TTP and Lashkar-e Taiba, and 100 Arabs, 100 Chechens and 100 Central Asians. During the winter their numbers shrank to just 60.[33] In Paktika too, over the summer about 800–1,000 foreign fighters would turn up to fight on the Haqqanis' side, mostly from Lashkar-e Taiba, Lashkar-e Jhangvi and TTP.[34] The foreign fighters were concentrated within the Miran Shah Shura's Delayez commission (see below), of whom 16 per cent were foreign fighters (Pakistanis, Tajikistanis, Uzbekistanis, Turkmenistanis, Chinese, Chechens, and Indian Muslims) as late as mid-2015, despite the amount of foreign fighters being well past its peak due to Pakistani pressure.[35]

The presence of Pakistanis extended all the way to the top levels of the Miran Shah Shura. By 2015 the surviving leadership included (apart from Serajuddin) Khalil Haqqani, Mawlavi Ghaus Haqqani, Qari Azizullah Haqqani and Mawlavi Hakimullah Haqqani. Surrounding this inner circle were another 30 members of the Shura, of whom eight were Pakistanis.[36]

The noticeable presence of volunteers from Pakistan and other countries contributed decisively to the Haqqanis' image as much closer to global jihadist currents like Al-Qaida, than were the Quetta Shura. Still, the average Haqqani field commander does not appear to have differed from those in other Taliban groupings.[37] As in other networks, even within the Haqqanis' ranks it was possible to find a few commanders reluctant to fight fellow Afghans and Muslims:

> We don't attack the police too much because we know they're Muslims too. Our main enemies are the foreign troops, the Americans. We attack American bases or convoys. We only fight the police if we come under attack ourselves.[38]

They were also able to exercise restraint when necessary:

> We have a policy to not use suicide bombers in tribal areas. If use them, we operate in areas where there are no civilians. This is because if we use suicide bombers in tribal areas, people will not want to help us.[39]

### Masters of asymmetric warfare

The Haqqanis have operated in areas with an American presence since the early stages of their jihad; their links to Al-Qaida and other foreign jihadist groups attracted American interest, effectively turning the group into a primary target for US counter-terrorism operations. As a result the Haqqanis have suffered major casualties over the years, including among their leaders. The three most notable deaths among the leadership were Mawlavi Sangin, Mawlavi Nazir and Badruddin Haqqani, all killed in 2013. Others have been detained, like Anas Haqqani and Hafiz Abdul Rashid (both in 2014).[40] Initially the 'night raids' were a major cause of concern, but the Haqqanis adapted faster than other Taliban, including by quickly procuring infrared goggles. Haqqani sources acknowledge that the biggest threat they were facing were drones:[41] 'If there were no drones and air forces, we would capture Afghanistan in one month.'[42]

In reality the Haqqanis have always been known, even within the Taliban, for their military focus on asymmetric tactics.[43] This focus on fighting a guerrilla war appears to have come at the cost of any concern for the overall strategic picture. At times they have made attempts to capture and hold territory militarily, which have then however been abandoned, not least because of tribal opposition. The high profile *fedayin* attacks in Kabul and the campaign of targeted assassinations have offset the lack of significant operations in rural areas in terms of ensuring the Haqqanis' public profile.

The Haqqanis entered the jihad in 2003 as an organised group, contrary to the fragmentation with which Taliban elsewhere were characterised. From the beginning, the network was committed to guerrilla tactics and deployed a military machine optimised towards harassment operations against a far superior enemy. The Haqqanis's inclination towards asymmetric warfare may have been further solidified by the influence of Iranian Revolutionary Guard advisers during 2012–15. One Haqqani source indicated that though there were Iranian advisers with the Haqqanis, the numbers decreased after 2013 due to Pakistani objections over their presence. Eventually in 2015 they all left as the Haqqanis reconciled with the Saudi authorities.[44] According to another source, during this period the Haqqanis even had two representatives in Mashhad, to liaise with the Revolutionary Guards.[45]

In the early days the Haqqanis relied exclusively on the so-called *zerbati* (fast) teams of 10 men. They were controlled in the field by *massuleen* (representatives) appointed for each province (Khost, Paktia, Paktika, Logar, and later Wardak and Ghazni) and district.[46] As the number of fighters grew, it became more difficult to handle them through just three layers of command: the *zerbati* commanders and the *massuleen* at the district and provincial levels. In 2005 it was decided to introduce larger groups that could handle large operations on their own, without the need for a *massul* to cobble together several *zerbatis* and lead them.[47] These became the *delayez*, groups of 100 men, tasked with carrying out larger operations. Among the *delayez* groups some were mobile, some were local militias and some were mobilised reserves based in Pakistan and ready to reinforce units in Afghanistan. In general, the *delayez* were more heavily equipped than the *zerbati*. Their mobility was in part assured by motorbikes; by mid-2015 the group had about 1,400 motorbikes available, but had plans to further increase the number, mainly through purchases in Iran.[48] The *zerbati*s survived as the main mode of organisation of village militias linked to the Haqqanis.[49]

The Haqqanis's military system differed from the Quetta Shura's even at its upper echelons. The Miran Shah Shura never had a single Military Commission, opting instead to create four different military-related commissions: Zerbati, Dalayez, Fedayi and De Mineno. Each of these Commissions would be in charge of distributing military supplies.[50]

- The Zerbati Commission would manage the village militias;
- The Delayez Commission would manage the full-time mobile units;

- The Fedayin Commission would manage special operations and suicide attacks;
- The De Minena Commission would manage the IED teams.[51]

The Delayez Commission was the largest of these four, which in 2014 had an administrative staffing of 200 in charge of paying salaries, registering new members, and liasing with other commissions, and which itself had several internal departments, including intelligence, logistics, recruitment, finance, villages and responsibility for mobile groups. Idris Haqqani was presiding over the Delayez Commission in 2015, with full powers to appoint and sack members.[52]

Already by 2005 the Haqqanis had established a *shura* tasked with handling suicide bombing. They then established a dedicated Fedayi Commission in 2011 to handle the training and deployment of suicide bombers. Fedayi Commission teams were deploying in small numbers throughout all territories to carry out specific operations, acting as something approximating a Taliban special forces.[53] Their specialisation was commando attacks and self-sacrifice (*fedayi*) operations; essentially complex suicide attacks. There was never an agreement within the Taliban that only the Haqqanis would deploy 'special forces', but rarely have other components of the Taliban been able to carry out operations of this type, so the leadership have usually relied upon the Haqqanis for this purpose.[54] As of 2017 this was still the only Haqqani Commission operating throughout of Afghanistan. It has branches covering the northern, southern, eastern and western zones and one cadre in charge of each province.[55]

The Fedayi Shura, and after it the Fedayi Commission, select their suicide bombers among madrasa students, inviting them to volunteer through the members of a mobile committee which tours the madrasa network. Those selected are then sent to training courses that last three months. According to a member of the Commission, there has never been any shortage of volunteers. Although recruitment happens in a large number of madrasas, 10 madrasas have been turned into specialised 'factories' for suicide bombers, all based in the FATA.[56]

Initially the Haqqanis would rely on adults and even the elderly for suicide attacks, but these suicide bombers were deemed ineffective and easy to spot. Gradually, therefore, the Haqqanis started relying on younger recruits, who proved to be much easier to train, indoctrinate and shape into effective suicide bombers. As of 2015, suicide bombing recruits were aged 10–35, with the majority being in the 14–23 age range.[57]

The Haqqanis then established the Mine Commission (De Nineno Komisiun), launched on 3 March 2011. This Commission deployed cadres at the provincial and district level and monopolised the use of mines within the Miran Shah Shura. Under its jurisdiction would operate tens of IED teams, of 10 members each.[58] The control over the IED teams was thus taken away from the provincial *massuls* of the Haqqanis and from the group commanders; this decentralised use of mines had been causing a high number of civilian casualties, according to a source within the Commission.[59]

The numerical growth of the Haqqanis was slow but steady. Haqqani sources put their strength at its peak at 50,000 in 2015.[60] Other Haqqani and Quetta Shura sources provided similar estimates of the network's strength.[61] Of these 50,000 combatants, over 20,000 were reportedly active fighters and the rest were reserves, of which typically 3–6,000 were mobilised at any given time, with a peak in the summer and a low during winter. Of those mobilised, almost 25% were mobile *delayez*, another 25% were local *delayez* militias or mobilised reserves, almost 20% were mobile *mahazes*, 2.5% were mine groups and just under 30% were *zerbati* village militias.[62] The Haqqanis used these figures in their meetings with other Taliban, to assert their claims of fighting power, but other groups often took these figures with a pinch of salt. A Quetta Shura cadre questioned whether all were genuinely mobilisable, and estimated that perhaps 20,000 of this figure were not actually rotated in and out of active duty.[63]

The Haqqanis also differed from the Quetta Shura system in that their structure was much more centralised. There was always a single chain of command and resources were allocated from the centre. For example, the more advanced weaponry was always managed centrally – the military commission decided how to distribute these resources to the fighting groups. Even specific requests for weapons by group commanders to the logistics commission would have to be authorised by the Military Commission. Groups tasked with fighting using guerrilla tactics would not, for example, be allowed to access heavy weaponry.[64]

A notable case was that of the Haqqani network's Kabul City front. The Haqqanis never had a complete monopoly over Taliban operations in Kabul, but from 2006 onwards they carried out almost all the complex attacks there. The Quetta Shura, the Peshawar Shura and other Taliban factions were each engaged in some level of activity in Kabul, but the Haqqanis were pre-eminent. Opening the Kabul front was the first large initiative of the Fedayi Shura. Over the years the Haqqanis developed in Kabul an organisation and a structure completely insulated from other groups of Taliban in and around the city, because they considered the others more liable to be infiltrated by the government and Western spies. As such, the Haqqanis maintained their own networks of spies, safehouses and planners. The structure was clearly accorded high importance as it was given the same status as the provincial-level structures of the south-east, despite maintaining only about 200 active fighters at any given time, plus *fedayin* teams which would deploy inside the city only days before striking. Haqqani sources claim that 70 per cent of all attacks in Kabul city had, as of 2015, been carried out by them, including the most notorious such as the 22 October 2006 attack, the 7 July 2008 attack on the Indian Embassy in Kabul, the two attacks on the Serena Hotel in Kabul, the attack on the American Embassy, the attack on the Hotel Intercontinental, the attack on Qargah, the attack on the Taverna du Liban and others.[65] Losses were heavy: in 2014 alone the Haqqanis admitted losing 104 men in Kabul city.[66]

Operations in Kabul were supported by Haqqani bases in Logar, Musayi, Khakijabar, Paghman, Charyaseyab, Bagrami and Lataband, as well as by advisers in Pakistan.[67]

## 3.2 The Rise of the Peshawar Shura

### *The formation of the Peshawar Shura*

The Quetta Shura's efforts to kickstart the jihad in eastern Afghanistan were not very successful, as discussed in Chapter 2. The few eastern networks already operational were divided and lacked a structure to coordinate and manage them. These flaws prompted a group of eastern Taliban to try to seize control of local operations from the southerners. The first to attempt to set up any eastern coordination centre for the jihad was the Ijraya Shura (Executive Council) in 2005, which had already been operating since 2002 as one of several Taliban networks in the east (see above).[68]

From the beginning of its existence the Ijraya Shura was organised in a more sophisticated fashion than a simple network based on personal relations. Its leader, Qari Khalid, a former mid-ranking Emirate official from Nangarhar's Khogyani, re-launched the Ijraya Shura on 5 April 2005 with the intention of turning it into a military coordination centre for eastern Afghanistan. This evolution of the Ijraya Shura was allegedly encouraged by the Pakistani ISI, already frustrated by Quetta's failure to intensify the jihad in the east. Around Qari Khalid were mostly former junior officials in the 1990s Emirate's loose hierarchy.[69]

The Ijraya Shura's signature military command structure aimed at exercising direct control over field units resembled that operated by Hizb-i Islami in the 1980s anti-Soviet jihad: a hierarchical model based on a capillary field presence of cadres deployed, and funded, by the central leadership.[70] For this reason it should not be a surprise that the second crucial step on this path came with a successful effort to co-opt elements of Hizb-i Islami, which had for years been historically predominant in the east. Faced with Gulbuddin Hekmatyar's inability to raise funds, or perhaps due to political calculations, the bulk of Hekmatyar's so-called Shamsatoo Shura, based in the Shamsatoo refugee camp near Peshawar and led by Qari Habibullah, joined this embryonic centralised military system. The Shamsatoo Shura had been created in 1998 on Gulbuddin's orders, as he was planning to restart his own military campaign in Afghanistan (unsuccessfully, as it turned out).[71]

High-level sources within the Peshawar Shura indicated that in 2005 the Shamsatoo Shura was offered Arab and Pakistani support on the condition that they joined the Ijraya Shura. Not everybody in Shamsatoo was in favour of the idea, but the decision was finally made, reportedly with the endorsement of Hekmatyar.[72] The majority of the Shamsatoo Shura split from Hizb-i Islami and became known from that time onwards as the Shamsatoo Mahaz.

Within the Taliban, the Shamsatoo Mahaz always had very distinctive features, not least among which was its focus upon recruiting in high schools and universities.[73] After its entry into the Taliban, the Mahaz also started recruiting madrasa students who had nothing to do with Hizb-i Islami, but the large majority of its cadres remained former 'Hizbis', who still made up an estimated 70 per cent of the group's fighting force as late as 2015.[74] Another estimate was that 80 per cent of the Peshawar Shura fighters in Nangarhar, Kunar, Nuristan and Laghman had a Hizb-i Islami background, with the other 20 per cent being madrasa students.[75] The relationship between the Shamsatoo Mahaz and Hizb-i Islami was a lasting subject of debate within the Taliban. Many members, even within the Peshawar Shura, still believed during 2012–15 that Hekmatyar still exercised control over the Shamsatoo Shura, and that Shamsatoo fighters were not 'real' Taliban and lacked a strong religious education background.[76] This contributed to make relations between Quetta and Peshawar more difficult.

It is clear that the main commanders of Hizb-i Islami went to the Peshawar Shura, and as the Quetta Shura thinks that they are not real Taliban, they therefore do not like the Peshawar Shura system.[77]

All the members of the Rahbari Shura think that the Peshawar Shura are not real Taliban. They say that all of them are Hizbi-i Islami. [...] So the Rahbari Shura does not want the Peshawar Shura to become powerful.[78]

In reality, over the years the boundaries between the former Hizb-i Islami and 'old Taliban' types blurred, as joining one or other of the *mahaz*es was a matter of choices available locally and of personal connections, as much as any sociological background. Common responses from interviewees were 'My friends invited me into this *mahaz*', 'In our area just this *mahaz* was active',[79] 'Our village elder had a relationship with them so I joined Shamsatoo',[80] 'My cousins and friends were there so I joined this *mahaz*',[81] and so forth.

The Shamsatoo Mahaz, accustomed to Hizb-i Islami's distinctly centralised style of operation, fit in well with the proponents of the centralising tendency, and in March 2005 formally joined the Ijraya Shura to establish what became known as the new Peshawar Shura. With its 17,000 members (largely unarmed at this point) it immediately became the largest component of the Peshawar Shura. The birth of the new Shura was not without its complications. Initially the Shamsatoo Shura imposed its men upon all the military leadership positions, but over time a compromise was negotiated, where other components such Toor-e Pagri (see below) and the Ijraya Shura would get their share of appointees too.[82] The Shamsatoo Shura became, however, the driving force behind Peshawar's pursue of autonomy from Quetta.[83] The network around Dost Mohammed, mentioned in Chapter 2, also joined the Peshawar Shura and was drawn closer to Shamsatoo.

By 2009, once the Peshawar Shura had taken shape, several of the key players within the Shura's higher ranks had a Hizb-i Islami background. Sources in Peshawar pointed to three of the most important personalities as Qari Baryal, who was to become the chief of the Peshawar Shura's Military Commission, Qari Habibullah (a nom de guerre, his real name being Abdul Rahman), who sat on the Peshawar Shura representing Shamsatoo and then rose to become the Shura's vice-head and a critically important figure, and Qari Atiqullah, who was for a period head of the Peshawar Military Commission.[84]

Within the Shamsatoo Mahaz different leaders had their own geographic constituencies. Qari Habibullah and his brother Qari Atiqullah dominated in Nangarhar, while Qari Baryal dominated in the north, north-east, Kapisa and – thanks to his alliance with Dost Mohammed – in Kunar and Nuristan as well.[85]

At about the same time as Shamsatoo joined the Peshawar Shura, the Toor-e Pagri Mahaz also joined. Established on 3 December 2001 in Hango as an eastern pendant to the Miran Shah Shura, it did not activate militarily for years because of its inability to raise funds. It attracted mainly madrasa graduates, students and staff from Nangarhar, Kunar, Laghman and Nuristan.[86] Toor-e Pagri (referring to the black turbans of the original Taliban) was a network of Pakistani madrasas scattered across Khyber-Pakhtunkhwa and the Federally Administered Tribal Areas (FATA), initially established in 2004 to support the Taliban indirectly.[87] These religious seminaries were key to Taliban recruitment, and many served to provide basic military training to their students. Toor-e Pagri was led by Mawlavi Abdul Saleh, a director of the vast 'Amir ul-Momineen' madrassa in Hangu, near Kohat, central to this network of seminaries. Saleh had a (well-deserved) reputation for being close to the ISI and for his international contacts, particularly in Saudi Arabia. He became a major fund-raiser for the Peshawar Shura and in 2008 was appointed as head of the Peshawar Shura, replacing Sheikh Amanullah.[88]

Toor-e Pagri contributed about 8,000 not-yet-mobilised men to the newly founded Peshawar Shura.[89] Within Toor-e Pagri, a minority objected to the creation of the Peshawar Shura outside the Quetta chain of command, but they were overruled.[90] Toor-e Pagri was more in the tradition of the classical Taliban than Shamsatoo, always recruiting its cadres exclusively through the madrasas. It continued to maintain relations with the Haqqanis throughout its existence.[91]

Most other Taliban actors operating in the east were also co-opted into the Peshawar Shura after its launch in 2005. A few commanders of the Spin Ghar Mahaz also joined.[92] The Tora Bora Mahaz initially resisted joining the Peshawar Shura, and its ranks were divided between those commanders sympathising with Quetta and those preferring Peshawar; eventually in 2009, under Pakistani pressure, the Mahaz became part of the Peshawar Shura, mostly merging with Toor-e Pagri. Its leader, Anwar-ul Haq, was detained by the Pakistanis for his opposition to the Peshawar Shura.[93]

More than 200 local and tribal *shura*s were connected with the Peshawar Shura by 2015.[94] Among them, the Safi Shura was the most important in terms of supplying fighters. A tribal outfit established on 21 August 2004 by clerical members of the Safi tribe who resided in Pakistan, the Safi Shura joined the Peshawar Shura in 2006 with about 4,300 men on their lists, according to internal sources; though the majority were probably inactive reserves. Branches were opened in Peshawar, Lahore, Karachi, Islamabad and Quetta. In Afghanistan the Safi Shura operated in Nangarhar, Kunar, Laghman, Kapisa, Parwan, Baghlan and Kunduz. Some of their members were appointed to senior positions, including a few provincial military leaders, but most sigmificantly Sheikh Amanullah Safi was twice head of the Peshawar Shura, in 2005–8 and in 2015–16.[95]

One key feature of the Peshawar Shura as it was emerging in those years was the comparatively young age of its leaders. The Pakistani members were the eldest: Saleh was 43 when he brought Toor-e Pagri into the Shura; Qari Habibullah, the leader of Shamsatoo, was 28 in 2007; Qari Khalid was 28 in 2005. Most of the other members were between 20 and 35.[96]

Initially, the head of the Peshawar Shura (Sheikh Amanullah at first) had the power to select the heads of the Commissions and the other senior members of the Shura; he would be expected to give adequate representation to all components, but had no constraints (except, allegedly, for those imposed by his Pakistani advisers). From 2009 onwards, a committee of five senior leaders was in charge of making these appointments.[97]

The Peshawar Shura were never effectively subordinate to the Rahbari Shura until 2016 and from its early days it competed with Quetta's representative in the east, Mawlavi Kabir (see Chapter 2 above). The Quetta Shura had never sponsored nor wished for the creation of the Peshawar Shura, whose emergence was a result of internal dynamics among the Taliban and other jihadist groups in the east, and the complicating factor of external financiers. Quetta tried to impose leaders of its own on the new Peshawar Shura, in exchange for full acceptance of the group by the Taliban's established leadership, but Peshawar rejected the offer.[98] The Peshawar Shura, in return, refused to recognise the authority of Quetta's governors over its men.[99] Until 2009, however, units loyal to Peshawar and Quetta coordinated and cooperated with each other in the field as peers.[100]

In 2008–9 Peshawar lobbied Quetta to appoint shadow governors in the east, the Kabul region and the north who hailed from those provinces, rather than continuing to fill these positions with southern Pashtuns, but Quetta resisted. By 2010 the Peshawar Shura felt strong enough to claim a monopoly of authority over a large portion of Afghanistan that initially encompassed all the east, the Kabul region with the exception of Kabul city, and all the northeast. In practice this meant that the governors appointed by Quetta were marginalised and subject to the authority of Peshawar's provincial military leaders, with their right to raise taxes and recruit taken from them.[101] Peshawar also created commissions to compete with Quetta's, including finance, education and health.[102]

Within the Peshawar Shura only two of the main leaders objected to the declaration of autonomy from Quetta: Mullah Mohibullah, linked to Quetta, and Mawlavi Hayatullah, linked to Miran Shah.[103] The rise of the Peshawar Shura was of course resisted by the Quetta Shura, as they remained intent on empowering eastern Pashtuns and eastern Taliban networks.[104] The incorporation of the Shamsatoo Shura into the Peshawar Shura was particularly contentious, Quetta dismissive of them as not genuine Taliban and at the same time wary of their potential influence.[105] The *loy mahaz*es of Baradar, Mansur and Dadullah were initially particularly hostile to the idea of working under the Peshawar Military Commission when deploying to areas under the group's effective jurisdiction, but by 2012 they had had to bow to Peshawar's financial superiority.[106] Then in 2012–13 there were instances of the Dadullah Mahaz trying to break free of the rules imposed by the Peshawar Shura, but after getting expelled from some areas of the north-east its rebellion ended.[107] In 2012–14 it was the turn of the Zakir Mahaz to try to establish an autonomous presence in the areas claimed by the Peshawar Shura; in 2012 some local agreements were negotiated after armed clashes (for example in Khanabad), but in 2013 the friction exploded again into widespread skirmishes.[108] According to sources in the Peshawar Shura, Zakir's units were first expelled from Kapisa, then from parts of Nangarhar, Kunar, Nuristan, Takhar, Laghman, Parwan and Wardak, while clashes also occurred in Baghlan, with tens of fighters killed.[109]

## Internal politics

After its formation, the Peshawar Shura banned the networks and insisted that it would operate as a single entity. The Shura even started accepting recruits directly, bypassing the component networks.[110] Still, there was nothing particularly meritocratic in how its leadership was formed. Close personal relations played an important role in the original formation and growth. Habibullah graduated as a mawlavi from Saleh's madrasa in Hango, where Saleh was his teacher for five years. Qari Khalid was rather close to Qari Atiqullah, Habibullah's brother and another key player in the Peshawar Shura.[111] There were however important ideological fault lines within the Peshawar Shura from the beginning. The practical difference between the Shamsatoo Mahaz and the Toor-e Pagri Mahaz were thus described by Taliban cadres:[112]

Toor-e Pagri is against schools, NGOs and all development activities. For example, one week ago they killed a teacher. Shamsatoo Mahaz is against this [doctrine]. They say that we should not make problems for doctors, teachers, NGOs, engineers and others because [these roles] are needed. We give permissions for NGOs [to operate] through our NGO Commission. After this no problem should be made for NGOs. After all, the local people need clean water, schools, hospitals, roads and other things.[113]

Ideologically the Safi Shura was closer to the Shamsatoo Mahaz than to Toor-e Pagri, accepting state education and NGO projects.[114]

In some instances these differences led to serious friction between Shamsatoo and Toor-e Pagri, for example in Nerkh district of Wardak in 2015, or in Kapisa, over issues like girls' schools.[115] Even clashes between the different components of the Peshawar Shura were not unheard of. Attacks by the Shamsatoo Mahaz on Toor-e Pagri were, for example, reported in Nangarhar.[116] Indeed, although the Peshawar Shura has always tried to present a façade of unity, in opposition to the endemic divisions of the Quetta Shura, its component groups have tended to maintain their own identity and even separate structures. For example, in 2012 the Shamsatoo Mahaz had several of its own offices, in Ghazni, Tagab (Kapisa), Sarobi (Kabul), Logar, Baghlan and Wardak.[117] In each province, Peshawar Shura cadres would know who belonged to Shamsatoo, Toor-e Pagri or any other groups.[118]

Moreover, many of the cadres appointed within the formal system of the military commission were given command of a relatively large number of men, often 100–200, who would then be incorporated in different *dilghay*s but maintain a relationship with their informal leader.[119]

In terms of groups' relative strength within the Peshawar Shura, in 2008–11 the Ijraya Shura had accumulated 35–40% of power in its hands. Geographically, the Ijraya Shura was most influential in Faryab and Baghlan.[120] Its influence gradually declined in subsequent years, mostly to the benefit of the Shamsatoo Mahaz: as of 2015 about 55% was in the hands of Shamsatoo, 30% in the hands of Toor-e Pagri and 9% in the hands of the Ijraya Shura, with the rest going to the other components.[121] The top positions of the Peshawar Shura were divided among the different components on the basis of their relative strength. The mid-2013 snapshot of the composition of the Peshawar Shura saw:

- seven of the top members coming from Toor-e Pagri; among them the top personalities were Mawlavi Saleh and Mullah Jahanzeb;

- nine of the top members from the Shamsatoo Shura, most prominent among them being Habibullah and Atiqullah;
- the Ijraya Shura represented by Qari Khalid alone.[122]

Qari Khalid of the Ijraya Shura was close to the Pakistani groups incorporated in the Shura, and reportedly to the Pakistani generals. Against him and his attempts to use Pakistani support to increase his and the Ijraya Shura's role were not only the Shamsatoo Shura and the Haqqanis, but also the representative from Quetta (Zakir) and Mawlavi Saleh with the Toor-e Pagri.[123] Qari Khalid was removed shortly afterwards, after having already been replaced at the end of 2012 by Qari Shah Mahmud as the leader of the Ijraya Shura. Shah Mahmud was the nephew of Dost Mohammad, the top Taliban military commander in the east, and belonged to a different faction within the Ijraya Shura.[124] The powerful Military Commission was usually the main preserve of the Shamsatoo Mahaz, and it also controlled the Education Commission most of the time. The Ijraya Shura had long controlled finance and recruitment, while Toor-e Pagri controlled the commissions for health, NGOs, Ulema and Hajj.[125]

Geographic expansion of the Peshawar Shura

Beyond the east, the Peshawar Shura's Military Commission found fertile ground in the Kabul region and in the north-east, where the southern *loy mahaz*es had established a presence but did not have deep roots (compared to the south), coalesced as they were around Pashtun pockets in a largely Tajik/Uzbek region. In the north, Peshawar focused on recruiting non-Pashtuns to the Taliban cause, as they tended not to be linked to any of the *loy mahaz*es. The north was virgin territory in this sense. From 2007 onwards the Peshawar Shura became gradually predominant in provinces that had once been under the Quetta's influence.[126]

Among them was Wardak province, where initially the Quetta governor, the Dadullah Mahaz and the Baradar Mahaz had been much stronger.[127] Here the Peshawar Shura first appeared in December 2006, rapidly attracting support thanks to its organisational strength and the widespread presence of Hizb-i Islami networks.[128] The governors, their men and the *loy mahaz*es resisted the take over,[129] but by 2010, once the superiority of the Peshawar Shura became clear, the *loy mahaz*es accepted the rule of the Wardak Military Commission.[130]

In Faryab, in the early years of the jihad, the Quetta Shura was predominant. Mullah Baradar invested a lot in the province and in neighbouring Badghis. After deploying a small contingent of 100 men in 2008, at the peak of his influence he had (according to local cadres) as many as 2,000 men in Faryab.[131] Existing divisions among the local insurgents who had joined the Taliban drove some of them to turn to the Peshawar Shura as an alternative source of support. Qari Salahuddin met Qari Baryal of the Peshawar Shura and obtained initial support to mobilise a force of 200 men; Mukhtum Ali and Dumullah Sadruddin also aligned themselves with Peshawar.[132] In the competition with Quetta, Peshawar had an edge because it was ready to offer more promotion opportunities to local Taliban in addition to better financial conditions.[133] The Peshawar Shura offered concessions to lure the Faryab Taliban in:

> Commanders are chosen by consultation within Faryab. We are not obliged to take orders from Peshawar. The situation in Faryab is different from other places. Faryab is very independent… we don't need Peshawar or Quetta. We just submit reports to Peshawar and consult with them; we talk to them by phone.[134]

As a result, many of Baradar's men joined the Peshawar Shura, which became the dominant *shura* in the province.[135] Uzbeks started opening their communities to Taliban recruitment, radically changing the nature of the Taliban phenomenon in Faryab; from an insurgency based on the local Pashtun minority it became an entity recruiting far and wide among all Faryabis. From then onwards the Taliban set sail in Faryab, but tension between networks affiliated with Quetta and those affiliated with Peshawar remained strong, as the latter were replacing the former as the area's predominant force.[136] The Peshawar Shura, and particularly Qari Baryal, being more open to including non-Pashtuns, benefited the most from this development.

As it became the predominant force among the Faryab Taliban, the Peshawar Shura tried to ban Quetta Shura forces, whether *loy mahaz*es or governor's groups, from recruiting locally. Unsurprisingly they resisted such an imposition, which would gradually have starved them of fighters.[137] Peshawar also tried to impose upon local rivals its chain of command, again encountering resistance.[138] According to one source, Quetta and Peshawar competed for control over Faryab because of the ease with which it was possible to import black market weapons from Uzbekistan through neighbouring Turkmenistan.[139]

Peshawar–Quetta disputes and ethnic competition were not unique to Faryab's Taliban, however. In Takhar, for example, Pashtuns resented the protection afforded by key players in the Peshawar Shura (such as Qari Baryal) to Tajiks and Uzbeks, and lobbied Quetta and Miran Shah to appoint Pashtuns in positions of power as a counter-balance.[140] The growth in strength of the Pashtun fronts in Baghlan, and their ability to secure support from the Taliban leadership, alienated the old Tajik commanders. Dad Khoda, the main Tajik commander in Baghlan, maintained good relations with the Taliban and Al-Qaida-linked Islamic Movement of Uzbekistan (IMU), but refused to cooperate with the leading Pashtun Taliban, Mullah Ruhollah. He demanded to be appointed military commander of the province and to have separate lines of supply from those of Ruhollah and his men.[141] This ethnic friction may have been the reason the Quetta Shura were able to maintain a significant presence in Baghlan, despite the Peshawar Shura's efforts.

Nonetheless in 2009–10 the competition between Peshawar and Quetta over predominance in Baghlan intensified, and during 2010 Peshawar managed to acquire a commanding position, thanks to its financial superiority. Until then loy mahazes, governor's groups and the Military Commission's dilghays had been coordinating with each other, but in 2010 the Peshawar Shura resolved to impose their chain of command and control. The loy mahazes linked to Quetta continued to resist Peshawar's power, until Quetta was no longer able to supply them.[142] Skirmishes between Quetta and Peshawar forces occurred regularly.[143]

As Peshawar attracted more and more funds at the expense of Quetta, it started offering the loy mahazes fighter salaries and supplies if they would fight under its orders.[144] The Peshawar Military Commission offered the loy mahazes Afs10,000 per fighter per month, in exchange for submission to its authority.[145] As elsewhere, the Peshawar Shura found it easier than Quetta to attract local Taliban; in no small part due to the group's superior organisational nous.[146] By 2009, Baghlan had acquired strategic importance for the Taliban, since the northern supply route leading through Baghlan had become ISAF's second artery after the route via Pakistan became increasingly insecure.

In the north the Taliban suffered from long supply lines and problematic logistics; Peshawar's superior organisation and resources, therefore, proved their efficacy more immediately than in the southern provinces, where sources of supply were relatively near, across the historically porous border with Pakistan. With the exception of suicide vests, remote control devices and some other special explosives, supplies were sourced from militia commanders aligned with the Kabul authorities. They would purchase a small amount directly from the black market.[147]

These internal problems were not so debilitating to prevent the Taliban from exploiting the opportunities offered by Kabul's weakness.[148] Because of the government's perceived vulnerability, significant sections of the population began cooperating with the Taliban to avoid trouble.[149] As a result, despite generating tension within the Taliban, the Peshawar Shura's expansion to the north contributed decisively to the destabilisation of government rule in the north/north-east from 2009 onwards. Only in Sar-i Pul and Jowzjan were the Peshawar Shura unsuccessful in unseating local networks connected to the Quetta Shura.[150]

The extent to which the Peshawar Shura was keen to establish its influence in the north/north-east is highlighted by the decision, made in late 2009, to establish a *mahaz* dedicated exclusively to non-Pashtuns, at the initiative of then Military Commissioner for the north-east, Qari Baryal. A Pashtun from Kapisa, Baryal had good relations with Tajik Taliban and had been arguing that only with greater Tajik involvement in the jihad could the Taliban bring the north-east under its influence. Baryal, who later became head of the Peshawar Military Commission and stayed in the job until early 2013, actively recruited Tajiks, Uzbek and Turkmen cadres into the new structure. Some important Peshawar Shura leaders like Saleh, Atiqullah and Dost Mohammed opposed the creation of a non-Pashtun *mahaz*, on the ground that it could one day lead to the split of the Taliban along ethnic lines.[151] Although different versions of the rationale for creating the *mahaz* – named Jundullah, or 'Soldiers of God' – are given, by the far the most common is the desire to advertise the fact that jihad in Afghanistan is not the prerogative of Pashtuns, but that all Afghans take part in it.[152] One Jundullah commander also mentioned the advantage of having units who all speak the same language.[153] The propaganda value of having a non-Pashtun *mahaz* was judged so great that the ban on all *mahaz*es within the Peshawar Shura (introduced at its inception) was exceptionally lifted.[154]

Another key rationale for the formation of Jundullah was to secure Iranian funding for the Peshawar Shura. Despite the relationship with the IMU, the Pasdaran funded and trained Jundullah from the beginning. Although Jundullah leaders tried to resist Iranian pressure to cut relations with the IMU, in the end Iranian funding proved more important than jihadist solidarity and during 2015 Jundullah cooled its relations considerably with the now badly splintered IMU.[155] Initially, Iranian help was provided through the Quetta Shura, but by 2015 it was sent directly to Jundullah. The Iranians also generously equipped Jundullah with better weapons than the average Taliban, smuggled through western Afghanistan, Turkmenistan and Pakistan.[156]

Initially a Tajik, Mawlavi Mohsin Hashami, was appointed leader of Jundullah while an Uzbek and a Turkmen were appointed as deputies and tasked with overseeing the Uzbek and Turkmen components of the group.[157] The claimed strength of Jundullah was 2,700 men at the end of 2012 and 6,000 at the end of 2013 (with another 1,000 being trained in Bajaur, Pakistan). All Taliban sources, even those hostile to the group, confirmed its rapid growth. This has been attributed to the abundant funds to which it has had access, enabling the *mahaz* to pay salaries to all its recruits.[158]

Another aspect of the expansion of the Jundullah Mahaz in the north-east was the co-optation of commanders of local militias linked to Kabul authorities, mostly members of Jamiat-i Islami.[159] The rising power of Jundullah led to clashes with the Zakir Mahaz in Baghlan, as Zakir and his men resented the fact that although 'Pashtuns hold power in the Taliban ... Tajiks are coming and giving orders to people'.[160]

> In Dandi Ghori District all the Taliban were Pashtun. If Tajik Taliban came from other districts like Andarab, Baghlani Jaded and Doshi, the Pashtuns would not behave well with them and [vice versa] when Pashtun Taliban would go to the Tajik Taliban areas.[161]

Jundullah accused the Zakir Mahaz and the governor's forces of killing a reputed cleric and of harassing the Tajik population of various districts in Baghlan.[162] A Taliban cadre hinted that both propositions were true: Jundullah groups were misbehaving towards Pashtun elders, and Zakir groups were misbehaving towards Tajik elders.[163] Later problems developed between Jundullah and Toor-e Pagri, the Atiqullah Mahaz and the Dost Mohammad Mahaz.[164] In Faryab too Jundullah became a source of friction, in particular with the Sattar and Mansur Mahaz.[165]

The southernmost point reached in the Peshawar Shura's expansion was Ghazni, where it started deploying forces in 2009, initially in Jaghatu, Nawur and Zana Khan, and then (from 2010 onwards) to other districts as well. Mostly the Peshawar Shura expanded by sending people in and recruiting new fighters, but it also 'stole' some commanders from the Quetta Shura.[166] The Quetta Shura resented the way in which Peshawar was making these inroads, and occasionally fighters from the two *shura*s even clashed in Ghazni;

provincial and district governors resisted the attempt to impose the authority of the Peshawar Shura's *nizami massuleen* (see *The military machine of the Peshawar Shura* below).[167] The fiercest opposition came from the Zakir Mahaz, but the Mansur Mahaz and the Dadullah Mahaz also opposed it.[168] In some cases the Ghazni Military Commission disarmed armed groups working for the governors or the *loy mahaz*es and expelled them from the area.[169] Taliban commanders in Ghazni described the Peshawar Shura in 2014–15 as better funded, better organised and more united than Quetta, a fact that seems confirmed by the data gathered in Figure 20 (in the Annex).[170] Even in Ghazni the superior financial resources and better organisation of the Peshawar Shura were seen by local Taliban as among the factors driving its successful expansion.[171]

### The Peshawar Shura and global jihadism

Like the Haqqanis, the Peshawar Shura relied extensively on foreign fighters. According to one source, in Kunar during the fighting season of 2015 there were over 1,200 Pakistani fighters and 170 others, including Arabs, Central Asians and Chechens.[172] In Logar, in 2013, a Taliban source reported the presence of 800 foreign fighters, of whom 500 were Pakistani and 300 were assorted Arabs, Central Asians and Chechens.[173] Many other interviewees confirmed they had significant numbers of foreigners fighting alongside them during the warmer months.

The inclusion of Toor-e Pagri in the Peshawar Shura resulted in several connected Pakistani organisations gradually joining the Shura formally, and being given a seat each:

- Jamiat ul Ulema, which had already joined by 2008;
- Sunnat-ul Jamiyat;
- Tehrik-e Taliban Pakistan (2012);
- Lashkar e Jhangvi (2012);[174]
- Tehriki-e-Nafaz-e-sharyat-e-Mohammadi;
- Lashkar-e-Islam;
- Jaish-e Mohammad (2013);[175]
- Sepah-e Sahaba (2013);
- Tehrik-e Taliban-e Punjab (2013).[176]

The Peshawar Shura therefore entertained close relations with a variety of organisations linked to Al-Qaida. The Shura also tried to establish close relations with the Haqqanis, even seeking to merge with them. As the influence of the Peshawar Shura began to spread, it soon expanded into the Miran Shah Shura's territory in Loya Paktya and Logar. The Peshawar Military Commission for a period even sent armed groups expressly with the aim of encroaching on Haqqani territory. Negotiations followed, and in 2008 a deal was struck in which the Miran Shah Shura formally allied with Peshawar and representatives of the Haqqanis were granted seats in the Peshawar Shura.[177] In 2010 the alliance was tightened into something approaching a merger, recreating the kind of relationship that Miran Shah had entertained with Quetta until 2007. After flirting with this arrangement for a short time, however, the Miran Shah Shura reclaimed its full autonomy, despite maintaining its seats in the Peshawar Shura, received in 2010. The Peshawar Military Commission was only able to exercise real power within the Haqqanis' turf for a few months in February–July 2010, before Serajuddin decided to cancel the agreement with Peshawar.[178] The Shura leadership did not object to Serajuddin's change of mind, worried that the relationship with the Haqqanis could be compromised.[179] The Haqqanis did accept the authority of the Peshawar Shura in areas outside Loya Paktia and Logar, where combat groups of the Haqqanis also deployed, except for Kabul city.

In October 2013 the Peshawar Shura once again tried to offer funds to Miran Shah in exchange for submission to its full authority, reportedly $120 million/year. The Miran Shah Shura would be subsumed into the same system and chain of command as the Peshawar Shura, and in exchange Miran Shah would be offered positions in the Peshawar Structure well beyond Loya Paktia and would be allowed to deploy armed groups in many provinces.[180] However, Serajuddin rejected this offer.

In October 2014 the Peshawar Shura tried one last time to convince Serajuddin Haqqani to allow them to expand their military apparatus to Loya Paktia, but Serajuddin only agreed to the Peshawar Shura deploying a modest presence there, who would have to remain under the authority of the Haqqanis's *massuls*.[181] While Serajuddin Haqqani maintained a good personal relationship with Qari Baryal and regular meetings occurred, the Haqqanis insisted they would remain masters of Loya Paktia.[182]

Despite all efforts, clashes between the forces of the two *shuras* did occasionally occur, for example in Logar over territorial control.[183]

## The funding underpinning the rise of the Peshawar Shura

The majority of the Taliban's foreign sponsors in 2010 had thrown in their lot with Peshawar, in part because of the growing military weakness of the Quetta Shura (see Chapter 4) and in part because of what the Pakistanis perceived as an attempt to gain more room for manoeuvre by some of the Quetta leaders (see Figure 3).[184]

In 2010 Pakistan and some other countries decreased or stopped support for the Quetta Shura. Their reasons were that we had started peace talks with the Afghan government, the Americans and some Western countries like Sweden and Germany. During that time Pakistan and some Arab countries turned to the Peshawar Shura because they were fighting well in Nuristan, Kunar, Laghman, Nangarhar, Baghlan, Kundoz, Takhar and Faryab. They captured many areas in these provinces, and therefore gained increased support. There was also support from China, one of the most financially strong countries in the world.[185]

As Figure 3 shows, 2009 was really the year Peshawar took off, with its revenue more than trebling. This gave the Shura leverage, with its Military Commission receiving the bulk of the Taliban budget. At the peak of its power, Peshawar was even in a position to partly fund the Quetta Shura:[186]

> The Peshawar Shura is the bridge between the Quetta Shura and the donors. Peshawar gets money from the donors and gives it to Quetta according to their needs.[187]

As described by Taliban sources, the Peshawar Military Commission dispensed money to the southern Military Commission, presided over by Mullah Abdul Qayyum Zakir, which in turn redistributed it to its cadres in the field or to the various networks that operated in the south.[188]

## The military machine of the Peshawar Shura

As of early 2013 the Peshawar Shura had the following structure:
- Commission for External Fundraising, led by Haji Nazir;
- Training Commission, led by Qari Janzeb;
- Military Commission, led by Qari Baryal;
- Health Commission, led by Dr. Qais and tasked with assisting Taliban fighters;
- Justice Commission, led by Mawlavi Atiqullah;

- Logistics Commission, led by Qari Habibullah;
- Education Commission, led by Abdul Ghani;
- Recruitment Commission, led by Qari Atiqullah;
- NGOs and Companies Commission, led by Mawlavi Faruq;
- Finance Commission, led by Saleh Mohammed.[189]

In order to give representation to the several components of the Peshawar Shura, deputies were appointed, with their number growing over time. In 2010–13 Abdul Qayum Zakir sat in the Peshawar Shura representing the Quetta Shura, while Mullah Ghausuddin represented Miran Shah.[190]

Of the commissions listed above, those directly involved in the military effort were military, training, logistics and recruitment. By 2007 the Peshawar Shura (often still referred to by its original name, the Ijraya Shura)[191] had already developed into something well beyond its original incarnation, not least because the establishment of the Peshawar Military Commission (Nizami Komisiun) had gone a step further in terms of controlling ground operations.

The idea of a *nizami massul* [military representative] came from the Shamsatoo Shura and their leaders; they said that we must have [such a position]. Toor-e Pagri did not support this idea at the beginning. When the leader of the Peshawar Shura was selected from the ranks of Toor-e Pagri, they then accepted the idea.[192]

The original opposition of Toor-e Pagri to the new system was confirmed by several sources. It was a reflection of the aversion of the 'original Taliban' towards centralisation of any kind.[193]

The Peshawar Military Commission had a leader, two deputies and five members, each one running a specific department, with portfolios covering the eastern provinces, the north and the north-east, the region of Kabul, logistics and finance.[194] At some point the Peshawar Shura started appointing supervisors for each province, or at least for some of them (in 2012, for example, there was one for Baghlan, one for Faryab, and one for both Kunduz and Badakhshan). Regional commands continued to exist at the layer above the provincial command.[195]

The Peshawar Military Commission was to take charge of managing the combat units of the Peshawar Shura through the *nizami massuleen* (pl., military representatives) – local officials whom the centre had the power to appoint at district and provincial levels. The Provincial Military Commissions were intended to become the core of the Taliban's new centralised command and control structure.[196] Their functions were thus described by one commander:

The duties of the Military Commission consist of making plans and strategies, developing new techniques, solving any complicated disputes, directing the fighting; in the provinces all the commanders are under the control of Military Commissions.[197]

A Taliban source described the *nizami massul* (military representative) as 'like the NDS [security services], he is responsible for security and knowing everything'.[198] Small-scale attacks would be left for commanders to deal with, with the *nizami massuleen* getting involved only for larger operations.[199] In practice, they were the equivalent of an officer corps, taking charge of all Taliban armed forces and coordinating them in large operations.[200] A source described the qualities required for a *nizami massul*:

He must be a member of the Peshawar Shura and must not have a relationship with any other *mahaz*.
He must be aged between 25–30.
He must be computer literate.
He must have a higher education – that is, from a madrasa – and he must have had a school education as well, [given he must deliver] daily, weekly and monthly reports.
He must not have committed any crime.
His relatives must not be working with the government.[201]

The *nizami massuleen* were first despatched en masse to the districts and provinces in 2007. Initially, they limited themselves to reporting back what they could observe – and readying the administrative infrastructure for the new system. It took some time before they started issuing orders. From 2008–9 onwards, this corps were systematically empowered throughout eastern Afghanistan and the Kabul region, where the influence of the Quetta Shura was very weak, and after that in the north-east and parts of the north as well. In this phase, where the new system was being established, the *nizami massul's* role resembled that of a political commissar: an official whose authority cuts across departments and hierarchies for the sake of military efficiency and effective centralisation. In addition to these representatives, occasionally, delegations of cadres would be sent by the Pakistan-based central leadership to inspect the Taliban in the field and report back.[202] Ultimately, however, the *nizami massuleen* were intended to become the officer corps of the Peshawar Shura's armed forces. By 2015 this is how they were seen:

The *nizami massul* will lead the Taliban in battle all the time, whether the fighters belong to a *mahaz*, the Rahbari Shura, or any other groups. This is the right of a *nizami massul*; no one else has this right. Under their control, *dilghays*, governor's groups and *mahazes* conduct operations. [...] Whether the operation is big or small, a *nizami massul* will direct it. A person cannot place a mine without the permission of the commission or a *massul*.[203]

Many of these new provincial operatives consisted of Afghans who had spent significant time in Pakistan, often studying at a madrasa and with their families living across the border. They were trained in Pakistan, not just in basic military skills such as weapons handling and small-unit tactics, but at times even in rudimentary IT, administration and English. Peshawar's Taliban cadres were not just trained to become field commanders, in charge of a combat unit; a new breed of official was also being trained to organise and run military operations at district or provincial level, or as members of an underground structure active far and wide throughout Afghan civil society. More likely to be recognised by other Taliban by their voice, call-sign or code name rather than their face, these operatives were to operate as the Military Commission's eyes and ears, particularly in the urban areas and district centres which remain the government's strongholds, and to report back either in person, by courier or by email. Even at district level, the *nizami massuleen* were trained to operate under cover.[204]

Their families all resided in Pakistan, particularly Karachi, where they had access to dedicated schools and hospitals. The *nizami massuleen* reportedly received training in Pakistani army bases as well as in the Peshawar Shura camp in Bajaur.[205]

With the advent of operatives of this kind, the Taliban insurgency turned into a professional guerrilla force for the first time, at least partially. Often holding both Afghan and Pakistani ID cards, they could travel freely across the border, an added benefit that made cross-border liaising with leaders easier and more reliable.[206]

Still, the *nizami massul* was no autocratic leader. He was supposed to act in accordance with Taliban rules, and he too could be reported to his superiors if seen to be misbehaving. The *nizami massul* was not legitimised by his proximity to a senior leader, thus making him untouchable, but was to act in accordance with the Taliban code of conduct and with the policy decisions dictated by the central Military Commission in Peshawar. The authority of the centralised system of command and control was inextricably linked to the rise of a new concept of affiliation to the Taliban movement: personal allegiance to charismatic mullahs was now being de-emphasized, in favour of membership of the movement as a whole. To a great extent, the new system appears to have succeeded in imposing a new military chain of command. Leveraging funds and logistics, these officials progressively enforced the new command system on the insurgency. A cadre in Wardak recounted:

[Interviewer:] How did the Military Commission manage to exert its will over the commanders, since they had been used to doing as they wanted?

[Respondent:] They got all the commanders together and told them; 'we are in control now, you are not to work autonomously.' They also spoke to all the local elders, explaining that the system had changed and that they were now the Taliban officials to deal with. They also told the commanders: 'if you disturb anyone or if you do anything wrong, we'll have you hanged or we'll cut your hands off.'

The commanders all went along with it, there were no instances of conflict...[207]

While this cadre may have understated the problems faced by the Military Commission in implementing the new system, by 2010 it was clear that it had consolidated its hold in the east and the central region surrounding Kabul, and was beginning to expand to north-eastern Afghanistan. As Quetta struggled financially in 2011–12, even the southern *loy mahaz*es ended up bowing (at least de facto) to the superiority of the Peshawar Shura, accepting the system of *nizami massul* authority and therefore no longer taking orders from the governors.[208] At the nadir of Quetta's financial quandary, an agreement was reached in March 2012 whereby Quetta *loy mahaz*es would send mobile fighters to areas under the control of the Peshawar Shura to fight under its orders, in exchange for the latter fully paying and supplying them.[209] This agreement was abrogated in the spring of 2014.[210] Until that point, each *loy mahaz* was getting paid 10,000 afs per fighter per month by Peshawar.[211]

In eastern, central and north-eastern Afghanistan, the *loy mahaz*es continued to operate alongside the units directly affiliated to the Peshawar Military Commission, which would issue orders through the *loy mahaz*'s chain of command. As of 2013, around 10–25 per cent of the Taliban's forces in these provinces belonged to a *loy mahaz*.[212]

The cadres of the Peshawar Shura bragged that under its authority 'there are rules and regulations, [...] not like in Kandahar and Helmand'.[213] But the agreement between the *loy mahaz*es and the Peshawar Military Commission was that the latter could order small operations at the group level without consulting the *loy mahaz* representative; for larger operations the consent of such a representative was a requirement, so a commander would need to receive the same order through two distinct chains of command.[214] This double chain of command, so far as the *loy mahaz*es were concerned, was rather unwieldy and sometimes led to confusion and accidents.[215]

Each *loy mahaz* was supplied and paid through the *nizami massul* – unlike under the Quetta Shura where they had had their own logistics and finance – and this gave the *nizami massul* more leverage than the average Quetta Shura governor. Importantly, in around 2010 the Peshawar Shura banned the southern *loy mahaz*es from recruiting in the areas under its control, thereby extending its monopoly to this realm as well.[216]

A *loy mahaz* would sometimes circumvent the rules imposed by Peshawar. In Wardak, where several southern *loy mahaz*es had a significant presence, a Taliban source estimated that 10 per cent of recruitment in 2012 still happened through the *loy mahaz* system, despite this practice having been banned by Peshawar.[217] Such subterfuge was not easy, however. The power of the Peshawar Shura in 2012–14 was such that any *loy mahaz* or governor's commanders who carried out attacks without the authorisation of the *nizami massul* were severely punished, after a first warning.[218]

The combat units of the Military Commission were usually spread around in order to intermix them with the *loy mahaz*es and the governor's groups to exercise control over them; they also had the authority to carry out inspections.[219]

## 3.3 The roots of polycentrism: different models or elite competition?

Both the Haqqanis and the Peshawar Shura had much more centralised systems of command and control than the Quetta Shura. Between these two there were still substantial differences: the Haqqanis had a highly patrimonial system centered around the family of Jalauddin Haqqani, with not just Serajuddin, but also all his brothers and half-brothers playing senior roles in the organisation. The Peshawar Shura, by contrast, was run by a collegial leadership, with regular rotation at the top.

Both systems differed greatly from the Quetta Shura's, raising the question of whether their desire for autonomy was driven by genuine differences over the most effective way to pursue the conflict, or by rivalries between different Taliban elites. Since the focus of this book is the evolution of the Taliban's military machine, the more political dimensions of the Taliban's polycentrism are not discussed to the same extent here. However, as we have seen in this chapter, tribal rivalries prevented the southern Taliban from establishing a firm foothold in the east.

Despite concerns about the compatibility of the Haqqanis' and particularly the Peshawar Shura's systems with the Quetta Shura, the latter managed to reach a modus vivendi with them relatively quickly. Although Quetta never explicity recognised either Miran Shah or Peshawar as peers, it in fact treated them as such: important meetings in Quetta started featuring the participation of delegations from both *shuras*, and Quetta negotiated agreements with Miran Shah and Peshawar over a territorial partition of responsibility, control, taxation and recruitment. The emerging horizontal polycentrism was not the result of a conscious decision of the Quetta leadership, but despite misgivings it was quickly accepted.

Through this accomodation, the Quetta Shura managed to expand the insurgency and to prevent the emergence of open splits within the Taliban. However, it also created internal competition for funds and recruits, as will be discussed in the following chapter.

# 4

# THE CRISIS OF THE QUETTA SHURA 2009–13

The autonomy afforded Miran Shah, and the emergence of the Peshawar Shura as another distinct entity within the Taliban movement, were signs that the Quetta leadership faced challenges. Then, from 2009 onwards the 'surge' ordered by US President Obama added immensely to the pressure Quetta was under, particularly in southern Afghanistan. US troops and marines pushed the Taliban back from the areas surrounding Lashkargah and Kandahar, bringing the war deeper into Taliban territory. The targeted killing and capturing of Taliban commanders and leaders intensified, and started taking a toll. At the same time, political and personal rivalries within the Quetta Shura started worsening, compounding the developing crisis. The Taliban's main sponsor, the Pakistani authorities, also started pressuring for reforms that would enable the Quetta Shura to use resources more effectively.

## 4.1 Misleading appearances: Taliban fighting in 2009 and 2010

To an external observer, the Taliban appeared to be holding strong during 2009 and the first half of 2010. The level of Taliban activity continued to rise. Their high-profile campaigns against the elections of 2009 and 2010 were much stronger than those of 2004 and 2005. By 2009 the Taliban were well organised, resourced, and able to exert considerable control over sections of the population, particularly in the south and east. As such, the 2009 Taliban campaign against the elections was different in both scale and style from 2005. Moderate persuasion and the exercise of soft power, which characterised most of the Taliban's efforts in 2005, gave way to active intimidation and coercion. One month before the elections, 'election commissioners' were appointed by Quetta to coordinate anti-election activities in the provinces. The number of foreign countries reportedly supporting the Taliban's campaign against the elections increased in 2009, with the addition of several Arab Gulf countries. Pakistani involvement in disrupting the electoral process also continued in 2009. Iranian help was also now forthcoming, as the Revolutionary Guards instructed their clients among the Taliban to disrupt the elections. Other countries from whence support came for specific Taliban networks or individuals in Quetta, earmarked for anti-election activity, included Saudi Arabia, Egypt, Oman, Qatar and others.[1]

In 2009, one Taliban interviewee claimed that the insurgency prevented elections from being held in 60 districts as well as many villages in other districts, mostly in the south, and that a total of 400 electoral staff were killed, and 10 trucks with ballots captured. Other Taliban sources claimed to have prevented elections in 85 districts and 1,200 other villages (roughly equivalent to 24 per cent of the countryside). Still other Taliban cadres claimed that, countrywide, more than 300 polling stations were attacked and 90 shut down. As the Taliban describe it, there was much more violence than in previous elections.[2]

Considering that the Independent Election Commission reported 700 polling stations unable to open on election day because of security issues, Taliban claims about the disruption of polling stations do not seem inflated. The veracity of the rest of the data appears dubious, however. According to the United Nations Assistance Mission in Afghanistan (UNAMA) and the Afghan Independent Human Rights Commission (AIHRC), a total of 20 IEC officials were killed, a far cry from the 400 claimed. Another 22 civilians were killed, some of whom were campaign staff of presidential candidates, but even if these were included, the gap between the two sets of data would remain huge.[3]

Despite the Taliban's exaggerations, elders in general agreed that violence was much worse in 2009 than in 2005 and in many districts people were hurt for the first time as a consequence of their desire to vote. Undoubtedly many areas that could vote in 2004 and 2005 were not able to in 2009. Elders interviewed confirmed at least some of these Taliban claims about declining rural participation.[4]

In 2009 the Taliban were still largely disinclined to make any compromise with regard to the elections, often rejecting approaches by candidates who sought leniency. Compared to 2005, however, there was greater willingness to shelve principles when tactically convenient. In Mohmand Dara, for instance, the Taliban stopped their anti-election campaigns after the first round, out of fear of aiding Abdullah Abdullah's victory – the predominantly Pashtun Taliban saw the possibility of a Tajik head of state more of a threat than the elections themselves.[5] Some of the Taliban interviewed admitted that in some instances elders may have influenced insurgents' actions. One fighter from Mansur's network admitted that his group had been contacted by elders in the past and secretly collaborated with them.[6]

During the 2010 parliamentary elections the level of Taliban violence was comparable to 2009. On election day, the Taliban claimed to have killed 65 police and 84 electoral staff, cut off the fingers of 35 people and closed 65 polling stations across three provinces. The significant difference with previous campaigns was that the Taliban allowed elections in certain areas and supported some candidates, allegedly at the direction of external sponsors. The most widely quoted case of the group supporting a candidate was in northern Helmand, where the brother of a prominent politician reportedly negotiated with some of the Taliban networks in Kajaki and Musa Qala districts to allow the vote to take place – whether the vote was fair or fixed (as was widely reported) is not clear. This deal was reportedly authorised by the external Taliban leadership. An elder in Daychopan (Zabul) reported that some Taliban were pushing for a particular candidate, while others were trying to sabotage the elections altogether – suggesting some local disunity and, in this case, the non-involvement of the top leadership. In some areas the support of the Taliban appears to have been proffered on a commercial basis. In Mohammad Agha and Baraki Barak (in Logar), elders believed that some candidates had made payments to some of the Taliban in exchange for being allowed to campaign, but this does not appear to have been a policy authorised by the Taliban leadership.[7]

With the Taliban allowing elections to occur in some areas, country-wide violence levels seem to have decreased in 2010, compared to 2009. However, where the campaign against the elections went ahead without compromise, the level of violence and intimidation was probably even higher than in 2009. In interviews, elders did indeed point to a rise in violence.[8]

The level of Taliban control, especially in rural areas, combined with the history of intimidation and punishment resulted in a greater number of villages being unable to vote than in years past. The most salient aspect of the elections was, however, the varying consensus among the Taliban on how to handle them. A Peshawar Shura interviewee stated that Quetta wanted to disrupt the elections, but was not sufficiently organised to achieve this. A Quetta Shura interviewee claimed that some leaders authorised local Taliban to tolerate the electoral process in certain cases in 2010; but that this was not a Taliban policy and no clear statements, either publicly or privately to front commanders and shadow governors, were made in this regard. Instead it seems to have been the result of high-level dealings between individual Taliban leaders and particular political elites in Afghanistan with family members running for office, or some other personal or economic stake in the electoral process.[9]

In addition to these internal, interest-based splits on whether to attack the polls, further differences arose in 2009 and 2010 between the Peshawar and Quetta *shuras*. According to the Peshawar source, in 2009 and 2010 the majority of the group was in favour of allowing the elections to take place, with the exception of a key military leader, Dost Mohammed, who insisted that he would carry out a campaign against the elections in Kunar and Nuristan regardless. Quetta, by contrast, was officially in favour of disrupting the elections, though it was willing to turn a blind eye when some leaders cut secret deals.[10]

Aside from the elections, the Quetta Shura continued to expand geographically in 2009–10. While it was forced to share space with the Peshawar Shura and the Miran Shah Shura in Ghazni and Wardak, in the north it established a presence in Jowzjan for the first time, appearing during 2009 in the districts of Darzab-Qush Tepa and Aqcha. Groups of mobile insurgents swept through the rest of Jowzjan during 2010, moving out from the two pockets to raid villages, preach, recruit and raise taxes. By the spring of 2010, the insurgents were active just a few kilometres from the provincial capital of Shiberghan; both the Mazar-e Sharif-to-Shiberghan and the Shiberghan-to-Faryab roads were deemed unsafe for travel at that time.

A remote cluster of three districts – Darzab, Sayyad and Qush Tepa – emerged as the most important Taliban enclave in northwestern Afghanistan in 2009, with large numbers of fighters operating from the area owing to its strategic location. The main Taliban commander in this area, Mullah Nadir (an Aimaq, like many others in the west and north) became an insurgent in 2006 before any of the *shuras* based in Pakistan reached out to him. Only in 2008 did Nadir reportedly link up with the Taliban leadership and travel to Pakistan. From there, he returned to his hideout near al-Malik village with weapons and fighters. Mullah Nadir recruited in Darzab, Qush Tepa and most of Sar-e Pol district, as well as in other provinces. By 2009, the Darzab–Qush Tepa–Sayyad enclave had developed into a Taliban stronghold in Jowzjan Province, from where the insurgency was spreading to the neighbouring districts of Belcheragh, Kohistanat, Sar-e Pol, Sozma Qala, Sangcharak, Gosfandi and Shiberghan. Although most of the insurgents operating in the area were locals, support lines and reinforcements also came from Badghis and Faryab. The Quetta Shura was also intensifying its presence in Faryab at about the same time. By early 2010, the insurgency was active in almost all parts of the province.[11]

## 4.2 The fall of Mullah Baradar

While the Quetta Shura in 2009 had not yet run out of steam, the declarations of autonomy by the Miran Shah Shura and the Peshawar Shura were major blows, even if neither *shura* went public with the rift and the Taliban as an organisation did not split altogether. In areas outside the control of the Quetta Shura, governors only had power over the few groups aligned with Quetta.[12] The rise of the Peshawar Shura carried the greatest threat because of its financial implications. The financial shift would eventually allow Peshawar to overtake Quetta in funding by 2010–12. This provided leverage to Peshawar and to the Peshawar Military Commission, which received the bulk of the Taliban's budget. According to a Helmandi commander, as early as 2010:

> When I went to Quetta, I met my commander and asked him for equipment and money. He said, 'We have nothing now, we're waiting for them to send over funds from Peshawar; there are some high-up leaders there who will send it.'[13]

The fact that the Quetta Shura struggled to centralise revenue collection – including from its main internal source of funding, the opium trade – strengthened the impact of the revenue shift.[14] The loss of some key poppy-growing areas in 2009–10 was an additional blow:

> Before, as Garmser district was a transit area for [drugs] traffickers, we received a lot of money from the traffickers as tax or *zakat*. At that time we didn't need our leaders or the Quetta Shura to support us; we had money for everything: weapons, ammunition, food, etc. Today it's completely different: we have few villages under our control and collecting *zakat* from those villages is not enough. Most of our supplies today come from Pakistan. We get our weapons, ammunition, petrol and whatever else we may need from Pakistan. That is our only source these days.[15]

The obvious strategic answer to ISAF's escalation in the south was to expand other fronts. The east, in this context, was the natural choice: the local Taliban were still weak, but there was believed to be strong anti-American sentiment there. Previous Quetta Shura failure in taking the jihad to the east convinced the Pakistani ISI and other backers of the Taliban that the Peshawar Shura would be better qualified for this endeavour. Consequently, support to Quetta from most foreign backers dwindled in 2010.[16] Peshawar was on its way to becoming the new primary centre of Taliban power.[17] By 2013–14 it was regularly taking higher casualties than Quetta, according to Taliban data, suggesting that it had overtaken Quetta in terms of share of operations (see Figure 6). It even worked towards finding allies in Quetta. The key character here emerged as Mullah Abdul Qayum Zakir, head of the Quetta Military Commission from 2009 onwards and a favourite of the Pakistani ISI. Zakir replaced Mansur Dadullah at the helm of the Military Commission thanks to his reputation as a capable and committed military commander, as well as due to Pakistani (ISI) support. Baradar initially accepted Zakir because he needed a charismatic military commander and because they had studied in the same madrasa.[18] Known as an able organiser and a committed jihadist, and as someone who had only recently been released from Guantanamo, Zakir's candidacy was hard to oppose.

From then on Zakir started cooperating closely with Peshawar and became a key recipient of funds from there, which he used in part to fund some of the new *loy mahaz*es, including his own, Sattar's and Ibrahim Alizai's.[19] Soon friction between Zakir and Baradar grew:

> He got a lot of support from the Pakistani government side. Pakistan knew that he was a bellicose commander, like Dadullah, but Mullah Abdul Ghani Baradar was opposed to him and was determined [that Quetta] continue with the system [as it had been]. When Mullah Abdul Ghani Baradar was arrested, it was because of Zakir. Zakir told Pakistan that if you want to get your way, you must arrest Baradar. So Baradar was arrested and Zakir [implemented the new] system.[20]

This may simply be a conspiracy theory, of the sort that abound among the Taliban. Zakir, in any case, was also detained at the same time as Baradar, and released after two weeks. However, Baradar was certainly opposed to Zakir's Peshawar-style reforms.[21] According to the sources, Baradar and his allies in Quetta had substantial differences with Peshawar over the power of the *nizami massul*, as they wanted the governors to remain the ultimate authority in the field, with the *nizami massuleen* to be under them.[22]

Soon after Baradar's arrest in 2010 by the Pakistani authorities in Karachi, Zakir formed his own *loy mahaz*, in the process attracting many of Baradar's men.[23] This split deepened the enmity between Zakir and Baradar's circle. To seal the arrangement between Zakir and the Peshawar Shura, the former was allowed to appoint some of his allies as deputies of the Peshawar Shura, Mawlavi Mohibullah being a notable example.[24]

Much has been written about Baradar's arrest by the Pakistani authorities in February 2010. The most common account of Baradar's arrest has it that he was spotted by Pakistani intelligence trying to establish communications with President Karzai. Baradar's decision to move towards some form of reconciliation without consulting with the Pakistanis created significant opposition against him within the Rahbari Shura for the first time: at least Ishanullah Rahimi, Abdul Qayum Zakir, Abdul Matin, Gul Mohammad and Abdul Majid were known to have opposed this strategy, and probably others felt likewise. Baradar's move toward reconciliation turned out to be the beginning of a serious political crisis in Quetta.[25] Most Taliban accounts were in agreement on this point, but it is also likely that the crisis in the relations with other *shuras*, and Quetta's declining finances, contributed to Baradar's downfall. As recounted by those affiliated with Peshawar and Miran Shah, Baradar represented the main hurdle to integrating Miran Shah and Peshawar within the Quetta power system on the terms they demanded (see Chapters 3 and 4).

The Taliban's donors were also increasingly sceptical of Baradar's military prowess and wary of the limitations of the system he presided over and defended. While the Quetta Shura was still expanding in some areas, from 2009 onwards the pressure on the Taliban had been intensifying, particularly in the south, and by early 2010 their gains started to be rolled back. The inability of the group to translate its gains in heavily populated rural areas around Kandahar and Lashkar Gah into the capture of district centres, even if the insurgents reached the outskirts of Lashkar Gah and Kandahar on several occasions, highlighted how the movement had reached a ceiling in terms of its existing capabilities.[26]

The arrest of Mullah Baradar did not just represent the loss of a charismatic leader. According to one source, after his arrest the Rahbari Shura stopped having plenary meetings, probably due to internal differences becoming unmanageable. The last full meeting was on 13 August 2009, the third or fourth meeting of that year, one of which occurred in Dubai and two in Saudi Arabia.[27]

## 4.3 Pakistan's interests start diverging with those of the Taliban

It was not just for the failure to consult with them that the Pakistani authorities opposed Baradar's initiative of seeking negotiations with Kabul. In fact, their main concern was that they considered negotiating in 2009–10 a premature move, which would not deliver Pakistan the political gains it was pursuing.

Among the Taliban's ranks, however, various efforts were underway to emancipate the organisation, or at least portions of it, from Pakistani tutelage. Pakistani advisers had played a major role during 2006–9 in improving the group's military capabilities.[28] By 2009–10 the Pakistani advisers were increasingly becoming aware that they were no longer the only source of advice. In addition to a few advisers from Al-Qaida and the IMU, accompanying selected groups of Taliban, the Iranian Revolutionary Guards were becoming a more pervasive presence. According to a Pakistani account, Pakistani pressure to remove such advisers had some success vis-à-vis the Arabs and the IMU, at least in southern Afghanistan, but not with the Iranians, whose cash and logistics was eagerly welcomed by the Quetta Shura.[29]

Another reason to appreciate the Iranian help was that the Pasdaran were more willing than the Pakistanis to transfer skills and training to the Taliban, aiming to engineer an organisational and technological upgrade of the insurgency:

> Most Taliban leaders and commanders are mullahs. They only studied in madrasas, not in schools or universities. Therefore, they are not qualified in organisational skills and technological skills. We help the Taliban in [this regard]. We are trying to recruit people [who have] modern educations; those who graduated from schools and universities.[30]

Taliban interviewees often ranked the Iranians as the best advisers, followed by the Arabs, with the Pakistanis only third.[31]

In 2012 many of the most important Taliban offices started being moved to Karachi, allegedly to make Afghan intelligence collection more difficult, but probably to increase the ISI's ability to keep the Taliban under strict watch. Taliban leaders had often been based in Karachi before, but now even the Taliban's 'bureaucracy' moved.[32] The operational branches of the various commissions, however, had to stay near the Afghan border for obvious reasons.

The most powerful control tool the Pakistani authorities had was the control they exercised over funding. Taliban sources related that the Quetta

Shura had seen its revenue continue to rise, despite rising challenges, until 2009 where it stagnated for the first time. External payments stayed the same as in 2008 (see Chapter 2), while tax collection may have started to decline due to a loss of territory in the south, although sources could not provide exact figures. The Taliban claimed the turning point was however in 2010, when funds transferred through the Pakistani authorities shrank by $120 million to just $30 million. The situation did not improve in 2011 and only started showing some sign of improvement in 2012, when funds transferred through Pakistan slightly increased. The impact of Pakistan withholding funds was devastating, but was nonetheless mitigated by new sources of funding. The sources said that the Iranians in particular started transferring cash to the Quetta Shura during these years, but only about $10 million/year were reaching the financial commission, with much of the money being spent on specific *loy mahaz*es, first and foremost Mullah Naim's. In 2013 Iran reportedly upped its contributions to $50 million, but in the meanwhile Quetta had burned through its financial reserves and the situation remained critical.[33] Commanders said of that time that 'we were lacking money. We did not have money for weapons, logistics or anything else.'[34] Collection of *ushr*, *zakat* and other contributions also became more difficult, as villagers objected more regularly.[35] The overlapping taxation by Mansur's and Zakir's factions, and also by rogue *loy mahaz* leaders, contributed to making villagers wary.[36]

## 4.4 Military pressure on the Taliban

The US surge that started in southern Afghanistan in 2009 resulted in significant Taliban territorial losses in the south in the following years, including in Kandahar Province, which had great symbolic importance for the Taliban. Here they were no longer able to collect taxes after 2009, having lost territorial control.[37] As Table 3 shows, no respondent in Kandahar reported any tax collection in the districts surrounding the provincial capital.

The damage was not limited to territorial losses in the south. The ISAF campaign to target the Taliban's chain of command started in earnest in 2007. The Taliban acknowledge that 2007 was possibly the hardest year for their chain of command in the field, with three of their most senior commanders killed: Dadullah, Faruq and Ibrahim.[38] The Taliban suffered heavily from NATO air power. Obituaries published in the Taliban's Arabic language monthly, *Al Somud*, confirm that air and drone strikes were the single most frequent cause of death for Taliban commanders and cadres, accounting for one quarter to one third of their casualties from known causes in 2004–9.

Taliban commanders in the field constantly referred to ISAF (in fact US) airpower as by far their greatest threat, and the only factor that prevented them from emerging victorious on the battlefield.[39]

> The foreign troops are also not so powerful, the only power that they have is air support, and otherwise they cannot stand against us.[40]
>
> Fighting the Americans is not easy. One night in the summer of 2007, my commander, Mullah Nurla, was killed in an American raid on his house. Other Americans killed 12 of our commanders. All the raids came between midnight and dawn.[41]

Taliban fighting groups began experiencing very high levels of attrition. The impact on morale was devastating:

> In our group in total there were 25 fighters. [...] Now from our group just seven people are alive, [all of whom have] left the Taliban. The other 18 fighters were killed.[42]
>
> Of the ten men in this group I joined in 2009, only I remain alive, the other nine were martyred. Another eight fighters who later joined our group were also martyred.[43]

The average fighter, having survived the war thus far, would have seen plenty of his colleagues die during its course. One interviewee had 83 comrades killed. Another joined as part of a group of 85 former Hizb-i Islami members; by the time of the interview, 35 of them had died, and of these 20 had been killed in airstrikes.[44] A former Taliban commander counted 45 of his friends and acquaintances among those who died in the Taliban's ranks.[45] In areas particularly affected by the conflict, like parts of Sayedabad, 'there is not a village that has not seen at least eight or nine people killed'.[46] Taliban sometimes quoted that 70 per cent of their casualties were due to air strikes.[47] A source estimated that in Kandahar province alone, 100–130 'great commanders' were killed in the years up to 2014.[48] Taliban data shows that the number of fighters killed in action peaked in 2009–10 (Figure 5).

The morale of many members of the Taliban was shattered. Many of those leaving had lost faith in the Taliban as a movement, or believed that the cause was not worth the losses and suffering incurred. Repelling the foreigners and/or bringing to power a more Islamic type of government did not (for those who left) justify the violence, the arbitrary killing and the destruction the group caused.[49] Even those who still had sympathy for the Taliban's cause believed that the price paid was too high.[50] The loss of faith in the Taliban in some cases meant that these fighters no longer believed the movement could win the war, and thought instead that Afghanistan would spiral towards state disintegration.[51] As they then left the Taliban, they also took their critical views and shattered morale with them, paradoxically helping the rest of the group to forge ahead. But even those who stayed were not unaffected.

The demoralising impact of airstrikes and drone strikes was acknowledged by several current and former Taliban members.[52] Many interviewees indicated that seeing comrades getting killed, particularly in air strikes, was the most traumatic experience to which they were subjected, all the more so since fellow members of the same groups were almost always friends, even relatives, or close acquaintances. The fact that corpses were pulverised was particularly shocking for them. The fact that the Taliban could not do anthing about airstrikes was a source of immense frustration.[53] It is quite likely that the interviewees understated the importance of family pressure (from fathers, mothers and wifes) in persuading them to leave the Taliban, probably because of the sense of shame involved. Although several interviewees did not list family pressure as a key factor in their exit from the movement, when pressed they did admit that this played a role:[54]

On 13 March 2010 my friend, Qari Fawad Amarkhel, was placing a bomb by the road when he was targeted by an American drone, which broke his body into small pieces. When I saw him, I became very sad and depressed. His father was also killed during the war against the Russians. He was the only son of his mother and father; he had no other brothers. All the villagers and relatives were unhappy about [what happened to] him. His mother is mentally sick now and is crying all the time. He once left the Taliban in 2009 because his mother told him to. In 2010 the *nizami massul* of Narkh district in Midan Wardag Province, Mullah Mustafa, brought Qari Fawad back to the Taliban by force.[55]

One night near Landakhel village Qari Nejad was [killed by an] airstrike; we only found small pieces of him. It was a very bad experience. Another friend was killed the same day. We discussed with each other; we started talking about taking revenge on the US, though some of us wanted to stop fighting.[56]

It is true that many people left the Taliban because of aerial bombing. They were very afraid of the drones. When these planes threw bombs [at our positions], and many fighters were killed and their dead bodies completely dismembered into small parts, their families would became crazy at the sight of the bodies of their sons. Other [fighters who saw this] were also afraid that if they were to be faced with such aerial bombardment, their dead bodies would also appear this way.[57]

Every time the Taliban attacked US or ISAF units, they knew an air strike would follow.[58] While it was more difficult to get even former Taliban to admit that the high level of casualties impacted upon their morale, they did sometimes admit that losing close friends in battle was traumatic. They also admitted that family pressure (from wives, parents and elders) was a key factor in getting many to quit.[59]

The night raids were another acknowledged source of pressure:

> I joined with the Peace Committee in 2009, that is to say that I left the Taliban at that time. To be honest, I became tired of fighting and war. I wanted to live in peace. Besides, during that time, the night operations and American air strikes were increasing in frequency. Even the Afghan forces had attempted many times to arrest me.[60]

More generally, the high risk involved in aligning with the Taliban was reportedly also a factor discouraging active engagement:

> They had the full support of local people in the past, but this has has decreased, because the American air strikes scared people away. The local people are also afraid of the foreign troops – they don't want to get killed in their operations. If the American troops arrest them [and they are] accused of supporting the Taliban, they will be jailed for many years in Bagram prison. So people are not supporting the Taliban like before.[61]

After peaking in 2006–7, however, losses inflicted from air strikes seem to have had gradually less impact, falling to 17.6% of recorded casualties in 2011 (see Figure 4). This might indicate some success at coping with their enemies' air superiority, although it is also due in part to the increased role played by kill and capture operations (the 'night raids'). Anecdotal evidence from interviews with commanders of smaller units also confirms that casualties were in decline by 2014. 30 out of 50 who answered the question said their casualties in 2014 were lower than in 2013.[62] Another 20 said their casualties in 2014 were actually higher than in 2013, but most of them qualified this by saying that this was because of the large-scale offensive launched by the Taliban in the wake of ISAF's troop reduction.[63]

The appearance of the Afghan Local Police (ALP) in 2011–12 contributed to weakening the Taliban, even if the ALP as an institution had a very mixed record. Since the ALP was drawn from local people and knew their areas, they could tell who were strangers. Before this, local Taliban had been able to operate without hindrance.[64]

Replacing dead cadres and leaders became more difficult after Mullah Baradar's arrest, as infighting among the Taliban leaders prevented consensus being reached on appointments.[65] Of the first generation of Taliban commanders, few were still alive in 2014, even those in the northern provinces who had come late to the insurgency. Most interviewees agreed that the task of replacing so many experienced leaders was difficult or impossible.[66] The main loss was the relationships that commanders and cadres had with the local communities, rather than any great amount of very proficient military commanders.[67]

Aside from combat casualties, the Taliban also suffered a heavy outflow of members who were tired of fighting. In Zherai alone, 75 local members quit at the height of US pressure.[68] The 18 former Taliban interviewed for this book mentioned various reasons for leaving the organisation. Issues related to abuse and killing of civilians were by far the most frequently mentioned (respondents mostly cited arbitrary killings, coercive tax collection, and forcing households to feed fighters), with 21 instances of these issues being mentioned between them. The risk involved in being associated with the Taliban and the family pressure to leave were other common causes, cited 10 times in total, as was were internal Taliban issues (disunity, the new generation of commanders being inferior to the earlier ones, and dependence on Pakistan) also mentioned 10 times.[69]

When asked about the more general reasons for members quitting the organisation, a mix of 23 current and former Taliban mostly cited 'family problems' (mentioned by 14 of them), with another three mentioning 'financial problems'. This is not surprising as the Taliban only permit one to quit the organisation, or take an extended leave, for these reasons. The next most common reason, mostly brought up by former Taliban, was the poor behaviour of others within the group (10 mentioned this). Risk and family pressure were cited as reasons by 9 interviewees.[70]

If a fighter can provide a suitable excuse, such as a family problem or the need to guarantee a livelihood for his family, Taliban commanders will normally allow him to quit the organisation, although they will typically contact him now and then to try to get him back. Being related to some senior members, especially a commander, or having friends still active within the Taliban, helps in finding a way out.[71] The interviewees who were former Taliban recalled how once given 'leave' they started receiving regular visits by their former colleagues, who would try to persuade them to return to the movement, or would assess the true extent of their 'family problems'. Members trying to quit would need to enlist the support of elders, or even better the mullah, in order to be left alone. Regardless, many former members had to leave their village and relocate out of reach of the Taliban. Few joined the commissions set up by the Afghan government for reconciling low-level Taliban, as they were all aware that the group would go after them if they did so. The Taliban commanders would sometime use soft techniques to lure these erstwhile fighters back. Other commanders used threats. In some cases the property of members who quit was damaged or seized. There were also instances of physical harm and even assassinations.[72]

Only in areas where the Taliban had been critically weakened, such as post-2010 Kandahar, were they in no position to forcibly maintain fighters in their ranks.[73]

Another example was in the winter of 2010–11 in southern Chahar Dara (Kunduz), where the militia of Mir Alam took control. The Taliban tried to retaliate using IEDs, but by the summer several senior commanders and the cadres of the commissions left for Pakistan.[74] Feeling squeezed and abandoned, a number of low-ranking Taliban commanders surrendered to the security forces in October, the most important among them Qari Zia, who controlled about a dozen villages with several dozen fighters.[75]

The elders who had encouraged villagers to join the Taliban were later to advise them to leave, once the interests of villagers and the movement no longer aligned. In some cases the Taliban executed elders who encouraged people to quit.[76] Although in interviews elders would often claim to have always opposed the Taliban, in fact former Taliban informants indicated their more pragmatic attitude:

> Some elders discourage people from joining the Taliban and say the village will be bombed. Other elders support the Taliban. [...] In XXX village the elders were unsupportive, but have now joined the Taliban, because the French and the US have left.[77]

Several interviewees who left the Taliban turned against the organisation afterwards, having realised that areas under Taliban control were left undeveloped, and also assuming that in the event of a Taliban victory they would be considered second-class citizens.[78] Although widely criticised in the West and in Kabul for its many flaws, development aid and emergency programmes of various kinds did place a lot of pressure on the Taliban:

> In 2005 a bad Afghan government made the Taliban popular. Now that the Taliban are strong, they behave like the Afghan government. My view of the

Taliban now is that it is clear they would do no good in Kabul. We can see that they are good at providing security, but they would not be good for the country as a whole. Schools are one problem – my son is in Shiberghan, where they closed the school.[79]

What community elders often described as the 'enslavement' of the Taliban to Pakistan's geopolitical interests also hurt their popular appeal.[80]

Aligning with the Taliban often turned out very costly in terms of property destruction and loss of human life, and many elders withdrew or reduced their support from 2007 onwards. By 2011–12, sources who were neutral or had no particular sympathy for the Taliban emphasised that locals supported the movement as a result of either expediency or fear, explaining how the majority of the population had no choice but to support whomsoever controlled their village, and had no active preference beyond who could lay definitive claim to their area and provide basic security. Just a single elder shared the Taliban's view that it commanded extensive popular support.[81] There were signs that, disillusioned as people were with the government, they were equally tired of the Taliban. According to one source:

> People don't see the Taliban the same way as before. They have lost the trust of the people. They are not real Taliban: there are thieves among them, they don't know about jihad, they don't know of the Taliban's laws, they have just picked up weapons to fight against the government. The Taliban will never again be trusted to rule Afghanistan.[82]

Sometimes the reasons one may have aligned with the group in the first place simply no longer applied. This was, for example, the case of the Alokozais of Sangin, whose elders withdrew their support from the insurgency when they were promised by the ISAF negotiators that their opium interests would no longer be interfered with.[83]

A distinction was often made between the new Taliban and the era of rule under the Emirate:

> When they returned after the [rise to power of the] Karzai government, at first people thought they were the same as before and welcomed them. But most of the ideological Taliban from years past now stay at home. It is only the youth who pick up weapons these days. No one will ever trust the uneducated youth to take control of the country.[84]

By contrast, local infighting among families associated with the government meant that many local Taliban tired of fighting would nevertheless need to stay with the group for their own protection. Unemployment has sometimes been cited as a factor pushing young villagers towards the Taliban, but not as a major reason.[85]

## 4.5 The crisis of Quetta's military system

After Mullah Baradar was arrested, the number of *loy mahaz*es further proliferated (see Figure 1). One reason was the ongoing power struggle at the top. Ibrahim Alizai's *loy mahaz* was, for example, supported financially by Zakir.[86] Many of Baradar's fighters dispersed after his arrest on 2 February 2010; the *loy mahaz*es of Zakir, Sattar, Naim, Ibrahim all benefited from this outflow, but at least ten of his senior commanders and their men withdrew from the fighting, in protest at Pakistani interference (see Chapter 5).[87]

Mansur reportedly established his *loy mahaz* to capture at least some of the fighters and commanders flowing out of the Baradar Mahaz,[88] as had Zakir. When the Dadullah Mahaz was re-launched in 2011, many commanders who had been with Dadullah before 2007 re-joined, as did many commanders who had never served with Dadullah (Map 1).[89] It was not just a matter of nostalgia for Dadullah: the re-launch of the *loy mahaz* was sponsored by various foreign donors, especially Arabs, some of which had ended their support in 2007.[90]

In 2010–14 the *loy mahaz*es were able to access more and more funding that bypassed the Rahbari Shura, whose power over them dwindled as a result.

According to the rules, the leaders of the Rahbari Shura are more important than the *mahaz* leaders. But now those leaders from the Rahbari shura are not as important [as the *mahaz* leaders].[91]

The *loy mahaz*es were becoming increasingly unruly.[92] Often meetings had to be called with the representatives of the *loy mahaz*es to resolve problems, making the system unwieldy.[93]

To counter-balance the power and indiscipline of the *loy mahaz*es in 2008 it was decided to create a new type of combat organisation, parallel to that of the groups and the *loy mahaz*es: the village *mahaz*.[94] The official rationale for the creation of the village *mahaz* was that they were meant to increase the capacity to carry out multi-group operations in the villages; the growing pressure on the Taliban in the south suggested that the Taliban's village roots needed to be consolidated in order to successfully resist. The standard size was fixed at 100 men, which was three or four times the size of a standard fighting group. The village *mahaz*es were, as a rule, a top-down creation: the Rahbari

Shura selected the leaders from among the most promising group commanders, and engineered the process.[95]

The village *mahaz*es were recruited from governors' groups among local communities aligned with the Taliban, with the intent of creating a bulwark around the governor against *loy mahaz* provocations. The governors would choose their commanders from among the pre-existing group commanders, but following the emergence of personal rivalries it was decided to have the group commanders select candidates, from which the governor would choose one. First rolled out in Kandahar, Helmand, Zabul and Uruzgan, the village *mahaz*es appeared in Ghazni, Wardak and Nimruz in 2009 and in Farah, Herat, Badghis, Ghor, Daykundi, Jowzjan, Sar-i Pul and Faryab in 2010. Although they were launched for the first time on 23 July 2008, the village *mahaz* were later also a response to the financial crisis of the Quetta Shura in 2010–13, as they were mostly funded through locally raised taxes and their expenses were lower, as the fighters would live in their family homes.[96] By early 2015, according to a senior Quetta Shura figure, the village *mahaz*es had 6,000 men in total, almost exclusively in southern and western Afghanistan.[97]

The village *mahaz*es differed from the groups because they were larger (100 men), while still being much smaller than the *loy mahaz*es and not mobile like them. It was a way of bringing several groups together under a single field commander. In fact the village *mahaz*es were created by merging the old groups together, but the groups were not completely replaced. The village *mahaz*es were also placed under the orders of the governor. There were therefore three different types of military organisations within the Quetta Shura's military structure at this point: governor groups, *loy mahaz*es and village *mahaz*es.[98] As a result of being used to counter-balance the rogue *loy mahaz*es, tensions between village *mahaz*es and *loy mahaz*es were frequent, as the latter needed the former's cooperation because of their local knowledge, but could not force them to cooperate without the governor's consent.[99]

Because the main rationale for the formation of the village *mahaz* was political (geared toward controlling the *loy mahaz*es), the recruitment criteria were loosened. Allegations started flourishing that criminal gangs and local militias were being brought into village *mahaz*es.[100] So in Badghis, for example, according to a Taliban critic, three of the six village *mahaz* commanders were smugglers and criminals, with one having been sacked from the police for drinking alcohol. Only two were 'decent guys' but even in their village *mahaz* criminal elements could be found.[101] In Nimruz shadow governor Ezatullah Baluch even took the decision to disband the village *mahaz*, and then killed or arrested several members.[102]

## 4.6 Political fractiousness

Between 2009 and 2013, the rising star of the Quetta Shura was Abdul Qayum Zakir, as discussed above. Zakir drew strength from his alignment with Peshawar, while the recalcitrant southern *loy mahaz* leaders, opposed to reform, coalesced around Akhtar Mohammad Mansur, Baradar's closest collaborator, and continued resisting the establishment of the Military Commission(s). These two strands, supposedly representing the expression of the political and military arms of the Taliban, were actually profoundly dissociated, and in practice behaved as self-standing entities replicating all the functions of a central *shura*. Mansur, naturally, did not eschew forays into military issues, and had his own military force (that is, his own *loy mahaz*), while Zakir's *nizami massuleen* in turn tried to replace the district and provincial governors as sources of military and political authority whenever possible.[103] Eventually, the enmity between Zakir and Mansur evolved into a confrontation between two distinct parallel governance systems, the former based on the authority of the *nizami massuleen* and styled after the Peshawar model (see Chapter 6), and the latter still following the old governors/*loy mahaz* system.[104]

Despite the military difficulties of the Taliban and the rationale behind military reform, opposition to Zakir came thick and fast. In late 2011 and during the first half of 2012, a number of Quetta political and *loy mahaz* leaders objected to Zakir's distribution of the Quetta Military Commission's resources. Zakir argued that he was distributing the resources on the basis of level of commitment to the jihad and competence of the various *loy mahaz*es. The opponents of the reforms accused Zakir and his allies of essentially riding the tiger of reform for the purpose of their own aggrandisement. Some *loy mahaz*es – including what was left of Baradar's – downscaled operations and came close to withdrawing from the battlefield in protest.[105] Zakir was accused of wanting 'to take the power from the Rahbari Shura and force all the *mahaz*es to work under the control of the military commission and *massuleen*.'[106]

There is evidence of Zakir exploiting reform in order to consolidate his personal position. Although in principle the *nizami massuleen* should have been appointed from out-of-area, in early 2012, six out of seven known Helmandi district *nizami massuleen* were local Taliban. Furthermore, three of the seven district *nizami massuleen* were relatives of Zakir.[107] Northern Helmand is a good example of an overlap between kinship-based networks and the new reformed system as it was applied in the south: in Zakir's case, the centralised command system simply replicated the command structure of Zakir's own *mahaz*. In many other cases, as in Kandahar, the *nizami massuleen* were appointed from the ranks of the Zakir Mahaz.[108]

Sources in Peshawar, confirmed by a UN source, related that in December 2011, following complaints by the southern fronts, a meeting took place in Pakistan to discuss the issue of the unequal distribution of funds among the *loy mahaz*es by the Quetta Military Commission. Allegations were voiced that the Commission was providing higher levels of funding to the eastern and south-eastern Taliban and, within the south, to commanders directly under the Military Commission's orders. Although a working group was established to report on the issue, by the spring 2012 supplies and payments to the southern *loy mahaz*es were reported to have been further reduced or even stopped in some cases. For a few months, support was largely confined to a few *loy mahaz*es believed at that time to be closely aligned with Zakir, such as Zakir's own, Sattar's, Janan's and Dadullah's, with the units responding to the Quetta Military Commission.[109]

Attempts were made on and off to reconcile the two Quetta factions; during such attempts Zakir had the opportunity to roll out his system more widely. In early 2011 an agreement appeared to have been worked out which established a diarchy at the top of the Quetta Taliban: Zakir and Mansur would both become deputies of the Quetta Shura as replacements for Baradar. Zakir would therefore be promoted, but the condition imposed by Mansur was that Zakir would have to quit the leadership of Quetta's Military Commission, where he would be replaced by Mullah Ismail, who was apparently considered easier to manage by Mansur. On this point the deal collapsed: Zakir appears to have refused to leave the Quetta Military Commission, probably because he knew that he would hold more power there, rather than as one of two deputies at the helm of the Quetta Shura.[110]

In the summer of 2012, another attempted rapprochement occurred between Mansur (with the majority of the Rahbari Shura behind him), and Zakir and his allies. It was agreed, again, that Zakir's *nizami* system would be accepted in exchange for reassurances that he would share power with Mansur. This fragile agreement was embodied by the long-delayed implementation of the decision originally made in late 2010 or early 2011 to appoint both Zakir and Mansur as deputies to the Quetta Shura. This truce between the two leaders, however, was short-lived, as in September 2012 they again started arguing over Zakir's efforts to impose new directives, as well as his alleged personal thirst for power. Zakir and Mansur clashed over the fate of Qari Ismail and several other Taliban accused of having negotiated with western diplomats without prior authorisation. Zakir had 17 of them arrested, but Mansur intervened (under Mullah Omar's name) to save Ismail from execution. Zakir responded by asking to speak directly with Omar, beginning the dispute over the role of Omar and his state of health.[111] In late 2012 several assassinations of Zakir's supporters took place in Quetta, allegedly at the hands of Mansur's supporters.[112] Mansur's supporters accused Zakir of having ordered the assassination of Mawlavi Abas, head of the Quetta Shura Companies and NGO Commission, who was killed by an IED in Pakistan.[113]

By autumn 2012 the split in Quetta was becoming public knowledge among the Taliban rank-and-file. A *nizami massul* from Nangarhar, deployed to Baghlan, commented disparagingly about the south:

> There are rules and regulation in Baghlan province. Baghlan is not like Kandahar and Helmand. Problems [such as exist there] never happened here. We once had a problem between Sattar's *mahaz* and the Jundullah *mahaz*, but we took care of it immediately.[114]

While the *loy mahaz*es of Zakir and Sattar were pushing for for the Quetta Military Commission (led by Zakir himself) to have full authority, Mansur, Dadullah, Naeem Janan and what was left of Baradar's *loy mahaz* refused to submit. Although *nizami massuleen* continued to exist in a number of southern districts and provinces, in much of the south and west the structure disintegrated as the coalition led by Mansur refused to recognise their authority. The two factions competed over tax collection and territorial control.[115]

In Helmand, for example, the *loy mahaz*es of Mansur, Dadullah, Naeem and Baradar organised themselves along a separate chain of command from Zakir's faction, which had the support of Sattar, Janan and Ibrahim Alizai's *loy mahaz*es. The tension between the two coalitions even devolved into open fighting.[116] Having lost hope in a settlement with Mansur, Zakir tried to consolidate his faction into what was nicknamed the 'New Quetta Shura'. It was first established in August 2012, as an attempt to create a new wider alliance within the Taliban against Mansur. Key players, apart from Zakir, were Idris Haqqani and Mansur Dadullah (who soon quit), as well as Abdul

Rauf, Abdul Sattar and Mullah Janan, who contributed the support of their *loy mahaze*s. Initially the new *shura* had a budget of $40 million, with about 50 commanders on its payroll, who had 'defected' from the Rahbari Shura.[117] In fact the New Quetta Shura did not have separate commissions, but had members within most of the commissions of the Quetta Shura, which remained paralysed by the factional infighting. The only Commission it controlled completely was the Military one.[118] However, Zakir had the support of several Rahbari Shura members and other senior 'old Taliban', such as Abdul Raziq Akhundzada, Ihsan Rahimi, Abdul Rauf, Abdul Majid and Ibrahim Alizai.[119]

In September 2013, a large meeting of senior Taliban took place in Quetta to once again discuss reconciliation between Mansur and Zakir. The meeting concluded the previous negotiations with the decision to re-merge the two parallel Quetta Shuras of Mansur and Zakir. According to a Quetta Shura cadre, in the areas ruled by Zakir and Peshawar, military power would be the exclusive prerogative of the *nizami massuleen*, and the *loy mahaz* field commanders deployed there would also comply with Military Commission directives. Conversely, in the provinces where Mansur was dominant, the governors reflected the balance of power between the local networks, and as such were better positioned to direct ground operations; the *massuleen* deployed their own units and were essentially in exclusive control over them. These two military systems were not integrated, but concurrent and dissenting.[120] Reportedly Mansur came under Pakistani pressure to agree to the deal, which was a success for Zakir.[121] By now Mullah Naeem, leader of a *loy mahaz*, had split from the alliance led by Mansur after a dispute, and had allied with Zakir.[122]

Among the Taliban commanders, views varied as to Zakir's credentials as a leader and a reformer. Some viewed him as a popular and capable military leader who was taking personal risks on the battlefield and could have led the Taliban to victory.[123] Others however saw him as a divisive leader blinded by personal ambition.[124] An example of Zakir's provocation was his recruitment of commanders and men from the *loy mahaz* of his ally Sattar, which in 2013 resulted in serious tension between the two men and a threat by Sattar to re-align with Mansur. Zakir had to promise to send Sattar's men back.[125]

Whether as a result of the fear that Zakir's charisma would lead to his complete takeover, or to resist his maneuvering, on 18 November 2013 the supporters of Mansur reportedly gathered in Quetta, following a meeting between the recovering Baradar (recently released from a Pakistani jail) and

Akhtar Mohammad Mansur. According to a participant's account, about 20 provincial governors, 180 district governors and 100 senior commanders attended, as well as Rahbari Shura and Commission members, for a total of 500 attendees. In that meeting Mansur reportedly hinted that Baradar would resume his leadership position and that Zakir's New Quetta Shura was illegitimate and its members were defectors as far as Mansur and Baradar were concerned, a crime punishable by death. The proposal to issue an ultimatum to the New Quetta Shura and then proceed with violent reprisals was put to the vote and passed with 360 votes in favour and 140 against.[126]

In January 2014 tension between Mansur and Zakir's factions resulted once again in violence, with former commanders of Baradar who had gone over to Zakir being assassinated. The most senior losses were Zakir's head of finance Mawlavi Farid Popalzai and his head of recruitment Mawlavi Atal Barakzai. Zakir's men retaliated by murdering the deputy shadow governor of Zabul, Mawlavi Saifullah and the head of the Quetta Ulema Council, both loyal to Mansur. A 'ceasefire' was unsuccessfully negotiated by emissaries of the Peshawar Shura and the Pakistani Jamaat ul Ulema.[127]

Meanwhile Zakir's activities in northern Afghanistan and the Kabul region caused growing friction with the Peshawar Shura and eventually ended his alliance with them.[128] Zakir was eventually removed from his position of head of the Central Military Commission in April 2014, following a disagreement with the majority view among other Taliban leaders and Saudi foreign backers regarding the Afghan presidential elections of 2014 and the planned Taliban campaign against it. Zakir wanted to go ahead with the campaign and try to disrupt the elections and prevent people from voting, while the political leaderships in both Quetta and Peshawar, as well as the foreign backers, wanted the Taliban to positively influence the electoral result.[129] As a result Zakir also lost his access to the budget of the Military Commission. A Quetta Shura cadre indicated how with his main rival marginalised, Mansur managed to acquire the loyalty of several main *loy mahaz* commanders who had previously sided with Zakir, such as Mullah Sattar and Mullah Janan, exponentially increasing his military reach countrywide. The balance of military power had now been turned on its head: with funding cut off, Zakir's *loy mahaz* started contracting and soon he could only entrench his forces in Helmand (see Map 2).[130] A purge of Zakir's supporters in the Military Commission started.[131] The removal of Zakir calmed the waters around the Quetta Shura, but not for long.[132]

## 4.7 The limits of polycentrism

In conclusion, we have seen how the Taliban's polycentric system, with its multiple lines of command and control, resisted the military pressure exercised upon it from 2009 onwards, but that the Taliban leadership could not prevent debates and criticism spreading rapidly. Hardliners started advocating reforms taking Quetta closer to the Haqqani or Peshawar model, while moderates started pushing for talks with the Kabul authorities aimed at some kind of reconciliation. The ensuing political paralysis highlighted the limitations of the polycentric system: nobody had the authority to push reforms through, in either direction. Throughout this period various failed reform efforts took place with some patching up of the old system in tow; it can aptly be described as a period of crisis.

Another limitation of polycentrism was that it made the Taliban easy prey to external manipulation. When the Pakistanis realised that the Taliban were taking an undesirable path, they started promoting younger military leaders like Zakir and the Peshawar Shura's leaders, who themselves thought they had found the key to military victory.

The polycentrism of the Taliban as a whole, and of the Quetta Shura internally, meant that skilled operators were needed to make the system function. This is why Mullah Baradar played such a key role in maintaining the Quetta Shura, and why his detention in Pakistan in 2010 was the main factor unleashing the subsequent crisis.

# 5

# THE TALIBAN'S TACTICAL ADAPTATION

While the Quetta Shura was entangled in a crisis, the Taliban were nonetheless attempting to adapt to new military challenges through changes in their tactics. Thus, the Taliban's guerrilla war effectively began in 2009. The Taliban could only make limited progress in upgrading their arsenal but, with external help, managed to put together a large-scale IED campaign, which became their key asset. While IED use began in 2002, it did not take off until 2006. Another important innovation was the intensification and growing sophistication of their intimidation and targeting campaign. Other innovations, such as the dramatic expansion in suicide bombing, had a comparatively modest impact.

## 5.1 The original tactics of the insurgency

Until the American surge of 2009–12, Taliban tactics were basic: gather some tens of men, occasionally hundreds, and attack government posts. Ambush tactics against police patrols were primitive, and suicide attacks were badly planned and organised. There was no capacity to carry out complex terrorist attacks. These unsophisticated tactics were enough when confronting the similarly poorly trained and disorganised Afghan government police and pro-government militias; however, they proved inadequate on the rare occasion when the Americans intervened (typically in the east and south-east, where they had a presence from 2001 onwards):

During the attack we didn't lose any fighters. Then American helicopters arrived, firing rockets and machine guns. We fought until sunset. We lost 12 Taliban to martyrdom, largely to the helicopter fire that comes down like heavy rain. We cannot compare our military strength to that of the Americans. But we have learned how to stay protected behind rocks and mountains. Even with all their advanced technology, we forced them to withdraw and captured that base.[1]

With ISAF's deployment in the provinces, which increased following the American surge, clashes with western armies, increasingly often accompanied by relatively better trained ANA units, became the new standard. As pressure mounted, the Taliban had to adapt to survive.[2]

## 5.2 The refining of guerrilla tactics

During the United States (US) surge, American Marines stationed in southern Afghanistan noted a regular pattern of adaptation. For the first few weeks, the Taliban would try to hold the ground against superior forces, using mud compounds, irrigation ditches and other fortifications, some of which would withstand multiple artillery strikes and 500 pound bombs.[3] Observers of Taliban operations pointed out their tactical clumsiness in the early days of the insurgency. An early 2006 assessment of their skills in Helmand recorded that they showed 'impressive aggression and determination, as well as an ability to organise, fire and manoeuvre'.[4] Despite having a basic grasp of infantry tactics, they could make 'stupid mistakes' like not changing position after firing. They 'always' placed their 'signature weapons' around their command and control centre, giving away its location, reportedly because leaders preferred to keep signature weapons close. As they gradually improved their skills, they masked their mortar positions and frequently relocated their mortars after firing a few rounds.[5] The Taliban also panicked whenever armoured vehicles were deployed, including light tanks like the British Scimitar.[6]

Later they would shift to asymmetric tactics like IEDs and long-distance sniping, fragmenting the tactical units from groups of fifteen to thirty men into teams of four to five. With the death of many experienced cadres, some inexperienced Taliban commanders chose to fight against immensely superior forces.[7] From 2010 onwards, the Taliban stopped trying to capture and hold exposed areas, and limited their engagements to approximately twenty minutes, to reduce the risk of air strikes.[8] In some areas the use of motorbikes and vehicles in exposed areas was banned, and so was the use of radios and mobile phones.[9]

There are changes in tactics, for an example we conducted big operations with large numbers of fighters involved, where we were losing many fighters in each fight. This was a totally wrongheaded perception and not a good plan, but now we have changed the strategy – we send small effective groups for different guerrilla attacks and they return with very positive results and without big casualties, also we have introduced IEDs, car bombs and so on... this is a very efficient way to fight and of course is cheap; it does not cost much. Suicide attacks are a new phenomenon; a new face of the fight, which was introduced recently.[10]

In 2009 the Taliban reverted from a system of mostly fixed bases (usually in remote valleys, caves, safe houses in villages, and so forth) and posts (in areas where they had superiority) to a system of mobile/temporary bases and posts. To facilitate this change, commanders and cadres were requested to shift their presence around as often as possible and to never to spend too many nights in the same place. Local Taliban could spend the night in their homes. Implementation of the new system occurred even in areas under de facto Taliban control, such as Gard Serai (Paktia). Interviews with Taliban commanders reveal that this change was a consequence of night raids and subsequent casualties.[11] One of the commanders stated:

Before, we were based in one place, and each week twice or thrice there were drone attacks on our military posts, so we took lots of casualties. From the time when we started moving bases around, we started having fewer casualties.[12]

This was a locally driven adaptation, with the same pattern repeated over and over as ISAF forces invested in one district after another. Similar patterns of local level adaptation had been previously noticed, for example in Ghazni.[13] Similarly, the British and others noticed a shift towards asymmetric tactics in the south no later than 2008, in particular with the abandonment of mass attacks.[14] The Taliban field commanders believed that they needed to demonstrate to their leaders that they made an effort to resist, even if it seemed pointless. As one of them said:

Of course we try to avoid direct clashes, otherwise they will kill us. But if we don't fight or show any activity, our leaders won't leave us alone. We have to maintain some kind of activity for the leadership.[15]

In some areas the local Taliban went 'overground' between 2006–8, shifting back to asymmetric tactics, as they believed that southern cities would be seized. After having mobilised large numbers of fighters locally, this change was not easy. What would the local villagers do once the Taliban moved back underground or even to the desert and the mountains? There is evidence that the Taliban tolerated, if not encouraged, their local fighters to reinsert themselves into society after the Taliban left an area or went back underground. In Helmand in 2011–12, for example, hundreds of former local Taliban flocked to courses organised by Mercy Corps, causing few issues from the Taliban.[16]

Figure 13 shows how the Taliban's reliance on different tactics changed from region to region, with Regional Command East (RC-E) and Regional Command Centre (RC-C) relying more heavily on indirect fire than the other regions. Similarly, the IED effort was proportionally greater in RC-E than elsewhere. However, the general trend was towards more asymmetric tactics. Here two commanders discuss the Taliban's diminishing ability to take over large areas in exposed positions (as in the Pashmul area in 2006) and assault district centres:

> Till 2011 [...] we fought a lot against the foreign troops and the Afghan army, but when they got tired of fighting they started bombing our area from the air, and the Americans started their drone operations every night in our area, and many Taliban commanders and fighters were martyred. Then our leadership decided to not fight face to face and turn to guerrilla fighting: suicide attacks, land mines, ambushes and other guerrilla fighting. We still use those tactics [and will do so] until we receive orders to fight with new tactics.[17]
>
> We lost many of our fighters in these drone attacks and night raids. That is why the Taliban leadership decided to become mobile and carry out guerrilla attacks against the foreign and Afghan troops.[18]

In reality, the Taliban had always used 'guerrilla tactics', but what these commanders meant was that the leadership imposed a more exclusive reliance on such tactics, while phasing out any tactics that led the Taliban to offer an easy target to enemy air strikes. For the average Taliban commander there was a continuum of tactics that ranged from the most asymmetric to the least, and were chosen according to the circumstance.[19] As one Taliban commander put it:

> There are no big differences in our fighting tactics, we have the same tactics in our fighting, only we have decreased face to face fighting against the foreign troops and Afghan forces and increased our IED attacks, ambushes and suicide attacks.[20]

Another noted:

> We know that fighting tactics differ from place to place, so in this case it is the area commander who must take effective decisions to get better results, because

they are in the area and know what to do – we cannot control every area with one strategy.[21]

After 2001, the Taliban regularly used ambush tactics.[22] However, the Taliban eventually dropped efforts to hold the ground altogether. During the Marjah operation of 2010, the local Taliban immediately went underground, while the mobile element pulled out.[23] From 2009 onwards, the Taliban pulled out their mobile, full-time units immediately and left behind local fighters, who could easily hide in the village.[24] This might have been the result of a decision made by Mullah Baradar:

> Soon after 4,000 U.S. marines flooded into Afghanistan's Helmand River Valley on July 2, Mullah Abdul Ghani Baradar called top Taliban regional commanders together for an urgent briefing. The meeting took place in southwestern Pakistan-not far from the Afghan border but safely out of the Americans' reach. Baradar told the commanders he wanted just one thing: to keep the Taliban's losses to a minimum while maximizing the cost to the enemy. Don't try to hold territory against the Americans' superior firepower by fighting them head-on, he ordered. Rely on guerrilla tactics whenever possible. Plant 'flowers' – improvised explosive devices – on trails and dirt roads. Concentrate on small-unit ambushes, with automatic weapons and rocket-propelled grenades. He gave his listeners a special warning: he would hold each of them responsible for the lives of their men.[25]

Western observers believed that attacks on fixed positions aimed to put foreign troops on the defensive.[26] These attacks were common in parts of Afghanistan Helmand, though not exclusive to this region. With this view, it is therefore incorrect to interpret Baradar's intervention in 2009 as an effort to introduce new tactics; rather, it was an attempt to convince field commanders, emboldened by having occupied densely populated areas in open ground, that they would not be able to retain these areas during an enemy offensive.

The Taliban were initially not very competent in underground organisation and therefore suffered a lot:

> One of the main tactics of the foreign troops was to pay local people to give them information about us, like spies. They recruited a lot of spies from among the villagers, so that they know where we are, what we are doing. This was one of the main reasons the Taliban suffered defeats in the area. [...] The Taliban found most of the spies. Some were sent to Pakistan, some were killed. This is the main way we reacted to the situation.[27]

The need to organise underground prompted a major organisational evolution of the Taliban; their counter-intelligence had to professionalise, and the court system had to further develop to contain abuses.[28] Recruitment of local Taliban, which had fallen out of fashion from 2005–8, became of great importance again.[29] When the Taliban moved into populated areas of Garmser, for example, they began filling their ranks by mobilising local sympathisers:

> When the Taliban came new to our district, they were not enough fighters, they told us to make groups of 10 to 15 and come to them, and they would give us weapons and supplies to fight against the local government and foreign fighters.[30]

In summation, there is evidence of the Taliban's tactical flexibility from the beginning of the insurgency as well as an effort to improve the implementation of asymmetric tactics, which intensified over time. By the summer of 2006, the Taliban's capability increased, as they employed more sophisticated tactics such as combined arms fire, multiple angles of attack, and fast reaction times. They also further developed their observation skills for enemy monitoring.[31] Quoting USMC assessments of the fighting in Helmand from 2010-11, Johnson highlights the following tactical changes:

- Improved Fire Control: 'The use of coordinated and disciplined volley fire of RPGs against specific targets with attacks coming from multiple firing positions.'
- Improved Fire Discipline: 'Engagements have lasted from two to forty hours of continuous combat, demonstrating the Taliban's ability to field, employ and sustain combat forces through disciplined and controlled application of resources.'
- More sophisticated tactical deployment to achieve interlocking fields of fire.
- Better fire coordination with combined arms and with manoeuvring units: 'Coordinated machine gun fire to suppress targets to enable them to be attacked with RPGs, rockets and mortars'; 'RPG and machine gun fire used to fix the enemy in position while fighters maneuver to the flanks';
- Improved Anti-Armor Tactics: The use of RPGs to disable and stop armoured vehicles, instead of attempting to penetrate them.
- Improved Cover and Concealment: 'The utilization of fighting positions built into "*Karez*" irrigation ditches which provide excellent

cover and concealment to maneuver around the battlefield and attack the Marines.'

- Improved planning and understanding of enemy tactics.[32]

The Taliban adopted the practice of planning attacks at least a week before carrying them out, sometimes together with foreign advisors.[33]

Not all Taliban members were happy with the shift back to guerrilla tactics, which explains the slow motion of the process. Some Taliban commanders had never implemented guerrilla tactics proficiently. Old-fashioned Taliban commanders sometimes argued that the Taliban should 'fight as a man' and be ready for martyrdom if necessary.[34] It seems that the pace of the shifts and its achievements were less than satisfying from the point of view of the Taliban leadership. In the spring of 2011 the Taliban leadership issued a new directive to shift towards asymmetric tactics. In the south this was rolled out with specific training courses.[35] Included in the directive was avoidance of 'face-to-face' fighting whenever possible.[36] The directive also placed emphasis on more sophisticated asymmetric tactics:

> It's almost one year since our training system changed and now we are focused on getting training for [using] IEDs, making suicide vests, preparing suicide bombers and conducting guerrilla warfare.[37]

However, with the emergence of new and more pragmatic cadres, often without a strong clerical background like the Shamsatoo Taliban, the new tactics were soon fully absorbed.[38]

The most important tactics introduced by the Taliban have indeed been mines, whether IEDs or industrially manufactured. IEDs were already in use in 2002, although on a small scale. The innovation is therefore not the use of IEDs per se, but the development of an organisation able to procure the components, assemble the IEDs and deploy them on a very large scale from 2006 onwards (see Figures 10–11).[39] Consultation about the use of mines on a large scale involved Pakistani and Arab advisers, as well as all the top Taliban military leaders.[40] British Army sources reported that in mid-March 2009 Mullah Taleb, then Deputy Shadow Governor, visited Nad Ali to inform fighters that the Taliban had learned lessons from fighting the British with conventional means and that in the future would focus on IEDs.[41] Some ISAF officers even argued that by 2010 the Taliban had gone beyond the 'cottage industry' stage and had developed a veritable industry of IED makings. In Helmand, the original workshops that produced IEDs in batches of ten which were then deployed were replaced by larger outfits able to produce an IED every fifteen to twenty minutes.[42] An ISAF general was quoted in 2010 saying: 'An enemy that can generate 8,000 IEDS and bring 8,000 IEDS to bear and have a major effect, we ought to hire the J-4, the logistician.'[43] Taliban sources claim that in 2014 they placed 20,000 bombs and mines in Kandahar province alone.[44] Taliban sources established a direct relationship between the use of IEDs and ISAF's reliance on air power.[45]

Until 2007 most IEDs were made with military explosives. According to the Afghan Ministry of Interior, by 2008 this production method accounted for just 38% of all IEDs, which shrank further to 20% in 2009.[46] JIEDDO (the Pentagon's 'Joint Improvised Explosive Device Defeat Organization') estimated in 2011 that 83% of IEDs used in attacks on U.S. troops were made with fertilizers produced in Pakistan.[47] In 2012 ammonium nitrate fertilizer, according to JIEDDO, accounted in 2012 for 59% of IEDs in Afghanistan and for 90% of casualties.[48]

Although improvements in the production of low-signature IEDs continued,[49] the Taliban's response to the new, more resistant troops transports could only be to increase the amount of explosives in each IED. The reliance on fertiliser to produce IEDs (as opposed to military explosives) hampered the development of very large IEDs, as it takes about 20kg of fertiliser to obtain an explosive power comparable to that of 1.5kg of military explosives. About 250–750kg of explosives derived from fertiliser were needed to destroy the new armoured vehicles deployed by the Americans and other ISAF contingents from 2008 onwards.[50] The deployment of improved designs of troops transports thus greatly reduced the effectiveness of Taliban IEDs in 2011–12, contributing to a reduction in IED-related casualties as the Taliban struggled to counter-escalate.

As a result, the Taliban only occasionally deployed such heavy IEDs. After a successful IED strike, fears that the Taliban had procured a more advanced IED technology emerged. However, until the summer 2012 there was no evidence of this, although the same does not apply to industrially manufactured mines (see below).[51] In the summer of 2012 there were reports indicating a new flow of significant quantities of military explosives to the Taliban. There was no evidence that such supplies were being used for the manufacturing of large quantities of IEDs, though it was clear that they were being used for suicide bombing and truck bombing operations; yet military sources described the supply as apparently 'unlimited'.[52] The use of industrially manufactured mines continued throughout the war and were back in vogue by 2015, although according to the Taliban usually not anti-tank or EFP mines:

> We have engineers in the Mines Commission of the Miran Shah Shura. Some ready-made mines we get from Pakistan and Iran. [...] The mines that are given to us from Pakistan and Iran are industrially produced mines and they are quite small. They are not enough [to take out] Americans tanks and big cars. We use them for the army and national police cars, but our [self-produced] mines are artisanal – they are heavy, have a lot of power and can damage any types military cars or tanks.[53]

Gradually the Taliban developed a panoply of mines for various circumstances:

> We use different types of mines now. For small cars we use small size mines, which have advanced technology, and for big cars and tanks we use wire-type mines that we build with material from Pakistan. We use another type for anti-personnel mines. The Americans have technology they use for countering bombs, but against that we use another type of mines that they cannot counter. [...] 70 out 100 mines are remote controlled and the remaining 30 are not. We can work well with remote control mines. [...] The remote control mines which are given to us by Iran, they are small and they do not work well against American cars – also sometimes their signals get blocked – but the wired mines are good and there is no risk of their signals being blocked. We get these mines from Pakistan and Iran, and we also use Russian mines.[54]

An important turning point was Iranian provision of industrially manufactured mines. The Haqqanis started receiving these in 2010 in small quantities and then on a much larger scale in 2011 and 2012.[55] A less advanced Iranian technology of mines had been in western and north-western Afghanistan from 2010 onwards, in smaller quantities. Compact and relatively light, they were basic mine models (no EFP), but still tactically superior to the IEDs previously in use, and much safer.[56] The Iranians also provided training on how to use the new mines effectively and with minimal collateral damage.[57]

The Taliban's effort to deploy IEDs on an ever-larger scale and with greater effectiveness was slowed down by ISAF's relentless hunting of their IED. While there were an estimated 330–335 IED makers in April 2011, JIEDDO had counted another 510 who had been killed, detained or were no longer active.[58] Taliban sources acknowledged heavy losses. The Miran Shah Shura's Mine Commission, for example, lost ninety-two men in 2013, and seventy-five in 2014, including twenty killed in the premature mine explosions, while the rest were almost all killed by drones.[59] This changed after the withdrawal:

Now we can use it so much easier with the national army and police because in the time of Americans, they had advanced technologies and they recognized mines so easily and eliminated them.[60]

During the peak of ISAF's efforts, following the killing of an IED specialist, IED activities declined for some time, indicating a scarcity of specialists. People sent from the leadership replaced them within weeks, which indicates a degree of central management of the IED effort, but the heavy losses potentially delayed the spread of the IED campaign.[61] So, as of 2011 a veritable IED industry had only appeared in Helmand, Kandahar and Khost. In 2011 initiatives to spread the industry to other provinces was still relatively new. Even in Kandahar province, in 2011 districts like Panjwai and Zhari had few IED specialists and there were often Punjabis, suggesting shortages.[62]

The Taliban needed to enlist external support to achieve expansion of their mine warfare capabilities. When the great IED campaign took off and the tactical and technological competition with counter-IED efforts began, foreign fighters gave way to Pakistani IED makers.[63] Gradually the Taliban organised training courses outside Afghanistan to train their own specialists, with the help of foreign trainers:[64]

If the foreign trainers had not helped us, and did not train our groups, then we could not train our people ourselves now. We have their support. Pakistan and Iran especially have supported us a lot [with regards to] mines.[65]

Indeed, several Taliban sources admitted that the main source of tactical innovation were the, Pakistani and Iranian foreign advisers, whose influence was felt mainly in the west, but also as far away as Nangarhar due to the training they provided to eastern Taliban.[66]

It is worth asking why the Taliban, while being able to source small arms, machine guns, rocket launchers, mortars, and recoilless guns, have long not been able to source significant quantities of TNT for IED manufacturing. Moreover, much of the military explosives being used was recovered locally from old stocks of artillery and mortar rounds, rather than imported into Afghanistan. This question links up with the difficulty of the Taliban to procure anti-aircraft weapons (see above). Perhaps cost considerations and the difficulty to deploy anti-aircraft missiles effectively limited Taliban access, but in the case of TNT there is no reason that the Taliban should not have bought it on the black market or procured somehow. This suggests that the ability of the Taliban to escalate the military technologies and supplies they use was somehow being constrained, perhaps by their Pakistani hosts.

Given these limitations, the Taliban have opted to invest in the quantitative escalation of their IED effort, with a focus on targeting dismounted patrols by setting up rings of IEDs in areas which they know ISAF troops visit regularly.[67] They have also adopted more sophisticated emplacement tactics:

> In the past it was just a single IED, it might be an old artillery shell dug into the middle of the road. Now we will see maybe two, three or even four IEDs in a cluster designed to ensure you strike one of them or to catch us as we respond.[68]

As IEDs are passive weapons, measuring the Taliban reliance on them is difficult, particularly in the presence of changing operational patterns, redeployment or changes in the force structure of their opponents. Statistics show that IED attacks increased until 2010 and then declined slowly in 2011 (see Figures 10 and 11).[69]

Due to their indiscriminate character, the widespread reliance on mines was a major compliant of elders against the Taliban.[70] The massive increase of mine use has always been politically controversial within the Taliban due to the high number of associated casualties among communities that cooperate with the Taliban. Even some relatively high level military commanders, such as two provincial *nizami massuleen*, opposed it.[71] Among the senior leaders, Akhtar Mohammad Mansur was an early opponent of mines (2006).[72] Local Taliban in particular tended to oppose it.[73] However, the large majority of Taliban eventually agreed that there was no alternative to the use of mines. As military head of Kandahar province, Akhtar Mohammad Mansur, who opposed the use of mines and suicide bombing, expressed the need for asymmetric tactics (including suicide bombing) on the open ground surrounding Kandahar city to the Taliban press.[74]

The backlash against the widespread reliance on mines first occurred in 2008, when provincial and district governors were asked to advise the mine layers to pay attention to civilians.[75] In 2012 the Rahbari Shura ordered a suspension of the mine campaign, to prevent losing political capital among the communities. The Military Commission did not accept the suspension, so only village *mahazes* and governor groups stopped the campaign. Six months later the southern Taliban received Iranian remote control mines, which could be targeted more effectively. This delivery prompted the Rahbari Shura to lift the suspension.[76] By 2013–14 the Taliban were shifting tactical control of IEDs and mines to local Taliban groups, who were better positioned to coordinate the mine campaign with the local population.[77] This change brought about the introduction of a one month prison sentence as punishment for mine layers who mistakenly killed civilians. The mine layers could then be reinstated.[78] In Paktika two major incidents of civilian casualties caused by mines led to a two-month ban on mines.[79] There were reportedly cases of local Taliban groups banning the use of mines locally.[80]

Not all elders were impressed by Taliban efforts to contain the collateral damage by mines:

> Even if the elders complained to the Taliban, they would not listen. They would say that these civilians who were killed in mine blasts were spies.[81]

After the withdrawal of western troops in 2014, Taliban use of mines declined. The Miran Shah Shura, for example, only planted 660 mines in Loya Paktia in 2014, down from 1,114 in 2013.[82] The Haqqanis, however, had no intention of giving up their use of mines:

> If there are no IEDs, we cannot defeat the Afghan army. [...] You can see that the army and the Americans say that 80 per cent of their casualties are from IEDs, so why should we stop [using them]? It is American and Western propaganda [about civilian deaths] – there are no civilian casualties [when we deploy mines].[83]

Another widely discussed tactical innovation by the Taliban is suicide bombing. While suicide bombings have not always been tactically successful, their use has eliminated key Taliban rivals in the police. More importantly, suicide bombings have a huge psychological impact, as they force the enemy to be on the defensive and on constant look-out.[84] The risk of suicide bombing has greatly impeded the work of Afghan government officials.[85]

The adoption of suicide bombing was controversial within the Taliban, as it was an import from Iraq. The Haqqanis began using suicide bombing in 2004. Since 2005 the annual number of suicide bombers and *fedayi* teams has grown significantly.[86] The main proponent of this tactic was Azizullah Haqqani, who received the support of Pakistani and Arab advisers. Indeed, in the early days it was Pakistani engineers who prepared the bombs. Azizullah served as head of the Fedayin Commission of the Miran Shah Shura until autumn 2016 (See Chapter 3). Other key proponents of suicide bombing were Serajuddin Haqqani, Qari Aziz and Qari Rauf Zakir.[87] The psychological value of the new tactics emerges clearly in this quote from a Taliban publication:

> Let the Americans and their allies know that even though we lack equipment, our faith is unshakable. And with the help of Allah the Almighty, we have created a weapon which you will not be able to face or avoid, i.e. martyrdom operations. We

will follow you everywhere and we will detonate everything in your face. We will terrify you, even from vacant lands and silent walls. We know we are inevitably heading towards death, so let it be a glorious death by killing you with us, [...]. We have thus prepared many suicide operations that even will involve women, and we will offer you the taste of perdition in the cities, villages, valleys and mountains with Allah's help.[88]

During its existence (up to February 2015) the Miran Shah Shura's Fedayi Commission deployed 1,160 suicide bombers in all of Afghanistan, according to an internal source. The Commission believed that 843 bombers achieved their task successfully, while the remaining individuals either were arrested, killed before they could detonate, or surrendered to the enemy. As of February 2015, the Fedayi Commission claimed to have 1,500 bombers ready to deploy, another 830 in training and 1,800 more waiting to start their training courses.[89]

The technology of suicide bombing improved over time, as the Haqqanis learned how to make smaller explosive-carrying waistcoats using plastic and developed other creative ways of hiding bombs on suicide carriers.[90]

The other sections of the Taliban showed less interest in suicide bombing than the Haqqanis. Specifically, the Peshawar Shura deployed few suicide bombers and, unlike the Haqqanis, never invested in the development of suicide bombers. The Military Commission would use them from time to time.[91] Suicide bombing was introduced in the Peshawar Shura in 2006 when the Shamsatoo Shura joined it; in particular, Qari Atiqullah sponsored it and Toor-e Pagri supported him.[92] Anwar ul Haq Mujahid and other early leaders of the Taliban in Nangarhar were against suicide bombing, as were the majority of Shamsatoo Mahaz and Safi Shura members.[93]

The Quetta Shura showed a strong interest in suicide bombing when Dadullah Lang was the military leader, but did not systematically organise suicide bomber recruitment like the Haqqanis did. The Taliban's *ulema* councils approved the use of suicide bombing against 'Kafir invaders', but the debate within the Taliban continued as some argued that collateral civilian casualties were unacceptably high. In the Quetta Shura there was never a dedicated structure for suicide bombing, and deployment was up to the discretion of each *loy mahaz*. After Dadullah was killed, Ihsanullah Rahimi became the main proponent of suicide bombing in Quetta.[94] While there was no opposition in the Miran Shah Shura some senior figures in the Rahbari Shura objected to the tactic, including Akhtar Mohammad Mansur and Mullah Baradar. Similarly, in most provinces several senior local cadres of the

Taliban showed reservations and opposition. In Ghazni Hazara and Tajik Taliban leaders opposed suicide bombing.[95] In Herat, Ghulam Yahya Akbari opposed the use of suicide bombers.[96] Local Taliban were less keen on suicide bombing than Pakistan-based Taliban groups.[97]

After Dadullah's death reliance on suicide bombing temporarily declined. This was a source of friction that eventually led to Miran Shah declaring its autonomy (see Chapter 3). The Taliban gradually re-absorbed the opposition in 2010-12 as high-profile suicide attacks in Kabul were the primary response of the Taliban to growing ISAF military pressure.[98]

In part the need for suicide bombing in the Quetta and Peshawar Shuras decreased because the Haqqanis were allowed to carry them out anywhere in Afghanistan, normally without even needing any authorisation. The Haqqanis only contacted the two *shuras* in a few specific circumstances before carrying out suicide attacks. A division of labour emerged, where the Haqqanis carried out the most controversial operations. According to the Taliban's own count, in 2015 almost 70 per cent of all suicide attacks were carried out by the Haqqanis, 18 per cent by the Quetta Shura and 13 per cent by the Peshawar Shura.[99] The Mashhad office did not deploy suicide bombers until the end of 2016, and in general Iranian advisers were reportedly unenthused by this tactic.[100] However, they were interested in *fedayeen* storm tactics, which the Mashhad-affiliated Naim Mahaz used for the first time in 2012 in a raid on Camp Bastion, in Helmand, after the team underwent extensive training by the Pasdaran.[101]

Once the Taliban adopted suicide bombing as primarily a military tactic (as opposed to a largely terroristic weapon in Iraq), patterns of improved tactical effectiveness became apparent. The early attempts were clumsy; later, however, efforts became much better planned and often relied on highly indoctrinated and trained individuals. By 2010 most suicide attacks were carried out with the help of support teams, as well as an increasingly widespread network of informers, infiltrated well into the government apparatus.[102]

Although isolated, clumsy attacks continued as training skills were unevenly distributed across the Taliban's networks, there was a strong tendency towards 'fedayeen tactics'; that is, integrated teams of attackers, well trained to fight and not just to blow themselves up, storming strategic or symbolic objectives. In achieving their multiple purposes, *fedayeen* tactics appear to have been meant to:

- Intimidate enemies into living in a state of siege;

- Demonstrate the utility of a centralised leadership and of the guerrilla professionalisation it advocated (see 'Enhanced command and control' in Chapter 6 below);
- Demoralise the enemy by penetrating well defended areas.

In other words, suicide bombing and *fedayeen* tactics were used in the pursuit of two goals: symbolic and tactical.[103]

After 2013 the debate re-opened as the impending withdrawal of ISAF combat forces removed the original legitimisation of suicide bombing, as authorised by the *ulema*. The *ulema* raised the issue of suicide bombing. Under pressure from community elders as well, the Quetta Shura decided to downscale the number of attacks.[104] In some areas, provincial level Taliban leaders banned suicide bombing altogether, as in the case of Faryab's *nizami massul* Salahuddin, though the Quetta Shura and the Haqqanis carried out attacks regardless.[105] The Haqqanis were at the forefront of those arguing that suicide bombing was still necessary:

> We will not reduce [suicide bombing], but will increase it. This is because we need it against the Afghan government. Also, as foreign troops [are not committed to a complete withdrawal], suicide bombers are needed. Basically, we want to use suicide bombers until the point at which Islamic governance is re-established in Afghanistan.[106]

Less widely discussed, but of much greater impact than suicide bombing was the Taliban's increasing resort to intimidation. The stronger the military pressure the heavier the Taliban relied on intimidation tactics to delay or prevent the consolidation of the Kabul government. In many areas where the Taliban were present, the Taliban would proactively target members of the Afghan security forces who refused to quit service by pressuring their families to force them to resign. Most members were gradually forced to relocate to safe areas under government control. Those who could afford to do so quit, and hundreds were executed over the years. Even those relocating were at risk of being caught travelling on the roads at a Taliban checkpoint.[107] The degree to which the Taliban proactively pursued members of the security forces was subject to tactical considerations. When the Taliban were trying to establish relations with local communities their approach was softer and they might show greater tolerance for the presence of members of the security forces.[108]

Targeted killing is easily measurable and has dramatically escalated over the years in retaliation to ISAF's 'night raids', with increased targeting of civilians (see Figure 9). While there is not UN data for targeted assassinations before

2008, the Taliban were already carrying them out in 2004 if not earlier, although on a small scale. USAID reported in 2006 that its Afghan staff had been targeted for three years, with a loss of about 100 staff members, while the assassination of pro-government clerics started in the summer of 2005 in the south.[109] The lack of precise data on previous years makes it difficult to evaluate where 2008 stood in terms of a trend in Taliban targeted assassinations, but overall Taliban-inflicted civilian casualties rose by more than half in that year. It is therefore plausible to estimate that targeted assassination also rose significantly. A small drop followed in 2009, while targeted assassinations almost doubled in 2010. This pattern continued as assassinations increased by 41 per cent in 2012 from 2011.

It should be noted that UNAMA data only includes civilian victims of targeted killings; police and army members are not included, though they have been priority targets of the Taliban. ISAF sources estimate that of the 190 recorded targeted assassinations that took place between in March–September 2011, fifty involved Afghan security force personnel, thirty-two involved government officials and the rest were individuals not working for the government.[110]

It is difficult to assess the extent to which intimidation was used as this type of data is notoriously difficult to collect. Since western militaries measure violence in conventional terms, they only capture a fraction of Taliban violence, particularly in regions like the north-west. However, for the Taliban's campaign, intimidation, proselytising (or, showing off their presence) and tax collection are as important as its more 'kinetic' aspects. Taliban activities in the eastern districts of Jowzjan, such as Mingajik, were ignored or undetected in 2011, because they were confined to small insurgent teams roaming around in motorbikes, entering villages, preaching in the mosques against foreign (Christian) occupation and inviting young men and boys to join.[111]

In Kandahar intimidation has been reported over several years.[112] The intimidation campaign has undoubtedly accompanied the spread of the Taliban as it is reported wherever the Taliban operate. What is unclear however is whether the Taliban have invested more resources into this type of activity, or whether there have been qualitative changes to the way they operate. Anecdotal evidence suggests that intimidation has gradually affected sections of the middle class in Kabul city.[113] Each team (*karwan*) was assigned a province and tasked with pursuing individuals willing to collaborate with Taliban intelligence. In most provinces, the team was made up of twenty men, though larger in places like Kabul.[114] The Taliban used their intelligence network inside the government apparatus to track down collaborators. According to Taliban sources, in 2016 the Kabul Military Commission had about 1600 members in Kabul, half of which were in support roles (recruitment, logistics, intelligence, and so forth). About 500 were spies and informers. This force claimed to have carried out sixty-five targeted attacks in Kabul in 2016, mostly through shootings and magnetic mines.[115]

Similar to suicide bombing and mines, targeted killing of government officials was also controversial among the Taliban, as some opposed targeting teachers, doctors or engineers.[116] Although former members often nostalgically recall the mythical early years of the insurgency as a time of restraint and rule of law among the Taliban, which ended as the old leaders were killed, targeted killing was actually at its most intense in 2005–10 in southern Afghanistan, despite the smaller size of the Taliban.[117] In Kandahar, violence was most intense, as hundreds of village elders were killed and more fled to the city.[118] After the initial wave of violence, arbitrary killings of suspect spies and government collaborators became a rarity, as few villagers would dare challenge the Taliban. Almost half of the elders interviewed in 2014–15 could not recall such instances.[119]

Of forty-one elders interviewed, nineteen could not recall any incident, while twenty-seven did. Of these twenty-seven elders, seven referred to the same three incidents of police captured and executed.[120] Targeting family members also occurred occasionally; the Taliban have restrained this practice after police and militia went after Taliban family members.[121] Of sixteen Taliban who answered the question, only three denied that arbitrary executions ever happened; another six admitted they were happened in 2014–15, but had not happened in previous years.[122]

The inability of the Taliban to respond airstrikes and night raids motivated some executions, as some local villagers were scapegoated:[123]

First from our own Amirkhel village, five people were killed by the Taliban. Three people were killed after being accused of working for the Americans as spies, and two people were killed under suspicion of working for the NDS. They never found any evidence.[...] They did not [conduct a trial]. In the case of two of these five, some Taliban had [previously] went to their homes to eat, where they were caught by the Americans and arrested. After this, other Taliban accused the two men of collaborating with the Americans and executed them as spies.[124]

Another Taliban innovation was the conscious, organised efforts to infiltrate the Afghan security forces. The escalation between 2009 and 2012 was obvious; before 2008 there is no record of this type of incidents.[125] What is certain is that green-on-blue attacks had a major demoralising impact on NTM-A and forced it to scale down its mentoring efforts.[126] But was this a result of a Taliban effort? In autumn 2011 the Taliban set up a *Dawat-o-Irshad* Commission, with the aim of encouraging the defections or realignment of members of the Afghan security forces.[127] Though the Taliban claimed any incident involving the so-called green-on-blue attacks as their own, ISAF claimed that evidence of direct Taliban involvement exists in only a small number of cases. In fact, for most green-on-blue and green-on-green attacks in Afghanistan there was insufficient evidence to assess the degree of Taliban involvement. In the few cases were evidence is present, it can be concluded that the Taliban were involved in most of these instances.[128]

The Taliban wanted to get their men into the Afghan security forces as well as recruit dissatisfied members of those forces, for example those who were publicly humiliated by US and other western soldiers.[129] When ISAF increased their attacks by shifting focus from combat operations to mentoring and building up the Afghan security forces, the Taliban effort (that is, its share in the crisis of mentoring caused by the green-on-blue attacks) became an example of military adaptation to changing circumstances.

One example of an adaptation is the banning of mobile phone communications. Despite the impact of targeted killing and capturing by ISAF (see Figure 6), within the Taliban's ranks many were not convinced that their liberal use of mobile phones facilitated targeting by ISAF. In 2013, of thirty-eight Taliban commanders in Helmand who answered questions about the impact of ISAF's radio and mobile phone intercepts (mostly at the *dilghay* level, some at the district level and some at the team level), eight (21 per cent) stated openly that they were worried, while another fifteen (39.5 per cent) stated that they were worried but were confident that measures taken to minimise the risk from such intercepts had largely been successful.[130] The remaining fifteen (39.5 per cent) were adamant that they did not consider radio and mobile phone intercepts a serious threat.[131]

Even those Taliban commanders who acknowledged being worried about mobile phone and radio interception often believed that the counter-measures taken had been sufficient in containing the threat:[132]

I am worried about this; we know that British troops have the technology to hear our mobiles and radios. We knew this before and that's why we change our numbers very often and most of the time we keep our mobiles off. Mostly we use Thuraya phones or satellite phones for communication, [as] British troops and Americans don't have the ability to listen to the satellite phones.[133]

Sources within the British army indicated that the Taliban's countermeasures are actually very ineffective, with the exception of couriers, and that the Taliban's coding system is far too simple to resist immediate decoding. Contrary to the Taliban's belief, even satellite phone are easy to intercept.[134] The Taliban however were successful in disseminating a large amount of unreliable information through loose communication, which confused their enemy and made it difficult to differentiate between truth and lies. For example, some believed that the Taliban might deliberately exaggerate their casualties to facilitate disengagement.[135]

Eventually the Taliban managed to enforce a stricter mobile phone discipline. Efforts to tighten phone use started no later than 2008.[136] Around May 2011 a new order was issued by the Taliban leadership to limit the use mobile phones:[137]

Before there were more airstrikes, now there are less. Everyone had a mobile phone, which allowed them to be tracked. Now, soldiers don't have mobiles and only one or two people, or just the commander, [carry them].[138]

The Taliban's practice of taking down cell towers, which also began during this period, might have been another way to pre-empt mobile use by Taliban members. The foreign trainers were instrumental in introducing some rationalisation in the management of Taliban communications (see also 'Training' below). Iran supplied satellite telephones and encrypted radios, and spent energy trying to make Taliban members understand the liabilities implicit in reckless mobile phone and radio usage.[139]

The Taliban believed that these concerns about unsecured communications were losing importance due to ISAF's withdrawal. A commander said:

I don't care if they listen our radio or mobiles, they cannot come to our area now even if they can hear us. Their airstrikes have also stopped.[140]

One case of deliberate Taliban investment in asymmetric tactics was a 2010 decision of the military leadership to develop sniping and sharpshooting skills (see also Equipment below).[141] Sniping inflicted significant casualties on enemy troops once fighters were adequately trained. Although few Taliban fighters ever qualified as a sniper by NATO standards, sharpshooting began increasing in 2010, though the average Taliban fighter remained a very poor shot. Data reported by Chivers shows that from June 2009 to March 2010 the lethality rate of Taliban small arms fire dropped to 12.3% from 15.6% in 2001–9, at a time when the lethality of IEDs increased from 14% to 18.9%.[142] Chivers reported a growing presence of Taliban sharpshooters in areas such as Marjah and Nuristan.[143] British army sources reported that in 2010 there was an increase in deaths from small arms fire (40% compared to 13% the previous year) as well as hits from single shots, presumably fired by sharpshooters or snipers, mostly in Sangin.[144]

Overall the impact of Taliban snipers has been limited and it is not clear whether there was a determined, large-scale effort to train combatants in sharpshooting techniques. Since deploying IEDs became more difficult due to ISAF restricting deployment in Taliban-held areas, after 2010 there were no reports of Taliban snipers and sharpshooters playing large roles. Taliban sources sometimes mention the existence of 'sniper fronts', but little is known about them.[145] It does not appear, therefore, that sniping has been a major feature of the Taliban's military adaptation.

Adaptation also means exploiting any kind of enemy weakness. According to a military blogger:

> The Taliban will force innocent women and children to stay close and act as human shields when they attack Americans. [...] The Taliban fighters will also shoot at our soldiers from concealed positions and then drop their weapons and stand out in the open because they know that we can't shoot at civilians who are not carrying weapons. Many times our troops can't return fire even though they know that the person standing there was just shooting at them.[146]

Elders confirmed that Taliban firing from village houses and sheltering themselves among the population was a major point of controversy between them and the Taliban.[147] The Taliban, however, do not like to discuss this issue.

## 5.3 New equipment

An interesting aspect of Taliban tactical adaptation is the minimal technological escalation since 2002. Up until mid-2012 the weapons used were largely the same: that is, various iterations of the Kalashnikov assault rifle, PKM or earlier models of machine guns, DSchK heavy machine guns

(12.7mm), RPG-7 rocket launchers, 107mm field rocket launchers, hand grenades and mines or IEDs. The innovations have been few, namely:

- The introduction of sniper rifles on a large scale;
- The introduction of 14.5mm anti-aircraft machine guns, with little actual impact;
- The introduction of longer-range ballistic rockets;
- The introduction of IEDs on a large scale;
- Suicide bombing;
- The introduction of heavy mortars;
- The introduction of advanced anti-armour weaponry, in small quantities.

By 2011 the Taliban introduced longer-range rockets (122mm), including the multi-barrelled version, which Iran supplied.[148] Before that the Taliban regularly used 107mm rockets, mostly in single and double launchers. As ballistic rockets are so imprecise, they are only useful for targeting cities or large encampments, which the Taliban decided not to attack on any significant scale. Their overall impact has been more than modest. Arguably long-range rockets are essentially just psychological weapons.

The use of mortars by the Taliban occurred on a more modest scale, because of the tactical limitations of these weapons (the 107mm rockets are available with disposable launchers). For most of the conflict, the mortars used were 82mm and in general they produced little casualties. Figures 12 and 13 show the limited impact of indirect fire among the Taliban's range of tactics. In some tactical situations, however, the mortars helped the Taliban achieve a degree of success when trying to overwhelm fixed enemy positions, like in the battle of Wanat.[149] Despite the low number of casualties inflicted by Taliban mortars, their impact in forcing defenders to take cover while Taliban fighters approached their positions should not be underestimated.[150] The Taliban's mortar firing skills left something to be desired; in order to hit fixed targets, they had to adjust fire gradually, observing where their rounds fell and they could not fire beyond visual range using coordinates.[151] The lack of education among the Taliban's mortar crew made it impossible for them to learn ballistics. This slow pattern limited the damage they were able to inflict and exposed them to counter-strike fire. By 2014–15 the Iranian government delivered 120mm mortars and a limited number of anti-tank missiles and rockets to loyal Taliban groups.[152] During this time the Peshawar Shura bought a few 120mm mortars on the black markets of Afghanistan and Uzbekistan.[153]

After 2010 the Taliban obtained a considerable number of Iranian copies of the Soviet Dragunov precision rifle and smaller quantities of the Daraskov long range, 14.5mm heavy rifle. Increasingly, sharpshooters have been procuring modern weapons with advanced optical equipment, such as the AK-74, M16 and M4.[154] The Iranians also delivered their long-range Shaher precision rifles.[155]

The agents of the Taliban's logistics commissions in Iran, China, Pakistan and Uzbekistan, charged with procuring military equipment, have been under growing pressure to procure more advanced weaponry, such as anti-aircraft missiles, heavy mortars, anti-tank weapons, etc. They procured this equipment either by lobbying the Taliban's allies or by purchasing them on the black market. As discussed above, they obtained tens of 120mm mortars from Iran.[156] The Taliban's greatest procurement ambition has been anti-aircraft missiles. Targeting enemy aircrafts with light weapons and RPG has always been quite common among the Taliban. At the peak of the conflict in 2009–10 there were between thirty to forty attacks, (see Figure 13 below), though few enemy aircrafts were successfully shot down. The Taliban consider better air defence a major priority. The 14.5mm heavy machine guns introduced around 2010 had a modest impact; they were obtained as a surrogate to more effective anti-aircraft weaponry, which the Taliban had problems sourcing. Although they constrained the reliance on helicopters by ISAF in some tactical situations, these heavier machine guns proved heavy and clumsy to deploy on the battlefield, and were usually destroyed by ISAF air power before entering the action.[157]

Between 2003 and 2014 the Taliban inherited, captured or bought on the black market ten anti-aircraft missile launchers. A few 9K32M launchers (NATO-coded SA-7b) made their way to the Taliban and might have been responsible for a few civilian helicopter losses. However, reporting on the use of anti-aircraft missiles by the Taliban has been inconsistent;[158] Taliban training manuals include pages on the 9K32M and the Taliban claim to be using such weapons in the field. Black market imports of these weapons were reported in the past from Tajikistan or China, through Badakhshan. The weapon systems were reportedly priced at $20–40,000 per launcher (with three missiles) in 2008–9. Iran has also been accused of transferring anti-aircraft missiles to the Taliban and training them to use the weapons, though the weapons were clearly not used on the battlefield. Sources within the Taliban are clear that there is a desire for more advanced portable anti-aircraft weapons.[159]

Taliban sources frequently reported attempts to purchase both advanced portable anti-aircraft missiles on the Central Asian black market and 'anti-aircraft weapons' from China in 2011–12.[160] A Taliban source indicated that the Chinese government agreed to deliver and dispatch the weapons systems, but was convinced by the Pakistani authorities to have them stored under Pakistani control until the Americans withdrew from the country. Reportedly, a major concern was the traceability of the weapons back to China.[161]

As of 2015 they were still trying to obtain newer anti-aircraft systems through Logistics Commissions agents. Efforts to purchase them on the Central Asian black market were largely unsuccessful due to their unavailability. In mid 2015 the Quetta and the Miran Shah Shuras lobbied the Iranians to deliver the weapons but were unsuccessful, despite significant compensation offered by the Taliban. According to some Taliban sources, the Pakistani intelligence vetoed the procurement of such weapons, as well as of any advanced or heavy weaponry, though the Taliban are trying to circumvent the ban. The Pakistanis told the Taliban that there was an agreement between the authorities of Pakistan and the Americans, whereby the Taliban would not get MANPADS and the Afghan government would not get a proper air force with combat capabilities. The Miran Shura eventually gave up such efforts in 2010, while the Quetta and the Peshawar Shura continued trying.[162] A Pasdaran adviser confirmed that the Pakistanis asked Pasdaran not to supply anti-aircraft missiles to Iran. The Pasdaran obliged, so as to create tension with Pakistan.[163]

Despite the failure to obtain significant numbers of anti-aircraft missiles, in 2015 the Taliban believed that the lack of such equipment would not dramatically hamper their ability to fight after the withdrawal of foreign forces, as they were assured that the Afghan air force would never be a major threat.[164]

Aside from anti-aircraft missiles, the only other advanced machinery obtained by the Taliban were anti-tank weapons. As of mid-2015 the Taliban of the Miran Shah Shura had succeeded in procuring a few advanced anti-tank weapons on the black market, including what they described as 'missiles'. They confirmed that these would have range of a few kilometres.[165] While the Chinese government rejected requests by the Miran Shah Shura to deliver advanced anti-tank weaponry, it reportedly delivered a few to the Peshawar Shura, before cutting relations with them.[166] Iran delivered a few anti-tank missiles to the Peshawar Shura.[167]

## 5.4 The impact of adaptation

The Taliban commanders believe that their new asymmetric tactics reduced their casualties while increasing the enemy's death toll:

> The only change I can tell you about is that before we were doing face to face fighting in which we had lots of martyrs, now we are using mines, which have two benefits: one is that we are successful in [their use] and second is that our death toll and casualties have decreased.[168]

The validity of this statement is difficult to assess. Taliban statistics suggest that after 2011 casualties fell dramatically (Figure 5), though in specific in cases numbers could still be high. In Helmand, a 2011–12 survey of twenty-eight Taliban commanders indicated that in the previous year on average about 20 per cent of their combatants were killed in action, with an additional number of fighters injured and arrested.[169] At the time, Helmand might have had the most acute military pressure on the Taliban, though samples from other provinces still suggest heavy losses. A commander in Imam Sahib (Kunduz) claims that twelve out of fifty men were killed in action in two years (24 per cent), with a further sixteen wounded (38 per cent).[170] Another commander in Baghlan Jadid lost twenty out of 135 men in one year, which is about 15 per cent.[171] The Taliban in the north-east were also bombarded heavily in 2011, so this region might also be above the average. However, an overall killed in action yearly ratio of 10–15 per cent seems plausible.

It is even more difficult to measure the impact of these new and refined tactics on the Taliban's enemies. Although as argued above the Taliban did not find an effective answer to the new mine-resistant vehicles, there are other factors that explain declining ISAF casualties:

- reduced operations by ISAF conventional troops (hence fewer targets), particularly in Taliban held areas as ISAF was focused on consolidating the areas grabbed in 2010 with the surge ordered by President Obama;
- reduced Taliban activity due to internal issues with respect to main IED deployment (south-south-west).[172]

At the same time, the casualties of the Afghan security forces were reportedly increasing, as they took on a larger role in the conduct of the war. An exact count is difficult to provide, as Afghan government data does not add up.[173] From the data that can be pieced together, it can be concluded that after 2014 casualties of the Afghan security forces escalated dramatically, reaching as high as 10,000 KIA in 2016.[174]

## 5.5 Sources of innovation

Tactical innovation was primarily driven by decisions taken at the leadership level, then transmitted down the hierarchy:

> Taliban have made lots of changes in their tactics since 2007, all these changes were made by the Quetta Shura and of course the Military Commission, local commanders cannot make any big changes in tactics. Roadside bombs and suicide attacks are some of those new tactics which are effective and easy to deploy against the enemy. Training is very important, in fact no one from new Taliban can join without good training, newcomers should get good training.[175]

Local commanders were only authorised to take such decisions in extreme situations, where coordinating with their field commanders was not possible:

> Sometime we also can bring changes, for example if I am in the battlefield with my group and we are in terrible situation and we need to bring some changes, because our leaders cannot help us in that case, then our group commanders have the authority to take an emergency decision an change our way of fighting.[176]

IED making skills might have been refined locally but were not originally developed by individual Taliban groups. The Taliban said that they had an IED development centre in Pakistan, where new techniques were developed and tested. ISAF officers confirm that the Taliban do experiment new IED concepts, although not always successfully.[177] ISAF officers also believe that the Taliban could not have developed the IED techniques alone. The help of the Iraqi insurgents is openly acknowledged by the Taliban, but ISAF sources believe that Iranian and Pakistani help also occurred.[178]

Indeed, Taliban commanders in Helmand sometimes said that the foreign advisers (Arabs, Pakistani, Central Asians and Iranian) were the real source of tactical innovation.[179]

> As I mentioned before, our Punjabi trainers work very hard and always find a solution when the enemies use new tactics against us. Our trainers in Helmand province found out that if were to continue fighting face to face, in a very short time all our fighters would be killed by foreign and Afghan forces, because they have different kinds of weapons. That's why they have told us to stop the face to face fighting and use more IEDs, ambushes and suicide attacks. [...] For sure when our trainers bring any changes regarding tactics, they first inform our leaders in Pakistan and get their permission.[180]

The Taliban did not develop an autonomous capacity to discuss and develop their military organisation and techniques. The foreign advisers interviewed for this book claim that played a crucial role in the debates that took place.[181] It is important to understand how some of these advisers assessed the Taliban's capabilities. A Pakistan ISI adviser believed that the Iranian Pasdaran transferred significant knowledge to the Taliban, which made the Mashhad Taliban the best trained of all. He then rated the Peshawar Shura Taliban as better trained than either Miran Shah Shura or Quetta Shura Taliban. He also rated the Taliban as superior to either Afghan police or ANA and hinted that the Taliban acquired the capacity to attack and take cities, and mentioned Kunduz, Lashkargah, Tarin Kot and Asadabad as future targets. He viewed the capacity of the Taliban to absorb large losses as one of their greatest strengths. He mentioned marksmanship as a weak spot of the Taliban, which had only made partial progress.[182]

A Pasdaran adviser to the Taliban described the Taliban as very capable and effective; he believed lack of innovative ideas and poor management as their weak spot. Interestingly, the Pasdaran officer rated the Peshawar Shura as the top performer among the Taliban. In his view, the Taliban was better than the Mashhad office, though he believed that the Mashhad office was on course to overtake the Peshawar Shura within a year or so. He viewed the Quetta Shura as lacking discipline, while he highly respected the Miran Shah Shura's leadership and management capabilities, rating them well above those of Quetta. Additionally, he rated Taliban intelligence as 'very strong', and admired their resilience and capacity to retaliate.[183]

# 6

# ORGANISATIONAL ADAPTATION

The previous chapter showed that tactical adaptation was controversial within the highly conservative Taliban. Predictably, in light of the Taliban's 'anti-Leninism' discussed in the introduction, organisational adaptation was even more controversial. This adaptation took multiple forms, but in general encompassed a systematisation and framing of Taliban activities through dedicated structures with rules and regulations – the shadow state. The Taliban also made major efforts to mobilise human and material resources more effectively. The most controversial aspect of this was the development of a more hierarchical, unified system of command and control.

## 6.1 Enhanced command and control

In Chapters 2, 3, 4 and 5 we discussed the evolution of the Taliban's military organisation from 2002 until 2009. We have shown how the rise of the Peshawar Shura was partially due to its promotion of a more centralised system, with a unified chain of command. However, when that system was first launched in 2007–8, the military pressure on the Taliban was far from reaching its peak. Initially the ideas promoted by the Peshawar Shura in the south were viewed as eccentric. When the American surge began 2009 this perspective changed. Even a member of the Rahbari Shura, a group that was hostile to the Peshawar Shura system, acknowledged that the Quetta Shura was not fighting efficiently in 2009–10 and that its military forces were undisciplined.[1]

In 2009, as Abdul Qayum Zakir took over the Quetta Military Commission, he immediately sought reform in order to emulate the Peshawar Shura Commission. Zakir's arrival at the top of the Quetta Military Commission was immediately followed by the appointment of *nizami massuleen* to the districts and provinces that were under the influence of the Quetta Shura: Kandahar, Helmand, Zabul, Uruzgan, Nimruz, Farah, Ghor, Herat, Ghazni, Faryab, Jowzjan and Sar-i Pul.[2]

Taliban sources believe that between 2010 and 2012 the Peshawar Military Commission dispensed money to the Quetta Military Commission to promote the new centralised system. Afterwards, Zakir began asserting his role as head of the Quetta Military Commission more aggressively, causing major friction with the defenders of the old system. Defenders included Akhtar Mohammad Mansur, the most prominent political figure in Quetta after Baradar's arrest. The vagaries of Quetta politics affected the roll-out of the *nizami* system (see Chapter 4), which never fully blossomed. The system was established in some parts of the south, but was suspended once Zakir and Mansur started openly competing for the control of the Quetta Shura. The system resumed when Zakir was removed from his job in April 2014. As of mid-2015, the *dilghays* of the Military Commission accounted for about 15,000 men, or 35–40 per cent of the fighting strength controlled by the Quetta Shura (excluding the *loy mahazes*).[3]

Aside from power struggles in Quetta, another other problem was that many Taliban resisted the regimentation implicit in the *nizami* system:[4]

> We do not want to implement the *layha* of the Peshawar Shura on ourselves. We are independent people and we do not want to work under someone's control. The Military Commission system is itself a problem. This system is the same as an army system. Therefore, we do not want this system.[5]

For many Taliban, the new system was incompatible with the ethos and ideology of the movement:

> We do not accept their authority, because they want to remove the culture of the Islamic Emirate of Afghanistan.[6]
>
> People respect the *loy mahaz* commanders and fighters more, because the *mahaz* system dates back to the very beginning of the Taliban movement, and people believe that these are the original Taliban.[7]

In Kandahar, the farthest the *nizami* system went was the appointment of *nizami massuleen* in just a few districts: Shah Wali Kot, Khakrez and Maruf.[8]

In Uruzgan, the *nizami* system did not take off at all.[9] In Helmand, it was abolished after a short experiment.[10]

In 2015, members of the Rahbari Shura viewed the Military Commission and its *dilghay*s as an effort to undermine its authority, sparking the need to increase the budget allocated to the governors' groups in order to counterbalance the power of Military Commission and *loy mahaz*es. Some members of the Rahbari Shura even argued for a return to the original structure, based exclusively on the governors' groups, disbanding *loy mahaz*es, village *mahaz*es and *dilghay*s.[11]

Even if not entirely successful in reshaping the Quetta Shura's forces, the Quetta Military Commission established its own system, overlapping with the pre-existing one. Within that system supplies and funding was better organised and managed:[12]

> The Taliban are more organised now as they are utilising the internet. In our times it was different. We would fight without eating for days, but now these new Taliban have breakfast, lunch and dinner and use computers and the internet. I don't know who provides them with all these facilities and money. It is very difficult to defeat these new Taliban.[13]

The Logistics Commission was the primary procurer of weapons, though received some assistance from the Military Commission.[14] The budget allocated to each *nizami massul* varied depending on the number of men and on the distance from the sources of supply – the farther, the more money received.[15] Where the Military Commissions fully or partially controlled the chain of supply, it enforced the new arrangements on the small armed groups, which had no choice but to comply, even if they were uneasy about the new system.[16]

Figures 14–16 illustrate the changes that occurred between 2006 and 2016. Where the Quetta Military Commission had clout, field commanders acknowledged that unified command and control was advantageous.[17]

The Military Commission in Quetta employed 760 staff, which included trainers, teachers and administrators, as of mid-2015. The administrative staff interacted with other commissions (recruitment, finance and logistics mostly), or contributed to intelligence activities.[18] The Military Commission had several departments:

- Commandos;
- Mines;
- *Fedayeen* operations;

- Special operations;
- Logistics;
- Finance;[19]
- Martyrs.[20]

The 2012 agreement on the division of labour between the Quetta and the Peshawar Military Commissions had Quetta responsible for all southern provinces, including Ghazni, and for all western provinces except Badghis. Zakir directly controlled the provinces of Kandahar, Helmand, Nimruz, Farah and Herat.[21]

In the original Peshawar Military Commission's model, the *nizami massuleen* were meant to be professional military leaders, flexible enough to deploy Taliban tactics as required by the local situation, based on the general guidelines provided by the leadership. Unlike the *nizami massuleen* of the Peshawar Shura, who were usually 'new men' selected on meritocratic ground, their Quetta Shura equivalents were usually old Taliban. For example, of those appointed in September 2013, not one was 'new' and all had served under the Taliban emirate, mostly as governors.[22]

The impact of the reforms centred around the creation of the Military Commissions was limited by the fact that the military organisations of the different *shura*s overlapped geographically. For years, the three main *shura*s, and eventually the Mashhad office as well, competed for territorial control. The Quetta Shura tried to maintain influence in Miran Shah's areas, particularly Paktika and Paktia, until a settlement was reached that allowed Quetta's forces to operate there, but under the formal command of Miran Shah. Similarly, a competition for control of Logar Miran Shah, Quetta and Peshawar was resolved with Miran Shah being recognised as formally in charge. There was also overlap in Wardak and Ghazni, and the Quetta Shura deployed a few combat groups to each province where it appointed a governor, even in areas under the Peshawar Shura.[23]

The new framework assigned command over a province to a specific *shura* and regulated access to that province for the other *shura*s; typically, it banned local recruitment and tax collection for the other *shura*s and requested the host units to clear military operations with the host's military command. Bilateral agreements between the *shura*s determined how many men the *shura*s could deploy over the territory of their counterparts.[24]

The framework did not work too well, particularly in the presence of political and strategic divergences between the *shura*s. Established in 2013, a Central Military Commission based in Karachi incorporated one representative from each *shura*'s military commission and was led by a head elected by the *shura*s. In March 2013 Abdul Qayum Zakir was selected to lead the Commission. In theory, this new Central Military Commission had power over the *shura*'s commissions, which were not authorised to take decisions autonomously and were receiving their budget by the Central Commission.[25] The Central Military Commission posted its own representatives to the subordinated military commissions. In principle, the Central Commission had the power to replace members of the subordinated Commissions.[26]

In practice, this reform had limited impact. The Peshawar Military Commission did not agree to implement its orders, and only appointed one representative with the Central Military Commission, for the purpose of coordination.[27] As one of its members commented, 'for us the Central Military Commission does not have any role, it is useless. But for Quetta and the Miran Shah Shura, it has a role and is useful.'[28] Similarly, a high level cadre from the Mashhad Office concurred in defining the Central Military Commission as 'useless'. The Central Commission was widely viewed as a tool created by the Pakistanis to exercise more control.[29] The main importance of the Central Military Commission might have been that it was the first sign of rapprochement between Quetta and Miran Shah, which came to full fruition in 2015 (see Chapter 7).

The problem of the Central Military Commission was that political authority did not underpin its power, which held similar sway over all the *shura*s. It could only function if its head was personally powerful, charismatic and well-connected.[30] Charismatic leaders like Zakir are however as likely to attract opposition as they are to attract support. In April 2014 Zakir was removed from the job, after he clashed with the Saudis over his refusal to downscale the campaign against the Afghan presidential elections. With the sacking of Zakir and the replacement appointment of Ibrahim Sadar, the plan to transfer power at the provincial level to the *nizami massuleen* was abandoned.[31] The *dilghay*s of the Military Commission were disbanded in several provinces, such as Kandahar.[32] The powers of the *nizami massuleen* were reduced to what they were before the reform, to the advantage of the governors.[33] In addition, the policy of appointing outsiders as *nizami massuleen* was abandoned, and local Taliban started being appointed to the position.[34]

Zakir took his job back at the end of 2014, under Pakistani pressure as the ISI was worried that the Taliban needed a capable military leader to make an impression on the battlefield in 2015. Zakir's second stint at the Central Military Commission was even less successful than the first:

> Zakir does not have the authority that he had before; he is only in name the head of the Central Military Commission. Because in the Peshawar Shura, in the Quetta Shura and in the Miran Shah Shura a lot of people are against him. So they do not listen to him a lot.[35]

In July 2015, opposition to his leadership led to his removal, even though many of those who voted him out rated him as a 'very expert and experienced' and 'strong commander', who could 'control the fighting well.'[36]

At the end of 2014, the establishment of a new Coordination Commission aimed to address the problems that the Central Military Commission had failed to resolve. The Commission was tasked to allow joint operations and avoid conflicts between the *shura*s. If imposing top-down command and control would not work, at least the different *shura*s could try to coordinate. Significantly, the Mashhad Office (see Chapter 7), which had refused to have any relationship with the Central Military Commission, accepted to be part of it. Offices were established at the provincial level, incorporating representatives from every *mahaz*, *shura* and military commission. In areas under the Peshawar Shura, one of the main tasks of the new commission was to avoid conflict between the groups led by the governors and loyal to Quetta, and the forces of the Peshawar Shura Military Commission.[37] The work of the Coordination Commission was initially rated as a success.[38]

The fate of one of the first main initiatives to come out of the new *nizami* system of the Taliban illustrates the difficulties of carrying out reform within the Taliban. The introduction of a generalised rotation system was meant to strengthen central control over the tactical units.[39] As already discussed, the initial agreement in 2008-9 on the *nizami massuleen* was that they should be out-of-area and rotated regularly. From 2010, however, the *dilghay* (combat group) commanders, the team commanders and the simple fighters were rotated on a large scale. Taliban commanders confirm that around 2010, following Mullah Baradar's arrest, the pace of rotation was greatly increased.[40] It was Abdul Qayum Zakir in Quetta who was promoting the policy of rotating commanders, on inspiration of the Peshawar Shura, which began this process even earlier.[41] Large scale rotation required a coordinating centre, with cadres on the ground to manage it (the *nizami massuleen*). The way it was implemented needed even more coordination, according to this commander:

If the Taliban leadership sends me to Faryab with my 40 people, we leave our weapons behind. Then when we reach Faryab, the local military commission will give us weapons that were left behind by the unit we are replacing, and when the new unit reaches Helmand, they will receive the weapons and vehicles we left behind.[42]

This ambitious change was intended to weaken the networks in the long run, uprooting them from their local constituencies and turning their commanders into a truly professional and mobile force, deployable where needed according to a military rationale.

At the peak of rotation, up to 60 per cent of fighters and commanders could be 'out-of-area', even in the southern areas where the Taliban had strong roots.[43] The 'experiment' however ran into major problems. Without the back-up provided by Baradar, the *loy mahaz*es were not going to subscribe to their own long-term demise. In practice, rotations in the south had to be negotiated with the *loy mahaz*.[44] Local Taliban commanders objected to rotation, as they wanted to stay close to their families.[45] Even after compromising with the *loy mahaz*es problems persisted.

In 2011 the pressure to rotate almost entirely disappeared, and rotation occurred every two to three years if at all, rather than every four to five months as before.[46] When Ibrahim Sadar eventually replaced Zakir at the Military Commission in 2014, rotation was disposed of altogether. Sadar was more in line with the political leadership who appointed him, and had to meet their desire of securing their patronage network among the local Taliban.[47] There are three reasons given for the reversion on rotation. Firstly, rotation greatly increased enemy threat from drones, which made rotation dangerous and difficult to implement.[48] The second reason was the resistance of the commanders who did not want to be posted away from their home area.[49] Here is how one of these commanders complained about being rotated:

I have been a commander in Marjah district for almost eight years. Certainly I have sometimes left the district for a while, but always I focused on [my command here]. Many times the leadership wanted to rotate me, but I told them that I wanted to stay in Marjah, and if they wanted to rotate me, I might leave the movement. Until now I have not been rotated.[50]

The third reason for the demise of the grand rotation plan is that the leadership might have developed a new awareness of the advantages of having local commanders, who knew their area of operations well.[51]

## 6.2 The strengthening of combat support

In the Taliban's military structure, combat support is managed at three distinct levels, which sometimes overlap. At the basic level, the combat groups had their own support elements, usually unpaid. In a couple of districts of Ghazni (Deh Yak and Andar), for example, American military sources estimated that about 400 Taliban fighters relied on support networks counting about 4,000 people 'provid[ing] food, shelter and part-time help, like passing false information to the Americans and signaling the movements of the battalion's patrols with mirrors or thick plumes of smoke'.[52] The large majority of these 4,000 people were local, unpaid supporters. The next level was either the governors or the *loy mahaz*es. Each governor or *loy mahaz* had people in charge of logistics and other support activities. For example, of the 5,000 men the Janan Mahaz had in Afghanistan in 2013, 700 worked in combat support or administration.[53] Finally, at the top level of the Taliban's organisation (the *shura*s) was the last level of combat support. Over the years, this level's organisation gradually improved and eventually evolved into bureaucratic structures called 'commissions'. As far as combat support was concerned, the most important commission was logistics.

In the early days of the Taliban insurgency (2002–4), the Taliban armed groups procured their supplies autonomously, either buying them on the market or obtaining them from sympathisers, in some cases through extortion. Traders and smugglers provided logistical services on a commercial basis. Taliban fighters and commanders active in those days recall how all they received from the Taliban was clothes, food and weapons. The latter were mostly procured in Pakistan and were either second hand Chinese and Russian or locally produced Pakistani copies. The quality was subpar and led to many complaints of malfunctioning weapons. Explosives recovered from the battleground or from old stocks again resulted in accidents and failures.[54]

By 2005 the Taliban started to improve their logistics. The Peshawar Shura Logistics Commission was established in that year, with the task of preparing such supplies as 'ammunition, weapons, food, clothes, motorcycles, explosive', etc.[55] The Miran Shah Shura Logistics Commission was established at about the same time, while the Quetta Shura Logistics Commission was established in 2006, with the same tasks.[56] A fourth Logistical Commission was established in February 2012 in Mashhad, subordinated initially to the Quetta Commission, but following the declaration of autonomy of the Mashhad office in spring 2014 it also cut off relations with Quetta. Subsequently, the

Mashhad office had to recruit virtually all staff from scratch.[57] Each Commission supplied Taliban forces to specific areas, but in some cases there was overlap in their areas of operations.

By 2015 the four commissions in Quetta, Peshawar, Miran Shah and Mashhad were paying around 6,000 permanent staff members to deliver logistics to the combat units in the field, usually deploying about 10-20 people per district. At this point the Taliban claimed to have extended their logistical net to the majority of districts.[58] The new structure was much more efficient than the old system, but it was also expensive to maintain. The annual cost in 2015 was $320 million between all *shuras*, making it the second most important commission in terms of expenditure.[59] Despite this massive development, as of 2015 some of the logistics were still handled by Taliban fighters (when moving between Pakistan and their assigned location), smugglers and traders on a commercial basis. A high-level source in the Peshawar Shura Logistics Commission estimated that of all supplies delivered to Peshawar Shura Taliban in 2015, 75% were delivered by the Commission, 10% by low level Taliban and 15% by smugglers and traders. Another high-level source in the Quetta Shura Logistics Commission estimated the split at 60% delivered by the Commission, 30% through smugglers and traders and 10% taken by Taliban units with them. A source working for the Miran Shah Quetta estimated that 80% was delivered by the Commission, 15% by travelling Taliban and 5% by smugglers and traders. Most of the weapons and ammunition deliveries were made by smugglers, who were better positioned than the Taliban to make deals with the police to ensure safe passage. Some of these smugglers are connected to government officials and enjoy political protection. Finally, a source in the Mashhad Logistical Commission indicated that it delivered 30% of its supplies through smugglers and spent a third of its budget in fees to them, with the remaining 70% supplied directly, of which four fifths from Iranian territory and one fifth from Pakistani territory. The Quetta Logistics Commission had a plan to handle all future deliveries and was planning to expand the staffing levels for this purpose. It was also planning and increasingly relying on IT technologies to handle supplies more efficiently. Smugglers in particular were difficult to replace in taking weapons across the borders. Food and most supplies, except weapons and ammunition, were procured almost entirely inside Afghanistan, but the black market price of weapons was usually too high for the Taliban to rely on local purchases exclusively. Deals were sometimes made with smugglers, who would have their due 'taxes' cancelled in exchange for providing transport services to the Taliban.[60]

During the fighting season, the demands for logistics increased and therefore exceeded the the capabilities of the Commission. The Taliban coped by allocating large budgets to be spent locally in remote areas:

> The provincial budget is determined both on the basis of number of men and also on the bases of distance. For example for Logar Province we allocated a greater budget because it is a little farther from the Pakistani border compared to the other provinces of Loya Paktia. [...] Sometimes in remote provinces if the number of fighters is small, the budget can be higher because they are far away and delivering there is expensive: such as Ghor, Daykundi, Badghis, Uruzgan and Sar-e Pul.[61]

The Taliban tend to deny buying any supplies from Afghan government officials, and say that these officials sell to black marketeers, from which the Taliban then sometime do business with.[62] The logistics commissions rely on vehicles and pack animals (horses and donkeys) to take supplies to the combat groups. Sources indicated that the Taliban had around 400 vehicles for deliveries in 2015, including lorries and pickups and, in the case of the Mashhad office, tankers. A source in the Peshawar Shura Logistics Commission claimed to have the capability to prepare supplies for a major attack, such as on a city, in just two to three days. The other Commissions had more modest claims: a source in the Quetta Shura Logistics Commission estimated the time required for gathering necessary supplies was one week, while for the Mashhad Logistical Office would need two weeks and one month for the Miran Shah Logistics Commission.[63]

Most of the needs of Taliban groups under the Peshawar Shura would be assessed by the Military Commission, or, where they operated, by the leadership of the various *loy mahaz*es, which would then make requests to the Logistics Commission. However, Taliban commanders were also able to send specific requests to logistics, usually for more advanced or heavier weapons. Under the Quetta and Miran Shah Shuras, all requests come straight from the combat group to the Logistics Commission. In recent years there have been persistent requests for Russian-made light weapons, which are better quality than weapons from China or Pakistan. Iranian weapons are also preferred to Pakistani ones. This has led to an increase of weapons purchases from or through Uzbekistan, as Russian-made weapons are rarely available in Pakistan. Other typical requests are for heavy anti-tank weapons, heavy mortars and anti-aircraft missiles, which the Logistics Commissions are mostly unable to procure. The Logistics Commissions have tried to obtain advanced weaponry from their donors, but with limited success (see also Chapter 5, *Improvements* *in Equipment*).[64] In general, the fighting units and their leaders chose from lists circulated by the Logistics Commission, which would then send their 'inspectors' to confirm with the units whether such requests were in line with actual needs. The fighting units tended to request greater quantities of machine guns, both PKs and DShKs.[65]

According to Taliban sources, over 25,600 weapons were sent into Afghanistan in 2014, typically made up of 10% RPG launchers, 30% machine guns and 60% assault rifles, plus a small number of heavier weapons. A source in Quetta indicated that the Quetta Logistics Commission was buying 30% of its weapons and ammunition on the Afghan black market, while supplying the rest from Pakistan. Source within the Miran Shah Shura and the Mashhad office also confirmed that most weapons were brought from Pakistan or Iran, rather than bought inside Afghanistan.[66]

Based on a formal agreement negotiated among them (signed on 3 March 2012), the three Shura Logistics Commissions became responsible for specific portions of territory and began delivering to units of other *shuras* when these operated in their territory. If this created an imbalance between different *shuras*, cash payments were made to offset the difference. The rationale for the agreement was the excessive cost of each *shura* having logistical structures in every area of Afghanistan. The exception to this rule was Ghazni, where both the Peshawar and the Quetta Logistics Commission remained independent, overlapping structures.[67] The Mashhad Logistics Commission was excluded from the agreement, due to its bad relations with Quetta. As a result, Mashhad only supplied its own armed groups.[68]

The Logistics Commissions enabled the Taliban to accumulate strategic reserves, which as of 2015 were estimated by Taliban sources to amount to two to three years' worth of fighting for the Quetta and Peshawar Shuras, two years for the Mashhad office and one year for the Miran Shah Shura. As an additional precaution, the Peshawar Shura Logistics Commission (but not by the Quetta Commission) created depots in locations unknown to the Pakistani authorities (which usually have the Pakistani army guarding Taliban stockpiles), in case a crackdown was ever to occur. As of 2015 the Peshawar and Quetta Shura Logistics Commissions planned to move some of their supplies into Afghanistan, in areas believed to be beyond the reach of the Kabul government. The Miran Shah Shura was still confident in their ability to maintain good relations with the Pakistani authorities, but it too had depots of which the Pakistani authorities were unaware of and was ready to move the remaining ones if needed. A source in the Peshawar Shura indicated that in early 2015 plans were drafted with smugglers and traders to move all the stockpiles into Afghanistan over the course of three months.[69]

Sources within the Logistics Commissions admitted to instances of corruption and claimed that the culprits were dismissed and punished. In one case the Taliban realised that they were buying black market weapons they had already registered. Thanks to the registration system and to their interrogation of the black marketeers, they managed to hold the Kandahar head of the Logistics Commission to account – he was tried in a Taliban court. The penalties included death for those who did not return the stolen weapons and jail for the others. In the case of the Miran Shah Shura, the black marketeers who bought from the Taliban were also arrested and their stock confiscated. Three sources indicated that the registration of weapons significantly reduced episodes of corruption. In this new system, all weapons were registered and the name of the commander to whom they were issued was noted; he was bound to report any weapon lost in the fighting and checks were made to verify that the records matched what was in the hands of the fighters.[70]

In winter the number of fighters deployed could drop by 60% in the coldest provinces, depending on the number of local fighters. Each *loy mahaz* would decide autonomously how many people to keep deployed and how many to pull out.[71] Over time, Taliban logistics improved at supplying fighting units in the field over winter with blankets, boots, coats, etc., even if capabilities remained uneven among *loy mahaz*es.[72] In some cases, this allowed the Taliban to more than double the number of men that could remain in the field over winter.[73] Moving supplies in the snow remained problematic, however.[74] Starting from spring, the mobile forces would deploy, together with short-time volunteers from the madrasa networks associated with the Taliban.[75]

Supplies to the Taliban initially originated exclusively from Pakistani territory. From 2005 Iran also began sending supplies, initially on a small scale but grew increasingly. By 2014 the Taliban in north-western Afghanistan and Ghor received 20–30 per cent of their supplies from Iran.[76] In western Afghanistan, Iran accounted for up to 80 per cent of supplies depending on the relations between any specific group of Taliban and the Pasdaran.[77]

Aside from logistics, the other main component of combat support was medical services. In the early years of the insurgency, very few medics were available to Taliban combat units and the only treatment available was usually in Pakistani hospitals.[78] Over the years the Taliban established Health Commissions (one per *shura*) over the years, primarily charged with providing health facilities to the Taliban's military effort. This was achieved in two ways:

- Develop the Taliban's own medical facilities;
- Co-opt existing medical facilities to treat injured Taliban.

As the budget allocated to the health commissions grew over the years, the number of facilities they were able to maintain grew as well. By the end of 2013/early 2014 there were about eighty fixed facilities, in addition to several mobile ones deployed by the Haqqanis. Of these 80, 12 were hospitals, mostly in Pakistan, and 68 were clinics inside Afghanistan (Table 4).

The nine largest Taliban's hospitals were in Pakistan. The distinction between hospitals and clinics is that the former is bigger and have real doctors, while the latter have nurses or semi-trained staff. Additionally, the Taliban had small mobile medical teams in each province as well as cadres in charge of managing the system and evacuating the injured to Pakistan. Overall, more than 4,000 Taliban were employed by the three health commissions at the beginning of 2014 (Table 4).

The Health Commission also organised mobile medic teams and approached NGO clinics and hospitals for the purpose of coercing or convincing their management to treat injured Taliban fighters or transfer them medicine. Some of the clinics coerced or co-opted by the Taliban suffered retaliation from ISAF units in the past. Government health staff who refused to collaborate with the Taliban were targeted for assassination. Each district health commissioner had twenty to twenty-five people under them, including nurses, doctors and assistants.[79]

## 6.3 The systematisation of recruitment

The Taliban have been recruiting both inside Afghanistan and inside Pakistan, and more recently inside Iran as well. Inside Afghanistan the recruitment effort was mostly focused on local militias, although not exclusively. Typically, the Taliban's recruitment groups would visit a village either when some local member of the Taliban had recently been killed, when the *ulema* were visiting, or where a wedding was taking place. These were the best of times for recruiting. Visits to the mosques were also a common pattern.[80] Recruitment of full-time volunteers took place mostly in Pakistan, particularly in the madrasas.

Recruitment was very fragmented in the early days, with each commander responsible for his own enlistment. Until 2006, group commanders carried out most Taliban recruitment in eastern Afghanistan, who regularly visited Pakistan, particularly the madrasas. There were also some madrasa representatives who had connections with specific commanders and were doing recruitment for them.[81]

Gradually all the Taliban's top *shura*s professionalised their recruitment and agreed on common recruitment rules. Agreements between the three *shura*s divided the thirty-four provinces of Afghanistan between them in terms of recruitment. In Pakistan, the pro-Taliban madrasas were made a recruitment reserve for the specific *shura* to which they belonged. Violation of the monopolies over recruitment was supposed to lead to serious incidents. There were also cases in which groups of Taliban opted out of the agreement – for example, in 2014 the *loy mahaze*s of Naim and Zakir broke relations with the Quetta Shura and started recruiting everywhere.[82] When Peshawar was financially stable (until 2013), it head-hunted commanders of other *shura*s, including from among the Haqqanis, offering better pay and promotions.[83]

The first form of centralised recruitment to appear in Quetta were mobile teams called Arshad-e Dawat, made up of about twenty members. At their peak there were thirty-two.[84] Finally, in April 2006 the Quetta Recruitment Commission was established, which allocated most of the recruits to the Military Commission's *dilghay*s and a minority of the recruits of the groups.[85] The Quetta Recruitment Commission represented a major investment in terms of human resources: it reportedly employed over 4,000 recruiters in 2015, distributed between Pakistan and thirteen provinces of Afghanistan.[86] In the south-east the Haqqanis were always better organised than the Quetta Shura. They deployed recruiters in the Pakistani madrasas quite early on, had mobile recruitment groups at the provincial level, and made agreements with some tribal elders to provide recruits.[87] The Miran Shah Recruitment Commission was established in August 2007 to expand their effort.[88] The Commission had a representative conducting recruitment in each of the 1805 madrasas connected to the Haqqanis; no other Taliban group was allowed to tap into these madrasas.[89] The Peshawar Shura Recruitment Commission was established in June 2006, the early history of the Peshawar Shura. The recruiters employed by the Commissions were a mix of imams, *ulema*, preachers, students, teachers and tribal *shura* members.[90] At the time of the Mashhad office's declaration of its autonomy from Quetta, the Mashhad Recruitment Commission was already in existence, as it was established in November 2012.[91] As of 2015 this Recruitment Commission was still in an early stage of development as it had to be re-staffed after the declaration of autonomy from Quetta.[92] Over time, the Iranian authorities granted the

Recruitment Commission more leeway for recruiting inside Iran. By 2015 it was able to tap into sixty-five Sunni madrasas in Iran, of which twenty had been opened by the Taliban, with Afghan teachers imported from Pakistan. However, no recruitment was allowed in Shi'a madrasas.[93] In 2015 the Taliban reportedly spent about $80 million for their Recruitment Commissions.[94]

Unsurprisingly, the most centralised recruitment took place in Pakistan. Data provided by a source inside the Quetta Recruitment Commission indicates that from 2006 onwards about a third of its recruits came from Afghanistan, with the rest from Pakistan, despite the fact that three-quarters of the recruits were deployed to Afghanistan. The source described recruitment inside Afghanistan as much harder than in Pakistan.[95] One reason was the small number of madrasas in Afghanistan. In total the Quetta Recruitment Commission recruited over 26,000 people from 2006 onwards, which is about one man per member of the Commission per year. This was hardly a resounding success. Clearly, the main purpose of the Recruitment Commission was not to expand recruitment, but to recruit independently of local commanders and governors. The existence of the Commission enabled the formation of larger mobile forces.[96] Similarly, the Miran Shah Recruitment Commission had 3,000 recruiters in 2015 and recruited around 3,000 men in both 2014 and 2015.[97]

Even as Taliban recruitment efforts became more sophisticated, recruitment was never fully centralised. The governors, once appointed, also became an important recruitment path for the groups and for the village *mahaz*es.[98] Despite being more centralised than Quetta from the beginning, the Miran Shah Recruitment Commission did not have a monopoly over recruitment. All the combat commissions (*Zarbati*, *Dalaez*, Mines and *Fedayeen*) could also recruit directly.[99] Similarly, in the Peshawar Shura, not only the *mahaz*es associated with the Peshawar Shura had their own recruitment efforts, as the Military Commission accepted volunteers without going through the Recruitment Commission.[100]

The main source of autonomous recruitment remained the *loy mahaz*es, because they were not assigned recruits by the Recruitment Commission. The *loy mahaz*es mostly recruited in Pakistan, relying on close networks of madrasas. However, some of the *loy mahaz*es developed their own recruitment networks inside Afghanistan. For example, in 2014-15 the Naim Mahaz and Zakir Mahaz, whose foothold in Pakistan became uncertain once they began their reliance upon the Iranians, invested heavily in establishing student recruiters inside state schools in western and southern Afghanistan.[101] The *loy* *mahaz* of Abdul Matinullah was formed in 2013. Matinullah was a close associate of Mullah Naim and often visited Iran with him. Encouraged by offers of Iranian patronage, Matinullah went to Pakistan and began approaching Taliban commanders and madrasas, collecting 'from some madrasas 50 recruits, from some 100, but 1000 madrasa students from the Shaikh Ketab Madrasa.' Taliban rules banned stealing commanders and fighters from other Taliban units, so Matinullah had to rely on commanders and fighters who had already left their previous job. Matinullah 'travelled to different provinces of Afghanistan and went to Quetta, Peshawar, Miran Shah, North Waziristan, South Waziristan, Alipor and Bajawar.' It took him five months to mobilise enough men to launch the *loy mahaz*.[102]

Another example is Abdul Majid's *loy mahaz*, formed in August 2012 following the decision of a group of Taliban *mawlavis*, who successfully approached the Pakistani ISI for funding. In this case, the *mawlavis* were dissatisfied with the conditions offered by the *loy mahaz* and groups to which they belonged (including financially). They did not hesitate to leave them with their men to join Abdul Majid, who therefore did not have to try hard to recruit people around Pakistan. Abdul Majid had been chief of the Quetta Shura's intelligence, so he had plenty of old contacts among field commanders. Most of the *mawlavis* and commanders joining came from the *loy mahaz* of Baradar (which faced a financial crisis after his arrest), Ibrahim and Faruq (which had disintegrated after their killings), and Dadullah (which was in crisis under the management of Mansur Dadullah). It took six months to get the *loy mahaz* organised. Although the *loy mahaz* who lost commanders to Abdul Majid complained, he managed to pacify them, which was helped by obvious Pakistani support.[103]

These examples illustrate how, despite being technically banned by the Quetta Shura, the competition for the loyalty of field commanders was not uncommon among *loy mahaz*es, and between them and groups.[104]

In 2012 and 2013 recruitment focused on Pakistan, but has since been re-focused on Afghanistan, because the cost of supporting local fighters is much lower.[105] Recruitment occurred either on an individual basis, or on a group basis. To join as a group, an aspiring commander would have to gather enough men (twenty-five for a *dilghay*, thirty for a group) and apply to the nearest *nizami massul*. Upon being accepted, the group receives enrolment certificates and starts receiving money, weapons and supplies.[106] The groups 'belonged' to the commander who recruited them.[107]

When the *loy mahaz*es were first introduced, the four original ones agreed not to steal each other's fighters and to impose sanctions on fighters and commanders switching *loy mahaz*. Later however these sanctions were abolished and it became common for the *loy mahaz*es to compete over fighters and commander offering better conditions. The size of the *loy mahaz*es started fluctuating widely, depending on their respective financial wealth.[108]

There is no evidence of the Taliban practising forced recruitment, except in cases of 'tribal' mobilisations agreed with the elders (or some of them). Often young recruits would join against family wishes, and the Taliban would try to convince (or pressure and threaten) the families to agree. Occasionally hard-line commanders would ignore the family's point of view. Recruits between age ten to eighteen could not in principle be sent to the battlefield, but were to be kept in madrasas for indoctrination (spiritual training), and given non-combat tasks.[109] Yet some commanders and elders admitted using fighters below eighteen, although usually not below sixteen.[110] Only three of the elders interviewed alleged the Taliban recruited children and used them in insurgency activities, particularly mine-laying, which suggests that the practice might have been the result of local decisions by Taliban commanders.[111] Recruits were supposed to be vetted by local mullahs and elders before being accepted.[112]

Personal relations influenced the individual fighter's decision to directly join one *mahaz* or another, or to go through the Taliban recruitment offices. He might follow friends into the Taliban, or follow the advice of a mullah or of the elders.[113] Often families opposed the decision of an individual to join, but friends and peers often proved more influential.[114] The reputation of leaders and commanders also played a role in the choice of the Taliban outfit.[115]

> I joined the Baradar Mahaz because it was a better *mahaz* compared to Ihsanullah Rahimi's and Mansur's. Their leaders were good and there were scholars, so I joined it. Another thing was that it was active in our area. This *mahaz* has a lot of power and authority.[116]

After 2009 the Taliban increasingly targeted state schools for recruitment, exploiting their co-option of teachers within the framework of deals aimed at re-opening schools. The Taliban gradually developed a network of teachers and student activists, which recruited volunteers for the Taliban.[117]

> The Taliban should recruit educated people who graduated from schools and universities. The recruitment commission tried, but they did not reach their target, so they should recruit more. When they recruit more educated people, the

problems they have in technology and organisational issues will be solved. Our advisers always told them to get better educated people, but at first they did not accept this. They hired only madrasa students. Now the leaders understand that if we do not hire educated people we cannot solve organisational problems.[118]

## 6.4 The improvement of training

The re-qualification of part-time support networks discussed above was only a small part of the Taliban's training efforts. In addition to a shifting focus in recruitment, the Taliban have been placing greater emphasis on training, again to improve the quality of their human resources and to make them more suitable for the deployment of more sophisticated tactics. Some Taliban stress training more than others (for example the Haqqanis) and have become more 'meritocratic' in appointing commanders. Rivalries and differences among the Taliban meant that the transfer of tactical skills from one network to another was difficult, even when the leadership actively encouraged it. For example, before 2011 only a few southern networks maintained direct relations with their south-eastern and eastern. Abdul Qayum Zakir had good relations with the south and encouraged the spread of the eastern model of guerrilla professionalism. From 2011 the resurgent network of Mullah Dadullah (now led by a cousin) and the network of Mullah Naim were also trying to import such tactics. For some time, Naim sent his men to be trained by the Haqqanis in Waziristan.[119]

The training capabilities of the Taliban developed gradually. There were none in 2003-4 when the insurgency started, but then short courses (typically a couple of weeks) were introduced to teach the use of weapons to inexperienced recruits, mostly inside Afghanistan.[120] Mostly Pakistan-based Taliban and commanders were trained before 2010. Eventually all Taliban recruits were sent to training courses. The rationale was that the Taliban were taking huge casualties due to their limited skills:

> Later in 2010 the new people who had joined were given training. In that time our casualties were so great that our leaders had a meeting and decided that all the Taliban must get training when they join.[121]

An additional rationale was the large-scale introduction of new techniques such as IEDs and suicide bombing, which required ever more specialists.[122] By 2015 and until the introduction of the Military Commission, three-month courses were standard and even compulsory. This was partially due to the growing pressure the Taliban faced, and in part because of the high losses that removed the bulk of the experienced fighters from the ranks.[123] By then, training incorporated courses in intelligence and other advanced skills.[124] Experienced Taliban could get away with no training or one month courses to familiarise themselves with the latest weaponry.[125] Foreign trainers, initially Pakistanis, were brought in.[126]

By 2012 the tactical training courses lasted fifteen to thirty days and took place every four months or so; it might therefore be that these were refresher courses, meant to instil new tactics in the minds of the fighters.[127] In the south, where training had been initially unpopular, the new emphasis was apparently welcomed. Among the Taliban of Helmand, for example, two thirds of those who were surveyed (26 out of 39) said that training is important. In some cases they even believed that without such training the Taliban would not have survived as a military organisation. Only about 5 per cent dismissed the importance of training, another 5 per cent stressed that training was only important for new recruits and 23 per cent dodged the question.[128] However, since training was strongly endorsed by the Taliban leadership, there might be a bias towards expressing support for training among these interviewees. Even with that consideration, doubts about the need for training were predominant in some areas, like Wardak and Ghazni.[129] Among those who rejected the idea of training, there was an assumption that Pashtun are natural warriors:

> Well... training is not very important for Afghan Taliban, because most of the Afghan Taliban are good fighters, they know how to fight, so there is no need to get extra training and waste time. But Taliban from other countries do need training so they do conduct some short training.[130]

Some argued that training only helps the Taliban in restricted matters, such as the production and deployment of IEDs, the training of suicide bombers, and some of the most innovative tactics.[131] Others argued that training suited new recruits, and that experienced fighters had little to gain from it.[132]

Interestingly, according to the Taliban training was usually imparted by foreigners.[133] 'What could the Taliban do without these foreigners? It is the foreigners who give the Taliban weapons, advice and support,' said one interviewee.[134] The investment in terms of foreign trainers was substantial, with up to fifteen to twenty 'Punjabi' trainers in some districts.[135] External observers also confirmed the impact of Pakistani trainers and volunteers. In Helmand, mortar skills improved with the introduction of the bracketing technique with help of foreign instructors. A Pakistani trainer was reportedly killed in Helmand in 2007.[136]

Apart from the training support of foreign volunteers and foreign advisers, the Taliban also benefited from the training imparted by deserters of the Afghan security forces. For example, the Quetta Shura training camps enlisted twenty to thirty deserters as trainers.[137] The Mashhad Office reportedly employed twenty-five defectors from the Afghan security forces as trainers, out of the 145 who had joined its ranks by July 2015.[138] The Peshawar Shura by contrast decided that it did not need the services of defectors from the Afghan security forces, except in administrative duties.[139]

The Haqqanis have always invested greater resources into training than the Quetta Shura. The mountainous geography of Loya Paktia allowed the Haqqanis to establish training camps inside Afghanistan.[140] The Haqqanis invested heavily in the preparation and training of *fedayeen* teams, establishing a system that produced hundreds of deeply indoctrinated fighters every year. This enabled them to mount the largest and most effective *fedayeen* campaign out of any Taliban component. Several madrasas were established specifically with the task of nurturing young boys as future *fedayeen*.[141]

The Haqqanis were sufficiently confident in their insurgent know-how and in the quality of their training that they did not try to use ANA and ANP defectors within their ranks for that purpose.

> We did not need their help in training because we have good trainers. But they are helping us in fighting tactics and administrative activities. They are very good in administrative activities, but they are not good in fighting tactics.[142]

## 6.5 The systematisation of intelligence

One of the most important components of underground networks is counter-intelligence. The Taliban's intelligence gradually became better organised and more professionalised. Before the intelligence departments were established, the units on the ground handled intelligence directly. The intelligence cadres of the various units were subsumed into the new department of intelligence when it was created.[143] The Quetta Shura was the first to establish an Intelligence Department of the Rahbari Shura in June 2006, placing the provincial and district branches under the authority of the governors.[144] The Peshawar Shura established its Intelligence Department within the Military Commission in April 2007 under the leadership of Sheikh Mohammad Amanullah, one of the main figures of the Peshawar Shura at that time.[145] The

Miran Shah Shura created an Intelligence Department within the Military Commission in November 2007. Finally, in August 2013 the Mashhad office organised its own Intelligence Department within Zakir's Loy Mahaz, and handed it over to the new Mashhad Military Commission in May 2015. This brought the the intelligence staff of the other *loy mahaz*es associated with the Mashhad Office together. Each department had teams of five to ten men led by representatives in each province and district.[146] To vet for reliability, the intelligence departments recruited seasoned Taliban members, who were then sent to three-month specialist training.[147] The Taliban spies could be shopkeepers, drivers, government officials, government staff, beggars, etc.[148]

Intelligence staff members were specially selected by senior Taliban leaders, such as Khalil Haqqani in the Miran Shah Shura or Zakir in the Mashhad Office, on the basis of their skills and loyalty and long-standing links to senior Taliban, who could guarantee for them. They were a mix of former fighters, fresh madrasa recruits, and villagers.[149]

A former Taliban commander in Musa Qala, now hostile to the movement, commented:

> [The Taliban] have agents in the government to inform them about the plans and programs of the officials. There were 200 to 250 agents of Taliban in the intelligence service of government when I was leader of a group of Taliban. Their number must have been increased by now. Same is the case of national army and police.[150]

Government officials in areas of weak Taliban presence still believe that the Taliban are informed of everything that happens.[151] In addition, the Taliban recruit informers at high levels of government, including army and police.[152] The Taliban's intelligence taps into the support networks, who usually provide information for free.[153] Apart from a number of permanent staff, the Taliban also relied on informers who were compensated for the information they provided. In the Quetta Shura, this type of informers is deployed beyond the provinces where the intelligence Department operates, that is, in areas under the control of the other *shura*s.[154] In 2015, sources in the Taliban's intelligence departments claimed to have a total of almost 900 informers inside the Afghan security forces and the government apparatus. In addition to financial remuneration, these informers were also granted immunity from the Taliban's targeting.[155]

The intelligence departments' mandate was to work for all branches of the Taliban, lay the ground for forthcoming operations and prevent threats from the enemy, including by detecting enemy informers. Other duties included investigating suspect government collaborators and selecting targets for the Taliban's hit lists, except in the case of the Quetta intelligence department, which was not part of the Military Commission. Finally, it recorded the Taliban's misbehaviour, such as abuses against the population and corruption.[156]

The intelligence departments of the three main military commissions signed a cooperation agreement in December 2010, which made the regular exchange of information possible. The agreement was not extended to the Mashhad office, reportedly because the Iranian Pasdaran encouraged the office to reject it. A source within the office claimed that it had informers within the other intelligence departments. Most of the information exchanged concerns government threats to the Taliban and the monitoring of individuals; other information, considered not to be of concern to the other *shura*s, is not exchanged. Some cadres, called Mamba, coordinated between the intelligence departments.[157] Like their Afghan government and ISAF rivals, the Taliban's intelligence was also affected by faulty intelligence driven by feuds and vendettas.[158]

## 6.6 Disciplining

Efforts to instil some discipline in the Taliban rank-and-file has been going on since the introduction of the first *layha* (code of conduct) in 2006. According to some sources,, the first *layha* was authored by Mullah Baradar and Ustad Yaser,[159] though some cite the Cultural Commission and the Ulema Councils.[160]

The first *layha* focused on drawing boundaries for when violence was authorised; it tried to shelter common civilians from violence and to protect some of their rights, for example by banning house searches.[161] Successive versions sought to regulate violence against authorised targets, for example by describing conditions in which enemy surrender is acceptable, excluding foreigners working for NGOs from the target list, and limiting the use of suicide bombers to specific conditions.[162] The *layha* explicitly states:

> [the] Mujahedin are obliged to adopt Islamic behaviour and good conduct with the people and try to win over the heart of the common Muslims and, as Mujahedin, be such representatives of the Islamic Emirate that all compatriots shall welcome and give the hand of cooperation and help. [emphasis added][163]

Independent Taliban fronts, not yet subsumed into any of the main *shura*s, simply ignored the *layha* of 2006.[164]

From 2009 the Military Commissions further tightened the rules of engagement. The Commissions took charge of writing and overhauling the *layha* in 2009.[165] The 2010 version specified that judges were to try Taliban members accused of serious misconduct or criminal activities, including gratuitous or negligent use of deadly force against civilians. Arbitrary executions were also banned and spies were to be tried in a Taliban court.[166] There are different lines of thinking about the actual relevance of the *layha*, with some observers arguing that its purpose was propagandistic.[167] The Taliban certainly realised the propaganda value of the *layha* and in recent years have even been posting it on their website. The 2006 version was passed on to a journalist by the then governor of Ghazni at the end of that year; while this was clearly a publicity stunt, it seems far-fetched to argue that this was the sole or main purpose of the *layha*.[168] The 2009 version became accessible after copies were captured on the battlefield by ISAF troops in 2009.[169] That hardly suggests a primarily propagandistic intent, with the aim to improve the Taliban's image without substantial impact on the way the Taliban function. There are therefore several reasons for considering the *layha* a genuine effort to discipline the Taliban.[170] Courses to teach the *layha* to cadres and commanders were organised in Afghanistan and Pakistan.[171]

The three Ulema Councils of the Taliban have played a substantive role in advising the Taliban leadership to restrain arbitrary violence (with limited success); they issued fatwas asking to restrain attacks on schools, suicide bombing and the use of mines. They also collaborated in the formulation of the *layha*.[172]

It is worth noting that by 2013 Quetta and Peshawar could not agree on the *layha* and two separate versions were produced.[173] The 2010 *layha* was controversial as not all leaders approved of it. It was also the last iteration as these divisions prevented the completion of new versions.[174]

The leadership publicly called for Taliban to respect the *layha*, and it was widely distributed among the commanders.[175] Interviews conducted over the years with Taliban commanders suggest that the *layha* was meant to be taken seriously by Taliban field commanders. The *layha* was widely circulated among Taliban field cadres (governors, *nizami massuleen* and mid-level commanders) and among the minority of simple commanders who were effectively literate. The Taliban cadres trained in Pakistan had to study the *layha* as part of their curriculum.[176] Another commander explained that when the *layha* was first released in 2006, there were clear instructions that the commanders and the fighters should read it together.[177] Johnson and Dupee also state that in 2010 the Alikozai tribe members in Sangin expected Taliban shadow governance officials to adhere to the *layha*.[178] Two Taliban governors were reportedly removed from Sangin following allegations of brutal behaviour, against the rules of the *layha*.[179]

The main problem in getting the rank-and-file to follow the *layha* was the very high illiteracy rate among the Taliban, including among the field commanders. Typical fighters are illiterate village youth, who are then deployed in small groups around the villages, a situation where supervision by team leaders and commanders (who usually have a madrasa background) is difficult. In theory, all Taliban field commanders are supposed to be educated, but few of them are functionally literate in practice. In October 2011 a commander in Imam Sahib stated that he was aware of the existence of the *layha* but refused to discuss its details, suggesting that he had at best a passing knowledge of it.[180] Both the commanders from Wardak and Imam Sahib mentioned above were much better educated than the average Taliban commanders.

In addition, the Taliban experienced difficulties in keeping their commanders focused on the *layha*. In October 2012, a source among the Taliban in Peshawar indicated that there was dissatisfaction within the leadership because of decreasing circulation of the *layha*, partly due to the loss of territorial control in many areas. The Taliban cadres trained in Pakistan had to study the *layha* as part of their curriculum, but once caught in the fighting the *layha* was not a high priority.[181] Angry Taliban commanders who had just lost comrades would often show little regard for the rules of engagement dictated by the *layha*: alleged spies would not be given the chance of repenting;[182] prisoners who should be exchanged with Taliban detained by the authorities were instead executed in revenge; alleged culprits who should be tried on the basis of evidence were instead executed arbitrarily.[183] For example:

> This boy was riding a bicycle in Kelagi Area and the Taliban asked him whether there were police over there. The boy said that there weren't any from where he had come. So, these five Taliban commanders went that way. Right at that moment the police came and killed the five [...]. The Taliban then called this boy a spy and killed him. He was a very small child in the fifth grade. He was the only son of his parents, the remaining three were daughters. We asked them what proof they had against this child, but they killed him with 60 bullets.[184]
>
> We also told you a story about a child who was bringing food from the ANA, and the Taliban killed him for spying. It is clearly mentioned in the Taliban *layha* that if the Taliban arrest a person for spying, they should find evidence and three

witnesses, and only after that can the person be killed. But these Taliban were killing straight away. They were not seeking evidence or witnesses.[185]

The district of Deh Rawood offers a good example of this trend. The Taliban took de facto control of Deh Rawood in 2007, except for the district centre. They brought in hundreds of fighters from the surrounding districts, including foreign fighters, as the Taliban had previously been weak in Deh Rawood and their local recruits were posted elsewhere. As the Taliban occupied the district, their lack of local roots and knowledge exposed them to 'bad tips' and to arbitrary behaviour. Local elders report that about eighty elders and villagers were executed in a spree of allegations of spying and collaboration with the government. The resulting backlash saw village elders collaborate eagerly against the Taliban when ISAF and ANSF escalated their operations in Deh Rawood in 2009–11; by 2011 the Taliban had lost control on all villages in the district. The Taliban leadership then ordered the transfer of all Taliban from Deh Rawood back to their home district. The Taliban's residual ability to operate in Deh Rawood derived from these local fighters and commanders, who collaborated with the remaining Taliban supporters underground and received support from the neighbouring Charchino district.[186]

The Taliban's growing reliance on mines also led to tension, because it endangered villagers.[187] The Taliban responded to this in some areas, working out agreements that restrained the use of mines in areas intensively used by civilians, or established rules of engagement that banned fighting inside the village.[188]

What is most effective in purely military terms is not necessarily productive in the general economy of a conflict. For example, for an ambush to have the best chances of success, the insurgents should not warn the local population, because the absence of civilians is a major warning sign for the enemy. However, the civilians could then be resentful against the insurgents for having involved them in a fire-fight without warning and then take revenge by tipping off the pro-government forces about the insurgents' whereabouts. Similarly, for IEDs, the insurgents face the dilemma of either informing the local population of their position, and therefore reduce tactical effectiveness as some civilians might tip off the enemy, or not inform the population and maximise short-term tactical impact at the expense of risking population hostility once civilians are accidentally killed. There are military intelligence reports that show on some occassions the Taliban went to great lengths and troubles to convince villagers to evacuate the area of future fighting.[189]

One former member in fact alleged that the commanders might be wary of introducing the *layha* to their fighters, fearing that they would hold the commanders accountable in the event of violation of the rules.[190] This does not necessarily imply that the average Taliban commander was ruthlessly violent. There was a desire to find scapegoats for losses incurred, but, for example, the Taliban refrained from committing rapes, and forced marriages were very rarely reported. Of twenty-four elders who were surveyed, twenty-three denied hearing of any cases of Taliban fighters imposing forced marriages on village households, and the one who responded affirmatively was unable to cite specific cases.[191]

Similarly, while villagers might have been unhappy to have to pay 'taxes' to the Taliban, few elders would accuse the Taliban of outright theft. Of twenty-nine elders surveyed, twenty-four denied hearing of the Taliban stealing, and the five who answered positively were mostly referring to Taliban pressure on wealthy people to 'donate' to the movement. Only one mentioned land seizure as an issue.[192]

A particular type of indiscipline was deal-making with the Afghan government forces. Of-the-records contacts with police officers, ANA officers, and Taliban showed that various types of local deals were common almost everywhere; usually these deals did not involve the upper echelons of either the Afghan security forces or of the Taliban.[193] The deals were mostly ceasefires, but information exchange was also common. Taliban sources tend to allege that the request for deals come usually from the Afghan security forces, who would offer information or other rewards in exchange for a ceasefire or for allowing supplies in.[194] The Taliban would sometimes tell the ANA that they would not be attacked unless they accompanied ISAF in operations.[195] These deals are different from the common Taliban practice of stopping operations during harvest time for about a month, based on a Fatwa of Mullah Omar allowing the suspension of hostility in order not to damage the interests of the villagers.[196]

The role of implementing discipline among the fighters and the commanders in the field belonged to the Taliban's *nizami massuleen* and to the Taliban judiciary. There have been cases of the Military Commission punishing unruly commanders.[197] As discussed above in 'Enhanced command and control', the new system brought a better discipline among the Taliban except in the south, where the Military Commission remained weaker.

Infighting carried sever punishments. For example, in July 2012 in Baghlan there were clashes between the Sattar network and Jundullah (IMU), following an attempt of Sattar's men to enter Jundullah's territory. The Military Commission intervened to stop the fighting, investigated and threatened the two networks with disbandment if any such incident was to be repeated.[198]

In parallel, the judiciary became a key tool for the central leadership to maintain order and discipline among Taliban combatants. The judges ruling over commanders was a delicate condition. The judges depended on the commanders for protection and sustenance, even if they were formally independent. The commanders provided the fighters to enforce the judges' verdicts. Therefore, each confrontation between judges and commanders represented a major dilemma and risked the broader relationship between the originally fragmented network-based military structure and the centralized top-down political structure of the Taliban.

Interviewees in Kandahar indicated that, while in the early years of the insurgency judges were too dependent over commanders to challenge them, a turning point occurred around 2006–7. As the Taliban were securing most of the provinces under their control, the judge, as a direct representative of Quetta, increased his power vis-à-vis the commanders, due to the backing of the leadership in Pakistan. He could effectively limit the latter's action, while gaining autonomy for himself.[199]

The governors and *nizami massuleen* were not subjected to the supervision of the judges, which incentivised them to strengthen the position of the courts over the commanders. Moreover, the Military Commissions (presided over by the *nizami massul*) added an element of centralisation in the military structure, which aligned it with the judiciary. Disagreements were often related to the treatment of alleged spies, whom the commanders would insist on convicting even in the absence of evidence, against the rules set by the *layha*. In areas where the Taliban have been weakened, the shortage of fighters might be another disincentive from cracking down heavily on undisciplined commanders.[200]

> In Shashgaw there was a 12-year-old boy with a piece of paper written in English – the Taliban shot him. When we saw that it was just a newspaper page, all the people became angry and unhappy about this, and then the elders of Shashgaw went to the *nizami massul* of Saydabad district of Midan Wardak Province. We told the *massul* that this commander must be fired from the job and taken to court, but he did not say anything to that commander.[201]

The persistent difficulties in having judges enforce discipline among the Taliban fighters occurred from 2009 until the establishment of new supervision instances on a different scale. So-called Provincial Judicial Commissions (*De Wilayat de Qaziano Komision*) covered multiple provinces each. The Commissions further broke down into provincial or multi-provincial teams. They dealt with misbehaving commanders, judges and other cadres of the Taliban, excluding *nizami massuleen* and governors. Claims were investigated by talking to local people in the mosques. The press reported on a case of intervention by a Regional Judicial Commission that led to the lashing and imprisonment of a commander.[202]

These commissions were established 'when the Taliban leadership was receiving complaints about Taliban commanders and judges disturbing civilians, requesting bribes from the people' and operated independently from the provincial structures of the Taliban. They directly reported to the *De Qaziano Komitah*.[203] According to one Commission head:

> As you know, most of the Taliban commanders and fighters are not educated and I am sure that there are lots of problems in their behaviour with the local villagers. If we don't try them [in court] and don't impose rules on them, it's very difficult to bring about a change in their behaviour. Every month our team receives three or four cases, mostly about Taliban commanders who misuse their positions and disturb or beat a villager. We also hear cases regarding Taliban commanders taking money by force from villagers, along with other problems; so according to their crimes we try them and punish them.[204]

Local sources reported that a judge in Wardak was removed in November 2011 by the Regional Judicial Commission after complaints that he had unfairly judged a 'doctor' accused of being a government spy, executed him and burnt his house down. The Taliban fighters who burnt the house were reportedly disarmed and a Taliban commander accused of instigating the judge was arrested and taken to Pakistan.[205]

The decisions of the regional Judicial Committees were implemented by the Provincial Military Commissions or the governors. A Taliban source stated that occasionally some Taliban commanders were tempted to resist the regional Judicial Committees, but the *nizami massuleen* were ordered to back their decisions.[206]

The September 2011 reform abolished the regional judicial commissions, effective from late 2012; the task of investigating and punishing abuses by the Taliban rank-and-file was transferred to the ordinary Taliban judiciary.

Transferring the task of disciplining the Taliban to the ordinary, fixed courts made it easier for common Afghans to lodge complaints, rather than rely on the provincial commission to seek cases of abuses through its local agents.[207]

The disciplining role of the judges in restraining the arbitrary behaviour of the commanders is most evident in cases of allegations of spying and collaboration with the government. The Taliban leadership, through implementation of the *layha*, authorised the assassination of government official and collaborators. If they occupied an official position and their identity was obvious, the intervention of the judges was deemed unnecessary. In the cases of uncertain identity, however, it was difficult to verify that the alleged culprits were indeed spies. These cases relied on the competence of the judges, according to the instruction of the Taliban leadership. Arbitrary executions continued, but mass executions like those that took place in Deh Rawood in 2007–8 are rare, and culprits have been punished. For instance, the October 2008 murder of twenty-seven labourers on a coach in Helmand, accused of being police on leave, resulted in the dismissal of the commander responsible for the attack, Mullah Adam. From 2008 onwards, reports about alleged spies being tried and acquitted surfaced, such as the case of Afghan TV reporter Nawab Momand, who was released after having been found innocent.[208]

There is anecdotal evidence of commanders and fighters disciplined for abuses, but also of on-going abuse. In particular, it is difficult for the Taliban leadership to punish anonymous attacks and abuses – the fear of being disciplined might have pushed abusive commanders to act undercover.[209] Reports of Taliban punished for violating the rules have been around for years.[210] Taliban interviewees recall various cases of fighters and commanders punished for breaking the *layha*, by taking money, kidnapping for ransom, beating people without authorisation and disobeying orders. The culprits would first be disarmed and taken away.[211] On the other hand, elders reported the continuation of extra-judicial executions by the Taliban.[212] In sum, while the intent is clear, it is difficult to say to what extent both the Taliban's judiciary and command and control system have been successful in restricting abuse.

## 6.7 The evolution of the combat forces

### *The expansion of the mobile forces*

As discussed in Chapter 2, the first type of fully mobile forces developed by the Taliban were the *loy mahaze*s. In principle, these mobile forces could be dispatched anywhere. In Chapter 3 we also discussed a different type of mobile force, the Delayez of the Miran Shah Shura, which like the *loy mahaz*es, was established in 2005. Then in Chapter 4 we discussed a third type of mobile force, the *dilghay*s of the Military Commission. All of these forces were better equipped than local Taliban groups, had machine guns in abundance (including heavy DSchK ones), and transport (mostly motorbikes).[213] The Mashhad Military Commission's mobile forces was ensured by about 1,300 motorbikes as of 2015, according to Taliban sources.[214] At about the same time the Peshawar Military Commission had 2,800 motorbikes, of which 1,000 were supplied by Iran.[215]

The commanders of groups and *dilghay*s (twenty-five to thirty men) were selected by their superiors, usually from among the ranks of the group. The group and *dilghay* members could appeal to the superiors to replace an inadequate commander, including ones who could not deal effectively with village elders.[216] There are three types of *dilghay*s: 'infantry', sapper and 'motorised'. Motorised *dilghay*s were better endowed with means of transport. Table 5 shows the strength of the *dilghay*s or equivalent forces (the Miran Shah Shura's *derabez*) in 2015. Not all the 'infantry' *dilghay*s were mobile units; for example, only 45 per cent Quetta Shura Military Commission was mobile in 2015. By contrast, 70 per cent of the Mashhad Shura Military Commission was mobile as of 2015.[217] The mobile *dilghay*s were often mixed in ethnic and tribal composition.[218]

A fourth type of mobile force, the 'mobile *mahaz*', was established in early 2016. Four of them were established under different *shura*s, with up to 3,000 men each. These forces were similar to the motorised *dilghay*s of the Peshawar Shura, which in fact merely relabelled them 'mobile *mahaz*'.[219]

From 2005 the mobile forces expanded, despite some temporary setbacks. After the departure of Zakir in 2015, Akhtar Mohammad Mansur allowed the expansion of the Quetta Military Commission's forces, in part to counterbalance the power of the *loy mahaz*es. The budget allocated to the Military Commission for the *dilghay*s rose $50 million in 2014 to $65 million in 2015, and was expected to increase again in 2016.[220]

Since the *dilghay*s offered better service conditions than the governor groups and most *loy mahaz*es, they attracted recruits, to the extent that the Military Commissions were often able to reject volunteers.[221]

There were several rationales for establishing mobile forces. One was the ability to concentrate forces based on strategic decisions, as discussed in Chapter 2. The other was to control and stiffen the motivation of the local

Taliban, who were not always keen to implement the orders and rules issued by the leadership. For example, one task that would fall on the mobile forces was the execution of members of the Afghan Security Forces, or their family members. Local Taliban were reluctant to do so because they feared a blood feud.[222]

*The development of the reserve system*

The Taliban military structure gradually developed two types of reserves.[223] The first type belonged to the Taliban's mobile forces, which relied on a system of reserves based in Pakistan to give them 'manpower depth'. This reserve system enabled the ability to absorb losses, to be flexible in terms of deployable forces, and to absorb any temporary decline in the number of volunteers. The reserve system also allowed the mobile forces to grant regular leave to the fighters. Each structure had its own rules concerning leave: sometimes three months a year, sometimes fifteen days every two months, sometimes six months on and six months off, and so on.[224]

The Recruitment Commission moved new recruits into the reserves until the mobile units called them in. In the case of the Miran Shah Shura, reserves accounted for 30–35,000 men.[225] In addition, each *loy mahaz* had its own reserve system.[226] For example, of Abdul Raziq's *loy mahaz* 5,300 men, just under half were mobilised for duty in Afghanistan in autumn 2014 and the rest were in reserve, mostly in Iran (60%) and Pakistan (40%), according to a senior member. The reserves would not be paid while inactive and would live with their families, eliminating the need for the Taliban of to feed and house them.[227] In the summer of 2013 the Mansur Mahaz had about 60% of its men deployed in Afghanistan, with the rest in reserve, recuperation, or leave in Pakistan.[228] Similarly, in the summer of 2014 the Matinullah Mahaz had over 60% of its manpower kept in reserve in Pakistan and Iran.[229] At about the same time Abdul Majid's *loy mahaz* had about 44% of its men in reserve, and the others fighting.[230]

The second type of reserve force was active inside Afghanistan, where the Taliban would register volunteers and enter them into a reserve list, so they were available to join the local Taliban units, either on a part-time basis or not. The reserves replaced losses, or expanded Taliban manpower when needed.[231]

## *The re-qualification of part-time fighters*

The local Taliban would mostly operate around their villages, usually no more than fifteen kilometers or one to three hours of walking distance away, and their maximum range for operations was a few districts away.[232] Typically these village-based groups were formed on the basis of negotiations between Taliban and village elders, or more likely village mullahs.[233] The majority of the part-timers attended to their own businesses, such as farming, when not mobilised.[234]

Another evolving aspect of Taliban human resources has been the recent re-qualification of the 'part-time' support networks. In the words of commanders, the advantages of having part-time fighters were the following:

- Cheaper than mobile groups;
- Knowledgeable about local area;
- Can operate underground; a particular bonus in areas of strong government/ISAF presence, where out-of-area Taliban would be very exposed;[235]
- Easier recruitment as fighters could stay with family.[236]

There were advantages for the villagers too. An elder summarised advantages and disadvantages of having a group of local Taliban in the village as follows:

- Disadvantages: girls schools not allowed, NGOs will not come to village, Afghan government will not deliver services;
- Advantages: local Taliban do not take food from villagers like out-of-area Taliban; no thefts or crimes will occur.[237]

The part-timers would support the mobile units with their local roots and knowledge, allowing them to operate in unfamiliar areas:[238]

> If there are no village groups and *mahaze*s, the out-of-area Taliban cannot do anything. Because we know the routes, police areas and bases. We are give places to the out-of-area Taliban. [...] We can give you a good example: in Zheray district, the Taliban were from outside and there were no locals among them, so 173 Taliban were martyred in one day. As such, local groups are very vital for the Rahbari Shura.[239]

By 2015 the Peshawar Shura had ordered each district under its influence to have at least fifty reserve fighters available.[240] Over the years, the Taliban tended to expand the number of part-timers, particularly once they experienced financial difficulties, as they were much cheaper than full-timers.[241]

The part-timers would participate in second line tasks such as:

- keeping an eye on the villages and on the prisoners;
- housing foreign fighters and out-of-area Taliban when needed;[242]
- Patrolling;
- Recruitment and propaganda;
- Spying;
- Enforcing Shari'a;
- Enforcing child attendance of Coranic schools;
- Interacting with the elders;[243]
- Accompanying out-of-area Taliban.[244]

Ever since the early days of the insurgency Taliban groups based inside Afghanistan had part-time fighters in their ranks. However, the new system that developed from the US surge imposed stricter organisational protocols for selecting commanders and handling weapons. The Taliban integrated the part-time system into their structure. For example, after they started issuing better quality weapons to the part-timers, both the Peshawar and the Quetta Military Commissions ordered weapons to be locked away from the part-timers when not in operations, and threatened fines for non-compliance.[245] The part-timers only fought once a week or month at the peak of the conflict.[246]

In winter most of the mobile full-time fighters would leave and Taliban presence on the ground would remain limited to the part-timers. During this time out-of-area Taliban accounted for less than 25–33 per cent of fighters in any province. At other times of the year there would be a mix of part-timers and full-timers.[247] During winter the percentage of out-of-area Taliban could drop by 80 per cent.[248] The part-timers would also continue to fight when the mobile units were forced to leave due to overwhelming enemy superiority. In Marjah, for example, when the 'full-time' Taliban units left before the Marines' onslaught, the Taliban remained active for several months due to their underground networks.[249]

The governors' groups were largely part-timers, and in some cases entirely so; the village *mahazes* were entirely made up of part-timers.[250] The *loy mahazes* were mostly composed of mobile forces, but had pockets of part-timers in areas where they were strongly rooted.[251] As discussed in *The expansion of the mobile forces* above, many *dilghays* of the Military Commissions were part-time too.

While the reliance on underground networks by the Taliban is not necessarily an innovation (they already existed in some form in 2002), the professionalisation of these underground networks is. In 2010-11 there was a major effort to train part-timers, so that they could participate in a real guerrilla war. Training camps started appearing well inside Afghan territory, in places such as Sangin and Nahr-i Seraj. While training continued to take place in Pakistani territory as well, the purpose of the training camps inside Afghanistan was solely to train part-timers, who were not expected to travel to Pakistan.[252]

The expansion of the part-timer system might have come at the cost of a decline in the stamina and commitment to these forces, despite improved training and organisation. Although they were ideally placed to fight a guerrilla war against superior forces, the strength of the 2009 repression has harmed their morale, according to local elders in areas such as Baghlan and Wardak. Madrasa students and graduates accounted for only a small percentage of those enrolled in the local groups, the bulk being simple villagers with little depth of commitment to the cause of the Taliban.[253] The best part-time fighters would be asked to join a mobile group for better pay and with the prospect of promotion.[254] This practice further diluted the ideological quality of the local Taliban.

The lower ideological purity and different sociological character of the part-time armed groups gave rise to friction between local and out-of-area Taliban. The politically correct Taliban response was to deny that such friction existed.[255] However, the majority of Taliban interviewees admitted divergences between the two types of Taliban, particularly when Pakistani Taliban were involved:[256]

> The out-of-area Taliban create problems for the villagers: they harrass them, close schools, and kill teachers, engineers and doctors. So the local Taliban do not like this and there are problems between the local Taliban and out-of-area Taliban. [...] The local Taliban do not want to use mines that kill locals and civilians. [...] The local Taliban are inclined to listen to elders, but the out-of-area Taliban show opposition to this [...]. The local Taliban do not want to create problems for government officials, [unlike those] out-of-area.[257]

There have been cases of local Taliban arrested by the organisation for allowing unauthorised NGO projects in their area.[258] Elders argued that these projects could influence local Taliban, unlike the out-of-area Taliban:[259]

> We tell local the Taliban to allow NGOs – sometimes they accept this and sometimes they do not. For example, the NSP had a 3 million Afs project in our

village for the water supply – in this project we gave 500,000 Afs to the local Taliban and they told us that we should finish the project in three months, and if not, Taliban from outside were coming and they had one commission which controls NGOs. They would certainly stop the project. So now we want to finish this project soon.[260]

From 2014 the local Taliban were tasked with laying mines because of their local knowledge and relations with the villagers (see Chapter 5, 'The IED campaign').[261]

### Seasonal volunteer forces

Throughout the history of their insurgency, the Taliban have relied to various extents on volunteers accruing to the battlefield for limited periods during the fighting season. Networks of madrasas in Pakistan would invite their students to rush to the battlefield during the holiday seasons, creating the largest number of 'volunteers', who were a mix of Afghans and Pakistanis. The students were deployed based on agreements between each madrasa network and a *loy mahaz* or Taliban leader. In 2012, efficiently managing the wave of students mobilised each summer, Bakht Mohammad, a brother of Dadullah Lang, launched Tehrik-e Taliban Afghanistan. Bakht Mohammed ran the Jamiat Ulema Afghan madrasa in Pakistan and was quite influential among pro-Taliban madrasas. Tehrik-e Taliban-e Afghanistan was a kind of 'jihadist stage agency', meant to give madrasa students the opportunity to taste jihad before deciding whether to turn into warrior mullahs and join a proper *mahaz*. The volunteers were assigned to existing local fronts and groups in Afghanistan. The ISI reportedly supported the project with $30 million each year.[262]

In addition, foreign fighters would go to Taliban units during the fighting season from all sort of countries and for varying period of times, on the basis of agreements with the various group (see also Chapter 3, 'The Haqqanis' jihadism', and 'The Peshawar Shura and global jihadism'). In southern Afghanistan, the deteriorating relations between the Quetta Shura and Al-Qaida and the regression of the Taliban to guerrilla warfare led to a declining presence of foreign fighters from 2010 onwards. Many foreign fighters moved to areas under the control of the Miran Shah and Peshawar Shuras.[263]

The foreign volunteers were never organised alongside the Taliban structures; they operated as independent groups of varying strength, and would attach themselves to a group of Taliban based on personal relations and sponsorships.[264] Some Taliban commanders openly stated that foreign fighters were not welcome and were often a liability; there were regular accusations of abuses against civilians and sexual harassment against women, affecting foreign volunteers.[265]

In areas where homogeneous groups of foreign fighters were no longer present, the foreign volunteers still existed in other, more discrete roles. We have discussed their important role in training (see 'Training'), but they are also involved in IED making.[266] Overall, the contribution of foreign fighters to the Taliban military effort was not insignificant, as shown by Taliban reports of their casualties (Figure 8).

As a rule, foreign fighters were not allowed to join the Taliban, but were treated as temporary hosts or allies. Only the Miran Shah Recruitment Commission recruited Pakistanis as well, but was banned by the Pakistani authorities from doing so in 2015. Even in the Miran Shah Shura, non-Pakistani foreign fighters were not recruited through the Commission; they were instead brought in as the result of Serajuddin's personal engagement with foreign jihadist organisations.[267]

### Taliban numbers

Despite the extent of their operations and the pressure they have been withstanding, the Taliban have expanded dramatically since 2003. Military intelligence estimates have always been scant, counting the number of full-time Taliban inside Afghanistan at a peak of 25,000 in the winters and early spring of 2010–11 and 2011–12. This figure perhaps increased to 35,000 in the summer. Taliban and NDS sources suggest that these figures are roughly correct, but underestimate the actual number of full-time Taliban fighters for two reasons:

a) some Taliban operated from across the Pakistan (and later even Iranian) border, so they were not counted when they in Pakistan even if on full war footing;

b) some remote areas were poorly covered by the intelligence, and some groups were not spotted.

More importantly, the full-time Taliban groups were only a fraction of Taliban manpower. As described above, the Taliban extensively used part-time guerrilla forces permanently based in their villages. They also had a system of rotation and reserves, which could be mobilised to various degrees for the fighting season, depending on the financial resources available. They also had a vast support system, providing logistics, intelligence and governance functions. Table 6 is based on Taliban, NDS and 'adviser' data and suggests that by the time ISAF disbanded, total Taliban manpower including reserves had reached over 200,000 men.[268] These figures should be interpreted as the Taliban's authorised force; actual numbers would be lower due to losses or to cheating by corrupt commanders (who might over-report numbers to cash salaries of ghost fighters). The Taliban tried to keep cheating under control by carrying out inspections and tasking their intelligence to report on this.

## 6.8 Improvement, but not enough

Reforms within the Taliban took place after complex negotiations, but the politicking of a divided leadership only allowed sub-optimal outcomes.

The Taliban massively improved their recruitment and management systems and became quite apt at managing their manpower. Their intelligence gathering became much more professional, and their military forces more mobile and better trained. Overall the Taliban experienced massive manpower growth, reaching over 200,000 by 2015. Considering their origins, this is undoubtedly an achievement. On the other hand, combat force disciplining was an area of more mixed achievements.

But overall the Taliban's organisational adaptation faced multiple obstacles and did not endow them with an adequate command and control system. The cost of this failure would become obvious after 2014 (see Chapter 7). The new centrally controlled mobile forces coexisted with both the *loy mahaz*es and the local forces controlled by the governors, adding considerable power, but at the same time further complicating an already convoluted command system.

# 7

# THE TROUBLED COMEBACK OF THE
# QUETTA SHURA 2014-

Four years of disgrace ended in 2014 for the Quetta Shura, due to a shift in the policies of the Pakistani authorities. As the Pakistani authorities believed it was time to reap the rewards of their long-term investment in the Taliban, they started pushing the Taliban towards opening negotiations with Kabul. The Quetta Shura's funding tap was re-opened, while the more 'militaristic' Peshawar Shura saw the end of its state of grace and its funding started declining. However, the polycentric structure of the Quetta Shura meant that increased funding did not automatically translate into political consensus towards the leadership, nor into battlefield successes. On the contrary, two new 'declarations of autonomy' by Taliban components took place during this period (Mashhad and the Rasool Shura), as the political crisis inside the Quetta Shura worsened.

## 7.1 Akhtar Mohammad Mansur consolidates control

By aligning with the Pakistanis in 2014, Mansur was able to turn the fortune of the Quetta Shura around. The death of Mullah Omar in 2013 (which was kept kidden for two years) gave Mansur power as the only 'interpreter' of the 'will' of the dead leader.[1] First of all he eliminated his rival Zakir from the scene. With his sacking from the Central Military Commission, Zakir had to pull his men out of Kandahar and eastward.[2] Zakir raised some funds from private Arab sources and eventually from Iran as well, but his *loy mahaz* shrank by more than half. His supporters working in the structures of the Quetta Shura had to re-align or were sacked.[3]

Once Akhtar Mohammad Mansur felt that he had firm control of the Quetta Shura by the summer of 2014 (having expelled Zakir and co-opted his allies), he abandoned the mantle of Taliban 'traditionalism' and took a sudden turn towards his own version of centralisation. He proposed the merger of all *loy mahazes* under a centralised military organisation, starting from his own *loy mahaz*. Zakir, who was still a member of the Rahbari Shura, resisted the idea, as did his allies Mullah Naim and Mawlavi Ihsanullah Rahimi, while Bakht Mohammad, Baradar and others agreed with Mansur.[4] The *loy mahaz* leaders were however mostly opposed to the idea and Mansur was not able to push it further.[5] However, he shut down the funding accruing to the *loy mahaz*es from the Quetta Finance Commission, while at the same time successfully lobbying Pakistanis and Saudis to stop directly funding the *loy mahaz*. Mansur effectively condemned the *loy mahaz*es to a slow death, unless they could find new external sources of funding.[6] At the same time Mansur was successful in reclaiming Quetta funds that went to Peshawar in 2010–13.

According to figures compiled from information provided by the Taliban, external funding to the leaderships of the different Taliban *shura*s peaked in 2014 and recorded a 8% decline in 2015. Increased local fundraising (+29% in 2015) offset the losses in external funding and the Taliban leadership were left with roughly the same revenue as in 2014. This increased local fundraising was not achieved easily: in 2014 the new head of the Military Commission, Ibrahim Sadar, ordered the execution of a few reluctant 'tax payers' in order to scare the others into paying.[7] As it can be seen in Figure 21, funding by foreign governments in 2014 accounted for almost 80% of centralised Taliban funding, up from 71% in 2012. In 2015 it fell back to 72%. Most of locally raised revenue was contributions from drug lords and others, with taxes accounting for single percentage digits at most. This is not surprising because, as explained above, most taxes and probably most contributions did not make it to the Taliban leaderships, but stayed with commanders and network leaders.

In 2015 the Taliban still raised more money than in any other previous year, except 2014. The drop in funding was painful for several reasons:

1. The Taliban knew that potential for raising more revenue locally was limited;

2. Raising money locally was pitting different Taliban *shura*s, networks and individual actors against each other, compounding existing divisions;
3. The Taliban expected a further drop in foreign funding;
4. the fall in funding was largely concentrated in the Peshawar Shura, with a 40 per cent drop, while the Quetta Shura saw a 35 per cent rise in funding, which allowed it to recover its financial pre-eminence after several years. The Mashhad Office saw its funding rise by 45 per cent in 2015; it should be noted that 2013 and 2014 were good years for Quetta, allowing it to gradually overcome the financial crisis that started in 2010;
5. The Taliban had recruited people and established structures and shrinking was painful.

Although it was not possible to collate complete sets of data for 2016, partial data suggested a further, strong decline in funding to the Peshawar Shura, eventually forcing it to fold up temporarily in August 2016 and then to surrender its autonomy. The Quetta Shura again improved its fundraising in 2016, but not enough to offset the decline in funding to Peshawar. The emergence of yet two more *shura*s in late 2015 and early 2016, the Rasool Shura (November 2015) and the Shura of the North, complicated the picture, but probably resulted in overall Taliban funding increasing again. The Shura of the North in particular was able to secure control or influence over some large mines in north-eastern Afghanistan, whose output it taxed.

Among the foreign 'donors', the four-years period saw a growing polarisation between Iran on one side and Pakistan and the Gulf countries on the other. The two poles competed for the loyalty of the Taliban and tried to carve out niches of loyalty, targeting increasingly their funding at autonomous fronts, more than to the established *shura*s. Until 2014 different Taliban groups obtained funds from rival sources, such as Iran and the Gulf countries, but from 2014 onwards these games became increasingly difficult and both Saudis and Iranians cut funding to Taliban who received funding from rival sources.

The consequence of this was that Mansur was able to rein in the *loy mahazes* to a greater extent than it had been possible since their initial establishment in 2005:

From 2010 till 2014 [...] Zakir was Head of the Military Commission and no one gave any importance to the Rahbari Shura as all the money was with Zakir. But now all the power and money is with the Rahbari Shura so *mahaz* leaders do not disobey them. [...] Those who take money from them must accept their orders.[8]

In his drive towards centralisation, Mansur also set out to merge all the village *mahaz*es into a single structure. The village *mahaz* experiment appears is considered unsuccessful so in 2014 Mansur merged all the village *mahaz*es into large province-based *mahaz*, called the Nafzai Mahaz. The order was implemented straight away in Kandahar and as of 2015 its implementation was planned for other provinces. The rationale was that a large formation would have been more effective in counter-balancing the *loy mahaz*es; the command of the Nafzai Mahaz was established at the provincial level and not at the district level as in the case of the village *mahaz*. The biggest difference between the *loy mahaz* and the Nafzai Mahaz was that the latter was not 'owned' by a particular Taliban military leader but depended directly from the Rahbari Shura – the governor's chain of command.[9]

Mansur's position was strengthened by the collapse of the alliance between Zakir and the Peshawar Shura in the second half of 2013. As major friction emerged, which resulted in armed clashes (see above), key Peshawar Shura figures such as Qari Baryal and Qari Atiqullah warmed to Mansur and established closer relations with him. When Zakir's forces were eventually expelled from the areas under the control of the Peshawar Shura, Mansur was invited to deploy his own men there.[10]

In September 2014 Qari Baryal, as head of the Peshawar Military Commission, negotiated a deal with Mansur's ally Ibrahim Sadar of the Central Military Commission to compel governor and *nizami massuleen* to cooperate in contested Faryab and Ghazni. The two men also agreed to establish liaison offices for each of the two commissions within the other, to facilitate coordination.[11]

Sadar was considered a supporter of military centralisation as advocated by Mansur, as was Bakht Mohammad and reportedly even Baradar after his release from detention. Despite the rejection of Zakir's approach to improving military efficiency, the losses suffered by the Taliban in the south and their inability to reclaim ground during 2014, particularly in Kandahar, made the return to the pre-Zakir status quo not an option. The slaughter of 173 inexperienced Taliban recruits in Zhirai in a single clash in 2014 catalysed a major debate among the Taliban.[12] The abolition of the *nizami* system after the sacking of Zakir was followed by a series of defeats.[13] The Taliban were so weak in Kandahar in 2014 that most of their recruits would concentrate in Shah Wali Kot or Uruzgan. Taliban activities in Kandahar were entirely underground.[14]

Another development that boosted Mansur's position in Quetta was the re-emergence of Mullah Baradar as a player in Taliban politics. In November 2013 Mullah Baradar met Mansur and some other key leaders of the Quetta Shura such as Abdul Majid and Mullah Naim. Baradar was bitter towards the Pakistanis who were still holding him under house arrest and criticised his associates for allowing Zakir to expand his power so dramatically after Baradar's arrest. Baradar also expressed his support for negotiations with Kabul, but not with the Americans. Baradar asked Mansur to move against Zakir and issued an ultimatum to all those commanders who used to support Baradar and joined Zakir, to return to the Baradar Mahaz or face punishment.[15] Mansur probably did not need to be invited by Baradar to fight against Zakir, but Baradar's endorsement is likely to have had a major legitimising impact on Mansur's status in Quetta.

Despite Mansur's 2014 winning streak, not all was well under his management. During the campaign against the elections, friction among different Shuras and factions reached a new high:

> During the elections last year we had problems with other Taliban. We had problems in Ghazni and Maydan Wardak Provinces. In Ghazni Province in Arjestan District, Jaghori District and Malistan District, we had problems with Peshawar Shura Taliban. In Maydan Wardak Province in Behsud District and Markazi Behsud District we had problems with Peshawar Shura Taliban. The Peshawar Shura was making problems in those areas where other ethnic groups were, which they would not do in those areas where Pashtuns reside. We told them that you must not discriminate. We told them that if you want to give permission for elections, you must give permission for elections anywhere and likewise if you do not want to give permission for elections, you must not give permission anywhere.[16]

The contrast between the authority of governors and *nizami massuleen* prompted the calling of a meeting in November 2014, where all three *shuras* and the Mashhad office attended. Mansur threatened retaliation against any Taliban group that created obstacles for the activities of the Taliban governors. He also threatened to seal the areas under control of the Quetta Shura from the other *shuras*. The Peshawar Shura dismissed Mansur's threats and instead proposed the creation of a coordination commission (*Hamahangi*). Zakir also accused Mansur of being the first to create problems, when he expelled the

THE TALIBAN AT WAR, 2001–2018

Zakir Mahaz from Kandahar and endorsed the idea to create a Hamahangi Commission. Serajuddin Haqqani also came out in support of the idea. Mansur had to agree to the creation of the Hamahangi Commission, with a budget of $20 million.[17]

Although Taliban diplomacy is not dealt with in this study, it is important to stress that Mansur's views on the need for reconciliation with Kabul still did not have majority support within the Taliban's ranks in 2014–15.[18] The military leaders in particular were adamant that they would reject any deal that did not meet their conditions:

> If Quetta Shura and Peshawar Shura political leaders deal with Ghani, we will continue the fighting. [...] I want to say that from the Peshawar Shura, Atiqullah and Baryal do not want to stop fighting, From the Miran Shah Shura, Sirajuddin Haqqani does not want to stop the fighting and from the Quetta Shura, Zakir does not want to stop fighting. [...] Our minimal demands are the changes in Afghanistan constitution, the complete withdrawal of foreign troops – meaning no single foreign fighter in Afghanistan – and all the contracts with NATO and ISAF and America must be cancelled, whether they are strategic or not. In the cabinet there must be big changes –Abdullah and Rasheed Dustam must be retired from their positions because they have killed a lot of Taliban.[19]

### A snapshot of the Taliban in 2014

Map 4 represents the relative weight of the different Taliban *shura*s as of 2014, just before Akhtar Mohammad Mansur consolidated his power in Quetta. The weakness of Quetta, even considering the two internal factions combined, is evident.

Map 3 represents the types of the Taliban's military organisations by region – governor's groups, village groups, Haqqani's system, *loy mahazes* and military commissions. The governor's groups, usually loyal to the Rahbari Shura (with the exception of some in western Afghanistan, co-opted by the Mashhad Office when it declared its autonomy in 2014), brought some Quetta Shura influence into every province, even in the Haqqanis' turf and in the areas under the Peshawar Shura. The Haqqanis had people everywhere, though in smaller numbers outside the south-east. In 2014 the Peshawar Shura challenged the traditional dominance of the Quetta Shura in Ghazni and in the north.

202

*Mullah Omar is dead: the succession struggle*

Rumours of Mullah Omar's death began circulating among the Taliban in August 2012, after the Pakistani authorities reportedly informed Abdul Qayum Zakir and Akhtar Mohammad Mansur (the two Quetta Shura deputies) that Omar had died in 2011. The news was kept secret to avoid endangering the Taliban's unity.[20] An alternative version of the story is that Abdul Qayyum Zakir was told in August 2012 that Mullah Omar died of a brain tumour a year earlier. Zakir had been aggressively trying to get an appointment with Mullah Omar to demand explanations for some of Omar's 'decisions', such as granting grace for Mullah Ismail. The Pakistanis explained to Zakir that Omar's Eid messages were recorded by an impersonator. Zakir was asked to keep the news secret, but it was leaked by members of his entourage.[21]

The Afghan security services (NDS) deliberated between confirming and denying the death of Mullah Omar, until they announced it in a December 2014 public statement. By 2010, after the arrest of Mullah Baradar, Mullah Omar's absence from the Taliban scene started raising serious questions. Why did he not intervene in the diatribe between Baradar's successor candidates (Zakir and Mansur)? Why did he allow this power struggle to go on unchecked for so long? Why did Mullah Omar not intervene in the past issues concerning relations between Quetta and Miran Shah, or Quetta and Peshawar? As these questions went unanswered for years, many Taliban doubted whether Omar was alive. The Taliban's internal turmoil worsened shortly after Mullah Omar was last seen.[22]

Eventually the deputy leader of the Quetta Shura, Akhtar Mohammad Mansur, decided to go public with the announcement of Mullah Omar's death in early summer 2015. After he informed his closest collaborators in early July, he reportedly leaked the information to Kabul, in order to prompt the government to announce Omar's death and provide a convenient excuse for Mansur himself to acknowledge it. On 29 July 2015 when the Afghan and US governments affirmed that he died, Quetta admitted it.[23]

The timing appeared odd to most observers. Kabul and the Taliban had just recently started meeting officially to discuss a peace process and acknowledging the death Omar was not going to help matters. The Taliban tried to gloss over the issue by claiming, through Omar's brother, Mullah Abdul Manan, and his son, Mohammad Yakub, that Omar had just died after a prolonged illness. It later became clear that he had died a couple of years earlier. In fact, Mansur circulated the news of Omar's death because of power struggles within the Taliban. By the summer of 2014, Mansur, Omar's deputy, had finally brought the Quetta Shura under his firm control by purging it of his main rival, Abdul Qayum Zakir, a Taliban member previously held in Guantanamo, and his followers. Mansur skilfully brought the majority of the Taliban's funding under his control, mostly through diplomatic manoeuvring, and the fact that his patronage system was unrivalled within the Taliban (see above).[24]

When Mullah Mohammad Yakub began his career within the Taliban in early 2015, he was adhering to Mansur's rules and siding with him. Mansur, in turn, appointed him to head the Quetta Shura's finance commission. Yakub regularly travelled to the Gulf for fundraising, where he was well received, which probably stimulated his ego. From the beginning Yakub entertained close relations with Serajuddin Haqqani. This relationship and perhaps the education Yakub received in a Pakistani madrasa predisposed him to object to Mansur's seemingly 'unprincipled' approach to the peace process, which was increasingly focused on power-sharing and spoils distribution, rather than on principles (establishing a 'more Islamic' system of government).[25]

According to sources within the Quetta Shura, friction first arose between Yakub and Mansur in April 2015, when Mansur first raised the possibility of publicising Omar's death. Mansur claimed that Kabul's demand to meet Omar to obtain an enthusiastic endorsement of the peace process left the group with no other choice. Yakub, however, also understood that Mansur was laying the ground for his own succession to Omar. Yakub probably did not appreciate Mansur's decision to issue an Eid ul Fitr message that endorsed the peace process at the end of Ramadan which was signed 'Mullah Omar'. His message broke the unwritten agreement that the Quetta Shura would not use Omar's name to promote policies that were still controversial among the Taliban.[26]

Then on 4 July, Mansur called a meeting of Taliban notables (governors, members of the various commissions, Quetta Shura members, top clerics, leading Taliban commanders, and the principals of the main madrasas) and announced that Omar had died and that he intended to make a public announcement within the month. He asked the notables to support his succession. It is likely that Mansur decided to proceed with the succession issue because he required full authority to move further with the peace process and take controversial decisions if needed.[27]

For weeks Yakub positioned himself as a key obstacle to Mansur and Mansur's approach to peace talks. He argued that the peace process should be slowed down, that Omar's death should not be announced, and that, in any event, he or Mullah Abdul Ghani Baradar, a cofounder of the Taliban, would be natural successors to Omar. In his bid for leadership, Yakub was supported by Serajuddin Haqqani and the Taliban's other two main military leaders, Abdul Qayum Zakir (allied with the Iranians) and Qari Baryal, Head of the Peshawar Shura Military Commission. Yakub's young age and inexperience was probably less important to them than the potential he offered to stop Mansur and prevent a reconciliation process that they did not like. As Yakub was gathering support, Mansur pre-empted him by accelerating the succession process. Perhaps Mansur believed that his international connections with major Taliban donors would give him a decisive edge.[28]

On 30 July, Mansur called for a general Taliban meeting to select Omar's successor. He was a 'shoo-in', since he staffed the Quetta Shura with protégés and allies and manipulated the selection process for the 1,500 delegates so that the assembled group (governors, *ulema*, members of the three *shura*s of Quetta, Peshawar and Miran Shah) was not representative of the Taliban movement or of its leadership. Although Mansur faced three alternative candidates (Serajuddin Haqqani, Gul Agha Ishaqzai and Mullah Hayatullah), none of them stood a chance. Together, Yakub and Abdul Manan stormed out of the meeting with the representatives of the Peshawar and Miran Shah Shura, when they realized what was happening. The Pakistani authorities warned Yakub and Manan two weeks earlier that Mansur would become leader, but they refused to endorse him. The gathering easily secured Mansur leadership, but the process won him new enemies, including Baradar, Omar's deputy until he was arrested by the Pakistanis in 2010. Temporarily released from house arrest, ailing Baradar reportedly made an effort to attend the meeting but did not vote. He sided with Yakub in rejecting Mansur's election as legitimate.[29] Mansur made even more enemies outside the Quetta Shura, where support for Yakub was even stronger.

Baradar's influence on the military ranks of the Taliban was actually quite modest. His *loy mahaz* was still in existence but a shadow of its former self, with just 3,000 men, only active in five provinces (Kandahar, Zabul, Uruzgan, Ghazni and Paktika) and totally dependent on funding from Mansur.[30] Still, Baradar's withdrawal of endorsement for Mansur's leadership campaign was a big blow.

Mansur managed to win back Serajuddin Haqqani's support by appointing him as one of his deputies—a successful attempt to co-opt one of Yakub's key allies. Serajuddin was under strong Pakistani pressure to align with Mansur and support the reconciliation process. The Pakistanis also supported Mansur and encouraged his bid to accelerate the peace process.[31]

Mansur moved quickly to consolidate his control over the Quetta Shura by replacing dissident members of the Rahbari Shura with loyalists. In particular, and controversially, he appointed fellow Ishaqzai tribesmen to key positions: Mawlavi Noorullah Ishaqzai became Head of the Finance Commission; Mawlavi Abdul Haq Ishaqzai became Head of the Logistic Commission; and Mawlavi Abas Ishaqzai became Head of the Recruitment Commission. Mansur appointed men loyal to his new ally Serajuddin Haqqani, most notably: Ibrahim Haqqani, who joined the Political Commission; Khalil Haqqani who joined the Finance Commission; and Ali Haidar who was appointed as the first deputy of the Military Commission.[32]

Yakub tried to undermine Mansur in the weeks following the 'election'. He resigned from the Finance Commission and campaigned to the clerical class and the Taliban leadership to convince them to resist Mansur. There was fertile ground for that. Many commanders and fighters were reportedly shocked that Mansur and the top leaders had been shamelessly lying for years, claiming to be endorsed by a dead man.[33]

Despite the successful co-optation of Serajuddin Haqqani, Mansur's gamble wrecked his multi-year efforts to re-unify the Quetta Shura under him; several senior Rahbari Shura members deserted him and joined Yakub's opposition. Even Zakir and Mansur Dadullah, who had been rivals since 2012, managed to find common ground and work together.[34]

Following the backlash from Mansur's rigged election, the leaders of the Peshawar and Miran Shah Shuras met with the internal Quetta apparatus in early August, where, following a mediation effort by Serajuddin Haqqani, it was decided to convoke a new 'election' for 15 August.[35] Pakistani authorities and senior Pakistani clerics also met and invited Mansur to offer senior positions to key opposition leaders in order to pacify them.[36] The Pakistanis also tried to convince the opposition to acknowledge Mansur as a leader for the sake of Taliban unity and image, though unsuccessfully.[37]

The new 'election' took place on 15 August 2015 in Quetta. Seventeen *shura*s and sub-*shura*s (the main ones out of over 300) were represented and voted as blocks. According to a Taliban account of the meeting, initially seven *shura*s supported Yaqub, six supported Mansur, three supported Zakir and one supported Mansur Dadullah. Zakir then pledged support to Yaqub and offered him his 'votes', giving him a majority. Akhtar Mohammad Mansur refused to acknowledge the result due to the arbitrary decision to invite selected *shura*s and to use the block votes. He demanded a full election with the whole Taliban constituency (*shura* members, governors and *nizami massuleen*).[38]

Throughout the dispute Serajuddin Haqqani was under conflicting pressures from his personal closeness to Yaqub and his hostility to reconciliation, and Pakistani pressure to support Akhtar Mohammad Mansur. Some of Serajuddin's brothers (Azizullah, Ibrahim and Khalil) reportedly pressured him to openly side with Yaqub.[39]

In early October the Pakistanis again tried to mediate between Akhtar Mohammad Mansur and Zakir/Mansur Dadullah, approaching moderate members of Akhtar Mohammad Mansur's opposition, such as Abdul Ghani Baradar and Sayed Tayab Agha. The Pakistanis advocated a repeat of the selection process, implicitly criticising Akhtar Mohammad Mansur's power grab in July, and offered financial support for the opposition if it abstained from openly opposing Akhtar Mohammad Mansur. The Pakistanis hinted that if an agreement was not reached, they would crack down on the opposition.[40]

A consequence of the internal conflict over the succession to Mullah Omar was a wave of desertions from the Taliban during the summer of 2015. Many Taliban were disgusted that they had not known about the death of their leader, despite being issued orders in his name for two years. A source in the Quetta Shura quantified 1,800 people from the ranks of the Quetta Shura defected, a third of which went home while the rest joined the Islamic State (see 'The Taliban's monopoly over the insurgency threatened', below).[41]

### The man of the narcos?

There is no need to review all the sources that claim the Taliban raise money from the drug trade,[42] as Taliban sources in Pakistan and Afghanistan confirm the importance of drug revenue for at least the Quetta Shura. Taxes on the poppy harvest, which Mansfield studied extensively, generally did not make it to the coffers of the Finance Commission, and were spent locally. In 2012 members of the Quetta Shura estimated that the southern Taliban made 40 per cent of their income from the drug trade, including resources that were not channelled through the Finance Commission.[43] Another Taliban source estimated that in 2014/15 the Taliban collected $225 million in drug revenue from Helmand alone, and another $60 million from Kandahar.[44] These figures cannot be verified, but considering that the Taliban officially reject making money from the drug trade, such claims are certainly not propaganda and might well reflect the reality. These sources stress that the 'voluntary contributions' of wealthy individuals and druglords often do not reach the Finance Commission in their entirety. According to sources in the drug trade, a range of Taliban actors raise taxes from them, sometimes in competition with each other.[45] In the south, for example, a drug lord reported paying to Akhtar Mohammad Mansur's official Quetta Shura and to his rival Abdul Qayum Zakir, as well as to several front leaders. In Nangarhar, a drug trader reported paying to the Peshawar Military Commission; others said they did the same in Kunduz and Takhar. In Badakhshan, several smugglers and traders said that a Taliban front known as Jundullah taxed them. Essentially, operators maintain relations with whichever Taliban component is active in the area.[46]

Drug smugglers claim tax rates that vary from 7–13 per cent, depending on who is taxing, who is being taxed and the Taliban's financial situation.[47] Higher taxation occurred when the Taliban were facing financial difficulties, for example in the east and north-east in 2015. In Quetta there is even a specialised 'drug office' within the Finance Commission, tasked with negotiating 'voluntary contributions' with operators in the narcotics trade. According to the same sources, drug revenue accruing to the finance commissions of Quetta and Peshawar was about $100 million in 2015, representing over 15 per cent of the combined revenue of the two commissions. The finance commissions of Mashhad and Miran Shah did not earn drug money, while the finance commission of the alternative Quetta Shura set up by Mullah Rasool in late 2015 was barely operational as the year ended.

Although the Taliban tried to enforce their drug tax wherever they were present, in many areas where the Taliban's control was not very firm smugglers sought to evade the tax. Several interviewees admitted to trying to evade Taliban taxes in provinces such as Balkh, Badakhshan, Kandahar, Nimruz and Nangarhar. In the south, taxes on opium had to be paid as the Taliban kept a close watch on the harvest, but heroin shipments could sometimes get away without being detected. If caught, smugglers are forced to pay their due taxes.[48] In some areas, such as Badakhshan, smugglers were able to negotiate lump payments for heroin (not opium), which saved the smugglers up to 7–8 per cent of the normal tax rate.[49]

While nobody among the Taliban had a drug revenue monopoly, it is clear that not everybody benefited equally. In 2010–15 Akhtar Mohammad Mansur was regularly accused by Taliban sources of diverting drug revenue to fund his own *mahaz*, as well as to fund his business activities in the Gulf.

Mansur Mahaz was the *loy mahaz* most dependent on drug money. In 2013 Taliban sources estimated that this *loy mahaz* relied on drug money for 50 per cent of its funding, with the remainder provided by external donors.[50] However, the role of Mansur's drug interests in his ascension to power in Quetta and/or in pushing him towards reconciliation talks with Kabul remains unclear.

## 7.2 The changing shape of the Taliban's centres of power

*The emergence of the Mashhad Shura*

Iran was a major player in Afghanistan in the 1980s, when it supported most Shi'ite insurgent groups against the Soviet army and the leftist regime, as well as some small Sunni groups. In the 1990s it supported the Rabbani regime, even against some of its own Shiite Khomeinist allies. From 1996 it supported opposition to the Taliban, including Shiite groups, Rabbani's Jamiat-i islami and Gen. Dostum's forces. From 2001 to 2005, the Iranians did not support any violent activities in Afghanistan and mostly tried to cooperate with the Karzai regime. Since 2005, however, this has changed. Initially on a small scale, agencies of the Iranian regime supported the Taliban, mostly with medical aid and small-scale military supplies. The purpose was to facilitate information gathering and communication with selected Taliban commanders.

In 2005–8, according to Taliban and local Afghan sources along the Iranian border, Taliban messengers were sent to Iran several times to meet with radical Iranian elements and discuss the issue of support to anti-government elements. Reportedly, Iran has been providing such elements with limited support including medicine, light arms, logistics, and training in Iran for some groups operating in western Afghanistan. When international actors tried to address this, officials in Tehran denied it and President Karzai supported this position.[51]

According to Taliban sources in Iran, Iranian support for the Taliban came primarily from the Revolutionary Guards (Pasdaran).[52] A Taliban command centre in Mashhad was established in 2007 to command operations in western Afghanistan.[53] Agha Jan Mohtasim was one of the chief negotiators of the extent of the support each year, before falling in disgrace in 2010 on allegations of unauthorised contacts with the Kabul authorities. Before the Syrian crisis began in 2012, the main Iranian objective was to avoid the use of Afghanistan as a base for operations against Iran. The Iranians wanted a complete Western withdrawal from Afghanistan, with no training mission left behind. They did not indulge the rumours that the Americans might leave Afghanistan in 2014, in the absence of an agreement over a strategic treaty with Kabul.

Iranian support for Taliban groups gradually and slowly increased from 2006–11. In this period most Taliban members had only occasional contact with Iran, including Mullah Qayum Zakir, who was receiving substantial Iranian aid for his fighting units in Helmand, particularly the Kajaki area.[54] In 2012 Iranian support doubled, largely due to worsening relations between Akhtar Mohammad Mansur of the Quetta Shura and the Pakistanis in autumn of that year. The Pasdaran saw an opportunity and offered Mansur support; this move created tension with the Pakistanis and delayed the negotiation of the strategic agreement between Iran and Pakistan, discussed above. Eventually the Pakistanis accepted the Iranian claim that they were trying to bring Mansur back to a path of collaboration with the Pakistanis.[55]

According to Taliban officials in Iran (tasked with keeping track of the money), the financial support provided by the Iranians over the years is as follows (excluding weapons and supplies):

- 2006: $30 million;
- 2007: $30 million;
- 2008: $40 million;
- 2009: $40 million;
- 2010: $60 million;
- 2011: $80 million;
- 2012: $160 million;
- 2013: $190 million.[56]

These figures may exclude payments made to Taliban commanders and fronts, which the Iranians might have wanted to keep hidden from the Taliban leadership. According to the Taliban, the material support provided by the Iranians has been modest, consisting of some thousands of Kalashnikovs, rockets of various types, explosives, long-range sniping rifles, night vision glasses, and a few guided missiles.[57] The Iranians had also promised to deliver anti-aircraft missiles, but did not. The new technologies transferred to the Taliban required relatively large numbers of advisers dispatched from Iran to teach the relevant skills to operate the devices.[58] From 2012, some Taliban groups operating from Iran were the first to receive remote control technology for their mines (see also Chapter 5, 'Improvements in equipment').[59]

As far as the various Taliban groups were concerned, the decision to tighten relations with the Iranians was taken in Quetta at a time when their Pakistani and Saudi funding were being reduced, to Peshawar's benefit.[60] Coinciding with the 2012 increase in financial support, the pre-existing Taliban liaison office in Mashhad was upgraded and two new Taliban bases were opened in Zahidan and Sistan. Zahidan became the operational base of the Taliban for the provinces of Nimruz, Farah, Herat and Badghis. The families of several leaders and cadres also resided in Zahidan. Zahidan's position next to the two borders (Pakistan and Afghanistan) facilitated Taliban movement between the three countries. The Iranian authorities encouraged the Taliban leaders and cadres to move their families to Zahidan.[61] The Sistan base of the Taliban was instead dedicated to training.[62] Iranian support allowed the Taliban to increase their presence in western Afghanistan significantly.[63]

It was the Iranians who approached the Taliban and proposed to open the office.[64] The Mashhad office was opened on 11 June 2012 with the consent of the Pakistani ISI, some of whose senior officials even attended the inauguration. Trilateral meetings between the Pasdaran and other Iranian authorities, the Pakistanis and the Taliban often took place in Mashhad. Pasdaran and ISI would often consult each other about their work with the Taliban. The office also maintained relations with the Arab Gulf governments and for a period with Al-Qaida's representatives in Iran, Samiullah and Yasin al Suri, who acted as recruiters and fundraisers in the region.[65]

Apart from playing a 'diplomatic' role, by 2013 the Mashhad office directed about 70 per cent of the Taliban's fighting forces deployed in western Afghanistan.[66] The leadership of the Mashhad Office included ten members, representing different components of the Taliban.[67]

The Iranians also allowed and encouraged the Taliban to recruit Sunni volunteers in Iranian madrasas. According to sources in Mashhad and to a Taliban cadre interviewed in Uruzgan, in early 2013 there were madrasas in Sistan, Mashhad and Bandar Abbas, where the Taliban were recruiting both Afghan and non-Afghan volunteers.[68] Sources in Mashhad indicated that as part of the intensified recruitment effort that led to the creation of two new Iranian-sponsored networks in May (see above), six new madrasas dedicated to Sunni students and staffed by Lebanese and Syrian teachers, were established in different parts of Iran.[69]

With Zakir in Mashhad, the office was powerful enough to declare its autonomy from Quetta. Quetta was of course unhappy about Mashhad's declaration, seeing it as a prelude to the emergence of yet another autonomous component of the Taliban.[70] The rise in power of the Mashhad Office soon prompted a demand that it be upgraded to full *shura* status, to be named perhaps the Sistan or the Mashhad Shura:[71]

> Now we are trying to change the Mashhad office to the Mashhad Shura. Because first there was one *mahaz*, the Naim Mahaz, then our *mahaz* was established, then the Abdul Mateen Mahaz and now there is Zakir's. If the number of *mahaz*es keeps increasing like this, it is possible that we will create a *shura*.[72]

In 2015 the Iranians were not ready to recognise Mashhad as a fully fledged Taliban *shura*, as this would have highlighted its role in supporting the Taliban.[73] One source pointed out how Mashhad was already behaving as a de facto *shura*.[74] Quetta was particularly incensed because the 'defection' of Mashhad dramatically weakened its hold on the Taliban in western Afghanistan.[75] Quetta threatened Mashhad supporters with harsh punishment,[76] but nevertheless accepted that representatives of the Mashhad Office would sit in top level all-Taliban meetings and even in the Doha office. Mashhad was in a position to retaliate against any exclusion by shutting off Quetta's logistics in the west.[77]

In total, according to Taliban sources, 8,000 Taliban of the Quetta Shura left with the Mashhad Office. This included about 100 governor groups with about 2,500 men; eighty-five *dilghay*s with over 2,500 men; six village *mahaz*es with about 600 men; and 1,300 men belonging to the four provincial governors, who themselves joined the Mashhad Office (these were the provinces of Herat, Nimruz, Farah and Badghis).[78] As a result, by 2015 70 per cent of the Taliban in Herat were under the control of the Mashhad Office, while 20 per cent stayed loyal to the Quetta Shura and 10 per cent belonged to other *shura*s.[79]

The Iranians convinced their long-term client Mullah Naim to relocate to Mashhad, followed by Abdul Qayum Zakir in the summer of 2014, after all his funding from Pakistan and Saudi Arabia had been cut off. Zakir negotiated with the Iranians and in a few months they agreed that he would join the Mashhad office and relocate part of his assets there.[80] A source in the Peshawar Shura estimated that as of summer 2015 60 per cent of the forces of Zakir and Naim were based in Iran, with the remaining 40 per cent in Pakistan.[81]

After Mashhad declared its autonomy, the Rahbari Shura continued appointing governors who were under the control of Mashhad (which paid them). As of 2014, after the governors' power declined and they eventually transitioned into an organisational role in 2010, power was concentrated in the *nizami massuleen*. Their role in Mashhad was therefore very similar to Peshawar.[82]

The ambitions of the newly autonomous Mashhad Office were not limited to the west. For instance, Zakir's priority remained recapturing the south,[83] which the Iranians encouraged.[84] Resulting from this was a major expansion of the activities and influence of Mashhad in southern Afghanistan.[85] Then, in 2015, the Mashhad Office started nurturing plans to expand its influence in northern Afghanistan, a plan presaging a more confrontational approach to other *shuras*.[86] This planned expansion might have been linked to the Iranians' push in 2015 for the Office to focus more on Islamic State activities in Afghanistan and particularly in the west. Iran asked the Taliban to gather intelligence and even participate in Iranian raids against these groups.[87]

The Pasdaran and the Mashhad Taliban suffered several blows in their efforts to co-opt whole Taliban networks. Abdul Matin cut off relations with the Pasdaran in 2014 and his *loy mahaz* was disbanded; many of its fighters crossed over to the Abdul Raziq Mahaz and the Mullah Naim Mahaz, which were more loyal clients of the Pasdaran.[88] Importantly, in April 2016 Zakir cut off relations with the Pasdaran following a clash over their negotiations with his arch-rival Akhtar Mohammad Mansur.[89] Money aside, the Pasdaran had problems retaining the support of ambitious Taliban leaders because associating with Iran was a major career hindrance. It was not conceivable that the path to Taliban leadership could pass through Iran, in opposition to the Pakistanis and Saudis. An alliance with Iran had its advantages, however. Iranian support was comparatively generous:

> Those Taliban who are in Iran get good facilities and benefits. So the Taliban in Iran are very happy compared to the Taliban in Pakistan.[90]

Additionally, before spring 2016 the Pasdaran never arrested or assassinated Taliban members when they disagreed with them:

> When we were in Pakistan, we lived in fear as the Pakistani government is not honest with the Taliban; they often arrest our members. The Rahbari Shura is also not well organised. But in the Mashhad office, our families are safe and they are supported financially – our children study in madrasas there. Iran does not blackmail us, while Pakistan tells us to do this thing otherwise our family would be under their control.[91]

In terms of organisation, the Mashhad Office was closer to Peshawar than to Quetta, as it was with regards to the *nizami massuleen*. The *loy mahaze*s were subordinate to the Military Commission like they were in the territory of the Peshawar Shura.[92] Mashhad also agreed to allow Quetta to appoint governors, so long as there was at least a pretence of them taking orders from Mashhad, in contrast to the Peshawar Shura, which allowed governors to issue orders only to the governor's groups and the village *mahaze*s.[93] One commander linked to Mashhad claimed that the Quetta governors would one day be expelled from western Afghanistan.[94]

The Mashhad Military Commission has several internal departments, including Commandos, Mines, Suicide Bombing, and Support for the Families of the Martyrs.[95] Zakir's arrival and his appointment as head of the Mashhad Military Commission strengthened Mashhad's inclination towards the *nizami* system.[96] While he was in charge, Zakir appointed the members of the Mashhad Military Commission and chose all the *nizami massuleen* at the provincial and district level. Zakir chose many members of his *loy mahaz*, followed by member of Naim's and Raziq's, as well as some people aligned with Sattar and Baradar.[97]

The Mashhad Office did not try to imitate the other Taliban *shura*s and re-create the same panoply of commissions as they did. By autumn 2014 Mashhad only had a Financial Commission, a Military Commission and a Political Commission. It was not interested in competing with Quetta in the delivery of services, and there were no plans to create more commissions.[98] As one of the leaders stated, 'the aim of the Mashhad Office is to defeat the Americans; we do not plan to make courts [or deal with] education or health.'[99]

Recruitment by the Mashhad Military Commission mostly took place inside Iran, attracting recruits with generous salaries. The *loy mahaze*s connected with the Mashhad Office instead relied on more traditional Taliban recruitment practices, including working through sub-*shura*s and refugee camps.[100]

Mashhad did not even try to collect taxes in the west and never developed a structure to do so. It left the meagre receipts to Quetta, reportedly after the Iranian Pasdaran reached an agreement with Quetta on the matter.[101]

High level Taliban sources associated with the Mashhad Office admitted that Iranian advisers played a key role:

> If the Mashhad office were making any decisions independently of Iranian advisors, it would not exist.[102]

One senior Pasdaran adviser, Hussain Moussavi, reportedly sat in the Mashhad Office permanently:[103]

> Of course they do play a great role in decision making, especially in military strategy. Their leader is Hussain Moussavi. He has a key role, similar to Hamid Gul in Pakistan.[104]

Other Pasdaran advisers sat with the commissions.[105] One former Taliban from western Afghanistan commented disparagingly:

> If the Iranian advisors tell them to not eat lunch or dinner, they will not eat it. It is clear their bosses are Iranian and these eight leaders are just their assistants. [This is the case] in all matters – military, political or any other types of decisions.[106]

The main beneficiary of Iranian support among the Taliban had always been Naim's network. As one of Naim's cadres said:

> With my groups there are ten Iranian Tajiks, who are tactical trainers. We do not forget that our *mahaz* was faced with defeat; it was the Iranians who got us back on our feet.[107]

Significantly the Mashhad Office was forbidden by the Iranians from collecting taxes, presumably as they wanted to keep it entirely dependent on Iranian support. Taxes collected in western Afghanistan were transferred to the Quetta Shura. If local commanders loyal to Mashhad did collect tax, they kept it for themselves and did not transfer it to the Office.[108]

### *The split of the 'High Council of the Islamic Emirate'*

On the strength of the endorsement of ten of seventeen Taliban *shura*s in August 2015 (see above), Yaqub tried to organise the opposition to Akhtar Mohammad Mansur in a parallel Quetta Shura; since Pakistan opposed his plans, he called a meeting in Garmser, just across the border in Helmand. While a few members of the Rahbari Shura and *loy mahaz* leaders, such as Mansur Dadullah, Mullah Abdul Manan attended, only one provincial governor (Mullah Salam of Kunduz) was there.[109] Pakistani hostility and the lack of an alternative safe haven stifled Yaqub's efforts, even though he reportedly raised about $200 million in the Arab Gulf to set up his own organisation. Yaqub had majority support among the Taliban in Uruzgan and Zabul, relatively marginal provinces, and he had some support in Farah, Badghis, Faryab and Kunduz. Akhtar Mohammad Mansur managed to mobilise additional funding from Pakistan and Saudi Arabia, allowing him to buy supporters, including Zakir's old allies such as *loy mahaz* leaders Sattar, Janan and Ibrahim Alizai.[110] Having secured complete Pakistani backing, by mid-October Akhtar Mohammad Mansur was preparing for war and was refocusing his intelligence apparatus efforts towards his opposition.[111]

Fearful that Akhtar Mohammad Mansur's opposition might reach an agreement with the Islamic State (IS), at the beginning of October the Iranians offered them support in exchange for not establishing relations with the Saudis and IS.[112] On 25 October 2015 the opposition launched its own alternative Quetta Shura with Iranian funding, having agreed to Mohammad Rasool as its leader. Initially, the main stakeholders were several Quetta Shura heavyweights such as Abdul Rauf, Abdul Majid, Ihsanullah Rahimi, Abdul Qayum Zakir, Mullah Naim, Mansur Dadullah and Abdul Raziq. The agreement was the outcome of negotiations between Zakir and Mansur Dadullah, who commanded the largest number of fighters. The creation of several commissions (political, logistics, recruitment and health) was immediately decided upon.[113]

Mullah Rasool was a compromise candidate; allied with the Iranians since 2012, despite having been expelled from Iran in 2002, he had support among the Noorzais of Farah, which added to the Alizai and Kakar support bases of Zakir and Mansur Dadullah.[114] In fact, the most popular leader of the High Council of the Islamic Emirate, as the new *shura* was officially called, was Mansur Dadullah, who had earned a new lease of (political) life thanks to his strident opposition to Akhtar Mohammad Mansur. He also contributed the largest number of men to the new Shura, excluding those Taliban leaders already associated with the Mashhad Office. For Mansur Dadullah the agreement with the Iranians represented a chance to re-launch his *loy mahaz*, which by the second half of 2015 was in its third straight year of decline. Its funding was down to just $32 million a year, gathered through taxes, private contributions in Afghanistan and Pakistan, and some donations from the Arab Gulf. His *loy mahaz* was cut off from the already declining contributions of the Rahbari Shura after the split, and none of the Taliban sub-*shura*s would any longer support it.[115]

Akhtar Mohammad Mansur identified the Dadullah Mahaz as a major threat, not least because in 2015 he was the only main stakeholder in the High Council (soon popularly known as 'Rasool's Shura') who had a significant presence east of Kandahar, particularly in Zabul. Faced with reports that Mansur Dadullah was trying to consolidate control over the northern districts of Zabul (presumably to secure supply lines into Zabul and Ghazni), Akhtar Mohammad Mansur ordered the first large scale offensive against the opposition. The fighting resulted in the killing of Mansur Dadullah, dealing a major blow to Rasool's Shura, but at the same time bringing discredit upon Akhtar Mohammad Mansur as the first Taliban leader to have killed a colleague.[116]

Naim's and Zakir's *loy mahazes* were key allies for Rasool because they also provided complete logistical support and partial financial support to Ihsan Rahimi's *mahaz* and Abdul Majid's *mahaz*.[117] Overall, the Rasool Shura attracted about 10 per cent of Taliban manpower by the time it was fully set up in January 2016.[118] The attempted assassination of Akhtar Mohammad Mansur on 2 December 2015 (he escaped, injured), which his supporters attributed to the Rasool Shura, and the killing of Mansur Dadullah by Akhtar Mohammad Mansur's men in November ended efforts to reconcile the two *shura*s. Soon, however, the Rasool Shura gradually lost its main stakeholders; by the summer they were all gone due to both the inability to raise sufficient funds and the detention of Rasool in Pakistan. Membership declined by over a third, but started recovering after the summer, when Arab Gulf donors replaced Iranian support.[119]

Although Rasool failed to conquer the top leadership of the Taliban, this episode represented the first instance of genuine fragmentation in the Taliban after the setting up of the Rahbari Shura in 2003 – the new *shura* having refused any collaboration with Quetta and repeatedly fighting against it throughout 2015–17.

*The crisis of the Peshawar Shura*

Cracks in the Peshawar Shura's cohesion were emerging in 2013, when despite the lack of unanimity it established two new autonomous *loy mahaz*es, Atiqullah's and Dost Mohammed's, in order to attract additional funding from China. This decision violated one of the rules held dearest to the founders of the Shura, sparking debate within the Shura on whether new *mahaz*es should be allowed. At one point, the names of ten likely applicants were in circulation, including one for each main tribal *shura*, such as the Safi Shura, and the Dawlatzai Shura. Hayatullah and Habibullah also explored the idea of forming their own *mahaz*. Although initially the proposals were rejected and it was decided not to authorise any new *mahaz*es, these decisions would not hold for long. In 2010 the Jundullah Mahaz was the only authorised *loy mahaz*-type structure authorised under the Peshawar Shura, though some members of the Peshawar Shura resisted it. The conflict did not lead to major consequences, despite rising unhappiness about the domination by the Shamsatoo Mahaz:[120]

> This decision was taken in 2005 that all the *mahaz*es to be under the control of the military commission. All the *shura*s agreed to work under the control of the Military Commission, including the Tora Bora Shura, Ijraya Shura, Safi Shura, Dowlatzai Shura, Jabarkhel Shura, Stanikzai Shura, and others. [...] But now they are not happy. The first time when we were uniting, the Shamsatoo Mahaz told us, 'we will take care of your *shura*', but they made the *shura*s weak and they promoted their own. Now, the Shamsatoo Mahaz is very powerful and we cannot do anything, so we need to work under the control of the Military Commission.[121]

Since the Shamsatoo Mahaz still controlled most of the funding, it managed to contain the rising opposition. However, these three new *mahaz*es (headed by Jundullah, Atiqullah and Dost Mohammed) established precedents, which made it easier in late 2015 and early 2016 for dissidents within the *shura* to establish their own *mahaz*es, sometimes without authorisation. In 2015 the Hayatullah Mahaz was formed, followed shortly by several other *mahaz*es: the Baryal Mahaz, Sabir Kuchi Mahaz, Safiyan Mahaz Lashkar Omari and the Shamsatoo Mahaz.[122]

Another manifestation of the incipient crisis was the sacking of Qari Baryal from the position of head of the Peshawar Military Commission in July 2013, under pressure from Zakir and the Pakistanis. Baryal, who had one of the largest personal constituencies within the Peshawar Shura, did not give up and took refuge in his native Kapisa, blocking access to Zakir's men and the Pakistanis. Efforts by the Pakistani authorities to buy off Baryal's commanders had minimal success.[123] At that time, the Pakistanis still opposed Akhtar Mohammad Mansur, so he linked up with Qari Baryal to stifle the rising power of his rival Zakir. Mansur deployed his men to eastern Afghanistan to shore up Baryal's men against Zakir. This was at a time when rumours were circulating among the Taliban that Baryal might align with the Quetta Shura.[124] In reality Baryal was not isolated in the Peshawar Shura, with Atiqullah, Habibullah and Mawlavi Saleh secretly supporting him.[125] In August 2013, when Zakir tried to go for Baryal's job, which would bring Peshawar under his direct control, he was defeated in the vote by Habibullah, twenty-five to seventeen.[126] Qari Baryal emerged in 2014–15 as one of the most 'nationalist' among the Taliban leaders. He insisted that even with no support from Pakistan and Saudi Arabia, the Taliban could continue fighting by raising taxes and seeking support in other countries.[127]

Financial crisis was at the root of the disintegration of Peshawar. Akhtar Mohammad Mansur's skilful diplomatic manoeuvring in 2014 left him in a comfortable position with most of the Taliban's donors, particularly in Pakistan and Saudi Arabia. This came mainly at the expense of the Peshawar Shura, which in addition to a curtailing of Pakistani and Saudi funding was also facing a complete cut in Chinese funding by the end of the year.[128] In areas like Baghlan the impact was significant, and a number of commanders and fighters had to be dismissed.[129] By the second half of 2014 the Quetta Shura was already in position to abolish the agreement whereby the *loy mahaze*s would deploy to eastern Afghanistan with financial support from the Peshawar Shura, and brought them back under its control.[130] One high level source estimated that as a result the Peshawar Shura went from controlling up to 60 per cent of the Taliban's military capabilities, to controlling just 35 per cent, while the Quetta Shura rose from 25 to 50 per cent.[131]

For Peshawar, the worst was to come in 2015. The efforts of the leaders of the Peshawar Shura to shore up support among private donors in the Arab Gulf showed that they too followed the same trend as their government, although more slowly and not unanimously. None of the donors agreed to increase support, while some even announced a gradual reduction due to pressure from their governments.[132] An increase in Iranian funding was not enough to offset all these losses. The formation of new autonomous *mahaze*s further reduced the funding streams as their leaders took their sources of funding with them. The Peshawar Shura was forced to implement major cuts. Initially the Shura leadership hoped to limit the cuts to non-military activities,[133] but despite the existence of financial reserves, in the end, the budget of the Peshawar Military Commission was reduced from $130 million in 2014 to $85 million in 2015. Plans to expand activities into Zabul and Badghis had to be dropped, and forces had to be withdrawn from Logar as well.[134] Plans to upgrade the Ulema Council and the Hajj and Awqaf Council to full commission status were put on hold.[135] Cuts were made to the funding of the Hajj and Awqaf Council and the Recruitment Commission, and the Education and Health Commissions were eventually closed down. At the same time, it was decided to increase taxes on economic activities as well as Zakat and Ushr, and to intensify fundraising among private donors.[136] The decision to increase tax collection was taken.[137]

The number of full time fighters deployed by the Peshawar Military commission in 2015 was about 17–18 per cent lower than in 2014, and in

2016 it shrunk by half compared to 2015.[138] Intelligence units were even ordered to participate in the fighting.[139] In addition, the two semi-autonomous *mahaz*es of Dost Mohammad and Atiqullah lost the bulk of their fighters in early 2015, as funding dried up.[140]

In 2015 the Quetta Shura started supporting Toor-e Pagri financially, while the Shamsatoo Mahaz and the other components bore the full brunt of the financial crisis. Toor-e Pagri handed over the cash to the finance commission, but in exchange it took over many key positions within the Peshawar Shura.[141] Toor-e Pagri had always been in favour of accepting the supremacy of the Quetta Shura, which Akhtar Mohammad Mansur started advocating for openly. Many Taliban started seeing this is a concrete possibility.[142]

Despite the crisis, the Peshawar Shura maintained strong positions in 2015 throughout the north, particularly in Kunduz, Badakhshan and Baghlan as discussed above. They also remained strong throughout Faryab, not only in districts exposed to infiltration from Badghis like Almar and Qaysar, but also in areas of recent Taliban penetration such as Khwaja Sabz Posh.[143] The decision to concentrate the remaining resources on the north-east left the Peshawar Shura weak in other areas, particularly Nangarhar where it faced a confrontation with the Islamic State and lost considerable ground to it in the summer of 2015.[144] In the summer of 2015 the financial situation worsened so quickly that the Peshawar Shura had to suspend operations for three months; it only re-opened in November after accepting a subordinate position to the Quetta Shura. Funding from Quetta resumed, but on a comparatively small scale. By the end of 2015 the Peshawar Shura was a shadow of its former self. Its commission was taken over by Quetta and turned into local branches, and Peshawar lost all independence. The defection of Qari Baryal, who went on to form the Northern Shura, taking with him thousands of cadres and fighters, further weakened Peshawar.[145]

## 7.3 Towards the war of the cities

During 2014, ISAF withdrew from the Afghan battlefield and limited itself to air support and occasional intervention in situations of crisis. The Afghan security forces started pulling out of rural areas, under Taliban pressure. As a result, the Taliban's 'war of the flea' became outdated. The population centres, which had until then been uncontested, began to appear vulnerable. Still in mid-2014 Taliban commanders could be heard arguing that what the Taliban needed was sappers and guerrilla tactics.[146] Other commanders, however, were beginning to recognise that the Taliban lacked the capacity to capture heavily defended locations, particularly when the enemy could receive close air support:

> Now the only thing that prevents us from capturing Baghlan Province is the support of the foreign troops, especially the air support and drone attacks. Honestly, still we cannot find any way to fight against American air attacks and we suffer a lot for this.[147]

The Taliban's military leadership decided that it would be premature to try to take the population and administrative centres, according to several accounts by Taliban commanders: [148]

> In fact, it depends on our leaders and authorities, because they haven't let us take districts centres yet, and I have no idea what the reason [for this] is.[149]
> The Quetta Shura has made a decision that nobody can [assault] districts and instead should use mines, suicide attacks and ambushes.[150]
> If we capture [areas], we cannot keep them and we cannot defend, because we do not have strong enough weapons to shoot down airplanes. We do not need to take district centres because now 70 per cent of Shindand district is with the Islamic Emirate. If the foreign forces leave Afghanistan, we will capture it, because there will be no air force [to support the] Afghan government.[151]

## The 2015 fighting season

The disengagement of US troops from combat operation at the end of 2014 appeared like a light at the end of the tunnel for the Taliban. The belief was that 'if there are no foreign forces with [the Afghan army], they can do nothing, if the foreign forces do not help them, they cannot compete for two days.'[152] A commander commented that 'whenever they carry out operations, they want support from foreign forces. If they were more capable, they would fight us face to face.'[153] Such views were widely shared among the Taliban.[154]

Even former Taliban who had grown critical of the organisation believed that a Taliban victory was likely, if not certain:

> When the Americans leave Afghanistan, the Taliban will win the war. The Afghan government cannot win the war, because they have problems between the senior officials. There are two presidents, Ghani and Abdullah. They cannot solve problems between themselves, so how can they win the war?[155]

Among elders, few of whom expressed any sympathy for the Taliban, the views were similar, particularly in eastern and south-eastern Afghanistan:

If the Americans withdraw from Afghanistan and the same corruption is present here, then the Kabul government will not survive; it will be damaged and collapse very soon. The Taliban are becoming more powerful day by day in the villages and districts.[156]

The main exception to this pattern was Kandahar, where almost all the elders interviewed appeared confident in the ability of the Afghan security forces to hold the line. Kandahar was also a province where several Taliban acknowledged that the Afghan security forces had improved their performance on the battlefield:

We now see that the Afghan police and army have become better at fighting. Six days ago they martyred 173 Taliban in Zheray district. So it seems they are better now than before.[157]

Elders and former Taliban tended to attribute the failures of the Taliban in Kandahar either to the charismatic leadership of the army's General Razziq, [158] or to the loss of motivation among Taliban fighters.[159] An observer however believed that the Taliban were using Kandahar as a safe haven for their leadership and fighters, which would explain the reduction in violence.[160]

It is not difficult to figure out the origins of the belief that the Afghan government was doomed. Elders in most of the provinces studied recounted how soon after the disengagement from combat operations of US troops, Afghan forces started appearing less and less often in their neighbourhoods.[161] The surge had been tactically successful, but the development of capable Afghan security forces had not, so the US withdrawal again left space for the Taliban to grow.[162]

The gradual drawdown which started in 2012 and ended with the withdrawal of almost all NATO combat troops led the Taliban to rethink their strategy. A Taliban intelligence cadre for example acknowledged that he was now spending much less effort on the Americans, as the priority had become gathering intelligence on the Afghan government.[163] The major effort set up by the Taliban to infiltrate Kabul with a network capable of carrying out regular high profile attacks against foreign targets was significantly downsized in 2015; the Miran Shura Intelligence Department reduced the number of its operatives from 250 to 100: 'we decreased the number of our people in Kabul city because we have the plans for attacks but not [the materiel].'[164]

The biggest strategic change derived from the international drawdown was the decision to start aiming to capture key ground: strategic targets such as district centres, poppy fields and even cities. With ISAF's disbandment in 2014, guerrilla tactics lost much importance for the Taliban and the issue was now to learn how to fight in large groups.[165] 2014 was a period of transition, with the Taliban experimenting with carrying out large-scale attacks against fixed government positions. The Peshawar Shura carried out several larger than usual attacks in Kunar, Nuristan, Baghlan, Kunduz, Badakhshan and Wardak.[166] According to a high-level source in the Peshawar Military Commission, the largest attack of 2014 was against Warduj district (Badakhshan), in which 1,200 Taliban took part. Other major operations took place in Dangam (Kunar), with 1,000 Taliban, in Chahar Dara district (Kunduz), with 800 Taliban, and in several other districts such as Qaysar, Dawlatabad, Andkhoy (Faryab), Sayed Gard (Parwan) and Batikot (Nangarhar), with hundreds of Taliban involved in each.[167]

Even the Miran Shah Shura decided that it would soon be time to escalate operations, but only once the American combat forces had completely pulled out of the country. Then the large reserves accumulated by the Miran Shah Shura (35,000 men) could be thrown into the battle:[168]

In 2015 we will carry out group attacks to capture district centres and provincial centres, and for this purpose we have set up two *mahaz*es. We need now to demonstrate our power and capture many areas. [...] Currently we do not have any plans for big, big operations to capture district and provincial centres, because the Americans are here and they will capture those areas back from us, and our casualties will also be heavy. We will continue guerrilla tactics, because we can defeat the government and the Americans this way. We will capture important areas when we are in a position to keep them for good, not like the Peshawar Shura and the Rahbari Shura who capture districts [only to] leave again.[169]

The Haqqanis developed their own replacement for the heavy weapons:

The *fedayi* team can break through defences and allow other Taliban to break through to police, army and other government zones. For example, when the Zarbati team and Dalaez groups want to take district centres, they request two suicide bombers from us. If we do not break through the checkpoints and security gates, they cannot enter those areas. They do not have heavy weapons to attack the concrete walls that protect government areas.[170]

Although a Miran Shah Shura military cadre claimed that the Haqqanis had the equipment to attack fortified posts if necessary, he implied that the preferred tactic was still to attack Afghan government forces while they were moving around.[171] Despite Haqqani claims of having a unique approach, the strategy advocated by the other *shuras* did not differ substantially. Until 2015 the strategy imposed by the leadership dictated that the district centres were not worth a major effort, because in the absence of heavy weaponry taking them would incur disproportionate casualties and then 'the jets and helicopters will come and they will capture it again'.[172] It was argued that it would be better to wait for the Americans to get out of Afghanistan.[173]

Preparations for a massive 2015 offensive included bringing back the best military commanders possible. At the beginning of September 2014, Qari Baryal was re-elected by the Peshawar Shura leadership as head of the Peshawar Military Commission, with fifteen votes against eight for Atiqullah. The hope was that Baryal would be more successful in fund raising than Ayatullah had been and better able to work together with the Quetta Shura, due to his strong relationship with Akhtar Mohammad Mansur; although the two professed friendship, Atiqullah refused to take the job of Baryal's deputy and instead tried to secure an appointment as head of the finance commission, hinting at future trouble (see 'The crisis of the Peshawar Shura' above).[174]

In December 2014 Zakir was also re-appointed without much fanfare as head of the Central Military Commission, a position from which he had only taken 'sick leave' in April 2014. The rationale for Zakir's reinstatement was that Ibrahim Sadar had a weak personality who could not impose his will; there was a sense that after a lacklustre year the Taliban had to put together a strong military showing in 2015. Taliban sources indicated that Mansur had to call Zakir back following heavy Pakistani pressure.[175] Zakir had at this point reconciled with Baryal, but not with Akhtar Mohammad Mansur.[176]

The Taliban's internal rivalries were however so deep at this point, that simply rehabilitating disgraced leaders would not suffice. In first half of 2015, Zakir was unable to recover his past strength. Of his old allies, only the Sattar Mahaz re-aligned with him, in addition to the Naim Mahaz which was already allied with him.[177] This time Zakir did not last long at the helm of the Central Military Commission. In June 2015, Akhtar Mohammad Mansur asked once again for his dismissal, on allegations of closeness to Iranian interests and of having started a war against the Islamic State, which was not in the Taliban's interests at that stage. Mansur warned that the support of Arab donors was at stake and that a pacification with IS was necessary (see 'The Taliban's monopoly over the insurgency is threatened' below).[178]

Another sign of Taliban desire to remove the image of military weakness that they had acquired in 2014 was the decision made in March 2015 to form four new mobile fronts, which were meant to be the most mobile Taliban front yet (see Chapter 6, 'The expansion of the mobile forces'). The fronts were named after their area of operations: the North, South, East and West *mahaz*es. The son of Mullah Omar, Mullah Yaqub, was appointed to lead the four fronts. This was his first senior military appointment. Each of the new mobile fronts had a projected strength of 3,000 men and senior Taliban leaders were appointed to lead each of them: Qari Baryal was given command in the east; Ishaq Faryabi was given command in the north; Mullah Yaqub took direct command of the south; and Zakir took command of the west. Each *mahaz* was given an extra $15 million to upgrade its equipment, reportedly paid by the Iranians, who also supplied military equipment. The negotiations over the funding for the mobile fronts also brought Mullah Yaqub in direct contact with senior Pasdaran and other Iranian officials for the first time.[179] The eastern mobile *mahaz* was created by renaming the existing *dilghay*s of the Military Commission, which were then authorised to enter any *shura* area.[180]

The Quetta Shura was party to the discussions about the 2015 fighting season strategy. The Quetta Military Commission agreed to take part in the offensive and aim for district and provincial centres. But the Quetta Military commission did not have the weapons required to take fortified positions. Until Zakir was head of the Central Military Commission, there was talk of getting the Iranians to supply heavier weapons to Quetta, but with his replacement these plans were dropped as the Quetta Shura leadership no longer had strong relations with Iran.[181] Modern anti-aircraft weapons were believed necessary only if the Americans remained involved in the fighting, as 'for [fighting] the Afghan government these weapons are sufficient – machine guns, Dahshaka [heavy machine guns], rocket launchers.'[182]

According to internal sources, in 2015 the Quetta Military Commission did not have a particular focus of operations and distributed its mobile *dilghay*s around in an even manner: twenty *dilghay*s were sent to each of the ten provinces where it was active (Kandahar, Uruzgan, Nimruz, Helmand, Zabul, Ghazni, Herat, Badghis, Farah and Paktika Provinces).[183] The Quetta Shura also had substantial numbers of governors' forces available. As of mid-2015, the thirty-two provincial governors appointed by the Rahbari Shura had a total of 644 groups under their orders, with a total authorised strength of over 16,000 men according to a member of the Rahbari Shura.[184] These groups were however not trained to fight together in large concentrations, and played a marginal role in the effort to take district centres and cities.

By late autumn and early winter in 2014 the Taliban were planning their biggest offensive ever. The driving forces behind the new strategic planning were the Peshawar Military Commission and the Central Military Commission, still under the leadership of Abdul Qayum Zakir in March 2015. The Zulfikar offensive was planned over the winter of 2014–15 and finalised in March. Baryal, Zakir and Sirajuddin Haqqani met in Hango (Waziristan) to agree to a new set of priorities, which were that the new offensive would have to try to make significant territorial gains in heavily populated areas, shifting away from the guerrilla tactics employed up to then. Establishing solid safe havens inside Afghanistan would have the added benefit of lessening their dependence on Pakistani support, as well as allow the Taliban to raise more tax. The new offensive was also the first one to be effectively coordinated among the three *shuras*. Importantly, the agreement among military leaders bypassed the political leadership of Peshawar and particularly Quetta.[185]

By March, the Pakistanis, which has suggested the expanded campaign in the first place, had changed their mind. Akhtar Mohammad Mansur was happy to align with the Pakistanis, while Serajuddin Haqqani was forced to because of his reliance on their support. Despite the growing financial difficulties of the Peshawar Shura, the budget cuts, Pakistan pressure to cancel the offensive and the failure of the Quetta Shura and of the Miran Shah Shura to follow up on their agreement, the offensive went ahead. In winter the logistical structures of the Peshawar Shura transferred supplies into north-eastern Afghanistan, also receiving new, heavier equipment from Iran.[186]

During the fighting season of 2015 the Taliban staged their first serious comeback in Uruzgan, with the Janubi (southern) Mahaz, Zakir Mahaz and Naim Mahaz all pushing hard in the districts and cleansing them of government presence.[187] In Helmand the fighting began in February and continued until the next winter, with short lulls to allow the Taliban to reorganise their supplies. In 2014 Zakir's *mahaz* was already very active in Helmand, reclaiming control over many villages, but in 2015 the Taliban closed in on Babaji, in Lashkargah district (and even briefly occupied it), Nad Ali, Marjah-Nawzad-Musa Qala (also all temporarily taken by the Taliban), Sangin, and even Girishk and Lashkargah. Contrary to what happened in 2014, and despite his aversion to the military offensive, Akhtar Mohammad Mansur's forces were also deployed to the battlefield, attacking from Kandahar towards Lashkargah, Marjah and Nad Ali. Mansur reportedly did not want to let his rival Zakir lay sole claim to any major gain on the battlefield. Although

Akhtar Mohammad Mansur remained committed to the reconciliation process, he reportedly dragged his feet when confronted with Pakistani pressure to downscale military operations, arguing that the Taliban would then be perceived as weak and lose leverage at the negotiating table. In August he reportedly asked the Pakistanis to allow three to four more months of intense fighting. The *loy mahaz*es of Naim, Ishanullah Rahim and Abdul Razaq also deployed to Helmand in support of Zakir's men. The Taliban performed particularly strongly in November 2015, with mobile forces of 300 men from the north taking Babaji and 235 men from the south reaching a suburb of Lashkargah, despite confronting much larger Afghan government forces on paper.[188]

The Taliban's most impressive achievement in 2015 was the seizure of the city of Kunduz for about two weeks, before being forced to pull out of the city under heavy American bombardment. The Taliban had been fighting in the surrounding of the city throughout 2014, seizing control over many villages and establishing networks of support near the city, which later enabled the mounting of a direct attack. Clearly the Taliban already viewed Kunduz as a long-term strategic objective in 2014. By the winter of 2014–15, the Taliban finalised their plans for Kunduz, which included securing some strategic districts of Badakhshan to secure the supply lines into Kunduz. Still, planning an attack deep into territory where anti-Taliban groups had deep roots, with long supply lines through districts once dominated by them, was indeed a daring plan. Taliban sources indicated that only approximately 20 per cent of the group's necessary supplies for the campaign could be purchased on the north-eastern black market. Consequently, the Taliban sent donkey caravans from Pakistan, through the provinces of Nuristan, Badakhshan, northern Panjshir, Takhar, and then Kunduz to enable the group's forces involved in the campaign to remain combat-effective. For the offensive, the Taliban mobilised all the forces they could rely on, including Central Asians, Lashkar-e Taiba and even some commanders now loyal to the Islamic State. In total around 7,000 Taliban and allies were mobilised for the campaign at its peak, including local militias mobilised by some Pashtun communities. After penetrating the defences of the city in April, the fighting grew to a standstill. The Pakistanis tightened the supplies and the Peshawar Shura started running out of cash, making Qari Baryal unable to organise the final push. Akhtar Mohammad Mansur came to Baryal's rescue over the summer. Badly in need of improving his image of leader of the Taliban, Mansur agreed to lobby the Pakistanis for the re-opening of the supply lines and to pay $40 million to Qari Baryal for the final push on Kunduz, on the condition that Mansur could claim the victory as his own. Baryal agreed and ordered his military leader in Kunduz, Mullah Salam, to pledge allegiance to Mansur shortly before the fall of the city. To symbolise the cooperation of Quetta and Peshawar in Kunduz, Salam was also appointed shadow governor of the province, the first Taliban to take the dual roles of governor and provincial *nizami massul*.[189]

Throughout most of the war, the Haqqanis were content to focus on the four provinces of Loya Paktia plus Logar, and then gradually expanded into Wardak and Ghazni as well.[190] In 2015 they extended their influence to the east and to the south.[191] The Haqqanis did not try to establish deep roots there, but contented themselves with deploying mobile forces out of Loya Paktia and Logar. In February 2014 another ad hoc structure was created to carry out larger scale special operations in Zabul, Uruzgan and Helmand, allegedly on the request of the Pakistani ISI, to strengthen a Quetta Shura which was still militarily weak.[192] Its operations had to be preliminarily cleared by the Quetta Shura on the basis of the territorial responsibility agreements between Quetta and Miran Shah. The new structure had an 'expeditionary' character and was therefore called *mahaz*, introducing a new type of structure in the Haqqani's military. With a strength of 1,000 men, it would multiply the average number of Haqqani special forces deployed in the three provinces by five. The new *mahaz* was allocated new funding and apart from drawing the top cadres from the Haqqanis was able to carry out new recruitment, but only in the Haqqanis' turf and not in the provinces of operation.[193]

In 2014 another *mahaz* was introduced, a somewhat larger one with perhaps 2,000 men. This mobile amalgamation of combatants was deployed outside the usual Haqqani turf; in 2015 it was deployed to Wardak. The two *mahaz*es were named after Mawlavi Sangin (the Sangin Shahid Mahaz) and Ibrahim Haqqani. As of 2015 the Haqqanis had not yet expanded their logistical net to either Wardak and the *mahaz*es depended on the support of the Peshawar Shura for their logistics.[194]

These developments were the prelude to a further consolidation of Haqqani presence in the south, due to Serajuddin Haqqani's appointment as deputy of the Quetta Shura in August 2015 and the appointment of several of his colleagues to the various commissions.

## 7.4 The Taliban's monopoly over the insurgency threatened: The Islamic State

As of spring 2015, the Taliban rated Bati Kot district as a strategic location where they wanted to strengthen their position, and from there threaten the Jalalabad–Torkham highway.[195] When they lost Bati Kot to the Islamic State in the summer of 2015, therefore, the Taliban did not surrender it because it lacked interest for them. The clashes in Nangarhar and their virulence came as a surprise and the weakened Taliban of Nangarhar (see above) could not contain a smaller number of former TTP fighters, who were trying to carve out a safe haven for themselves in Afghanistan. The fact that several local Taliban commanders joined the Islamic State contributed to the debacle. The Taliban could only recover most of the ground lost in January 2016, after mobilising funding abroad through Iranian help.[196]

In reality, the Taliban's attitude towards the Islamic State had been initially positive. IS's emissaries tried to accredit the organisation as just another jihadist group which wanted to establish a presence alongside the Taliban; like Al-Qaida and others, they stated their readiness to contribute to funding the jihad in exchange for the Taliban's consent to establish a presence there. Friction began between IS and Taliban when the Taliban discovered that IS was actively trying to co-opt Taliban commanders and fighters to its side. The Haqqanis, the Quetta Shura and the Peshawar Shura all suffered from defections to IS; Dost Mohammed and the Atiqullah Mahaz were hit particularly hard due to their very heavy financial difficulties.[197]

The fighting between Taliban and IS then occurred at various locations and times. The Taliban of Zakir helped the Iranians crush some IS groups in Farah and destroy their training camp in Kajaki. IS however was able to exploit Taliban rivalries and earn at least some tolerance for some Taliban groups. In autumn 2015, for example, when Mansur Dadullah was attacked by superior Quetta Shura forces in the north of Zabul, he appealed to his contacts in IS for help, who defended him against Akhtar Mohammad Mansur's forces for three days. However, when IS heard that Rasool and Mansur Dadullah were negotiating with the Iranians, it immediately cut off relations and allied instead with Akhtar Mohammad Mansur, contributing to the decisive defeat of Dadullah.[198]

Defections of Taliban fighters and commanders to IS were driven considerably by the organisation's disunity and inability to act in a cohesive way, as well as by the offer of better financial conditions. By 2015 the Taliban were going through an identity crisis; the obvious enemy, the Americans, were now playing a modest role. Different international patrons were pulling the organisation in different and even incompatible ways.[199]

The failure of the Taliban to crush or at least contain IS certainly compounded their image and credibility problems, and negatively impacted the morale of the rank-and-file.

## 7.5 The Taliban at the end of 2015

In terms of perceptions among the village elders, the Taliban were definitely past their peak as NATO combat forces were packing up. Among elders and former Taliban the predominant view is that in 2014–15 the Taliban were far from the peak of popular support that they had at least in their old territory, but were more powerful organisationally and militarily.[200] Seventy elders interviewed for the project leading to this book between summer 2014 and winter 2015 in eleven provinces had mixed views about the state of the Taliban, but 53 per cent of them described the Taliban as in decline, with almost 39 per cent describing them as a strong as ever. Just under 9 per cent saw them as essentially stable. Of sixteen former Taliban interviewed for this project (mostly not on good terms with the organisation anymore), over two thirds stated that the Taliban were in a position to win the war, and three quarters stated that they viewed the Taliban as stronger than when they left them.

Against the Taliban militated the fact that almost universally elders and many former Taliban viewed one main factor undermining support for the Taliban to be the Pakistani states' major influence over the Taliban.[201] These views were partially offset by the feeling that the Taliban at least protected Pashtun interests against a government believed to be dominated by non-Pashtuns, even if this grievance was of declining importance after the early years of the Karzai government.[202]

In part, the loss of Taliban roots among the local population was the result of the high casualty rate in 2007–13. The better-connected local leaders were difficult to replace.[203] One Taliban commander for example sang the praises of Ibrahim, one of the first *loy mahaz* leaders:

> The fighters joined with Ibrahim because he was trustworthy – he was working for Islam. He was not a thief and was not, like the current *mahaz* leaders, working for their own pockets and positions.[204]

Similarly, the fear of getting caught in the fighting or in the retaliation of government forces discouraged potential supporters:[205]

> They had full support of the people some time ago, but during that time, support has decreased because they are afraid of the foreign troops' operations. This is why they don't want to work with the Taliban anymore. The Taliban are not strong like [they were] before and they are weaker now because they have lost the support of the people.[206]

As late as 2012 the tribal sections favoured by the government continued to feel entitled to control all government posts, exclude their local rivals, and push government and foreign troops for a more aggressive posture against the Taliban and the communities which supported them.[207] However, perhaps under Western pressure, the Afghan authorities tried to contain the abuses, apparently with at least a degree of success. By 2014–15, the extremes of abuse by government officials of 2002–5 were now a rarity, luring many elders back towards opposing the Taliban:[208]

> Currently, people are witnessing a better situation because the government has realised their mistake. Now, they maintain Pashtun rights in our area. They appoint honest and good workers to positions, [who are] Pashtuns.[209]
>
> The first time the Taliban appeared in the district, they appeared in Joy Now village. There, the villagers who were victims of Andarabi and Tajik crimes came and visited the Taliban and then announced their support. [...] The villagers only stopped their support for the Taliban [due to] Abdul Rahman Rahimi, who was the commander of the police in the province. After Mr. Rahimi was appointed as police chief, he did a very good job for the people in our district. As police chief, after hearing the villagers he understood their problems and supported the villagers.[210]

Even where the perception was one of worsening government abuse, the Taliban were still seen as a weakening force and therefore of little use, at least in Kandahar.[211] Another reason for the Taliban's declining popularity was that they had become more violent and abusive, as they expanded ranks and came under heavy military pressure; their internal disunity also started showing:

> I do not think badly of the Taliban but there is one bad thing, in that they are not united now. They are divided in factions, all working for themselves and not for the emirate. They should stop [using] mines and suicide attacks because civilians are killed in them. They collect taxes from the people by force and they eat in people's houses by force, even when a family cannot feed itself. However, in our time there were no such activities.[212]

In many locations the Taliban had some pockets of core support, which continued to host Taliban even at the most challenging times. For instance, in Baghlan province, which had certainly not been a Taliban stronghold in earlier days, they managed to find roots from 2006 onwards not only in places such as Gadya (Baghlan Jadid),[213] or the Pashtun settlements in Dand-e Ghori,[214] but also among some Uzbek communities in Burka district. These communities even reached out directly to IMU leaders in Pakistan for support, allowing the IMU to establish a direct presence in Baghlan by 2008–9.[215] Due to the inactivity of ISAF troops, the Taliban expanded undisturbed in the northern districts of Baghlan-e Markazi, Baghlan-e Jadid and Burqa. Non-Pashtun districts of Baghlan increasingly came under Taliban influence due to their exploitation of disputes over land and pasture rights, which sometimes dated back decades. Increasingly, a quarrelling party would request their involvement to strengthen the disputant's position. This occurred in the districts of Nahrin, Tala wa Barfak and Burka.[216]

Other examples of such areas included Charshaka, a cluster of thirteen Noorzai villages, and Nedai, another cluster of Ishaqzai villages, both in Zhirai, Kandahar.[217] From those areas the Taliban tried to expand their presence again in 2015. The outcome varied significantly. In 2014–15 the Taliban in the south had not yet recaptured all the areas lost during the surge of 2009–11. They made big gains in Helmand and in Uruzgan, but in other areas the situation appeared to stabilise, as it did in the west.[218] In Kandahar in 2015 the Taliban mostly operated underground:[219]

In some small villages, people still support the Taliban, and are connected with Taliban commanders. I believe the Taliban [won't be able to regain their] strength unless big villages and tribes start supporting them again. I believe this support has significantly decreased from previous years. But overall, the Taliban do still have some people in the villages, working with them secretly.[220]

The loss of active support was partially offset by the fact that the weakening presence of the Afghan government in many areas prompted many elders and villagers to passively support the Taliban. In many areas the government simply had no access, making the Taliban the only option:[221]

The Taliban are strong enough now, they don't need support of local people anymore. Currently, they can do whatever they want, and there is no one to help the local people. [...] Now, if it was up to the people, they would not support the Taliban, but, of course, they have to do what the Taliban say.[222]

The nadir of support for the Taliban was in 2012–13, when the effect of the surge reached its apex and the Taliban were perceived as weak in the south and north-east, while state governance was showing signs of improvement:

> It is worth mentioning that Taliban are still contacting people and encouraging them to join their ranks, but people are rejecting them, because they are tired of fighting and they don't want to get killed by foreigners.[223]

By 2015 the Taliban controlled more of Afghanistan than ever before (see Map 5 for a visual estimate). One Pakistani adviser estimated that in mid-2015 they controlled 55% of Afghanistan's territory,[224] while another cited 60% control.[225] In terms of population, the Taliban controlled of course much less; US military sources conservatively estimated that around 10% of the population lived under Taliban control, with another 20% in contested areas as of September 2016.[226]

## 7.6 The Taliban reunite?

In 2014–15 there was certainly an awareness among the Taliban that their internal divisions were at least slowing their path to victory, if not preventing victory altogether.[227] The Taliban were already discussing their own political leadership in the summer of 2014. Reportedly, on 27 August the three *shura*s met in Quetta to discuss a matter raised by Ibrahim Sadar, then head of the Central Military Commission. Sadar highlighted the fact that without a unified political leadership, the Central Military Commission was pointless, and would exacerbate internal divisions. If united, he hinted, they could be as successful as the Islamic State in Syria. The Quetta Shura then proposed to organise the election of a Taliban leader, unless Mullah Omar reappeared and stated his intention to assume the day-to-day leadership of the movement. The three leaders agreed in principle to have an election in October, but could not agree on the mechanism for selection. The Quetta Shura proposed to invite all Taliban leaders to the election, with the implication that a majority of the grand electors would be from the Quetta Shura. Serajuddin Haqqani proposed a fixed number of grand electors for each *shura*, who would choose the new leader. The Peshawar Shura endorsed his position. Atiqullah of the Peshawar Shura also hinted that Quetta should bring Zakir back to the fold to have a fully legitimate selection process.[228] In parallel, negotiations were going on for a reunification between Quetta Shura and Miran Shah Shura.[229]

None of this happened as planned. In May 2015 one of the leaders of the Peshawar Shura remained pessimistic about the prospects of reunification:

> It is impossible that there will be a united Taliban leadership for all the Taliban. Because the policies and the *layha* [differ by] *shura*. One thing more, the Taliban [constituent groups] are influenced by different countries and their sources of money are different, so those countries also will not give them permission to reunify. [...] The Quetta Shura wants a new all-Taliban political leadership, but the Peshawar Shura and the Miran Shah Shura do not want it. Moreover, inside the Quetta Shura there are issues and they cannot control their own organisation, so how can they control the whole Taliban? [...] They should not give all the power and authority to the Durrani tribe only, there must be Ghilzais too, and those from other tribes.[230]

Only the Mullah Omar affair, as explained above, compelled Akhtar Mohammad Mansur to act in July 2015. Akhtar Mohammad Mansur's financial wealth, which improved again in 2015 after a substantial recovery in 2014, allowed him to reach out to several other Taliban components and seek their recognition for his leadership. Mansur's co-optation of Serajuddin Haqqani was mentioned above; apart from making him his deputy, Mansur also transferred funds to him, recreating the relationship which had existed between the two *shura*s until 2007. The relationship went beyond that, as Mansur brought a substantial number of Haqqani leaders and cadres into the Quetta Shura. Pushing Taliban reunification further proved harder. After the tactical agreement on Kunduz with Qari Baryal in August 2015 (see below), Mansur tried to convince Baryal to support him as a leader in exchange for Mansur's support for his appointment as leader of the Peshawar Shura and for the right to appoint *nizami massuleen* in every province. Since the beginning of 2015 Mansur had funded the Toor-e Pagri within the Peshawar Shura, which allowed them to expand their influence and role at the expense of the cash-stripped Shamsatoo. Always a shrewd financial operator, Mansur insisted that Baryal give up his remaining Iranian funding, in exchange for generous funding to be routed through Quetta (that is, through Mansur himself). Baryal did not accept Mansur's terms, demanding instead to keep his independent sources of funding.[231]

Similarly, in September 2015 Mansur offered Zakir his old job at the Central Military Commission, in exchange for acknowledging his leadership, but negotiations continued until the end of March without achieving anything. Mullah Naim refused to negotiate with Mansur altogether.[232]

The acknowledgement that Mullah Omar was dead in 2015 made Taliban cohesion even harder. The first formal split took place with the so-called Rasool Shura opting entirely out of the 'Taliban consensus', waging war against them. Mansur's skilful monopolisation of financial resources helped him co-opt the Haqqanis, but he lost complete control of the Mashhad office. It is doubtful that the co-optation of the Haqqani network had a significant impact, as they maintained strong de facto autonomy, despite having formally bowed to the authority of the Quetta Shura.

## 7.7 Three models, three cultural milieus

In sum, by 2015 Akhtar Mohammad Mansur, who had previously led the opposition against Zakir's reforms, accepted that the Quetta Shura's military system required an overhaul and believed that more political power had to be concentrated in the hands of the leader (himself). Characteristically, however, Mansur's attempt backfired and ended up weakening the Quetta Shura. The Quetta Shura's polycentric system, deeply rooted in the Taliban's political culture, proved to be incompatible with centralisation.

Meanwhile, the Taliban's inability to mount well organised, synchronised conventional operations cost them a unique opportunity to score major victories against Kabul, at a time when the Americans were strongly disinclined to respond after the big 2014 withdrawal. That contributed to the weakening of the Quetta Shura, delegitimising its leadership.

Mansur's centralisation plan resembled the Haqqani's system: patrimonial in nature, with the Ishaqzai tribe replacing the Haqqani family (given the larger size of the Quetta Shura). The Haqqani' system might have been more appropriate for the cultural milieu of the Quetta Shura than the Peshawar Shura's system, which was heavily influenced by the Hizb-i Islami model. But clearly it was not enough given the reaction elicited.

Mansur's failure suggests that the differences between the three models (Quetta, Miran Shah/Haqqani, and Peshawar) were deeply rooted in the respective areas of operations, and not just the result of the capriciousness of different Taliban leaders.

# 8

## CONCLUSION

### THE IMPOSSIBLE CENTRALISATION OF AN
### ANTI-CENTRALIST MOVEMENT

**Many little conflicts merging into a big war**

Thanks to their polycentric organisation, the Taliban proved apt at acting as a catalyst of resentment, grievance and local interest groups. Their alliances with tribal groups illustrate this point well. Some tribes or tribal segments (among the Noorzais, Alizais, Barakzais, Ishaqzais and so forth) supported the Taliban for their own reasons, mainly due to perceived favouritism of the central government towards rival tribal segments and in some cases this mobilised *lashkar*s to fight alongside the Taliban.[1] Often the village elders sponsored the creation of local Taliban groups in order to gain the opportunity to influence the Taliban, or protect some of their interests by keeping the out-of-area Taliban away from the village.[2]

Many who joined the Taliban, the Afghan army or police, were motivated by a personal desire to avenge wrong. For example, a Taliban commander in Ghazni admitted that while some of his colleagues had joined 'for God's sake', others like him joined because they wanted personal revenge.[3] Factional, ethnic and personal rivalries also fuelled the prolongation of the conflict:

> In government there are some people who do not want peace like Jamiat, Dostum, Abdullah, Attah, Ahmadzia Massud and others from Jamiat, Junbish and the Shura-e-Nizar members. Therefore, the Taliban do not want to join the the peace

process. [...] How will Taliban achieve peace when this government is assassinating their people and calling them enemies. For example, I went to Baghlan province, where the new director of the NDS is arresting people because they are Pashtun, wear turbans or have a beard. He calls them Taliban. So how will peace come? [...] The government must fire such people from their jobs. They must change their policy so that peace can be possible.[4]

Once this 'catalysing' process took off and the Taliban reached the critical mass needed to be the dominant force in vast regions of the country, they relied on social pressure to affect the choices of many:

>...if someone did not join the Taliban, the villagers did not think well of that person. They would find excuses to fight me and beat me, because most of them were with the Taliban. [...] At the beginning the elders would also convince us to join the Taliban. [...] The Taliban were also insulting and beating the elders. The elders, out of fear, were building relationships with the Taliban and campaigning for them.[5]

## From spontaneity to organisation

As discussed in Chapters 1 and 2, harassment and persecution by pro-government groups and by US forces was a major factor in the original mobilisation of the Taliban insurgency. The persecution of individuals formerly associated with the Taliban was mentioned as a primary cause of the development of the insurgency by 13% of 140 interviewees, both field operative Taliban and village elders. Among the elders, the percentage was even higher, at 14.5%. Abuse by police and foreign troops against the wider population was mentioned by 68% of interviewees as a primary cause. Among elders the percentage was slightly higher, nearing 70%.[6] Harassment and violence of pro-government groups and of the security forces continued to drive recruits to the Taliban even in 2014–15.[7]

Much has been said about the thousands of young Afghans lured into joining the Taliban for money. Undoubtedly over the years the Taliban have improved the financial package they offer to volunteers. In the early years of the jihad, Taliban fighters and commanders did not receive regular salaries. This was only introduced gradually by the military commissions and by the best-funded *loy mahazes*. Whenever funds became available through taxes or donations, or booty was captured, the members of the group would receive a share of the capital. The *shuras* began their support by sending in shoes and clothes on top of weapons. Gradually salaries were introduced with the decisive help of the *shuras* based in Pakistan. By 2007 it was common for the main Taliban *shura*s to pay salaries to their fighters, initially Afs5,000 (equivalent to $65.90 USD in March 2019)/month per fighter, rising later to Afs7–10,000. That was one of their attractions, and one of the reasons why the independent Taliban fronts mostly disappeared as the *shura*s expanded their reach. By 2015 part-timers received 10,000 Pakistani rupees, part-time small commanders 14,000 and full-timers twice that. A 5,000 Pakistani rupees hazard pay bonus was paid while on operations. By 2014 almost all Taliban interviewees agreed that few Taliban would be willing to serve anymore without being paid their salary. Some interviewees also mentioned 'prizes' paid for each police or soldier killed, up to Afs50,000.[8]

As salaries became increasingly regular, the attraction of the Taliban to the average villager increased. Many unemployed 'normal persons and fathers' joined the local Taliban's forces.[9] Even a Taliban group commander admitted that some of his colleagues were motivated by the prospect of looting.[10]

Still this does not mean that the Taliban are mercenaries, any more than any soldier fighting for any government, who also receives a salary. By 2014 the Taliban's salaries were roughly in line with what the Afghan government paid, but volunteers joining the Taliban faced a much higher risk of getting killed, maimed or injured than the average Afghan policeman or soldier. In fact, as we have discussed in Chapter 4, Taliban losses were heavy, and many Taliban saw tens of comrades killed and injured. Although improving, the financial conditions offered by the Taliban were modest considering the risk. The status of insurgent or 'warrior' was perhaps a stronger factor in attracting recruits. As an elder put it:

> The students of the schools are young, and they are not able to differentiate between wrong and right. The Taliban can easily attract them by providing them with a motorcycle, money, a mobile and so on. Of course, a young person around 15–18 would accept this offer, take the weapon and start working for the Taliban.[11]

One Haqqani fighter commented:

> Most of the youths are jobless and they think that it is better to join the Taliban. They say that rather than being jobless it is better to wage jihad. And then they also earn some money.[12]

The elders described the increasingly loose village youth as 'dodgy guys',[13] but, from another perspective, the elders' social control was breaking down and the Taliban (among others) found plenty of willing recruits among young villagers who could not see a better future for themselves.

The Taliban by contrast tend to suggest that Afghans were joining the insurgency primarily to express their opposition to Western presence in the country, as well as to establish a genuinely Islamic government in Afghanistan and, in some cases, fight 'northern domination'. The impact of Western withdrawal in 2014 tested the extent to which this was a motivating factor. As the withdrawal took place, the Afghan army and police dramatically curtailed their patrolling of rural areas. This removed the other often stated reason for Taliban mobilisation, that is, harassment and persecution by government forces. Almost all Taliban and former Taliban interviewed had a low opinion of the fighting abilities of Afghan police and army and believed these forces would not be able to resist the Taliban once the western forces had left the country.[14] Most local Taliban interviewees suggested that they would continue fighting.[15] Some, however, indicated they would quit.[16]

## From conservative rebels to professional insurgents

The 'ideological' motivation of Taliban recruits was not necessarily the result of high awareness of the texts or of a sophisticated indoctrination process; it was often more from conservative views:

> We do not accept that our daughters, wives and sisters will go to work and university or school without an Islamic hijab. We don't want our daughters and sisters to study together with boys in one class. If we were to take control of Afghanistan we would make a separate university with female teachers for our sisters and daughters. Afghanistan is going to face a crisis if this situation continues, I believe that if the situation carries on like this, the culture of Afghanistan will change and its people will copy Western culture.[17]

The radicalism of the Taliban commanders often looked like the hardened views of combatants who believed they were fighting for a superior cause, had endured a lot and had little patience for the petty interests and concerns of the villagers:

> I told [the elders] that instead of coming and joining us in the jihad, instead of buying weapons for us to continue the jihad against the foreign troops and the Afghan government, you come and ask us to let the elections happen. [...] It was a very funny request; they all know that we have been fighting against this shit government for a long time. Many of our friends were martyred and wounded in this battle but those villagers, without thinking, came and asked us to let the elections happen.[18]

This would seem to suggest that ideology was a crucial factor driving mobilisation into the Taliban, but it might also suggest the gradual development of a 'military professional' ethos, separating at least the full-time Taliban from the society that originated them. In the mobile Taliban forces, recruits experienced a different environment and were fully socialised into the Taliban organisation. Whatever their reasons for joining, the Taliban would turn the recruits into 'real Taliban'.[19]

## Nostalgia of the old days

Among the Taliban interviewed there were two different views on what was the Taliban's most difficult period. Many interviewees indicated that the early days of the insurgency had been very tough because of the lack of funding and equipment, as well as of local support. In the words of a fighter from Nangarhar:

> The worst time for the Taliban was from 2001 up to 2006 and 2007. In this time we were faced with financial problems, logistical problems, and many other problems. In that time one good thing was the support of the local people. Nowadays that support for the Taliban has decreased a lot.[20]

Others instead insist on 'how good the old times were'. The nostalgia for the first generation of field commanders of the post-2001 Taliban is often mentioned by the surviving first generation of fighters.[21] For example:

Q: Do you think that if Ibrahim were still alive, things would be different now?

A: Yes, everything would be better, firstly because there would not be disunity among the Taliban. The Taliban would have advanced so much further and they would not be in this stage where they are now. From 2003 till 2007 the Taliban grew quickly and if we are not growing now, it is because we lost good leaders.[22]

Q: What type of *mahaz* leader was Faruq?

A: He was a great leader. He was always smiling and all the people were happy because of him. People respected him. Truly, he was undertaking jihad without any [ulterior motives], not like nowadays with commanders who [answer to the] money of foreign countries.[23]

The former Taliban were united but now they are divided in different groups. Before the Taliban were not disturbing people and were only working for jihad, but the current Taliban are disturbing people and taking food forcefully from the people. Before, the Taliban accepted the *layha* of the Rahbari Shura, but the current Taliban do not work according to the *layha*. Before, the Taliban were fighting for jihad and Islam – the current Taliban are fighting for their own [enrichment].[24]

If these leaders were alive – Mullah Dadullah, Ibrahim, Faruq – they would never let the Taliban to be divided [as it is, into the] Peshawar Shura, Quetta Shura and Miran Shah Shura. Now there are three *shura*s and [each is divided further]. [...] If they do not give money to the Taliban fighters, they will not fight for one day. So we cannot truly call them Taliban, we can call them salary-takers. Those who [are here just to] take a salary, we cannot call this jihad. In jihad one must sacrifice their sons and their own money. They don't spend their own money; they even take money from people.[25]

In the early days of the insurgency, there was an aura highlighting the Taliban as Robin Hood-type figures who were fighting thieves and protecting the communities from militia commanders. Their aims were 'pure jihad' and 'justice'. Then the taxation, the arbitrary killings, the dependence of foreign funding, the obsession with raising more funds, the campaign against schools, Taliban infighting, the massive reliance on mines and using civilians as sheilds combined to spoil their reputation.[26] The institutionalisation of the Taliban, with the introduction of regular, standardised pay, was seen by many of the first generation as evidence that the character of a genuine jihad movement had been lost.[27] One former commander from Kandahar province put it this way:

From 2004 till 2008 we did not give salaries to the men and none requested money. They even they brought their own money to spend in the way of Allah. But now you can say all the fighters and Taliban are getting their salaries. [...] We can say now there is fighting of business and chairs.[28]

For other Taliban, this institutionalisation is instead the very sign of the groups's success:

We are no longer like before. [...] Before, nobody around the world knew us, they didn't know who the Taliban were at the beginning, but now the whole international community and America seek to make peace with us. They don't even know how to stand against us. [...] We can carry out our attacks wherever we want; we even carried out attacks near the presidential palace. The government is increasingly getting undermined and losing their confidence and international credibility.[29]

Now the Taliban are more powerful than our time because in those days people did not know of the Taliban. They carried out operations in secret. But now that they have foreign countries' support, financially they are strong, logistically they are strong, and they have a lot of people. From any perspective they are strong.[30]

The quotes cited above highlight the trade-offs of the transition from a spontaneous rebellion towards a shadow state, with all its requirements in terms of 'realpolitik'.

## Foreign funding and the end of romantic rebellion

In the world of realpolitik, politics and war cost money. This book has discussed the history of Taliban funding, though the picture is incomplete as there are significant gaps, particularly for the first few years of the insurgency. The main trends are however clear. Over the years the Taliban leaderships developed their capacity to raise tax at the *shura* level, but as of 2014 tax revenue was modest, contributing only around 8–9 per cent of total Taliban leadership revenue (that is what accrued to the Finance Commissions of Quetta, Peshawar and Miran Shah). Contributions by drug smugglers contributed a similar amount, as much of the revenue was captured by a variety of Taliban actors before it reached the Finance Commissions. Other contributions by Afghan donors, typically businessmen, accounted for another 4 per cent of the Finance Commission's revenue. For the three *shuras* of Quetta, Peshawar and Miran Shah Taliban, almost 80 per cent of the revenue available to the leadership came from abroad. This figure excludes the Mashhad Office, which was exclusively funded by the Iranian Pasdaran, as well as the *loy mahaz*es and everybody else raising funds outside the Finance Commissions. This external flow of funds can be distinguished into three types:

- funding from foreign governments: 54%;
- funding from private donors abroad: 10%;
- funding from other jihadist organisations, mostly Al-Qaida and, for a short period, Islamic State: 16%.

Notably, foreign governments accounted for the bulk of the money received by the Finance Commissions by 2014. Taliban finances therefore largely mirrored the finances of the Kabul government, which in 2014 was 71 per cent dependent on aid for funding its budget, without counting direct expenditure by donors.[31]

In 2014, while the leadership was satisfied with the funds accruing to the Finance Commissions of the three *shuras* (close to $900 million in 2014), many Taliban local leaders, *loy mahaz* leaders and individual political leaders still had an unquenched thirst for funding, to enable them expand their own group, *mahaz* or faction, or for personal benefit. This thirst often led to competition and even infighting among Taliban.

Episodes of corruption are known to have taken place among the Taliban. Some have been discussed already throughout the book. Sales of weapons on the black market for example were discussed in 'Strengthening of Combat Support' (Chapter 6).

Cases of governors removed due to corruption or rule breaking are known. The governor of Badghis Mullah Lal Mohammad, for example was sacked because he was found stealing the salaries of local Taliban. The governor of Faryab, Salahuddin, was sacked after he was found to be taking money from NGOs to allow projects that did not satisfy to the Taliban's rules.[32] The military commissions were not exempt from corruption either. In 2013 in eastern Afghanistan, three provincial *nizami massuleen* were sacked following allegations that they misused Chinese funding.[33]

The most intense competition was a case of unaccounted revenue sources belonging to the Taliban apparatus. In some cases for example the competing Taliban *loy mahaz*es clashed over the control of drug revenue:[34]

> There is also fighting among the Taliban themselves. Like in Nawa district where Mullah Janan and Mullah Qayum Akhund are fighting for control. [...] Maybe in around 12 districts they are fighting for control... it's because of the opium.[35]

There were even reports of Taliban commanders lobbying their bosses for appointment to lucrative posts in the Taliban system.[36] When Zakir clashed with Akhtar Mohammad Mansur within the Quetta Shura in 2010, he was cut off from receiving any drug revenue.[37] It was not until much later that Zakir managed to extract revenue from the drug smugglers. In 2014–15, Zakir offered extra services to smugglers, such as securing caravans. This enabled him to impose a 25 per cent tax on narco-trafficking, compared to the 15 per cent levied by Akhtar Mohammad.[38] Some Taliban interviewees portrayed the fighting as often driven by the desire to control smuggling routes:

> The fighting [in Marjah] was because of the opium. People grew opium, but moving the opium was very difficult because of government control. One of the reasons was to open the way, to move the opium to Pakistan. Not just the opium grown in Marjah, but in other districts as well. The routes were blocked.[39]

This tension of course only applies to parts of Afghanistan where substantial revenue was available, such as Helmand, parts of Kandahar, and Sayedabad (Wardak). In Sayedabad the competition was concerned with spots on the highway where Taliban groups could prey on convoys or make escort deals with security companies in exchange for cash. The Taliban sometimes try to contain this unauthorised extortion, though with little success. In the race to secure the best spots on the highway, skirmishing between competing Taliban groups was common.[40]

In most districts of Afghanistan there were no major resources that would attract the attention of Taliban powerbrokers. Despite this, as discussed in 'Local Fund Raising' (Chapter 2), the Taliban Finance Commissions were surprised by the revenue raised by Zakat and Ushr, and eventually allowed local Taliban to keep a modest amount for their own use.

Overall, how did the Taliban leaders fare in monopolising total revenue? There is a dearth of studies focused on revenue generation in insurgencies, and therefore no real source for comparison. Certainly there have been plenty of accusations of Taliban embezzling funds, and bypassing official Taliban channels to channel funds towards a particular *mahaz* or faction. Even before 2010 there were accusations that Mullah Baradar was manipulating Taliban funds to the advantage of his own *mahaz* (see 'The Establishment of the Loy Mahaz' in Chapter 2). The tenure of Akhtar Mohammad Mansur as deputy of a dead or dying man (2010–15) and then as supreme leader (2015–16) represented a new level of controversy over handling funds from leaders. Mansur controlled the 'drug office' of the Quetta Financial Commission and was routinely accused by his colleagues of siphoning funds for his *mahaz*, the fastest growing Quetta-based *loy mahaz*es in 2010–15, and for his family. Today, individuals who were close to Mansur acknowledge that he accumulated large funds, which he passed on to his political heir (his cousin Obeidullah Ishaqzai) after his death in May 2016.[41]

Reliance on external support could not remain secret for long. The Taliban developed a reputation for being stooges of first Pakistan and then Iran. This compromised their legitimacy as a resistance movement against a puppet government supported by the West. The abundance of funding destroyed the original romantic ethos of the Taliban and turned them into simply a colossal fighting machine, unsure of its overall aims.

## The impossible centralisation

During the period covered by this book, two attempts to centralise power within the Taliban's military took place. The Peshawar Shura began the first attempt when it launched its new Military Commission model. The Peshawar

Shura implemented the model fairly successfully in eastern, central and north-eastern Afghanistan at least for several years, before it imploded due to a collapse in funding. The model survived in the Northern Shura, however. The Peshawar Shura tried to export its model to the Quetta Shura, allying with some local 'reformers'. This attempt failed and it also deepened the crisis of the Quetta Shura.

The other attempt was launched by Akhtar Mohammad Mansur, the main opponent of Peshawar-style centralisation, when he consolidated power within the Quetta Shura in 2014. His approach to centralisation was probably meant to be a continuation of what Mullah Baradar was trying to achieve in 2009–10, that is, a patrimonial model of concentration of power in the hands of one person at the top (the operational leader of the Taliban). There are similarities between this model and the Haqqani's, though the latter have been much more successful in putting it into practice. One reason for the Haqqanis' success might be that they adopted a centralised system from the beginning and have been using this same system since the 1980s. Their cadres were familiar with the approach. In addition, the Haqqanis slowly built it up by generating their own cadres and recruiting at the grassroots level, instead of going down the Quetta Shura path of co-opting existing armed groups from diverse backgrounds.

Mansur's attempt to seize overall control in 2015 looked like a coup to many of his colleagues. He caused stark opposition to his rule with his efforts to move away from the classical polycentrism of the Taliban. The legacy of this attempt is the seemingly permanent breakaway of the so-called Rasool Shura and the persistent divisions within the Quetta Shura, with large groupings of Taliban commanders and leaders refusing to cooperate with the leadership.

The Peshawar and Northern Shuras were run primarily by former members of Hizb-i Islami, who opportunistically jumped on the Taliban's bandwagon. They brought their Muslim Brotherhood-esque political culture to the group, including a belief in the virtues of centralisation. Their ability to put in practice a centralised command system is the classical exception that proves the rule.

## Managing polycentrism

In practice, the 'original' Taliban's system did change after 2009, but more to improve or patch up the management of polycentrism, rather than replace it.

A typical result of this was the establishment of the Coordination Commission at the end of 2014. This change only had a limited impact, however. Another even less successful example was the establishment of the Central Military Commission at the end of 2013. Talks of reunifying the Taliban under a single chain of command, common after 2010, focused on the imposition of a limited degree of authority of control over the different top-level *shura*s, and never to abolish polycentrism.

The Taliban sought to create a range of institutions that would regulate polycentrism at various levels. The various commissions used funding and supplies to impose adherence to some rules and regulations by the Taliban, for example. Unable or unwilling to create a unified chain of command, the Taliban gradually created new semi-autonomous structures which at least had a stronger internal chain of command: the Quetta Military Commission is a classic example. These new structures co-existed with the old ones. In essence, the Taliban abolished or suspended polycentrism in specific sections of their military structure, particularly when these sections were created anew. But at the top polycentrism was never seriously challenged, not only as far as the different *shura*s were concerned, but also as far as the different structures of the Quetta Shura. So, the *loy mahaze*s were established alongside the governors' groups, and then the Military Commission was established alongside both. Finally, the village *mahaze*s were established again under the authority of the governors.

## The missing 'collegial leadership'

The difficulty the Taliban experienced in centralising revenue can be ascribed to the lack of a strong hierarchy among leaders, who at the same time failed to establish a genuinely collegial leadership. That perhaps would have been the only way to successfully manage polycentrism. As a Pashtun-centric movement, the Taliban absorbed Pashtun political culture, which is hostile to hierarchy even for the south. Even a supreme leader would only be a *primus inter pares*, with little coercive power and authority to take decisions on their own. The very moment Akhtar Mohammad Mansur tried to consolidate his leadership in 2014–15, resistance against him built up, even among former allies. The exception to this rule was the Haqqanis, who remained a family business throughout the 2002–15 period. The Haqqanis maintained cohesiveness by insulating themselves from society and expanding their networks downwards through recruitment among Afghan communities in

Pakistan. Of the main Taliban *shura*s, the Haqqanis had the poorest community connections in Afghanistan, and the smallest number of local Taliban forces compared to their whole armed cohort. The Mashhad Office was also cohesive, but likely due to the total control exercised over it by the Iranian Pasdaran, who brooked no dissent.

Defined as 'a set of continuing political leadership structures and practices through which significant decisions are taken in common by a small, face-to-face body with no single member dominating their initiation or determination,'[42] 'collegial leadership' could have been the solution to fill this leadership vacuum. Max Weber identified among the factors leading to the rise of collegial leadership the need to represent status groups and territorial entities, the absence of a leader due to mutual jealousies among those competing for leadership or to antipathy to the individual strongman, and the need to reconcile divergent interests.[43] This would seem to fit the Taliban well. Indeed, the Peshawar Shura had a functional collegial leadership in 2005–14, before the Pakistani ISI started interfering, pressuring the group to favour the minority Toor-e Pagri and hand control over the Peshawar Shura to them.

Some of the structures required for exercising collegial leadership in Quetta were also developed over time. In the early days of the Rahbari Shura, its members would sit together with tea and discuss matters. Mullah Baradar was acknowledged as leader by virtue of his skills as a mediator and a persuader, and never had the strength to coerce his colleagues. Indeed, the very accusations of hidden manipulations and murder plots, whether true or not, confirm if nothing else that he did not have the power to dismiss or expel fellow leaders like Mullah Dadullah, Faruq and others. There were no formal checks and balances in place, however, and it all rested on shared views of how leaders should behave.

When Akhtar Mohammad Mansur tried to break with these traditions in 2015 and accumulate the power to make decisions quickly and authoritatively, his colleagues discovered that there were no written rules on how to select a successor to Mullah Omar, as well as on many other aspects of the Taliban's organisational structures. The reluctance to formalise rules is not an exclusive feature of the Taliban and might have to do with late state development in Afghanistan; after all, leadership problems have long been a feature of Afghan political organisations.

This begs the question of why collegial leadership functioned better in the Peshawar Shura than in the Quetta Shura. The leadership of the Peshawar

Shura was cohesive enough to need polycentrism no longer – they opted for centralisation. The political culture of former Hizb-i Islami cadres mattered but was not the only factor. Once the Peshawar Shura started losing its cohesiveness at the top, its centralised command and control system also started disintegrating. Another reason might be that for several years (2005–14) external donors to the Peshawar Shura were aligned in their intent and the Shura leadership agreed with those, so there was no incentive for donors to meddle with the decision-making process of the *shura*. The same did not apply to the Quetta Shura, which started clashing with its donors in 2009. As discussed in Chapter 5, the internal struggles of the Quetta Shura did have external patrons, even if internal reasons for infighting existed. Another confirmation that this was a principal factor can be found in the fact that in 2015, as the convergence of donor and leadership aims ceased, the Peshawar Shura started experiencing dysfunctionality akin to what the Quetta Shura experienced since 2010 (Chapter 7, 'The crisis of the Peshawar Shura').

Whatever the exact sources of disunity among Taliban leaders, divergence at the top weakened the efforts to centralise revenue, making the Taliban less effective and more dependent on external donors. In turn this dependence on donors emerged as a major factor threatening not only the Taliban's ability to win the war, but also their own viability as the hegemonic insurgent movement in Afghanistan. As donors started becoming critical of the Taliban's failure to bring the conflict to a close despite the withdrawal of almost all NATO troops, it became increasingly difficult for the Taliban to reconcile the support of donors bitterly opposed to each other. As discussed in Chapter 7, Iran and the Gulf monarchies, involved in an increasingly bitter confrontation in Syria, Iraq and Yemen, by 2014 were beginning to view Afghanistan as another battlefield for their proxy wars. Demands that Taliban factions paid by either Iran or the Gulf monarchies cut off relations with colleagues paid by their opposition became increasingly common, making coherent action impossible for the Taliban. The 2014 elections, discussed in Chapter 7, were a case in point.

### The downsides of polycentrism

Unable to establish a genuinely collegial leadership, representative of the different centres of power within the movement, the Taliban remained trapped in a somewhat dysfunctional polycentrism. The downsides of polycentrism were not apparent as long as the Taliban were confronting ill-trained and equipped militias, whether these were police, army or other militarised groups. With the deployment of ISAF to the provinces, particularly in the south in 2006, and with the gradual deployment of newly trained Afghan army and police, the old Taliban approach to fighting became inadequate.

Extensive tinkering with old style polycentrism in 2010 added new life to the Taliban's military model. The Taliban rightly saw the withdrawal of Western combat forces in 2014 as their success: they had convinced their enemies that they were vulnerable to defeat. The resilience of the polycentric model was fully demonstrated. But this very success also laid the ground for the deficiencies of that very model to be exposed. After 2014 the Taliban wanted to go on the strategic offensive and start seizing Afghanistan cities. Despite occasional tactical successes, however, the Taliban as a whole were not able to exploit the initiative they gained, and were locked into a strategic stalemate with the Afghan government's forces, supported by US air assets and special forces. In fact, as western and Afghan forces started pulling out of large parts of Afghanistan in 2014, additional tensions within the Taliban started surfacing: the external threat that had been keeping the Taliban more or less united seemed was disappearing.

The idea of a full centralisation was dead by 2015; nobody tried to revive it in Quetta, after its supporters had been crushed decisively in the previous months. By the end of 2015, the Taliban were faced with the erosion of the near monopoly over the insurgency that they had established in previous years (due to the emergence of the Islamic State in Afghanistan); and with a forthcoming upswing in US participation in the conflict, they missed their best opportunity to end the war in their favour.

# EPILOGUE

The war did not end in 2015, it just changed its nature. If anything, it became even more intractable. For the Taliban, the problem in 2015 was that the juncture of ISAF's disbandment and the presidential elections in 2014 created opportunities to seek a political settlement with Kabul, which the group's main sponsor, Pakistan, insisted they should pursue. While the Taliban started fighting each other over the prospect of a peaceful settlement, the new administration of Ashraf Ghani in Kabul gained precious time.

## 2016: Back to war

The failure of the 2015-pre-talks, and the near collapse of the Quetta Shura, pushed the Taliban (and their Pakistani sponsors) back towards the battlefield. Some of the Taliban decided that negotiations would not deliver them any positives. Others, however, and likely their sponsors, wanted to strengthen the Taliban's negotiating position after a year of obvious and debilitating infighting.

The trend had already been visible in the autumn of 2015, when the battle of Kunduz signalled that the previously downscaled Taliban military campaign had resumed and expanded. The main signal of a change among the Pakistani handlers of the Taliban was the appointment of Serajuddin Haqqani as responsible for the military campaign for the Quetta Shura, with clear ISI backing. As a result, he was able to concentrate so much power (he had oversight over all the military related commissions) that speculation circulated that he was the de facto leader of the southern Taliban. Akhtar Mansur must have been upset by this trend and have felt sidelined by the Pakistanis, as in March 2016 he fled to Iran to negotiate an agreement for support with the Revolutionary Guards. What might have become of this will never be known, as he was killed by an American drone in Baluchistan while on his way back to Quetta, on 21 May 2016.

The death of Mansur removed a controversial leader, but also eliminated one of the few Taliban leaders who had the resources to rule over the movement, if not fully legitimately lead it. His successor Haibatullah Akhund tried more successfully to strike a balance between Iran and Pakistan. He travelled to Iran two days after being selected as leader, on 25 May, but came back straight away and to work with the Pakistanis to sustain the momentum of the Taliban's offensive. This would be the hallmark of Haibatullah's 'donor management strategy' for the coming two and a half years.

A cleric with no experience of military leadership, Haibatullah could only let his far more experienced first deputy Serajuddin continue the pursuit of capturing cities. During 2016 the Taliban repeatedly assaulted Lashkargah, the capital of Helmand, and came close at least once to overwhelming its defences. The Taliban also entered Kunduz again, and Tarin Kot, the capital of Uruzgan.

In terms of headline-catching assaults, 2016 stood out as the Taliban's most successful year. But in terms of getting any closer to winning the war, the attempted capture of several cities only showed that the Taliban had missed the opportunity in 2015, when the US political leadership was keen to keep the training mission Resolute Support a strictly non-combat operation. After the fall of Kunduz, the Americans agreed to recommit to the battlefield, and increasingly did so, with airstrikes and the deployment of small units of special forces, to aid Afghan units on the ground. All the Taliban assaults of 2016 were repulsed even before they managed to completely seize control of any city.

It became clear during 2016 that the Taliban's frontal assaults, whether by day or night, in good or bad weather, could not beat the Americans. The Taliban would take high casualties on approaching the target city, and then in a matter of days the Taliban would be repulsed by a counter-attack. Entering a city would embarrass Kabul and the Americans, and highlight the weakness of the Afghan armed forces, but not win the war.

The Taliban's efforts were compounded by their ever more complicated internal dynamics. Thanks to the realignment of various donors, 2016 saw the final demise of the Peshawar Shura as an autonomous centre of Taliban power. In autumn 2015 Shura shut down for three months, having run out of funding, and then re-opened as a subsidiary of Quetta, de facto controlled by the Haqqanis. But a good half or even more of its members abandoned it, and many sought to re-organise into a new Shura. The Shura of the North, as it became known, took shape between the end of 2015 and early 2016, under the leadership of Qari Baryal, the former head of the Peshawar Military Commission. The former Hizb-i Islami element of the Peshawar Shura quit en masse to disperse or to join the Shura of the North, which received Iranian and Russian support and remained hostile to the Pakistanis, as Baryal had been in previous years. The net result was a serious weakening of Taliban activities in eastern Afghanistan.

In the meantime, Haibatullah finally recognised the Mashhad Office as a full 'Shura'. Despite this, the Mashhad Shura refused to bow to Haibatullah and remained fiercely autonomous from Quetta (but under the control of the Iranian Revolutionary Guards).

With the arrival of Haibatullah at the top of the Taliban in May 2016, the influence of the Iranians at the centre of the Taliban power structure massively increased. In the coming months and year, the Iranians might well have overtaken Pakistan as the top source of Taliban funding. 2016 also signalled, as already hinted, the beginnings of Russian sponsorship of the Taliban. Initially limited to the Shura of the North, Russian support soon extended to the Mashhad Office, and most importantly to Haibatullah. The Russians also started providing direct supplies and facilities (especially medical ones) in Tajikistan. The Russians operated in strict coordination with the Iranians, who introduced them to the Taliban, and might at least in part have been motivated by the desire to counter the rising influence of the Islamic State.

The ability of the Islamic State to keep inflicting resounding defeats on the Taliban, despite the overwhelming numerical superiority of the latter, is likely to have raised concerns in Moscow, as well as in Iran. These two countries viewed IS as a 'Saudi project' aimed at undermining their influence and their allies in the region. Haibatullah managed to inflict a bloody defeat on the Islamic State in Zabul in the first few months of his mandate but IS recovered promptly and fought back. By the end of 2016 it was clear that the Taliban were going to be fighting on two fronts for the foreseeable future.

## 2017: A year of indecision

The failure of the campaign against the cities to produce results in 2016, and a new turn in Pakistani attitudes towards Afghanistan, resulted in the freezing of the campaign and a return to the default asymmetric tactics at which the Taliban over the years had become quite adept.

The Pakistanis, worried by newly elected US President Trump's bellicose statements, did not want the Taliban to assault cities just weeks after Trump's August 2016 speech. All major operations were frozen. At the same time some serious re-thinking was going on among the Taliban about the tactics that they had been using to assault the cities, with great loss of men and little permanent gains. A consensus emerged that the Taliban should develop infiltration tactics in order to enter the cities without getting exposed to US airstrikes. Once inside the city, smaller but better trained Taliban forces could hide in buildings and mix with the population. To make these tactics implementable, the Taliban formed new units called Sare Qeta, essentially special forces units trained to operate in small groups.

Although the Taliban were inflicting possibly heavier casualties than ever on the Afghanistan security forces, thanks to a renewed commitment to asymmetric tactics, their internal debates were largely about an ongoing power struggle between Haibatullah and Serajuddin. Serajuddin embodied the widespread opposition within Taliban ranks towards close relations with Russia and towards the campaign against the Islamic State, which was still just another jihadist organisation. He also embodied the militarist approach, that is the belief that decisive military victory was possible.

Haibatullah, on the other hand, took a centrist position within the Taliban. He side-lined a group of 'reconcilers' who wanted to end the war soon and at any cost, perhaps betting on the transformation of the Taliban into a political movement. These reconcilers had the sympathy of Saudi Arabia, and considerable support among the local Taliban units, under the control of the governors. He also fought to contain the influence of hardliners like Serajuddin, who were in abundance, especially in the east. He argued instead for reconciliation and ending the war only at certain conditions, set high enough to make progress in negotiations either unlikely or slow. Clearly, Haibatullah was waiting for the green light of his sponsors (at least Pakistan) before engaging seriously in negotiations.

Haibatullah was not elected in a proper Taliban congress and therefore his legitimacy suffered. Throughout 2017 the pressure on him to hold congress and receive a proper investiture increased greatly, as Serajuddin openly challenged him. Haibatullah hesitated, uncertain of whether he had the support to make it in the face of powerful opposing candidates like Serajuddin. In retaliation for Haibatullah clinging on to his half legitimate position,

Serajuddin suspended all military cooperation of his men with those of Haibatullah. By mid-2017 Pakistanis and Taliban agreed in principle that it was time to resume assaults on cities, lest the Taliban be perceived as weakened. But Haibatullah was at this point unable to mount major operations without Serajuddin on board. The Taliban's image suffered from their perceived inactivity.

From the point of view of the Taliban, 2017 was a wasted year and it had the potential to worsen as Taliban cohesion vis-à-vis the Islamic State frayed. The Haqqani network reached agreements and even formed alliances with the Islamic State in Khorasan (IS-K) towards the end of 2017, at a time when it was being challenged by Haibatullah.

## 2018: War of attrition

In 2018 Iran-Pakistan relations, already far from their peak in 2017, worsened. The Iranians were far from assured that any kind of cooperation with their eastern neighbour in handling the Taliban would be possible in the future. They assumed that eventually, ever increasing Saudi pressure on the Pakistani army would force it to dump any type of cooperation with Iran.

As a result, in late 2017 to early 2018 the Iranians, who since 2015 had been cautious to encourage their Taliban – hosted in Mashhad – to take active part in major operations against Kabul's forces, decide to help the Taliban mount a large campaign for taking control of Farah province, in western Afghanistan. The main rationale of the campaign was to open better supply lines to southern Afghanistan, allowing the Iranians to support Taliban allies in the absence of Pakistani cooperation. The new campaign resulted in the successful resumption of the Taliban's campaign against the cities. The Taliban entered Farah city twice in 2018, in February and May. Most importantly, it was taken without frontal assaults due to the more sophisticated infiltration tactics of Taliban special units.

The same tactics were deployed effectively again in the assault on Ghazni city in August, supported this time by the Pakistanis. In Farah and in Ghazni the Afghan security forces clearly demonstrated the inability to cope with the Taliban without US support. At the same time the Taliban were running their asymmetric campaign with increasing effectiveness, thanks to improved training and tactics. The campaign against the cities had resumed, but was no longer central to the Taliban efforts as it was in 2016. Instead, the Taliban campaign was now a war of attrition, punctuated by assaults against cities, meant to demonstrate the Taliban's military proficiency even to the most distracted observers. In 2018 the casualties taken by the Afghan security forces reached a new high.

In 2018 the Taliban also seemed to finally start get a grip on their Islamic State enemy. The Taliban were able to destroy an IS-K base in Derzab (Jowzjan) in July 2018. They were also able to increase pressure on IS-K throughout Afghanistan, after years of being on the defensive. Haqqani network cooperation with IS-K was reduced and pushed underground.

## Towards 2019: Talk and fight

By spring 2018 there were already signals that a new season of diplomatic contacts around the issue of reconciliation in Afghanistan was about to begin. The Trump administration, keen to quit Afghanistan before the 2020 presidential elections in the US, started to view accelerated negotiations as the only feasible way out. It even started pressuring President Ghani to do more to entice the Taliban to the negotiating table, and then to offer a deal that would appeal to them.

The Taliban were intrigued by the news that President Ghani was now ready to offer more substantial concessions to them, in exchange for a ceasefire and for an immediate start of formal talks. However, they also felt that Ghani was in a weak position, and would have to offer more if he wanted to spark serious negotiations before the presidential elections, planned for spring 2019. In the meantime, the Taliban did their best to remind everybody's of Ghani's weakness. Not only was their military campaign relentless, but the strike on Ghazni humiliated Ghani's military command. Similar to what had happened months earlier in Farah, the Taliban's plans for Ghazni city were not a mystery. Military intelligence and even casual observation revealed a growing concentration of Taliban forces around the city in the weeks and months prior to the attack. Still, the Afghan security forces protecting the city were caught by surprise.

For some time the new 'talk and fight' strategy managed to unite Haibatullah and Serajuddin. The former was in no hurry to start formal talks, but wanted to keep the door open for the future. The latter was not unduly worried about the prospect of talks, if they remained remote enough and the Taliban's combat forces had free rein to carry on fighting. The Pakistani ISI worked hard during the summer of 2018 to force Haibatullah and Serajuddin to collaborate again, seemingly with at least a degree of success.

## What to look for

Since this book is primarily concerned with the evolution of the Taliban's military machine, it is fitting to conclude it with an outline of the evolution of the Taliban's military machine post-2015.

As mentioned already, the appearance of the Sare Qeta 'special forces' has been the main military innovation of the Taliban in recent years. These elite units incorporate battle-tested commanders and fighters, who are retrained and deployed with the best equipment the Taliban can source, including night vision goggles. After early tests showed that the new units and their tactics were highly successful, the Taliban's military command decided to expand the size and the role of these units. Gradually the Sare Qeta have become the cornerstone of the Taliban's strategy. The local militias that had endured most of the war against ISAF have started being neglected and downsized, while within the Taliban's mobile forces the emphasis has been increasingly placed on elite formations. Much of the increased casualty rate of the Afghan security forces appears to have been due to this shift of the Taliban towards greater military professionalism. In 2018 the Taliban reportedly sent some of their best men to Lebanon for training by Hizbollah, thanks to a the sponsorship of the Iranian Revolutionary Guards.

As the Taliban were losing interest in 'people's war', they redoubled their efforts to obtain more advanced military equipment. Night goggles were a game changer, but the Taliban thought they needed more. In particular, they continued their search for anti-aircraft missiles. As of November 2018, Taliban sources hinted that they had obtained a few launchers in Pakistan and had used them to target Afghan air force helicopters.

A highlight of the Taliban's 'special forces' was that their creation and gradual expansion removed at least in part the need for a unified, centralised command and control system. Simply, most of the old Taliban military machine, with its multiple chains of command, became redundant or suitable at most for secondary and support roles. The neglect experienced by much of the old Taliban military machine translated however into political friction; declining funding encouraged the leaders of local Taliban units to sympathise with those Taliban leaders, such as Mullah Yakub, who advocated an immediate peace settlement. The episodes of fraternisation between local Taliban fighters and Afghan security forces during the Eid ceasefire of June 2018 highlighted this trend, to the embarrassment of the Taliban leadership. In reality, many of those local Taliban units had not been participating in the

Taliban's military campaign for a good couple of years. In Helmand, for example, the Taliban shadow governor pulled his local forces out of the campaign to take Lashkargah in 2016.

The implications of this worsening dichotomy between mobile forces becoming increasingly professionalised, and local forces becoming increasingly marginal, are yet to be explored. As of 2018, pro-reconciliation Taliban leaders have tried to connect with these local forces and their leaders as well as with external donors, in order to form a well-organised lobby, able, if not to take over the leadership, at least to force Haibatullah to compromise. At a time when Haibatullah has at least temporarily pacified the hardliners, he has been threatened by the rise of a 'moderates' faction.

As 2019 loomed, the embattled Islamic State looked less threatening to the Taliban, even if it did not intend to disappear from Afghanistan anytime soon. Having weathered the IS storm, the Taliban looked set to gain from this confrontation. By fighting IS and by appearing relatively moderate in comparison, the Taliban gained legitimacy internationally and internally, especially in areas of strong IS activity (such as Nangarhar). Their dealings with Russia added to a growing sense of Taliban pragmatism. The Taliban strengthened this trend by downscaling terrorist attacks in Kabul after January 2018. They could now potentially use this legitimacy to smooth their glide towards a political settlement favourable to them.

# ANNEX 1

## FIGURES

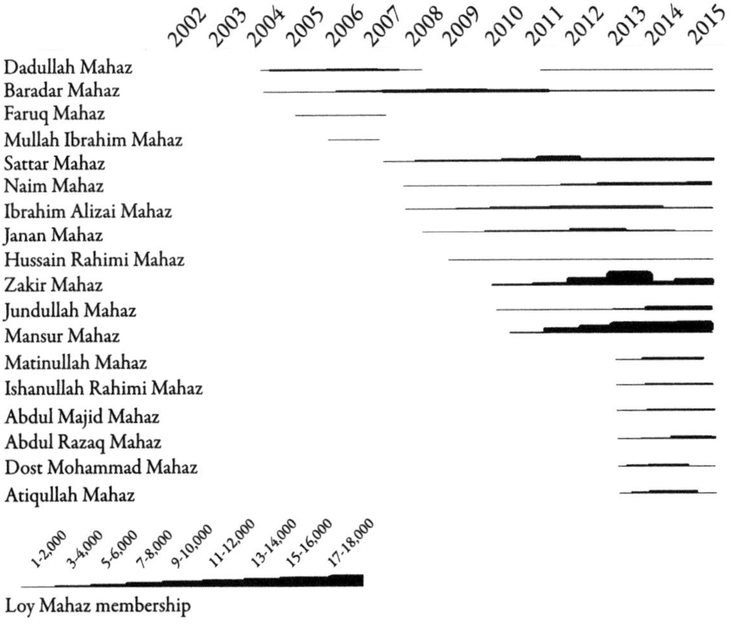

FIGURE 1: Chronology of Loy Mahaz establishment

*Source:* Interviews with Loy Mahaz members, 2013–15.

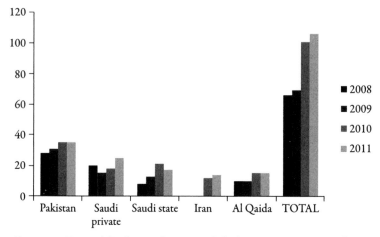

FIGURE 2: External funding to the Miran Shah Shura, 2008–11, in $ millions
*Source:* Interviews with finance cadres of the Miran Shah Shura, 2012.

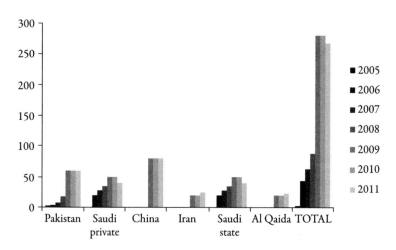

FIGURE 3: External funding to the Peshawar Shura, 2005–11, in $ millions
*Source:* Interviews with finance cadres of the Peshawar Shura, 2012.

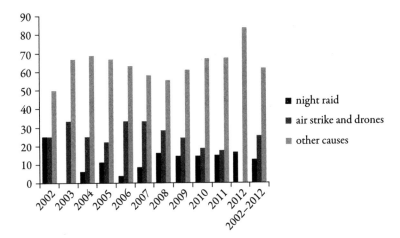

FIGURE 4: Causes of Taliban casualties according to *Al Somud*'s obituaries

*Source: Al Somud.*

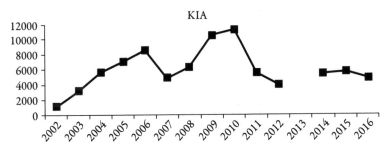

FIGURE 5: Numbers of Taliban members killed in action, 2002–16

*Source:* Contacts with administrative cadres in the shuras of Quetta, Miran Shah and Peshawar.

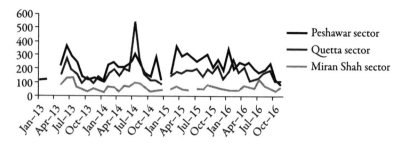

FIGURE 6: Monthly Taliban losses (KIA) by regional command, 2013–16

*Source:* Contacts with administrative cadres in the shuras of Quetta, Miran Shah and Peshawar.

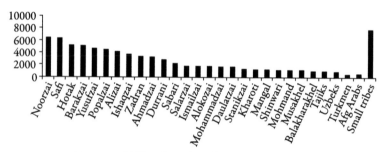

FIGURE 7: Taliban losses by tribe and ethnic group

*Source:* Contacts with administrative cadres in the shuras of Quetta, Miran Shah and Peshawar.

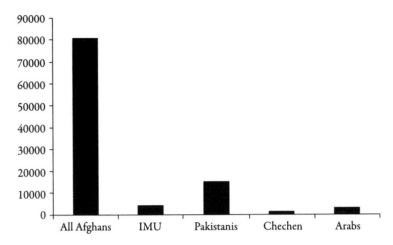

FIGURE 8: Taliban and allied losses by nationality

*Source:* Contacts with administrative cadres in the shuras of Quetta, Miran Shah and Peshawar.

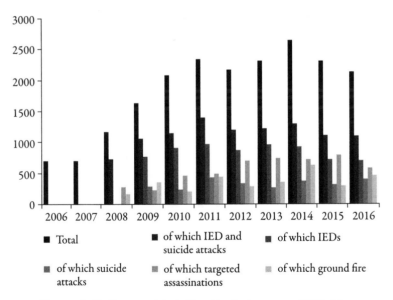

FIGURE 9: Civilian casualties inflicted by the insurgents, 2006–16

*Source:* UNAMA.

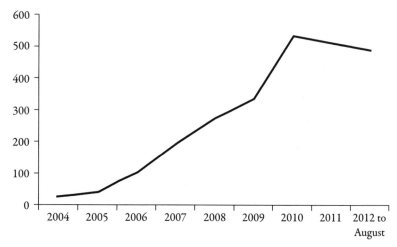

FIGURE 10: IED events in Afghanistan according to ISAF data, 2004–12 (August).
*Source:* ISAF.

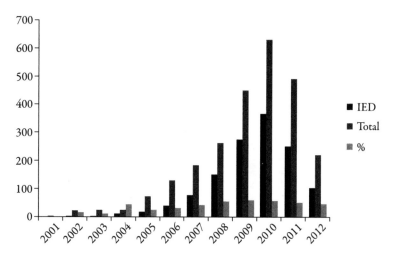

FIGURE 11: IED fatalities, ISAF and OEF forces
*Source:* http://icasualties.org/oef/

ANNEX 1

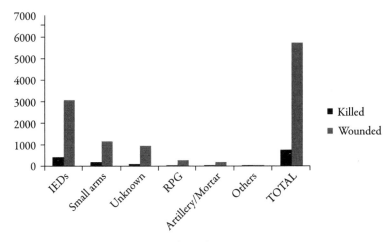

FIGURE 12: US losses by cause, 2001–10

*Source:* OEA Team report, 15 June 2010, in 'Taliban Top 5 Most Deadly Tactics Techniques and Procedures', TRADOC G-2 Intelligence Support Activity (TRISA), Ft Leavenworth, June 2010.

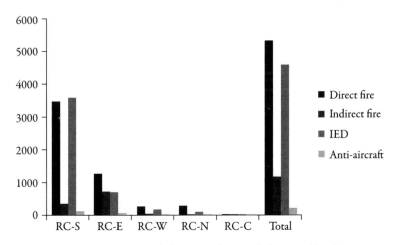

FIGURE 13: Insurgent attacks by region (Regional Command) and type, October 2009–March 2010

*Source:* ISAF officer, 2010.

## The Taliban's Chain of Command (2006)

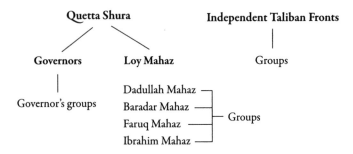

FIGURE 14: The Taliban's chain of command (2006)

*Source:* Interviews with Taliban leaders and cadres, 2013–15.

## The Taliban's Chains of Command (2013)

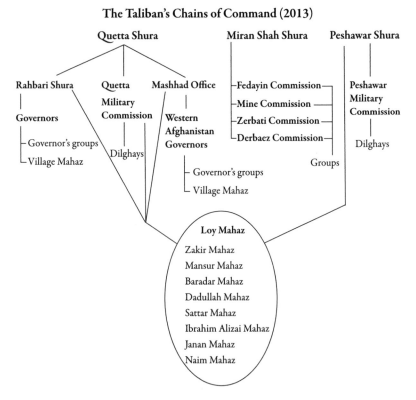

FIGURE 15: The Taliban's chains of command (2013)

*Source:* Interviews with Taliban leaders and cadres, 2013–15.

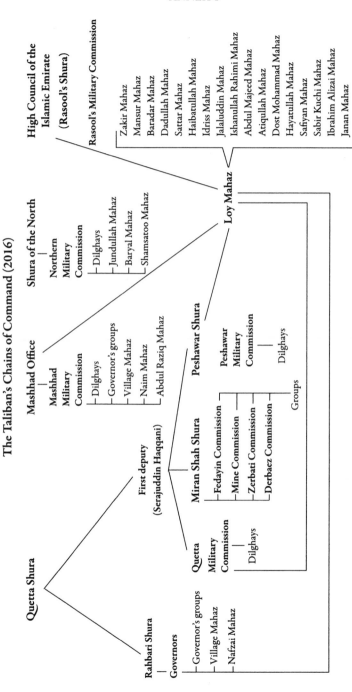

FIGURE 16: The Taliban's chains of command (2016)

*Source:* Interviews with Taliban leaders and cadres, 2013–15.

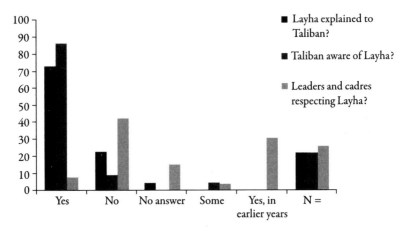

FIGURE 17: Taliban and the *layha*

*Source:* Interviews with commanders, former commanders, fighters and former fighters of the Taliban, 2014–15.

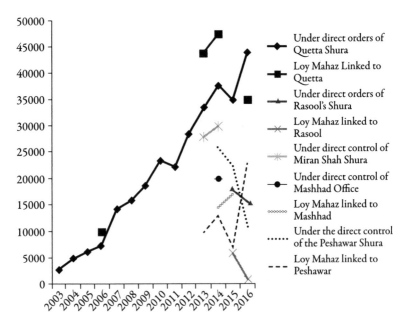

FIGURE 18: Taliban combat forces by *shura*, 2003–16

*Source:* Interviews and contacts with Taliban cadres and leaders, 2012–16.

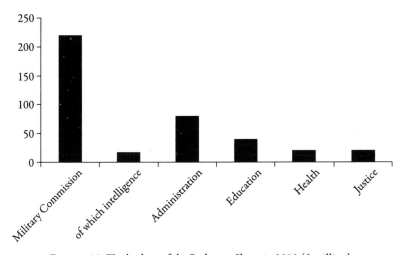

FIGURE 19: The budget of the Peshawar Shura in 2013 ($ million)

*Source:* Source in the administration of the Peshawar Shura, August 2013.

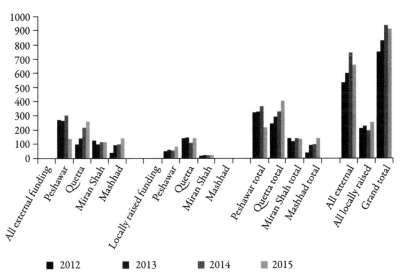

FIGURE 20: Funding to the *shura* leaderships, 2012–15

*Source:* contacts and interviews with members of the Finance Commissions of Quetta, Peshawar, Miran Shah and Mashhad, 2013–16.

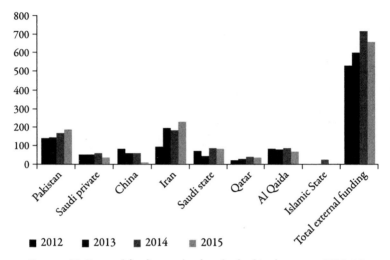

FIGURE 21: External funding to the *shura* leaderships by source, 2012–15

*Source:* contacts and interviews with members of the Finance Commissions of Quetta, Peshawar, Miran Shah and Mashhad, 2013–16.

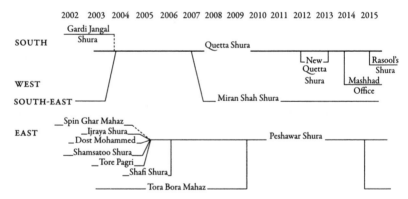

FIGURE 22: The Taliban insurgency tree

*Source:* Elaboration based on the interviews carried out for this study.

# ANNEX 2

## MAPS

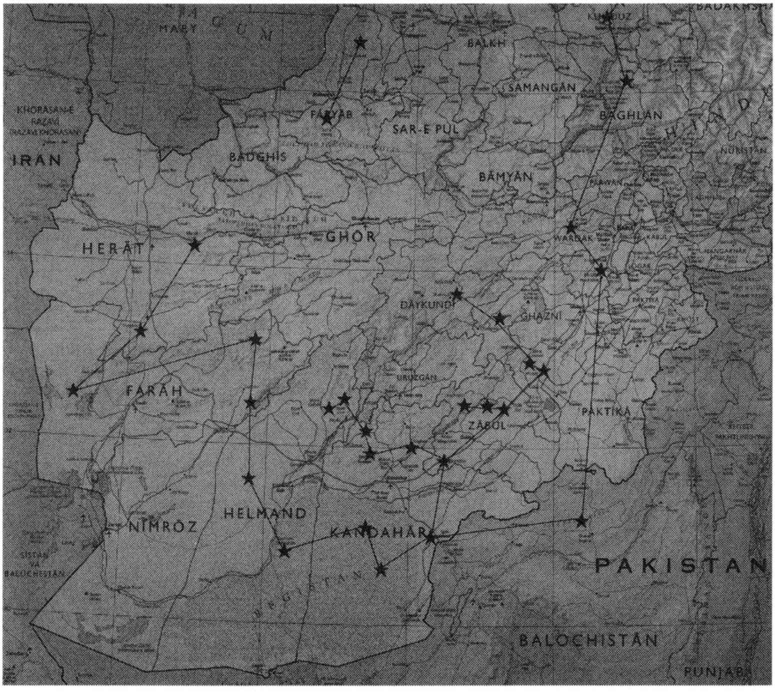

MAP 1: Main fronts of the Dadullah Mahaz, December 2012.

*Source:* Contacts with cadres of the Dadullah Mahaz, 2013.

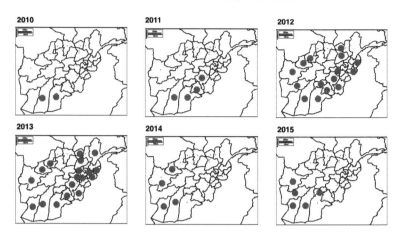

MAP 2: Expansion and contraction of the Zakir Mahaz, 2010–15

*Sources:* Interview with cadres of the Zakir Mahaz, 2013–16.

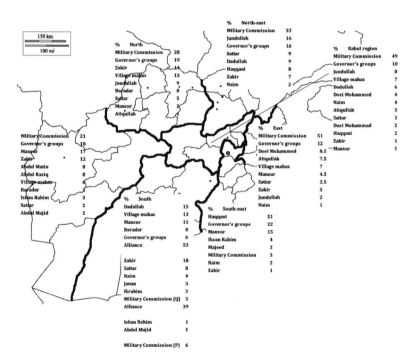

MAP 3: Taliban *mahaz*es, Commissions, Governor's groups and Village *mahaz*es by region, 2014

*Source:* interviews and contacts with Taliban cadres and leaders, 2014–15.

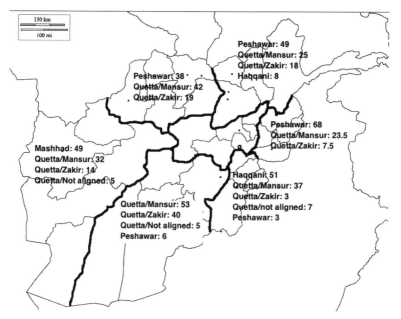

MAP 4: Taliban *shura*s and factions by region, 2014 (% of Taliban fighters)

*Source:* Interviews and contacts with Taliban cadres and leaders, 2014–15.

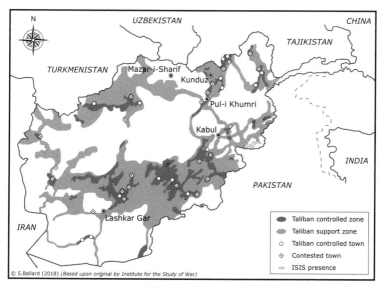

MAP 5: Taliban presence in Afghanistan in December 2015, according to the Institute for the Study of War.

# ANNEX 3

## TABLES

TABLE 1: Number of Taliban interviews for the ESRC project, 'The Taliban at War', 2013–15

| Province | Former Taliban | Fighters | Activists | TB cmdrs | TB cadres | Local elders | Leaders | Non-Taliban: smugglers, advisers; splinters | Women activists | Total |
|---|---|---|---|---|---|---|---|---|---|---|
| Kandahar | 7 | 4 | | 8 | 3 | 14 | | | | 36 |
| Ghazni | | | | 10 | | 10 | | | | 20 |
| Kapisa | 1 | | | | | | | | | 1 |
| Haqqani | 1 | 2 | | 3 | 5 | 2 | | | | 13 |
| Helmand | 1 | | | | 1 | 1 | | | | 3 |
| Baghlan | 3 | | | 12 | 3 | 10 | | | | 28 |
| Herat | | | | 7 | 1 | 7 | | | | 15 |
| Nangarhar | 4 | | 1 | 2 | 3 | 10 | | | | 20 |
| Faryab | | | | 5 | 2 | 8 | | | | 15 |
| Ghazni | 2 | | | 3 | 2 | 10 | | | | 17 |
| Uruzgan | 1 | | | | | | | | | 1 |
| Wardak | 3 | | 1 | 9 | 2 | 7 | | | | 22 |
| Pakistan | | | | | | | 44 | 7 | | 51 |
| Arab Gulf | | | | | | | | | | |
| Zabul | | | | | 1 | | | | | 1 |
| Kabul | | | | | | | | 1 | 6 | 7 |
| TOTAL | 23 | 6 | 2 | 59 | 23 | 79 | 44 | 8 | 6 | 250 |

Table 2: Interviews used for this book and for other projects, including the Helmand pilot study, 2011-2017

| Province | Elders | Former Taliban | Taliban fighters | Taliban commanders | Taliban leaders | Taliban cadres | Total |
|---|---|---|---|---|---|---|---|
| Badakhshan | | | | 3 | | 4 | 7 |
| Badghis | | | | | | 4 | 4 |
| Baghlan | | | 1 | 1 | | 1 | 3 |
| Bamyan | | | | | | 1 | 1 |
| Farah | | | | | | 4 | 4 |
| Faryab | | 1 | | | | | 1 |
| Ghazni | | | | 2 | | 4 | 6 |
| Ghor | | | | 1 | | 5 | 6 |
| Helmand | 13 | 1 | | 33 | | 3 | 50 |
| Jowzjan | | | | | | 1 | 1 |
| Kabul | | | | | | 4 | 4 |
| Kandahar | 3 | | | 1 | | 4 | 8 |
| Kapisa | | | | | | 1 | 1 |
| Kunar | 2 | | | | | 6 | 8 |
| Kunduz | | | | 1 | | 3 | 4 |
| Laghman | | | | | | 3 | 3 |
| Logar | | | | | | 1 | 1 |
| Nangarhar | | | | | | 3 | 3 |
| Nimruz | | | | | | 6 | 6 |
| No location | | | | 2 | | 2 | 4 |
| Nuristan | 2 | | | 2 | | 3 | 7 |
| Pakistan | | | | | 14 | 3 | 17 |
| Paktia | | | | 4 | | 1 | 5 |
| Paktika | | | | | | 3 | 3 |
| Panjshir | | | | | | 1 | 1 |
| Parwan | | | | | | 5 | 5 |
| Samangan | | | | | | 1 | 1 |
| Sar-i Pul | | | | | | 5 | 5 |
| Takhar | | | | 1 | | | 1 |
| Uruzgan | | | | | | 3 | 3 |
| Wardak | 2 | | | 7 | | 2 | 11 |
| Zabul | 2 | | | 4 | | 1 | 7 |
| TOTAL | 24 | 2 | 1 | 62 | 14 | 88 | 191 |

TABLE 3: Elders' responses on Zakat and Ushr, 2014–15

|  | Zakat collected? % | People coerced to pay? % | Should the poor get Zakat? % | N= |
|---|---|---|---|---|
| Baghlan | 100.0 | 66.7 | 16.7 | 6 |
| Ghazni | 80.0 | 10.0 | 0.0 | 10 |
| Helmand | 100.0 | 100.0 | 0.0 | 1 |
| Herat | 100.0 | 71.4 | 28.6 | 7 |
| Kandahar | 0.0 | 0.0 | 8.3 | 12 |
| Nangarhar | 100.0 | 75.0 | 25.0 | 8 |
| Faryab | 100.0 | 100.0 | 0.0 | 8 |
| Wardak | 42.9 | 28.6 | 0.0 | 7 |

*Source:* Project interviews (see Introduction).

TABLE 4: Taliban health data

|  | Budget 2012 $ million | Budget 2013 $ million | Budget 2014 | Total staff 2013 | Clinics 2013 | Hospitals 2013 |
|---|---|---|---|---|---|---|
| Health Commissions all | 88 | 93 |  | 4050 | 68+ | 12 |
| Peshawar Shura | 35 | 50 | 80 | 2200 | 40 | 7 |
| Quetta Shura | 45 | 35 | 20 | 1400 | 28 | 3 |
| Miran Shah Shura | 8 | 8 |  | 450 | some mobile ones | 2 |

*Source:* Contacts with members of the Taliban's Health Commissions.

TABLE 5: Specialisation of the forces of the Military and Derbaez Commissions, 2015

| 2015 | Quetta Shura | Peshawar Shura | Mashhad Office | Miran Shah Shura |
|---|---|---|---|---|
| Mine (sapper) dilghays | 1800 | 1500 | 600 | 460 |
| Infantry dilghays/derbaez | 13200 | 18000 | 4200 | 10000 |
| Motorised dilghays |  | 3000 |  |  |
| Special forces dilghays |  |  | 1200 |  |

*Source:* Interviews with members of the Taliban's Military Commissions, 2015.

TABLE 6: Taliban manpower 2003–15

| | ISAF estimate full-time | ISAF Estimate Part time | Authors' estimate Full time | Authors' estimate Part time | Authors' estimate Reserve | Authors' estimate On leave | Authors' estimate Support element | Authors' estimate Support element in Pak/Iran | Authors' estimate Intelligence | Authors' estimate TOTAL manpower |
|---|---|---|---|---|---|---|---|---|---|---|
| Winter 2004-5 | 2000 | 3000–4000 | 3,500 | 4,000 | 4,550 | 1,200 | 1,200 | 600 | 1,400 | 16,690 |
| Winter 2005-6 | 3000 | 4000–7000 | 5,000 | 6,500 | 7,000 | 1,750 | 2,000 | 800 | 2,500 | 25,810 |
| Winter 2006-7 | 6000 | | 8,500 | 11,900 | 12,750 | 3,000 | 3,800 | 1,100 | 4,000 | 45,370 |
| Winter 2007-08 | 10000 | | 14,000 | 19,600 | 22,400 | 4,900 | 6,800 | 1,400 | 7,000 | 76,460 |
| Winter 2008-9 | 15000 | | 21,000 | 25,200 | 35,700 | 7,350 | 10,400 | 2,200 | 10,000 | 112,250 |
| Winter 2009-10 | 20000 | | 28,000 | 33,600 | 50,400 | 9,800 | 15,000 | 3,150 | 14,000 | 154,370 |
| Winter 2010-11 | 25000 | | 30,500 | 37,500 | 57,950 | 10,675 | 19,500 | 4,100 | 18,000 | 178,665 |
| Winter 2011-12 | 25000 | | 30,500 | 39,000 | 61,000 | 10,675 | 21,000 | 4,400 | 20,000 | 187,045 |
| Winter 2012-13 | | | 30,500 | 41,000 | 64,050 | 10,675 | 22,000 | 4,600 | 22,000 | 195,325 |
| Winter 2013-14 | | | 33,000 | 45,000 | 72,600 | 11,550 | 25,000 | 5,500 | 23,000 | 216,180 |
| Winter 2014-15 | | | 36,000 | 50,000 | 80,000 | 12,500 | 27,000 | 6,000 | 24,000 | 235,500 |

*Sources:* Interviews and contacts with Taliban cadres and leaders, 2012–16; contacts within ISAF, 2006–14; press reports.

# NOTES

## INTRODUCTION

1.  S. Yousufzai, 'The Taliban's Oral History of the Afghanistan War', *Newsweek*, 25 September 2009.
2.  See admissions of Taliban's resilience from the American side in 'Report on Progress Toward Security and Stability in Afghanistan', Report to Congress, Washington: DoD, 2010, p. 42; Vahid Brown and Dan Rassler, *Fountainhead of Jihad*, London: Hurst, 2013, p. 124.
3.  Jeremy Weinstein, *Inside Rebellion*, Cambridge: Cambridge University Press, 2006.
4.  Alex Strick van Linschoten and Felix Kuehn, *An Enemy We Created*, London: Hurst, 2012.
5.  Anand Gopal, 'The Battle for Afghanistan', in Peter Bergen and Katherine Tiedemann (eds), *Talibanistan*, New York: Oxford University Press, 2013.
6.  Anand Gopal and Alex Strick van Linschoten, 'Ideology in the Afghan Taliban', Berlin: Afghanistan Analysts Network, June 2017.
7.  Mike Martin, *An Intimate War: An Oral History of the Helmand conflict*, London: Hurst, 2014.
8.  In particular Thomas Ruttig, 'How Tribal Are the Taliban?' Berlin and Kabul: Afghanistan Analysts Network, 2010.
9.  Yoshinobu Nagamine, *The Legitimization Strategy of the Taliban's Code of Conduct*, New York: Palgrave, 2015; Kate Clark, 'The Layha: Calling the Taliban to Account', Kabul/Berlin: Afghanistan Analysts Network, 2011; Thomas Johnson and Matt Dupee, 'Analysing the new Taliban Code of Conduct (Layeha): An assessment of changing perspectives and strategies of the Afghan Taliban', *Central Asian Survey*, vol. 31 issue 1, 2012, pp. 77–91.
10.  Brown and Rassler, *Fountainhead of Jihad*.
11.  Matt Waldman, 'The sun in the sky', London: Crisis States Research Centre, 2010.

12. Gretchen Peters, *Seeds of Terror*, London: Oneworld, 2001; David Mansfield, 'Understanding Control and Influence: What Opium Poppy and Tax Reveal about the Writ of the Afghan State', Kabul: AREU, 2017.

13. Theo Farrell, *Unwinnable: Britain's War in Afghanistan*, London: Bodley Head, 2017.

14. Carter Malkasian, *War Comes to Garmser*, London: Hurst, 2013.

15. Sean Rayment, *Bomb Hunters*, London: HarperCollins, 2011.

16. Antonio Giustozzi, 'The military adaptation of the Taliban, 2002–2011', in T. Farrell et al. (eds), *Military adaptation in Afghanistan*, Stanford: Stanford University Press, 2013.

17. Theo Farrell and Antonio Giustozzi, 'The Taliban at War: Inside the Helmand Insurgency, 2004–2012', *International Affairs*, July 2013; Antonio Giustozzi and Christoph Reuter, 'The Insurgents of the Afghan North', Kabul/Berlin: Afghanistan Analysts Network, May 2011; Claudio Franco and Antonio Giustozzi, 'Revolution in the Counter-Revolution: Efforts to Centralize the Taliban's Military Leadership', *Central Asian Affairs*, 3 (2016), pp. 249–86; Antonio Giustozzi, 'Afghanistan: Taliban's organization and structure', Oslo: Landinfo, August 2017; Antonio Giustozzi, 'Afghanistan: Taliban's Intelligence and the intimidation campaign', Oslo: Landinfo, August 2017.

18. The term polycentric has been used thus far to describe Al-Qaida's organisational strategy: see David Ronfeldt, 'Al-Qaeda and its affiliates', Santa Monica: RAND, 2008, p. 45.

19. See A. Olesen, *Islam and the State in Afghanistan*, London: Curzon, 1995.

20. See Anand Gopal and Alex Strick van Linschoten, 'Ideology in the Afghan Taliban', Berlin: Afghanistan Analysts Network, June 2017.

21. Support from sources other than Pakistan was sometimes hinted at in the press and in some analytical reports, especially in the case of Iran. On Pakistani support see: 'Pakistani military admits links between ISI and militant groups', *Khaama Press*, 6 October 2017; Joshua Partlow, 'Karzai accuses Pakistan of supporting terrorists', *Washington Post*, 3 October 2011; Barnett R. Rubin, 'Saving Afghanistan', *Foreign Affairs*, January–February 2007; Sherard Cowper-Coles, *Cables from Kabul*, London: Harper Collins, 2011, pp. 21, 50–1, 68–71, 73; Ahmed Rashid, *Descent into Chaos*, pp. 229, 241, 259, 364, 369; Matt Waldman, 'The sun in the sky', London: Crisis States Research Centre (LSE), 2010; Jayshree Bajoria and Eben Kaplan, 'The ISI and Terrorism: Behind the Accusations', Council on Foreign Relations, 26 July 2010; 'Pakistan's ISI still linked to militants, U.S. says', *Reuters*, 28 March 2009. On Iranian support see: Leah Farrall, 'Interview with a Taliban Insider: Iran's Game in Afghanistan', *The Atlantic*, 14 November 2011; Palash R. Ghosh, 'Why Is Iran Building Ties With The Taliban?', *International Business Times*, 2 August 2012; Ben Farmer, Taliban opens office in Iran, *The Telegraph*, 1 August 2012; Ahmad K. Majidyar, 'Iran's hard and soft power in Afghanistan', Washington: American Enterprise institute, August 27, 2012; Frud Bezhan, 'Tensions Simmer Between Tehran, Kabul', *Radio Free Europe*, 15 May 2012. On China see: Joshua Kucera, 'China's Military Aid to the Taliban?', *Eurasianet.org*, 20 December 2010. On Saudi support see: Carlotta Gall, 'Saudis Bankroll Taliban, Even as King Officially Supports Afghan Government', *The New York Times*, 6 December 2016; US Embassy Kabul

Cable, TERRORIST FINANCE: ACTION REQUEST FOR SENIOR LEVEL ENGAGEMENT ON TERRORISM FINANCE, SECRET STATE 131801, 30 December 2009; Declan Walsh, 'WikiLeaks cables portray Saudi Arabia as a cash machine for terrorists', *The Guardian*, 5 December 2010; Nic Robertson, 'Saudis discover new funding channels for Taliban, al Qaeda', *CNN*, 27 January 2011.

22. See for example Ghaith Abdul-Ahad, 'Syria: the foreign fighters joining the war against Bashar al-Assad', *The Guardian*, 23 September 2012.

23. Afghan translators are often not professional translators, and so are inclined to add words or phrases to help westerners understand what locals are getting at; we discouraged our translator from doing this, nonetheless, our transcripts do contained phrases that would be alien to Afghan locals.

24. On principles for field research see Diana Kapiszewki, Lauren M. Maclean and Benjamin L. Read, *Field Research in Political Science: Practices and Principles*, Cambridge: Cambridge University Press, 2015, pp. 26–31. Both the pilot and main project received approval from the King's College London Research Ethics Committee prior to each commencing.

25. This included protocols for the secure transmission and storage of data.

26. Theo Farrell and Antonio Giustozzi, 'The Taliban at War: Inside the Helmand Insurgency', *International Affairs*, vol. 89, no. 4 (2013), pp. 845–872.

27. Interview with Taliban, Garmser 7, 2012.

28. Interview with Taliban, Ghazni 1, 2014.

29. Interview with Taliban, Garmser 1, February 2012.

30. See also in this regard Joseph V. Micallef, 'Follow The Money: The Taliban's Growing Criminal Empire', Military.com, 3 April 2017.

## 1. THE COLLAPSE OF THE EMIRATE AND THE EARLY REGROUPING, 2002–4

1. Anand Gopal, *No Good Men Among the Living: America, the Taliban and the War Through Afghan Eyes*, New York: Metropolitan Books, 2014, pp. 17, 19.

2. Michael E. O'Hanlon, 'A Flawed Masterpiece', *Foreign Affairs*, vol. 81, no. 3 (2002), pp. 48, 55.

3. Sami Yousufzai, 'The Taliban's Oral History of the Afghanistan War', *Newsweek*, 25 September 2009.

4. Yousufzai.

5. Malkasian, *War Comes to Garmser*, pp. 72–3.

6. Interview with former member of the Rahbari Shura, September 2014 (Leadership 7).

7. Interview with former member of the Rahbari Shura, September 2014 (Leadership 7).

8. Interview with member of political commission, Miran Shah Shura, September 2014 (Leadership 4); Interview with senior member of Abdul Majeed Mahaz, September 2014 (Leadership 2).

9. Van Linschoten and Kuehn, *An Enemy we Created*, p. 249; Anand Gopal, 'The Battle for Afghanistan: Militancy and Conflict in Kandahar', New York: New America Foundation, November 2010, p. 11; Gopal, *No Good Men Among the Living*, location 3157ff.

10. Gopal, 'The Battle...', pp. 34–5.
11. Ibid.
12. Jason Burke, *The 9/11 Wars*, London: Allen Lane, 2011, locations 5803-5805.
13. Interview with former member of the Rahbari Shura, September 2014 (Leadership 7).
14. Gopal, 'The Battle...', pp. 34–5.
15. Interview with commander of Faizani front, Taliban Ghazni 1, August 2014; Gopal, 'The Battle...'.
16. Yousufzai.
17. Gopal, 'The Battle...'.
18. Interview with former commander of Faruq Mahaz, Maywand, December 2014 (Kandahar Taliban 11).
19. Interview with Achakzai elder, Helmand, Nahri-i Seraj, June 2012, OP elder 1.
20. Interview with Mahaz representative, Ghazni, December 2014, Ghazni Taliban 11; Interview with district governor, Ghazni Taliban 13, January 2015.
21. Interview with Commander, Ghazni (Andar), August 2014, Ghazni Taliban 10.
22. Interview with Kandahar elder 11, Ishaqzai tribe, February 2015.
23. Interview with Toor-e Pagri commander, Bati Kot, Nangarhar Taliban 4, April 2015; Interview with commander, Bati Kot, Nangarhar Taliban 5, April 2015; Interview with Nangarhar Taliban 3, Bati Kot, April 2015; Interview with Nangarhar Taliban 3, Bati Kot, April 2015.
24. Interview with senior member of Ijraya Shura, Taliban leadership 21, May 2015.
25. Mid-level cadres in Kunar reported that at the time the existence of a military structure in Peshawar was known to a limited number of leaders, who appeared keen to keep it as low-profile as possible (interviews, Kunar, September 2012).
26. Interview with commander, Bati Kot, Nangarhar Taliban 5, April 2015; Interview with former Tora Bora Mahaz commander, Nangarhar Taliban 7, April 2015; Interview with Nangarhar Taliban 3, Bati Kot, April 2015.
27. Interview with former commander of Kabir, Hissarak, Nangarhar Taliban 1, April 2015.
28. Interview with Nangarhar elder 3, Bati Kot, March 2015.
29. Interview with Nangarhar elder 6, Shirzad, March 2015.
30. Interview with Nangarhar elder 8, Shinwar, March 2015; Interview with Nangarhar elder 10, Bati Kot, March 2015.
31. Interview with member of Safi Shura, Nangarhar Taliban 2, April 2015; Interview with Toor-e Pagri commander, Bati Kot, Nangarhar Taliban 4, April 2015; Interview with commander, Bati Kot, Nangarhar Taliban 5, April 2015; Interview with Shamsatoo Mahaz cadre, Hissarak, Nangarhar Taliban 6, April 2015.
32. Senior cadre of Dost Mohammad Mahaz, Taliban OP146, December 2013.
33. Interview with provincial cadre of the Haqqani networks, February 2015, Haqqani 8; Interview with *dilghay* commander, Behsud, Wardak Taliban 10, March 2015; Interview with Taliban cadre in Wardak, March 2015, Wardak Taliban 11.
34. Interview with provincial cadre of the Haqqani network, February 2015, Haqqani 8; Interview with *dilghay* commander, Behsud, Wardak Taliban 10, March 2015; Interview with Taliban cadre in Wardak, March 2015, Wardak Taliban 11.

35.  Interview with Haqqani elder 1, Baraki Barak, Logar, February 2015; Interview with Haqqani elder 2, Mohammad Agha, Logar, February 2015.

36.  Interview with former commander, Baghlan Taliban 16, May 2015; Interview with Taliban cadre, Dandi Ghori, Baghlan Taliban 13, March 2015; Interview with commander, Baghlan-e Jadid, Baghlan Taliban 3, September 2014.

37.  Malkasian, *War Comes to Garmser*, p. 108.

38.  Interview with Kandahar elder 2, Daman, November 2014.

39.  Interview with Uruzgan Taliban 1, Shahid Hassas, commander, March 2015.

40.  Interview with former Taliban member, Helmand, July 2015, Helmand Taliban 2; Interview with former senior member of Gardi Jangal Shura, Kandahar Taliban 19, July 2015.

41.  Interview with Helmand elder OP2, March 2012.

42.  Interview with Achakzai elder in Nahr-i Seraj, OP elder 3, June 2012; Interview with Khalozai (Alizai) elder in Musa Qala district, OP elder 4, March 2012.

43.  Interview with Commander, Helmand, OP Taliban 2, December 2011.

44.  See: Martin, *An Intimate War*; Malkasian, *War Comes to Garmser*; Farrell and Giustozzi, 'The Taliban at War'; Gopal, 'The Battle for Afghanistan: Militancy and Conflict in Kandahar', New York: New America Foundation, November 2010, pp. 8ff.

45.  Interview with senior member of Janan Mahaz, OP Taliban 3, January 2013; Interview with Helmand commander, Nad Ali, OP Taliban 4, December 2011; Interview with senior member of Ijraya Shura, Taliban leadership 21, May 2015; Yousufzai; Interview with former Tora Bora Mahaz commander, Nangarhar Taliban 7, April 2015; Interview with Wardak elder 4, Sayed Abad, July 2014; Interview with group commander, Wardak Taliban 3, July 2014.

46.  Yousufzai.

47.  Interview with Ghazni Taliban 5, August 2014.

48.  Gopal, 'The Battle for Afghanistan', p. 10.

49.  Interview with adviser to Serajuddin Haqqani, Leadership 13, January 2015.

50.  Interview with former group commander of Mansur Mahaz, Ghazni Taliban 16, May 2015.

51.  Malkasian, *War Comes to Garmser*, p. 76.

52.  Interview with former Taliban cadre, Kandahar, July 2015, Kandahar Taliban 18; Interview with former Taliban member, Helmand, July 2015, Helmand Taliban 2; Interview with former senior member of Gardi Jangal Shura, Kandahar Taliban 19, July 2015.

53.  Interview with former Taliban cadre, Kandahar, July 2015, Kandahar Taliban 18.

54.  Interview with former Taliban cadre, Kandahar, July 2015, Kandahar Taliban 18; Interview with former Taliban member, Helmand, July 2015, Helmand Taliban 2; Interview with former senior member of Gardi Jangal Shura, Kandahar Taliban 19, July 2015.

55.  Interview with former Taliban cadre, Kandahar, July 2015, Kandahar Taliban 18; Interview with former Taliban member, Helmand, July 2015, Helmand Taliban 2; Interview with former senior member of Gardi Jangal Shura, Kandahar Taliban 19,

July 2015; Interview with former commander, Daddullah Mahaz, Kandahar Taliban 22, July 2015.

56. Interview with former Taliban cadre, Kandahar, July 2015, Kandahar Taliban 18; Interview with former Taliban member, Helmand, July 2015, Helmand Taliban 2; Interview with former senior member of Gardi Jangal Shura, Kandahar Taliban 19, July 2015.

57. Interview with former Taliban cadre, Kandahar, July 2015, Kandahar Taliban 18; Interview with former Taliban member, Helmand, July 2015, Helmand Taliban 2; Interview with former senior member of Gardi Jangal Shura, Kandahar Taliban 19, July 2015.

58. Interview with former Taliban cadre, Kandahar, July 2015, Kandahar Taliban 18; Interview with former Taliban member, Helmand, July 2015, Helmand Taliban 2; Interview with former senior member of Gardi Jangal Shura, Kandahar Taliban 19, July 2015.

59. Interview with adviser to Serajuddin Haqqani, Leadership 13, January 2015.

60. Interview with adviser to Serajuddin Haqqani, Leadership 13, January 2015.

61. Steve Coll, *Directorate S*, London: Allen Lane, 2018, p. 127.

62. Interview with adviser to Serajuddin Haqqani, Leadership 10, January 2015.

63. Yousufzai.

64. Ibid.

65. Ibid.

66. Ibid.

67. Ibid.

68. Ibid.

69. Ibid.

70. Interview with provincial cadre of the Haqqani network, February 2015, Haqqani 8.

71. Interview with member of political commission, Miran Shah Shura, September 2014 (Leadership 4).

72. Interview with adviser to Serajuddin Haqqani, Leadership 13, January 2015.

73. Interview with senior member of Miran Shah Shura Commission, Leadership 14, February 2015.

74. Interview with member of political commission, Miran Shah Shura, September 2014 (Leadership 4).

75. Interview with senior member of Miran Shah Shura Commission, Leadership 14, February 2015.

76. Interview with adviser to Serajuddin Haqqani, Leadership 13, January 2015.

77. Interview with former member of the Rahbari Shura, September 2014 (Leadership 7).

78. Interview with former member of the Rahbari Shura, September 2014 (Leadership 7).

79. 'Afghan Taliban leader reported as setting up resistance council', *The News*, 24 June 2003.

80. Interview with former member of the Rahbari Shura, September 2014 (Leadership 7).

81. Interview with former member of the Rahbari Shura, September 2014 (Leadership 7).

82. Interview with member of Commission in Quetta Shura, Leadership 1, September 2014; Interview with senior member of Abdul Majid Mahaz, September 2014 (Leadership 2).

83.  Interview with Baradar Mahaz cadre, August 2014 (Kandahar Taliban 4).

84.  Interview with provincial cadre of the Haqqani network, February 2015, Haqqani 8; Interview with Taliban cadre, Baghlan, May 2015, Baghlan Taliban 14; Interview with Mahaz representative, Ghazni, December 2014, Ghazni Taliban 11.

85.  Interview with Rahbari Shura member, August 2015, Taliban Leadership 40; Interview with former member of the Rahbari Shura, September 2014 (Leadership 7); Interview with member of political commission, Miran Shah Shura, September 2014 (Leadership 4).

86.  Taliban cadre in the Finance Commission of the Quetta Shura, contacted in September 2012.

87.  Interview with Baradar Mahaz cadre, August 2014 (Kandahar Taliban 4); Interview with Taliban cadre in Wardak, March 2015, Wardak Taliban 11.

88.  Interview with Baradar Mahaz cadre, August 2014 (Kandahar Taliban 4).

89.  Interview with former member of the Rahbari Shura, September 2014 (Leadership 7).

90.  Interview with former member of the Rahbari Shura, September 2014 (Leadership 7).

91.  Yousufzai.

92.  Interview with Taliban commander, Ghazni Taliban 9, August 2014; Interview with Kandahar elder 3, Panjwai, February 2015.

93.  Interview with Kandahar elder 3, Panjwai, February 2015.

94.  Interview with Ghazni elder 5, Andar, August 2014; Interview with Kandahar elder 3, Panjwai, February 2015; Interview with Kandahar elder 7, Daman, February 2015; Interview with Kandahar elder 8, Dand, February 2015; Interview with Kandahar elder 10, Daman, February 2015; Interview with Kandahar elder 11, Ishaqzai tribe, February 2015.

95.  Interview with Kandahar elder 14, Dand, February 2015.

96.  Interview with senior member of Abdul Majeed Mahaz, September 2014 (Leadership 2); Interview with former member of the Rahbari Shura, September 2014 (Leadership 7); Interview with senior Taliban active in western Afghanistan, Leadership 5, October 2014.

97.  See for example Joshua Partlow, 'In northern Afghanistan, a small, stubborn Taliban', *Washington Post*, 2 October 2011; also: Ashley Jackson and Antonio Giustozzi, forthcoming report on humanitarian access in Afghanistan, for examples of elders reporting negative Taliban propaganda on NGOs and UN.

98.  Abdulhadi Hairan, 'A Profile of the Taliban's Propaganda Tactics', *Huffington Post*, 1 February 2010.

99.  Michael Semple, 'Rhetoric of resistance in the Taliban's rebel ballads', March 2011: http://www.hks.harvard.edu/cchrp/research/working_papers/Semple_RhetoricOfResistanceInTheTalibanTuranas.pdf; Alex Strick van Linschoten and Felix Kuehn, *Poetry of the Taliban*, London: Hurst, 2012; Thomas Johnson, *Taliban Narratives*, London: Hurst, 2018.

100. Interview with adviser to Serajuddin Haqqani, Leadership 10, January 2015.

101. Interview with adviser to Serajuddin Haqqani, Leadership 10, January 2015.

102. T. Ruttig, 'The Haqqani network as an autonomous entity', in A. Giustozzi (ed.), *Decoding the New Taliban*, London: Hurst, 2009.

103. Interview with former member of the Rahbari Shura, September 2014 (Leadership 7).

104. Personal communication with several field commanders between 2011 and 2013; Tom Coghlan, 'The Taliban in Helmand', in Giustozzi (ed.), *Decoding...*

105. Interview with Taliban commander, Jagatoo district, Wardak, Taliban OP 1, September 2011.

106. Interview with Rahbari Shura member, August 2015, Taliban Leadership 40.

107. Interview with Rahbari Shura member, August 2015, Taliban Leadership 40.

108. Interview with cadre, Nimruz, Taliban OP36, January 2014.

109. Interview with fighter, Kandahar Taliban 1, August 2014; Interview with fighter, Kandahar Taliban 7, Zherai, August 2014; Interview with fighter, Kandahar Taliban 8, Spin Boldak, August 2014.

110. Interview with former member of the Rahbari Shura, September 2014 (Leadership 7).

111. Interview with Dadullah Mahaz, July 2013, Kandahar Taliban 3, August 2014; Interview with Baradar Mahaz cadre, August 2014 (Kandahar Taliban 4); Interview with cadre, Kandahar Taliban 5, August 2014.

112. Interview with member of political commission, Miran Shah Shura, September 2014 (Leadership 4); Interview with former member of the Rahbari Shura, September 2014 (Leadership 7).

113. Interview with former member of the Rahbari Shura, September 2014 (Leadership 7).

114. Interview with former member of the Rahbari Shura, September 2014 (Leadership 7).

115. Interview with member of Commission in Quetta Shura, Leadership 1, September 2014.

116. Interview with former member of the Rahbari Shura, September 2014 (Leadership 7).

117. Interview with Baradar Mahaz cadre, August 2014 (Kandahar Taliban 4).

118. Interview with former member of the Rahbari Shura, September 2014 (Leadership 7).

119. Interview with member of Commission in Quetta Shura, Leadership 1, September 2014; Interview with former member of the Rahbari Shura, September 2014 (Leadership 7).

120. Source in the Taliban structure in Pakistan, January 2013; Interview with member of Commission in Quetta Shura, Leadership 1, September 2014; Source in the Taliban structure in Pakistan, January 2013.

121. Interview with senior member of Abdul Majeed Mahaz, September 2014 (Leadership 2).

122. Interview with member of political commission, Miran Shah Shura, September 2014 (Leadership 4).

123. Yousufzai.

124. Ibid.

125. See A. Giustozzi, 'The Splintering Taliban: Examining the proliferation of dissident factions in Afghanistan', *Jane's Terrorism & Insurgency Monitor*, 6 March 2015.

126. See A. Giustozzi and Silab Mangal, USIP 2014.

127. Stephen Graham, 'U.S.: Taliban rift over failure to crash vote', *The Herald-Sun* (Durham, NC), 21 October 2004.

128. Interview with senior member of Quetta Shura, June 2014, Taliban OP 144.

129. Ahmed Rashid, *Descent into Chaos*, London: Allen Lane, 2008, p. 259.

130. Interview with Rahbari Shura member and Loy Mahaz commander, June 2014, Taliban OP145.

## 2. THE APOGEUM OF THE QUETTA SHURA, 2005–9

1. Source in the Taliban structure in Pakistan, January 2013.
2. Interview with commission member, Quetta, Taliban leadership 1, September 2014.
3. Interview with former member of the Rahbari Shura, September 2014 (Leadership 7).
4. Kandahar elder 1, Zhirai, November 2014.
5. Interview with Kandahar elder 7, Daman, February 2015; Interview with Kandahar elder 10, Daman, February 2015.
6. Interview with Baradar Mahaz cadre, August 2014 (Kandahar Taliban 4); Gopal, 'The Battle for Afghanistan', p. 4.
7. Interview with former member of the Rahbari Shura, September 2014 (Leadership 7).
8. Interview with senior member of Abdul Majid Mahaz, September 2014 (Leadership 2).
9. Interview with Helmand elder, OP elder 5, June 2012; Interview with commander in Helmand, Taliban OP2, December 2011; Interview with Popolzai elder in Nowzad district, June 2012, Elder Op 6; Martin, *An Intimate War*, p. 147.
10. Interview with senior member of the Quetta Shura, Taliban OP147, June 2014; Interview with senior Quetta Shura cadre, Taliban OP148, June 2014. See, on Directorate S: Coll, *Directorate S*, in particular pp. 218–19.
11. Interview with Rahbari Shura member, Taliban OP 149, June 2014.
12. Community elders interviewed in various locations, 2013–14.
13. Interview with Taliban cadre in Ghazni, June 2014, Taliban OP 150.
14. Yousufzai, cit.
15. Interview with former member of the Rahbari Shura, September 2014 (Leadership 7).
16. Interview with senior member of education commission, Peshawar, December 2012, OP Taliban 4.
17. Kate Clark, *The Layha: Calling the Taliban to Account*, AAN Thematic Report 6/2011, (Kabul, Berlin: Afghanistan Analysts Network, 2011); sources close to the Taliban in Pakistan, 2009.
18. Jason Straziuso, 'Slaying of Teachers in Afghanistan Follows New Rules From Taliban', *The Washington Post* (10 December 2006).
19. 'Taliban Attacks Killed Over 700 Afghan Civilians this Year: NATO', *Agence France Presse* (2 November 2006).
20. UNAMA JMAC, A review of the Taliban and Fellow travelers as a movement, Kabul, 23 August 2007.
21. Interview with Herat elder 1, Pashtun Zarghun, April 2015; Interview with Herat elder 3, member of Peace Committee, April 2015.
22. Interview with UN official, Mazar-e Sharif, 22 April 2010.
23. A small, nomadic group originating in India – similar to Europe's Sinti and Roma.
24. Interview with Afghan informer connected to the Taliban, May 2010.
25. Interview with security officer, Mazar-e Sharif, April 2010.
26. Interview with UN official, Kabul, 25 April 2010.

27.  Interview with Taliban cadre, Baghlan, May 2015, Baghlan Taliban 14; Interview with Taliban cadre, Dandi Ghori, Baghlan Taliban 13, March 2015.

28.  Interview with district governor, Ghazni Taliban 13, January 2015.

29.  Interview with Wardak elder 6, Jaghatu, July 2015.

30.  Interview with district governor, Ghazni Taliban 13, January 2015.

31.  Interview with *dilghay* commander, Behsud, Wardak Taliban 10, March 2015; Interview with Taliban cadre in Wardak, March 2015, Wardak Taliban 11; Interview with provincial cadre of the Haqqani networks, February 2015, Haqqani 8.

32.  Interview with *dilghay* commander, Behsud, Wardak Taliban 10, March 2015; Interview with provincial cadre of the Haqqani network, February 2015, Haqqani 8.

33.  Interview with senior Taliban active in western Afghanistan, Leadership 5, October 2014.

34.  Interview with senior Taliban active in western Afghanistan, Leadership 5, October 2014; Interview with former cadre of Ghulam Yahya Akbari, Herat Taliban 1, December 2014; Interview with commander of Amanullah Khan, Herat Taliban 2, December 2014; Interview with commander, Shindand, Herat Taliban 5, December 2014; Interview with commander of Abdullah Zekria, Herat Taliban 6, Shindand, December 2014; Interview with group commander, Cheshti Sharif, Herat Taliban 3, December 2014.

35.  Interview with group commander, Cheshti Sharif, Herat Taliban 3, December 2014.

36.  Interview with group commander, Cheshti Sharif, Herat Taliban 3, December 2014; Interview with group commander, Shindand, Herat Taliban 5, December 2014; Interview with commander of Abdullah Zekria, Herat Taliban 6, Shindand, December 2014.

37.  Interview with group commander, Cheshti Sharif, Herat Taliban 3, December 2014.

38.  Interview with former cadre of Ghulam Yahya Akbari, Herat Taliban 1, December 2014.

39.  Interview with former commander, Shindand, Herat Taliban 8, December 2014.

40.  Interview with senior Taliban active in western Afghanistan, Leadership 5, October 2014; Interview with former cadre of Ghulam Yahya Akbari, Herat Taliban 1, December 2014; Interview with commander of Amanullah Khan, Herat Taliban 2, December 2014; Interview with commander, Shindand, Herat Taliban 5, December 2014; Interview with commander of Abdullah Zekria, Herat Taliban 6, Shindand, December 2014; Interview with group commander, Cheshti Sharif, Herat Taliban 3, December 2014.

41.  Interview with Herat elder 1, Pashtun Zarghun, April 2015.

42.  Interview with Herat elder 1, Pashtun Zarghun, April 2015.

43.  Interview with Herat elder 2, Obeh, April 2015.

44.  Interview with group commander, Shindand, Herat Taliban 5, December 2014.

45.  Interview with commander of Abdullah Zekria, Herat Taliban 6, Shindand, December 2014; Interview with former cadre of Ghulam Yahya Akbari, Herat Taliban 1, December 2014.

46.  Interview with commander of Amanullah Khan, Herat Taliban 2, December 2014.

47.  Interview with senior Taliban active in western Afghanistan, Leadership 5, October 2014.

48.   Interview with Herat elder 1, Pashtun Zarghun, April 2015.

49.   Interview with Herat Taliban 7, commander, December 2014; Interview with Herat Taliban 2, commander, December 2014; Interview with Herat Taliban 1, cadre, December 2014; Interview with Herat Taliban 5, commander, December 2014; Interview with Herat Taliban 3, commander, December 2014; Interview with Herat Taliban 6, commander, December 2014; Interview with Herat Taliban 4, commander, December 2014; Interview with Taliban leadership 6, October 2014.

50.   Interview with former cadre of Ghulam Yahya Akbari, Herat Taliban 1, December 2014.

51.   Interview with German officer, Kunduz, October 2009.

52.   Personal communication with Martine van Bijlert, Afghanistan Analysts Network analyst, May 2010.

53.   Interview with cadre, Faryab Taliban 4, December 2014; Interview with cadre, Mansur Mahaz, Faryab Taliban 5, December 2014; Interview with Taliban cadre, Almar, Faryab Taliban 1, December 2014; Interview with cadre, Mansur Mahaz, Faryab Taliban 3, December 2014.

54.   Interview with cadre, Faryab Taliban 4, December 2014.

55.   Interview with UN official, Kabul, 25 April 2010.

56.   Interview with cadre, Faryab Taliban 4, December 2014.

57.   Interview with cadre, Mansur Mahaz, Faryab Taliban 5, December 2014; Interview with group commander, Sattar Mahaz, Faryab Taliban 6, December 2014.

58.   Interview with Faryab elder 3, Qaysar, May 2015.

59.   Interview with cadre, Faryab Taliban 4, December 2014.

60.   Personal communication with UN official, 5 April 2008.

61.   Interview with former commander of the Tora Bora Mahaz, Nangarhar Taliban 7, April 2015; interview with senior member of Dost Mohammed Mahaz, Taliban OP 146, December 2013.

62.   Interviews with Taliban cadres and commanders in Nangarhar, Nangarhar Taliban 1–7, April 2015; Interview with former member of the Rahbari Shura, September 2014 (Leadership 7).

63.   Interview with former commander Of Kabir, Hissarak, Nangarhar Taliban 1, April 2015; Interview with member of Safi Shura, Nangarhar Taliban 2, April 2015.

64.   Interview with senior member of Ijraya Shura, Taliban leadership 21, May 2015.

65.   Interview with former commander of Kabir, Hissarak, Nangarhar Taliban 1, April 2015; Interview with member of Safi Shura, Nangarhar Taliban 2, April 2015; Interview with Nangarhar Taliban 3, Bati Kot, April 2015; Interview with cadre, Shirzad, Nangarhar Taliban 8, April 2015; Interview with Toor-e Pagri commander, Bati Kot, Nangarhar Taliban 4, April 2015; Interview with commander, Bati Kot, Nangarhar Taliban 5, April 2015; Interview with Shamsatoo Mahaz cadre, Hissarak, Nangarhar Taliban 6, April 2015; Interview with former Tora Bora Mahaz commander, Nangarhar Taliban 7, April 2015; Interview with cadre, Shirzad, Nangarhar Taliban 8, April 2015; Interview with senior member of Ijraya Shura, Taliban leadership 21, May 2015.

66.   Interview with commander, Sorkhrod, Nangarhar Taliban 9, March 2015.

67.   Interview with former commander of Kabir, Hissarak, Nangarhar Taliban 1, April 2015.

68.  Interview with Nangarhar Taliban 3, Bati Kot, April 2015.
69.  Interview with Toor-e Pagri commander, Bati Kot, Nangarhar Taliban 4, April 2015.
70.  Interview with Shamsatoo Mahaz cadre, Hissarak, Nangarhar Taliban 6, April 2015.
71.  Interview with former commander of Kabir, Hissarak, Nangarhar Taliban 1, April 2015.
72.  Interview with former member of the Rahbari Shura, September 2014 (Leadership 7).
73.  Interview with member of political commission, Miran Shah Shura, September 2014 (Leadership 4).
74.  'Sallust', *Operation Herrick: An unofficial history of British military operations in Afghanistan 2001–2014*, published by the author, 2015, location 13026.
75.  Malkasian, *War Comes to Garmser*, p. 152.
76.  Interview with Kandahar elder 8, Dand, February 2015.
77.  Malkasian, *War...*, p. 88.
78.  Ibid., p. 91.
79.  Martin, *An Intimate War*, p. 149.
80.  Interview with former member of the Rahbari Shura, September 2014 (Leadership 7).
81.  Gopal, 'The Battle for Afghanistan', pp. 18–20. See also: Andrew Garfield and Alicia Boyd, 'Understanding Afghan Insurgents Motivations, Goals, and the Reconciliation and Reintegration Process', Philadelphia: Foreign Policy Research Institute, The Philadelphia Papers, NO. 3, July 2013.
82.  Malkasian, *War Comes to Garmser*, p. 85; Martin, *An Intimate War*, p. 147.
83.  Yousufzai.
84.  Interview with cadre, Baghlan Jadid, Baghlan Taliban 7, July 2014; Interview with commander, Dahan-e Ghori, Baghlan Taliban 8, July 2014.
85.  Interview with commander, Baghlan Jadid, Baghlan Taliban 4, September 2014; Interview with Baghlan elder 8, Dandi Ghori, July 2014; Interview with Baghlan elder 10, Dandi Ghori, July 2014; Interview with Baghlan elder 3, Baghlan Jadid, July 2014; Interview with commander, Baghlan Taliban 6, Baghlan Jadid, September 2014.
86.  Interview with Baghlan elder 2, Baghlan Jadid, July 2014.
87.  Interview with intellectuals from Jowzjan and Sar-e Pul, April 2010.
88.  Gopal, 'The Battle for Afghanistan', p. 16.
89.  Ibid.
90.  Interview with Commander, Helmand, Taliban OP18, March 2012.
91.  Interview with Nangarhar Taliban 3, Bati Kot, April 2015; Interview with Nangarhar elder 9, Khogyani, March 2015; Kandahar elder 9, Panjwai, February 2015.
92.  Interview with Helmand elder, OP elder 5, June 2012; Interview with Achakzai elder, Helmand, Nahri-i Seraj, June 2012, OP elder 1. See also: Gopal, *No Good Man among the Living*; Farrell and Giustozzi; Martin, *An Intimate War*; Carl Forsberg, 'Politics and Power in Kandahar', Washington: Institute for the Study of War, 2010; Gopal, 'The Battle for Afghanistan'.
93.  Interview with Ghazni elder 5, Andar, August 2014.
94.  Interview with Ghazni elder 3, Qarabagh, August 2014.
95.  Interview with Wardak elder 7, Sayed Abad, July 2014.
96.  Martin, *An Intimate War*, p. 131.

97.　Interview with commander, Ghazni Taliban 8, August 2014.

98.　Interview with commander, Wardak Taliban 2, Jaghatu, June 2014.

99.　Malkasian, *War Comes to Garmser*, p. 84.

100.　Interview with intellectuals from Jowzjan and Sar-e Pol, Mazar-e Sharif, 20 April 2010; Interview with elder in Nahr-i Seraj, Elder OP21, 10 June 2012.

101.　Kandahar elder 9, Panjwai, February 2015.

102.　Ralf Beste, Matthias Gebauer, Holger Stark and Alexander Szandar, 'Tot oder lebendig,' *Der Spiegel* (2009) 22, p. 34; Interview with security officer, Mazar-e Sharif, April 2010. Interview with intellectuals from Jowzjan and Sar-e Pol, Mazar-e Sharif, 20 April 2010.

103.　Interview with elder in Nad Ali, Elder OP15, March 2012.

104.　Interview with Commander, Helmand, Taliban OP2, December 2011.

105.　Interview with Commander, Helmand, OP Taliban 2, December 2011.

106.　Interview with former commander, Taliban Kandahar 20, May 2015.

107.　Gopal, 'The Battle for Afghanistan', p. 13; Interview with Kandahar elder 11, Ishaqzai tribe, February 2015.

108.　Malkasian, *War Comes to Garmser*, p. 111.

109.　Interview with elder from Sangin, Taliban OP16, April 2012.

110.　Interview with commander, Kapisa Taliban 1, March 2015.

111.　Interview with AREU research staff, Kabul, October 2009.

112.　Interview with UN official, Faryab, April 2010.

113.　Malkasian, *War Comes to Garmser*, p. 128.

114.　Ibid., p. 105.

115.　Interview with UN official, Kabul, 4 April 2010.

116.　Interview with elder from Nad Ali district, Elder OP17, March 2012; Interview with Mullah from Musa Qala district, Elder OP18, June 2012.

117.　Interview with elder from Garmser district, Elder OP19, 11 June 2012.

118.　Interview with elder from Garmser district, Elder OP19, 11 June 2012; Interview with Mullah from Musa Qala district, Elder OP18, June 2012.

119.　Interview with elder in Nad Ali, Elder OP20, March 2012.

120.　Malkasian, *War Comes to Garmser*, p. 78.

121.　Interview with security officer, Mazar-e Sharif, April 2010.

122.　Conversation with Krystóf Gosztonyi, Analysis Research Consulting, Berlin, via Skype, 18 December 2009.

123.　Geert Gompelman, 'Winning Hearts and Minds?: Examining the Relationship Between Aid and Security in Afghanistan', Boston: Tufts University, January 2011. Personal communication with UN official in Kunduz, October 2006. Interviews with a mawlawi, Maimana, April 2009. Interview with intellectuals from Jowzjan and Sar-e Pol, April 2010. Interview with Syed Azizullah Sayead Olfaty, deputy secretary of the Meshrano Jirga from Jowzjan, Kabul, 25 April 2010.

124.　Ibid. Interview with Sayed Azizullah Olfaty, a Wolesi Jirga member from Jowzjan, Kabul, 25 April 2010.

125.　Interview with TLO analyst Kabul, 5 April 2010. Interview with NGO security official in Kunduz, May 2010.

126.　Martin, *An Intimate War*, p. 144.

127. Malkasian, *War Comes to Garmser*, p. 86.

128. Interview with senior Taliban active in western Afghanistan, Leadership 5, October 2014.

129. Interview with Wardak elder 7, Sayed Abad, July 2014.

130. On Taliban propaganda more in general see 'The Taliban's propaganda activities: How well is the Afghan insurgency communicating and what is it saying?', Stockholm: SIPRI Project Paper, June 2007; 'Taliban propaganda: winning the war of words', Bruxelles, Crisis Group, 2008 and Joanna Nathan, 'Reading the Taliban', in Giustozzi (ed), *Decoding the New Taliban*, pp. 23–42; Johnson, *Taliban Narratives*.

131. Interview with former member of Rahbari Shura, Taliban leadership 7, September 2014.

132. Source in the Taliban structure in Pakistan, May 2015.

133. Source in the Taliban structure in Pakistan, May 2015.

134. Gretchen Peters, 'Haqqani Network Financing', West Point: CTC, 2012, pp. 51, 57.

135. *Al-Somood*, Issue 55.

136. Interview with deputy, Quetta, Taliban Leadership 14, July 2015.

137. Yousufzai.

138. Yousufzai.

139. Interview with former member of the Rahbari Shura, September 2014 (Leadership 7); Interview with member of political commission in Miram Shah shura, Taliban Leadership 4, September 2014.

140. Source in the Taliban structure in Pakistan, December 2013; Interview with Ibrahim, leader of Ibrahim Mahaz, Taliban OP52, February 2013.

141. Source in the Quetta Shura, contacted April 2013.

142. Interview with senior member of Hussain Rahimi Mahaz, Taliban leadership 11, January 2015.

143. Interview with Baradar Mahaz cadre, August 2014 (Kandahar Taliban 4); Interview with cadre, Kandahar Taliban 5, August 2014.

144. Interview with Dadullah Mahaz cadree, Kandahar Taliban 3, August 2014.

145. Source in the Taliban structure in Pakistan, October 2012.

146. Source in the Taliban structure in Pakistan, August 2012.

147. Interview with cadre, Uruzgan, Taliban OP98, May 2013.

148. Interviews with Taliban commander, Helmand, Taliban OP19, September 2011.

149. See Thomas Ruttig, 'How Tribal Are the Taliban?', Berlin and Kabul: Afghanistan Analysts Network, 2010; Interview with former commander, Kandahar Taliban 16, Spin Boldak, December 2014; Interview with commander, Zherai, Kandahar Taliban 14, December 2014.

150. Interview with cadre, Kandahar Taliban 5, August 2014.

151. Interview with member of political commission, Miran Shah Shura, September 2014 (Leadership 4).

152. Interview with Dadullah Mahaz, July 2013, Kandahar Taliban 3, August 2014; Interview with cadre, Kandahar Taliban 5, August 2014; Martin, *An Intimate War*, p. 146.

153. Interview with former commander of Faruq Mahaz, Maywand, December 2014 (Kandahar Taliban 11).

154. Interview with former commander, Faruq Mahaz, Kandahar Taliban 10, Maruf, December 2014.

155. Interview with commander, Kandahar Taliban 13, Zherai, December 2014.

156. Source in the Taliban structure in Pakistan, December 2013; Interview with senior cadre of Ibrahim Mahaz, OP52, February 2013; Source in the Taliban structure in Pakistan, September 2013.

157. An interview with cadre of Zakir Mahaz in Uruzgan province, Taliban OP 154, May 2013.

158. Interview with Mahaz representative, Ghazni, December 2014, Ghazni Taliban 11.

159. Interview with commander, Jaghatu, Taliban OP57, January 2013; Interview with Dadullah Mahaz, July 2013, Kandahar Taliban 3, August 2014; Interview with Baradar Mahaz cadre, August 2014 (Kandahar Taliban 4).

160. Ron Moreau, 'America's New Nightmare', *Newsweek*, 3 August 2009; Taliban Layha, 2006 edition.

161. Interview with senior member of Abdul Majid Mahaz, Taliban leadership 2, August 2014.

162. Interview with member of political commission in Miran Shah Shura, Taliban Leadership 4, September 2014.

163. Interview with Dadullah Mahaz, July 2013, Kandahar Taliban 3, August 2014; Interview with Baradar Mahaz cadre, August 2014 (Kandahar Taliban 4); Interview with cadre, Kandahar Taliban 5, August 2014; Interview with former commander of Faruq Mahaz, Maywand, December 2014 (Kandahar Taliban 11); Source in the Taliban structure in Pakistan, December 2013; Interview with senior member of Abdul Majid Mahaz, Taliban Leadership 2, September 2014.

164. Source in the Taliban structure in Pakistan, August 2012.

165. Source in the Taliban structure in Pakistan, October 2012.

166. Source in the Taliban structure in Pakistan, July 2013.

167. Source in the Taliban structure in Pakistan, September 2013.

168. Source in the Taliban structure in Pakistan, December 2013.

169. Ibid.

170. Ibid.

171. Interview with senior Taliban active in western Afghanistan, Leadership 5, October 2014; Interview with former cadre of Ghulam Yahya Akbari, Herat Taliban 1, December 2014; Interview with commander of Amanullah Khan, Herat Taliban 2, December 2014; Interview with commander, Shindand, Herat Taliban 5, December 2014; Interview with commander of Abdullah Zekria, Herat Taliban 6, Shindand, December 2014; Interview with group commander, Cheshti Sharif, Herat Taliban 3, December 2014.

172. Interview with cadre, Mansur Mahaz, Faryab Taliban 5, December 2014.

173. Interview with Mahaz representative, Ghazni, December 2014, Ghazni Taliban 11; Interview with district governor, Ghazni Taliban 13, January 2015.

174. Interview with district governor, Ghazni Taliban 13, January 2015.

175. Interview with *dilghay* commander, Behsud, Wardak Taliban 10, March 2015; Interview with Taliban cadre in Wardak, March 2015, Wardak Taliban 11; Interview with provincial cadre of the Haqqani networks, February 2015, Haqqani 8.

176. Interview with Taliban commander in Kunduz, July 2011, Taliban OP 6; interview with Taliban commander in Baghlan, September 2012, Taliban OP 7.

177. Interview with senior member of Abdul Majid Mahaz, September 2014 (Leadership 2).

178. Interview with commander, Kandahar Taliban 13, Zherai, December 2014; Interview with former commander, Faruq Mahaz, Kandahar Taliban 10, Maruf, December 2014; Interview with Baradar Mahaz cadre, August 2014 (Kandahar Taliban 4).

179. Interview with former commander of Faruq Mahaz, Maywand, December 2014 (Kandahar Taliban 11).

180. Interview with commander, Kandahar Taliban 13, Zherai, December 2014.

181. Bernd Horn, *No Lack of Courage*, Toronto: Dundurn Press, 2010, p. 31. It should be noted that these estimates are at odds with ISAF's estimates of total Taliban strength, which in 2006 placed their numbers at 3–4,000 core and 4–7,000 non-core fighters (see: Antonio Giustozzi, *Koran, Kalashnikov and Laptop*, London: Hurst, 2008, p. 35).

182. Horn, p. 39.

183. Horn, pp. 31, 39; Rusty Bradley and Kevin Maurer, *Lions of Kandahar*, New York: Bantam Books, 2011; interviews with two former commanders of Dadullah Mahaz in Zabul and Kandahar, summer 2011.

184. Horn, p. 35.

185. Stephen Grey, *Operation Snakebite*, London: Viking, 2009, p. 291.

186. Interview with two former commanders of Dadullah, Taliban OP 155 and Taliban OP 156, Helmand, 2012; Interview with cadre, Kandahar Taliban 5, August 2014.

187. Interview with senior member of Janan Mahaz, OP Taliban 3, January 2013; Interview with Uruzgan Taliban 1, Shahid Hassas, commander, March 2015.

188. On cross-border support networks for the Afghan Taliban immediately after the Emirate's collapse, see C. Franco, 'The Tehrik-e-Taliban Pakistan', in A. Giustozzi (ed.), *Decoding...*

189. Interview with senior member of Matinullah Mahaz, Taliban leadership 3, August 2014; Interview with member of political commission, Miran Shah Shura, September 2014 (Leadership 4); Interview with Dadullah Mahaz, July 2013, Kandahar Taliban 3, August 2014; Interview with Baradar Mahaz cadre, August 2014 (Kandahar Taliban 4); Interview with cadre, Kandahar Taliban 5, August 2014.

190. Interview with veteran Taliban field commander in Helmand, September 2011.

191. Taliban source in Quetta, contacted June 2013; Martin, *An Intimate War*, pp. 153–4, 170.

192. Interview with Taliban cadre, Naim Mahaz, Taliban OP22, January 2013.

193. Interview with Dadullah Mahaz cadre, July 2013, Kandahar Taliban 3, August 2014.

194. Interview with former commander of Faruq Mahaz, Maywand, December 2014 (Kandahar Taliban 11); Interview with former commander, Taliban Kandahar 20, May 2015; Interview with former commander, Faruq Mahaz, Kandahar Taliban 10, Maruf, December 2014.

195. Interview with former commander, Dadullah Mahaz, Kandahar Taliban 22, July 2015.

196. Interview with former commander, Taliban Kandahar 20, May 2015; Interview with commander, Kandahar Taliban 13, Zherai, December 2014.

197. Interview with Wardak commander Taliban OP 13, Sayed Abad, December 2011.
198. Ron Moreau, 'Americas New Nightmare: If you thought the longtime head of the Taliban was bad, you should meet his no. 2', *Newsweek*, 3 August 2009.
199. Ibid.
200. Interview with commander, Helmand, Taliban OP4, December 2011.
201. Interview with former commander of Faruq Mahaz, Maywand, December 2014 (Kandahar Taliban 11); Interview with former commander, Faruq Mahaz, Kandahar Taliban 10, Maruf, December 2014.
202. Interview with commander, Kandahar Taliban 13, Zherai, December 2014.
203. Communications with Taliban sources in Quetta and Peshawar in spring 2012; interview with Taliban commander in Babaji, Helmand, December 2011.
204. See: Ruttig, 'How tribal...'.
205. Taliban commander in Deh Rawood, interviewed in autumn 2011.
206. Moreau, 'America's New Nightmare'; Interview with Kandahar Commander, Taliban OP8, Zhirai, January 2012; Interview with Nuristan Commander, Taliban OP9, Zhirai, January 2012; Interview with former member of Rahbari Shura, Taliban leadership 7, September 2014; Interview with member of political commission, Miran Shah Shura, Taliban leadership 4, September 2014; Interview with senior member of Matinullah Mahaz, Taliban leadership 3, September 2014; Interview with Commander, Sayed Abad, Tliban OP 16, December 2011; Interview with Commander, Daychopan, Taliban OP 17, January 2012.
207. Interview with Commander, Daychopan, Tliban OP 15, August 2011; Interview with cadre, Baghlan Taliban 11, March 2015.
208. Interview with Wardak commander Taliban OP 12, Sayed Abad, December 2011.
209. UN Security Council, Letter dated 4 September 2012 from the chair of the security council committee pursuant to resolution 1988 (2011) addressed to the President of the Security Council.
210. Source in the Taliban structure in Pakistan, February 2013.
211. Interview with former member of Rahbari Shura, Taliban leadership 7, September 2014.
212. Interview with fighter, Kandahar Taliban 7, Zherai, August 2014; Interview with fighter, Kandahar Taliban 8, Spin Boldak, August 2014.
213. Interview with group commander, Kandahar Taliban 2, August 2014.
214. Interview with Paktia Commander, Taliban OP10, Gard Serai, March 2012.
215. Interview with Nangarhar Commander, Taliban OP11, Khogyani, January 2012.
216. Interview with commander, Ghazni Taliban 6, August 2014; Interview with group commander, Wardak Taliban 3, July 2014.
217. Interview with commander, Baghlan Taliban 1, September 2014.
218. Interview with Herat elder 2, Pashtun Zarghun, April 2015.
219. Interview with Wardak elder 1, Jaghatu, July 2014.
220. Interview with Ghazni elder 4, Qarabagh, August 2014.
221. Commander, Wardak Taliban 5, July 2014.
222. Interview with Kandahar commander Taliban OP 14, Panjwai, December 2011. On the taxation of the mining sector see: Matthew C. DuPée, 'The Taliban Stones Commission and the Insurgent Windfall from Illegal Mining', *CTC Sentinel*, March

2017. On the relationship between Taliban and businessmen, see also: Fazal Muzhary, 'Finding Business Opportunity in Conflict: Shopkeepers, Taleban and the political economy of Andar district', Berlin: Afghanistan Analysts Network, 2 December 2015.

223. Interview with Wardak elder 1, Jaghatu, July 2014; Gopal, 'The Battle for Afghanistan...'; Gretchen Peters, 'Haqqani Network Financing', West Point: CTC, 2012, pp. 34, 39.

224. Gopal, 'The Battle for Afghanistan...'.

225. Gopal, 'The Battle for Afghanistan...'.

226. Interview with commander, Wardak Taliban 7, Daimirdad, July 2014; Interview with commander, Kandahar Taliban 9, Shorabak, August 2014.

227. Interview with Wardak elder 7, Sayed Abad, July 2014.

228. Peters, *Haqqani Network Financing*, pp. 40ff; Interview with Wardak commander Taliban OP 13, Sayed Abad, December 2011.

229. Interview with group commander, Wardak Taliban 3, July 2014; Interview with Kandahar commander Taliban OP 14, Panjwai, December 2011.

230. Interview with Wardak commander Taliban OP 12, Sayed Abad, December 2011.

231. Ron Moreau, 'Feud Splits the Taliban', *Daily Beast*, 17 August 2011.

232. UNODC estimates for the annual drug revenue accruing to the Taliban from 2003 to 2008 (UNODC annual reports); UN Security Council, Letter dated 4 September 2012 from the chair of the security council committee pursuant to resolution 1988 (2011) addressed to the President of the Security Council; Personal communication with ISAF official, September 2011.

233. Gretchen Peters, *Seeds of Terror*, New York: St Martin's Press, 2009, p. 14.

234. David Mansfield, 'From Bad They Made It Worse', Kabul: AREU, May 2014; David Mansfield, 'The devil is in the details: Nangarhar's continued decline into insurgency, violence and wide spread drug production', Kabul: 2016; David Mansfield, 'Understanding...'; David Mansfield, *A State Built on Sand: How Opium Undermined Afghanistan*, London: Hurst, 2016.

235. Interview with commander, Gard Serai, Taliban OP93, April 2012; Interview with commander, Gard Serai, Taliban OP94, April 2012; Interview with commander, Sayed Abad, Taliban OP95, December 2011; Interview with Kandahar commander Taliban OP 14, Panjwai, December 2011; Interview with commander, Daychopan, Taliban OP96, January 2012; Interview with Kandahar Commander, Taliban OP8, Zhirai, January 2012; Jason Burke, *The 9/11 Wars*, Location 6988-6996. For a denial: Interview with commander, Ghazni Taliban 4, August 2014.

236. Taliban source in the Quetta Shura administration, contacted October 2013.

## 3. THE EMERGENCE OF ALTERNATIVE CENTRES OF POWER TO QUETTA

1.    Interview with Logar elder, Baraki Barak, Haqqani elder 1, February 2015; Interview with Haqqani elder 2, Mohamamd Agha, Logar, February 2015.

2.    Interview with Haqqani elder 2, Mohamamd Agha, Logar, February 2015.

3.    Interview with senior member of Miran Shah Shura Commission, Leadership 14, February 2015. Interview with provincial cadre of the Haqqani network, February 2015, Haqqani 8.

4.    Interview with provincial cadre of the Haqqani networks, February 2015, Haqqani 8.

5.    Interview with provincial cadre of the Haqqani networks, February 2015, Haqqani 8; Interview with Taliban cadre in Wardak, March 2015, Wardak Taliban 11.

6.    Brown and Rassler, *Fountainhead of Jihad*, p. 137.

7.    Syed Saleem Shahzad, 'Revolution in the mountains Part 3: Through the eyes of the Taliban', *Asia Times Online*, 5 May 2004.

8.    Interview with former member of Rahbari Shura, Taliban leadership 7, September 2014.

9.    Interview with cadre, Paktia, Haqqani 4, February 2015.

10.   Interview with adviser to Serajuddin Haqqani, Leadership 10, January 2015; Interview with senior member of Zerbati Commission, Miran Shah Shura, Taliban leadership 14, January 2015; Interview with former member of the Rahbari Shura, September 2014 (Leadership 7); Interview with former member of Rahbari Shura, Taliban leadership 7, September 2014; Interview with commission member, Quetta, Taliban leadership 1, September 2014.

11.   Brown and Rassler, *Fountainhead of Jihad*, p. 135.

12.   Interview with Logar elder, Baraki Barak, Haqqani elder 1, February 2015; Interview with Haqqani elder 2, Mohammad Agha, Logar, February 2015.

13.   Interview with group commander, Khost, Haqqani 2, January 2015; Interview with cadre, Paktia, Haqqani 5, February 2015; Interview with cadre, Paktia, Haqqani 4, February 2015.

14.   Interview with fighter, Paktika, Haqqani 6, February 2015.

15.   Interview with commander, Logar (Mohammad Agha), Haqqani 9, February 2015.

16.   Interview with fighter, Paktia, Haqqani 3, February 2015.

17.   Interview with commander, Logar, Haqqani 7, February 2015.

18.   Interview with adviser to Serajuddin Haqqani, Leadership 13, January 2015.

19.   T. Ruttig, 'Loya Paktia's insurgency', in A. Giustozzi (ed.), *Decoding the New Taliban*; Interview with former member of the Rahbari Shura, September 2014 (Leadership 7).

20.   Interview with adviser to Serajuddin Haqqani, Leadership 10, January 2015; Interview with member of Miran Shah Military Commission, Taliban leadership 38, June 2015; Interview with cadre, Paktia, Haqqani 4, February 2015.

21.   Interview with adviser to Serajuddin Haqqani, Leadership 10, January 2015

22.   Interview with adviser to Serajuddin Haqqani, Leadership 10, January 2015; Interview with senior member of Zerbati Commission, Miran Shah Shura, Taliban leadership 14, January 2015; Interview with provincial cadre of the Haqqani networks, February 2015, Haqqani 8.

23.   Interview with adviser to Serajuddin Haqqani, Leadership 10, January 2015.

24.   Interview with senior member of Miran Shah Shura Commission, Leadership 14, February 2015.

25.   Source in the Taliban structure in Pakistan, December 2013.

26.  Interview with Mahaz representative, Ghazni, December 2014, Ghazni Taliban 11; Interview with cadre, Mansur Mahaz, Ghazni Taliban 12, January 2015; Interview with district governor, Ghazni Taliban 13, January 2015.

27.  Interview with former member of the Rahbari Shura, September 2014 (Leadership 7).

28.  Interview with member of central council of Miran Shah Shura, May 2017, Taliban OP 166; Interview with Haqqani network commander in Daychopan, May 2017, Taliban OP167.

29.  See on this point Antonio Giustozzi, *The Islamic State in Khorasan*, London: Hurst, 2018.

30.  Interview with member of central council of Miran Shah Shura, May 2017, Taliban OP 166; Interview with Haqqani network commander in Daychopan, May 2017, Taliban OP167. See also Brown and Rassler, *Fountainhead of Jihad*; Duncan Fitz et al., 'Central Asian Militancy: A Primary Source Examination', Washington: CSIS, 2014, p. 10; Jeremy Binnie and Joanna Wright, 'The Evolving Role of Uzbek-led Fighters in Afghanistan and Pakistan', *CTC Sentinel*, August 2009.

31.  Brown and Rassler, *Fountainhead of Jihad*, p. 219.

32.  Interview with adviser to Serajuddin Haqqani, Leadership 10, January 2015.

33.  Interview with cadre, Logar, Haqqani Network, Taliban OP102, February 2014.

34.  Interview with cadre, Mansur Mahaz, Paktika province, Taliban OP103, February 2014.

35.  Interview with member of Miran Shah Military Commission, Taliban leadership 38, June 2015.

36.  Interview with adviser to Serajuddin Haqqani, Leadership 10, January 2015.

37.  Personal communication with BBC journalist Dawood Azami, London, September 2017; personal communication with Pakistani journalist, London, 2013; Lars W. Lilleby, 'The Haqqani Network: Pursuing Feuds Under The Guise Of Jihad?', *CTX Journal*, Vol. 3, no. 4, November 2013.

38.  Interview with commander, Wardak, Taliban OP13, December 2011.

39.  Interview with deputy, Miran Shah Shura, Taliban leadership 15, February 2015.

40.  Interview with adviser to Serajuddin Haqqani, Leadership 13, January 2015.

41.  Ibid.

42.  Ibid.

43.  Interview with cadre, Mansur Mahaz, Helmand, Taliban OP 99, June 2013; Interview with Cadre, Satta Mahaz, Helmand, Taliban OP100, May 2013.

44.  Interview with cadre, Paktia, Haqqani 4, February 2015.

45.  Taliban source contacted in Mashhad, summer 2013.

46.  Interview with senior member of Zerbati Commission, Miran Shah Shura, Taliban leadership 14, January 2015; Interview with cadre, Paktia, Haqqani 4, February 2015.

47.  Interview with adviser to Serajuddin Haqqani, Leadership 13, January 2015; Interview with group commander, Khost, Haqqani 2, January 2015; Interview with cadre, Paktia, Haqqani 4, February 2015; Interview with cadre, Paktia, Haqqani 5, February 2015; Interview with commander, Logar, Haqqani 7, February 2015.

48.  Interview with member of Miran Shah Military Commission, Taliban leadership 38, June 2015.

49. Interview with adviser to Serajuddin Haqqani, Leadership 13, January 2015; Interview with member of Miran Shah Military Commission, Taliban leadership 38, June 2015.

50. Interview with member of Miran Shah Military Commission, Taliban leadership 38, June 2015; Interview with senior member of Zerbati Commission, Miran Shah Shura, Taliban leadership 14, January 2015

51. Interview with senior member of Mine Commission, Miran Shah Shura, Taliban leadership 16, February 2015.

52. Interview with member of Miran Shah Military Commission, Taliban leadership 38, June 2015.

53. Interview with cadre, Naeem Mahaz, Ghazni province, Taliban OP101, May 2013; Interview with senior member of Mine Commission, Miran Shah Shura, Taliban leadership 16, February 2015.

54. Interview with commander, Haqqani network, Kabul province, December 2014, Haqqani 1.

55. Interview with deputy, Miran Shah Shura, Taliban leadership 15, February 2015.

56. Ibid.

57. Ibid.

58. Interview with senior member of Mine Commission, Miran Shah Shura, Taliban leadership 16, February 2015.

59. Ibid.

60. Interview with senior member of Zerbati Commission, Miran Shah Shura, Taliban leadership 14, January 2015.

61. Interview with senior member of the Miran Shah recruitment commission, Taliban Leadership 18, February 2015; Interview with advisor of Sirajuddin Haqqani, Taliban Leadership 10, January 2015; Taliban cadre of the Quetta Shura, contacted October 2013.

62. Interview with member of Miran Shah Military Commission, Taliban leadership 38, June 2015; Interview with senior member of Zerbati Commission, Miran Shah Shura, Taliban leadership 14, January 2015.

63. Quetta Shura cadre, contacted in November 2016.

64. Interview with member of Miran Shah Military Commission, Taliban leadership 38, June 2015.

65. Interview with commander, Haqqani network, Kabul province, December 2014, Haqqani 1.

66. Ibid.

67. Ibid.

68. Communication with Taliban cadre in Jalalabad, July 2012.

69. Interview with senior member of Ijraya Shura, Taliban leadership 21, May 2015; Communications with high-ranking Peshawar Shura cadres, July-August 2012; personal communication with tribal elder associated with the Ijraya Shura, Nangarhar, September-October 2011; interview, senior field commander, Wardak, October 2011.

70. Communications with Taliban cadres in Peshawar, summer 2012; interviews with commanders in Helmand, December 2011, and Wardak, October 2011. On Pakistan and Hizb-i Islami see Peter Tomsen, *Wars of Afghanistan*, New York: Public Affairs,

2011; Olivier Roy, *Islam and Resistance in Afghanistan*, Cambridge: Cambridge University Press, 1989; Interview with senior member of Ijraya Shura, Taliban leadership 21, May 2015.

71. Source in the Taliban structure in Pakistan, November 2012.
72. Interview with senior member of Peshawar Military Commission, Taliban leadership 22, April 2015.
73. Interview with deputy, Peshawar Shura, Taliban leadership 23, May 2015.
74. Interview with Taliban cadre, Baghlan, May 2015, Baghlan Taliban 14; Interview with cadre, Baghlan Taliban 11, March 2015; Interview with Taliban cadre, Dandi Ghori, Baghlan Taliban 13, March 2015; Interview with former commander, Nawur, Ghazni Taliban 17, May 2015; Interview with provincial cadre of the Haqqani networks, February 2015, Haqqani 8; Interview with cadre, Wardak Taliban 12, March 2015; Interview with former fighter, Wardak Taliban 14, May 2015; Interview with commander, Baghlan Taliban 17, May 2015; Interview with senior member of Peshawar Military Commission, Taliban leadership 22, April 2015.
75. Interview with member of political commission in Miram Shah shura, Taliban Leadership 4, September 2014.
76. Source in the Taliban structure in Pakistan, November 2012; Interview with former fighter, Baghlan Taliban 15, May 2015; Interview with former commander, Baradar Mahaz, Ghazni Taliban 15, May 2015; Interview with former commander, Nawur, Ghazni Taliban 17, May 2015; Interview with senior member of Matinullah Mahaz, Taliban leadership 3, August 2014.
77. Interview with former member of Rahbari Shura, Taliban leadership 7, September 2014.
78. Interview with former commander, Faruq Mahaz, Kandahar Taliban 10, Maruf, December 2014.
79. Interview with former commander, Nawur, Ghazni Taliban 17, May 2015.
80. Interview with former fighter, Wardak Taliban 14, May 2015.
81. Interview with former commander, Wardak Taliban 15, May 2015.
82. Interview with Shamsatoo Mahaz cadre, Hissarak, Nangarhar Taliban 6, April 2015.
83. Interview with member of Safi Shura, Nangarhar Taliban 2, April 2015; Interview with senior member of Ijraya Shura, Taliban leadership 21, May 2015.
84. Communications with Taliban cadres in Peshawar, summer 2012; Interview with Shamsatoo Mahaz cadre, Hissarak, Nangarhar Taliban 6, April 2015.
85. Interview with senior Peshawar Shura cadre in Nangarhar Province, Taliban OP 157, August 2013.
86. Interview with cadre, Shirzad, Nangarhar Taliban 8, April 2015.
87. Source in the Taliban structure in Pakistan, November 2012.
88. Confirmed by multiple sources within the Taliban and by sympathisers within Pakistani Deobandi circles, contacted in 2011–12.
89. Interview with cadre, Shirzad, Nangarhar Taliban 8, April 2015.
90. Ibid.
91. Interview with senior member of Peshawar Military Commission, Taliban leadership 22, April 2015; Interview with deputy, Peshawar Shura, Taliban leadership 23, May 2015; Interview with Taliban cadre, Dandi Ghori, Baghlan Taliban 13, March 2015.

92. Interview with Nangarhar Taliban 3, Bati Kot, April 2015.
93. Interview with former Tora Bora Mahaz commander, Nangarhar Taliban 7, April 2015; Interview with Shamsatoo Mahaz cadre, Hissarak, Nangarhar Taliban 6, April 2015; Interview with senior member of Peshawar Military Commission, Taliban leadership 22, April 2015.
94. Interview with Nangarhar Taliban 3, Bati Kot, April 2015; Interview with Shamsatoo Mahaz cadre, Hissarak, Nangarhar Taliban 6, April 2015; Interview with deputy, Peshawar Shura, Taliban leadership 23, May 2015; Interview with commander, Bati Kot, Nangarhar Taliban 5, April 2015; Interview with Taliban cadre, Baghlan, May 2015, Baghlan Taliban 14; Interview with member of Safi Shura, Nangarhar Taliban 2, April 2015; Interview with Toor-e Pagri commander, Bati Kot, Nangarhar Taliban 4, April 2015; Interview with former Tora Bora Mahaz commander, Nangarhar Taliban 7, April 2015; Interview with cadre, Wardak Taliban 12, March 2015; Interview with senior member of Ijraya Shura, Taliban leadership 21, May 2015.
95. Interview with member of Safi Shura, Nangarhar Taliban 2, April 2015.
96. Source in the Taliban structure in Pakistan, September 2012.
97. Interview with Nangarhar Taliban 3, Bati Kot, April 2015; Interview with Toor-e Pagri commander, Bati Kot, Nangarhar Taliban 4, April 2015; Interview with commander, Bati Kot, Nangarhar Taliban 5, April 2015; Interview with Shamsatoo Mahaz cadre, Hissarak, Nangarhar Taliban 6, April 2015; Interview with former Tora Bora Mahaz commander, Nangarhar Taliban 7, April 2015; Interview with cadre, Shirzad, Nangarhar Taliban 8, April 2015; Interview with senior member of Ijraya Shura, Taliban leadership 21, May 2015.
98. Interview with member of Safi Shura, Nangarhar Taliban 2, April 2015.
99. Interview with Nangarhar Taliban 3, Bati Kot, April 2015; Interview with Toor-e Pagri commander, Bati Kot, Nangarhar Taliban 4, April 2015; Interview with commander, Bati Kot, Nangarhar Taliban 5, April 2015; Interview with former Tora Bora Mahaz commander, Nangarhar Taliban 7, April 2015; Interview with senior member of Ijraya Shura, Taliban leadership 21, May 2015.
100. Interview with senior member of Ijraya Shura, Taliban leadership 21, May 2015.
101. Interview with former commander Of Kabir, Hissarak, Nangarhar Taliban 1, April 2015; Interview with member of Safi Shura, Nangarhar Taliban 2, April 2015; Interview with commander, Bati Kot, Nangarhar Taliban 5, April 2015; Interview with cadre, Shirzad, Nangarhar Taliban 8, April 2015; Interview with Shamsatoo Mahaz cadre, Hissarak, Nangarhar Taliban 6, April 2015; Interview with former Tora Bora Mahaz commander, Nangarhar Taliban 7, April 2015; Interview with former commander, Baghlan Taliban 16, May 2015; Interview with cadre, Mansur Mahaz, Taliban OP104, August 2013; Interview with senior member of Ijraya Shura, Taliban leadership 21, May 2015.
102. Interview with member of Safi Shura, Nangarhar Taliban 2, April 2015; Interview with Toor-e Pagri commander, Bati Kot, Nangarhar Taliban 4, April 2015.
103. Interview with Shamsatoo Mahaz cadre, Hissarak, Nangarhar Taliban 6, April 2015.
104. Interview with former member of the Rahbari Shura, September 2014 (Leadership 7); Interview with Nangarhar Taliban 3, Bati Kot, April 2015.
105. Interview with cadre, Shirzad, Nangarhar Taliban 8, April 2015.

106. Interview with commander, Baghlan Taliban 17, May 2015; Interview with cadre, Dadullah Mahaz, Taliban OP105, December 2012.
107. Interview with Commander, Jundullah Mahaz, Taliban OP106, January 2013.
108. Interview with cadre, Dashti Archi District, Taliban OP 107, December 2012.
109. Source in the Taliban structure in Peshawar, August 2013, source in the Taliban structure in Peshawar, July 2013.
110. Interview with cadre, Baghlan Taliban 11, March 2015; Interview with Taliban cadre, Dandi Ghori, Baghlan Taliban 13, March 2015; Interview with provincial cadre of the Haqqani networks, February 2015, Haqqani 8.
111. Source in the Taliban structure in Pakistan, November 2012.
112. Interview with commander, Sorkhrod, Nangarhar Taliban 9, March 2015; Interview with cadre, Baghlan Taliban 11, March 2015; Interview with former commander, Baghlan Taliban 16, May 2015; Interview with cadre, Shirzad, Nangarhar Taliban 8, April 2015; Interview with commander, Jundullah Mahaz, Baghlan Taliban 11, March 2015.
113. Interview with Shamsatoo Mahaz cadre, Hissarak, Nangarhar Taliban 6, April 2015.
114. Interview with member of Safi Shura, Nangarhar Taliban 2, April 2015; Interview with senior member of Ijraya Shura, Taliban leadership 21, May 2015.
115. Interview with former fighter, Wardak Taliban 14, May 2015; Interview with commander, Kapisa Taliban 1, March 2015.
116. Interview with commander, Sorkhrod, Nangarhar Taliban 9, March 2015.
117. Source in the Taliban structure in Pakistan, November 2012.
118. Interview with Shamsatoo Mahaz cadre, Hissarak, Nangarhar Taliban 6, April 2015.
119. Interview with commander, Bati Kot, Nangarhar Taliban 5, April 2015.
120. Interview with deputy, Peshawar Shura, Taliban leadership 23, May 2015.
121. Interview with senior member of Peshawar Military Commission, Taliban leadership 22, April 2015; Interview with deputy, Peshawar Shura, Taliban leadership 23, May 2015.
122. Source in the Taliban structure in Pakistan, June 2013.
123. Source in the Taliban structure in Pakistan, November 2012.
124. Source in the Taliban structure in Pakistan, January 2013; Source in the Taliban structure in Pakistan, November 2012.
125. Interview with senior member of Peshawar Military Commission, Taliban leadership 22, April 2015.
126. Interview with commander in Dadullah's loy Mahaz, September 2012.
127. Interview with *dilghay* commander, Behsud, Wardak Taliban 10, March 2015; Interview with Taliban cadre in Wardak, March 2015, Wardak Taliban 11; Interview with provincial cadre of the Haqqani network, February 2015, Haqqani 8.
128. Interview with *dilghay* commander, Behsud, Wardak Taliban 10, March 2015; Interview with Taliban cadre in Wardak, March 2015, Wardak Taliban 11; Interview with cadre, Wardak Taliban 12, March 2015.
129. Interview with former commander, Wardak Taliban 15, May 2015.
130. Interview with former fighter, Wardak Taliban 14, May 2015.
131. Interview with commander, Andkhoy, Faryab Taliban 7, December 2014; Interview with Taliban cadre, Almar, Faryab Taliban 1, December 2014. The 2,000 estimate

seems however high for the period in which Baradar was dominant in Faryab. Other sources put total Taliban strength at just over 2,000 for 2013.

132. Interview with Taliban cadre, Almar, Faryab Taliban 1, December 2014; Interview with cadre, Almar, Faryab Taliban 2, December 2014.

133. Interview with commander, Andkhoy, Faryab Taliban 7, December 2014; Interview with cadre, Faryab Taliban 4, December 2014; Interview with group commander, Sattar Mahaz, Faryab Taliban 6, December 2014; Interview with cadre, Almar, Faryab Taliban 2, December 2014; Interview with cadre, Mansur Mahaz, Faryab Taliban 3, December 2014.

134. Interview with Military Commission cadre for Faryab province, December 2011.

135. Interview with cadre, Mansur Mahaz, Faryab Taliban 5, December 2014; Interview with Taliban cadre, Almar, Faryab Taliban 1, December 2014; Interview with cadre, Faryab Taliban 4, December 2014; Interview with group commander, Sattar Mahaz, Faryab Taliban 6, December 2014; Interview with cadre, Almar, Faryab Taliban 2, December 2014.

136. Interview with commander, Andkhoy, Faryab Taliban 7, December 2014; Interview with cadre, Faryab Taliban 4, December 2014; Interview with cadre, Mansur Mahaz, Faryab Taliban 5, December 2014; Interview with group commander, Sattar Mahaz, Faryab Taliban 6, December 2014; Interview with Taliban cadre, Almar, Faryab Taliban 1, December 2014; Interview with cadre, Almar, Faryab Taliban 2, December 2014; Interview with cadre, Mansur Mahaz, Faryab Taliban 3, December 2014.

137. Interview with commander, Jundullah Mahaz, Baghlan Taliban 11, March 2015.

138. Interview with cadre, Faryab Taliban 4, December 2014; Interview with cadre, Mansur Mahaz, Faryab Taliban 5, December 2014; Interview with commander, Andkhoy, Faryab Taliban 7, December 2014; Interview with cadre, Mansur Mahaz, Faryab Taliban 3, December 2014; Interview with cadre, Almar, Faryab Taliban 2, December 2014.

139. Interview with Taliban cadre, Almar, Faryab Taliban 1, December 2014.

140. Personal communication with Afghan analysis from Takhar, 2012.

141. Interview with Afghan informer connected to the Taliban, May 2010; Interview with former fighter, Baghlan Taliban 15, May 2015; Interview with former commander, Baghlan Taliban 18, May 2015.

142. Interview with Taliban cadre, Baghlan, May 2015, Baghlan Taliban 14; Interview with Taliban cadre, Dandi Ghori, Baghlan Taliban 13, March 2015; Interview with former commander, Baghlan Taliban 18, May 2015.

143. Interview with former commander, Baghlan Taliban 16, May 2015; Interview with commander, Jundullah Mahaz, Baghlan Taliban 11, March 2015.

144. Source in the Taliban structure in Pakistan, August 2012.

145. Interview with Taliban field commander in Badakhshan, September 2012.

146. Interview with Taliban cadre, Dandi Ghori, Baghlan Taliban 13, March 2015.

147. Personal communication with Afghan analyst, 2012.

148. Interview with resident of Baghlan Markazi, April 2010.

149. Interview with UN official, Mazar-e Sharif, 21 April 2010.

150. Interview with cadre, Mansur Mahaz, Sar-e-pul province, Taliban OP40, March 2014.

151. Interview with Nangarhar Taliban 3, Bati Kot, April 2015; Interview with senior member of Ijraya Shura, Taliban leadership 21, May 2015. On Taliban recruitment of Tajiks in north-eastern Afghanistan see also Obaid Ali, 'The Non-Pashtun Taleban of the North: A case study from Badakhshan', Berlin: Afghanistan Analysts Network, 3 January 2017 and 'The Non-Pashtun Taleban of the North: The Takhar case', Berlin: Afghanistan Analysts Network, July 2017.

152. Interview with commander of IMU in Chahardara District of Kundoz, December 2013; Interview with IMU commander in Takhar province, December 2013; Interview with IMU cadre, December 2013; Interview with Jundullah Mahaz high level cadre, December 2013; Interview with Jundullah Mahaz cadre, December 2013.

153. Interview with Commander, Jundullah Mahaz, Taliban OP115, October 2012.

154. Interview with Jundullah Mahaz senior cadre, Taliban OP116, December 2013.

155. Interview with commander, Jundullah Mahaz, Baghlan Taliban 11, March 2015.

156. Ibid.

157. Interview with Jundullah Mahaz leader, Taliban OP117, December 2013; Interview with Jundullah Mahaz senior cadre, Taliban OP116, December 2013, Interview with Jundullah Mahaz leader, Taliban OP114, December 2013; Interview with Jundullah Mahaz leader, Taliban OP118, December 2013.

158. Interview with leader of Jundullah Mahaz, Taliban OP116, December 2013.

159. Interview with Iranian adviser with Jundullah Mahaz, Advisers 2, July 2015.

160. Interview with Taliban cadre, Baghlan, May 2015, Baghlan Taliban 14; Interview with cadre, Baghlan Taliban 11, March 2015; Interview with former commander, Baghlan Taliban 18, May 2015.

161. Interview with former fighter, Baghlan Taliban 15, May 2015.

162. Interview with commander, Jundullah Mahaz, Baghlan Taliban 11, March 2015.

163. Interview with Taliban cadre, Dandi Ghori, Baghlan Taliban 13, March 2015.

164. Interview with former fighter, Baghlan Taliban 15, May 2015; Interview with former commander, Baghlan Taliban 18, May 2015.

165. Interview with cadre, Faryab Taliban 4, December 2014; Interview with cadre, Mansur Mahaz, Faryab Taliban 5, December 2014; Interview with group commander, Sattar Mahaz, Faryab Taliban 6, December 2014.

166. Interview with cadre, Mansur Mahaz, Ghazni Taliban 12, January 2015.

167. Interview with Mahaz representative, Ghazni, December 2014, Ghazni Taliban 11; Interview with former commander, Nawur, Ghazni Taliban 17, May 2015; Interview with former commander, Baradar Mahaz, Ghazni Taliban 15, May 2015.

168. Interview with cadre, Naeem Mahaz, Ghazni province, Taliban OP101, May 2013; Interview with former commander, Baradar Mahaz, Ghazni Taliban 15, May 2015.

169. Interview with cadre, Nawa District of Ghazni province, Taliban OP117, May 2013.

170. Interview with Mahaz representative, Ghazni, December 2014, Ghazni Taliban 11; Interview with cadre, Mansur Mahaz, Ghazni Taliban 12, January 2015; Interview with commander, Jaghori, Ghazni Taliban 14, January 2015; Interview with district governor, Ghazni Taliban 13, January 2015.

171. Interview with commander, Jaghori, Ghazni Taliban 14, January 2015.

172. Interview with cadre, Kunar, Taliban OP32, January 2014.

173. Interview with senior Taliban cadre in Logar province, Haqqani Network, Taliban OP102, February 2014.

174. Source in the Taliban structure in Pakistan, November 2012.

175. Source in the Taliban structure in Pakistan, February 2013.

176. Source in the Taliban structure in Pakistan, June 2013.

177. Communications with a high-level Taliban cadres in Miran Shah and Peshawar, October 2012 and March 2015; Interview with Haqqani commander, Sayedabad district, Wardak, September 2011.

178. Interview with cadre, Paktia, Taliban OP108, February 2014; Interview with member of Miran Shah Military Commission, Taliban leadership 38, June 2015.

179. Source in the Taliban structure in Pakistan, September 2012.

180. Source in the Taliban structure in Pakistan, October 2013.

181. Source in the Taliban structure in Pakistan, October 2014.

182. Interview with senior member of Peshawar Military Commission, Taliban leadership 22, April 2015.

183. Interview with former Taliban commander, Mohammad Agha (Logar), Haqqani Taliban 11, March 2015.

184. Source in the Taliban structure in Pakistan, June 2012.

185. Interview with former member of Rahbari Shura, Taliban leadership 7, September 2014.

186. Interview with commander, Helmand, Taliban OP 21, September 2011.

187. Interview with commander, Helmand, Taliban OP2, December 2011.

188. Taliban sources in Quetta and Peshawar, contacted July–September 2012.

189. Taliban source in Peshawar, contacted March 2013.

190. Source in the Taliban structure in Pakistan, June 2012.

191. Source in the Taliban structure in Pakistan, May 2015.

192. Interview with senior member of Ijraya Shura, Taliban leadership 21, May 2015.

193. Interview with member of Safi Shura, Nangarhar Taliban 2, April 2015; Interview with commander, Bati Kot, Nangarhar Taliban 5, April 2015; Interview with Shamsatoo Mahaz cadre, Hissarak, Nangarhar Taliban 6, April 2015; Interview with cadre, Shirzad, Nangarhar Taliban 8, April 2015.

194. Source in the Taliban structure in Pakistan, August 2013.

195. Source in the Taliban structure in Pakistan, November 2012; Source in the Taliban structure in Pakistan, February 2013.

196. Tens of interviews with Taliban cadres in eastern and central Afghanistan in 2013-15 have all confirmed the role of the Military Commission and of its local Massuleen.

197. Interview with Taliban field commander based in Khakriz district, Kandahar, September 2011.

198. Interviews with Taliban commanders, Helmand, Taliban OP18, 3 March 2012.

199. Interview with commander, Wardak, Taliban OP13, December 2011.

200. Interview with Taliban cadre, Baghlan, May 2015, Baghlan Taliban 14; Interview with cadre, Baghlan Taliban 11, March 2015; Interview with Taliban cadre, Dandi Ghori, Baghlan Taliban 13, March 2015; Interview with commander, Andkhoy, Faryab Taliban 7, December 2014; Interview with Mahaz representative, Ghazni, December 2014, Ghazni Taliban 11; Interview with cadre, Mansur Mahaz, Ghazni

Taliban 12, January 2015; Interview with provincial cadre of the Haqqani networks, February 2015, Haqqani 8; Interview with fighter, Kandahar Taliban 1, August 2014; Interview with group commander, Kandahar Taliban 2, August 2014; Interview with commander, Kandahar Taliban 9, Shorabak, August 2014; Interview with member of Safi Shura, Nangarhar Taliban 2, April 2015; Interview with Toor-e Pagri commander, Bati Kot, Nangarhar Taliban 4, April 2015; Interview with Shamsatoo Mahaz cadre, Hissarak, Nangarhar Taliban 6, April 2015; Interview with cadre, Shirzad, Nangarhar Taliban 8, April 2015; Interview with cadre, Wardak Taliban 12, March 2015.

201. Interview with cadre, Nuristan, Taliban OP30, August 2013.

202. Mentioned in multiple interviews with Taliban cadres in various provinces throughout 2012 and 2013.

203. Interview with senior member of Ijraya Shura, Taliban leadership 21, May 2015.

204. Interview with district *nizami massul*, Maidan Wardak, July 2013.

205. Source in the Taliban structure in Pakistan, February 2013.

206. For more detail, see: Claudio Franco: 'The evolving Taliban: Changes in the insurgency's DNA', Afghanistan Analysts Network, 19 May 2013: www.afghanistan-analysts.org/the-evolving-Taliban-changes-in-the-insurgency-dna/

207. Interview with Taliban field commander, Jagatu district, Wardak, Taliban OP 158, September 2011.

208. Interview with Taliban cadre, Baghlan, May 2015, Baghlan Taliban 14; Interview with Taliban cadre, Dandi Ghori, Baghlan Taliban 13, March 2015; Interview with cadre, Faryab Taliban 4, December 2014; Interview with cadre, Mansur Mahaz, Faryab Taliban 5, December 2014; Interview with group commander, Sattar Mahaz, Faryab Taliban 6, December 2014; Interview with commander, Andkhoy, Faryab Taliban 7, December 2014; Interview with cadre, Almar, Faryab Taliban 2, December 2014; Interview with cadre, Mansur Mahaz, Faryab Taliban 3, December 2014; Interview with Mahaz representative, Ghazni, December 2014, Ghazni Taliban 11; Interview with Taliban cadre, Dandi Ghori, Baghlan Taliban 13, March 2015; Interview with provincial cadre of the Haqqani networks, February 2015, Haqqani 8; Interview with fighter, Kandahar Taliban 6, Maruf, August 2014; Interview with fighter, Kandahar Taliban 8, Spin Boldak, August 2014; Interview with member of Safi Shura, Nangarhar Taliban 2, April 2015; Interview with Toor-e Pagri commander, Bati Kot, Nangarhar Taliban 4, April 2015; Interview with commander, Bati Kot, Nangarhar Taliban 5, April 2015; Interview with Shamsatoo Mahaz cadre, Hissarak, Nangarhar Taliban 6, April 2015; Interview with cadre, Shirzad, Nangarhar Taliban 8, April 2015; Interview with Taliban cadre in Wardak, March 2015, Wardak Taliban 11; Interview with cadre, Wardak Taliban 12, March 2015.

209. Source in the Taliban structure in Pakistan, August 2012.

210. Interview with former member of Rahbari Shura, Taliban leadership 7, September 2014.

211. Interview with Sattar Mahaz Leader in Badakhshan province, Taliban OP159, January 2013.

212. Interviews with Taliban cadres and commanders, 2013-15.

213. Interview with cadre, Nahrin, Taliban OP109, January 2014.

214. Interviews with Taliban commanders, Helmand, Taliban OP18, 3 March 2012; Interview with senior field commander, Wardak, Taliban OP 160, October 2011.

215. Interview with cadre, Satter Mahaz, Baghlan, Taliban OP110, October 2012.

216. Interview with Taliban field commander, Baghlan, October 2012.

217. Taliban sources in Quetta and Peshawar, contacted June-July 2012.

218. Interview with commander, Taliban OP82, January 2013; Interview with cadre, Jundullah Mahaz, Shahri Bozorg, Taliban OP111, November 2012; Interview with Commander, Taliban OP112, November 2012; Interview commander, Taliban OP82, January 2013.

219. Interview with commander, Faryab, Taliban OP113, July 2012.

4. THE CRISIS OF THE QUETTA SHURA 2009–13

1.    Antonio Giustozzi and Silab Mangal, 'Violence, the Taliban and Afghanistan's 2014 elections', Washington: USIP, 2015.

2.    Ibid.

3.    Afghanistan: AIHRC-UNAMA Joint Monitoring of Political Rights, Presidential and Provincial Council Elections, Third Report, 1 Aug – 21 Oct 2009.

4.    Giustozzi and Mangal, 'Violence…'.

5.    In reality Dr. Abdullah is of mixed Tajik and Pashtun ethnicity, but was widely seen by Pashtuns in 2009 as a 'Tajik' candidate.

6.    Giustozzi and Mangal, 'Violence…'.

7.    Ibid.

8.    Ibid.

9.    Ibid.

10.   Ibid.

11.   Antonio Giustozzi and Christoph Reuter, 'The Insurgents of the Afghan North', Berlin: Afghanistan Analysts Network, 2011.

12.   Interview with senior member of Zerbati commission, Quetta, Taliban Leadership 14, July 2015.

13.   Interview with Helmandi field commander, September 2011.

14.   Communications with Taliban cadres in Quetta, summer 2013. Regarding press reports on the Taliban's revenue from opium being affected, see for example: Jim Michaels, 'Afghan poppy crops down 40% since '08 as key towns secured', USA Today, 17 June 2012; Guillaume Lavallee, 'Taliban changing strategy in Kandahar: governor', AFP, 7 Jun 2011.

15.   Interview with Taliban commander, Garmser district, Helmand, March 2012. In general, interviews in Helmand in 2011–12 saw Taliban members admitting to having been pushed out of the areas of most intensive poppy cultivation, with consequent losses in terms of tax revenue, although the smugglers continued to contribute to the Taliban's coffers.

16.   Communication with district-level nizami massul in Faryab, summer 2012.

17.   Interview with former member of the Rahbari Shura, September 2014 (Leadership 7).

18.   Source in the Taliban structure in Pakistan, March 2013.

19. Interview with former commander of Faruq Mahaz, Maywand, December 2014 (Kandahar Taliban 11); Interview with commander, Kandahar Taliban 13, Zherai, December 2014; Interview with former commander, Faruq Mahaz, Kandahar Taliban 10, Maruf, December 2014; Interview with former member of Rahbari Shura, Taliban leadership 7, September 2014; Interview with member of political commission in Miran Shah shura, Taliban Leadership 4, September 2014; Interview with senior member of Matinullah Mahaz, Taliban leadership 3, August 2014; Interview with senior member of Abdul Majid Mahaz, Taliban leadership 2, September 2014; Interview with member of Quetta Political Commission, Taliban Leadership 1, September 2014.

20. Interview with former member of Rahbari Shura, Taliban leadership 7, September 2014.

21. Interview with member of Quetta Political Commission, Taliban Leadership 1, September 2014.

22. 79 interviews with Taliban cadres and commanders of the Quetta Shura in 2012–14 for a project mapping the Taliban networks highlighted the differences between the Quetta Shura and the Peshawar Shura systems.

23. Interview with Taliban field commander from Kunduz, October 2011.

24. Communication with Taliban cadre in Peshawar, June 2013.

25. Interview with Dadullah Mahaz, July 2013., Kandahar Taliban 3, August 2014; Interview with Baradar Mahaz cadre, August 2014 (Kandahar Taliban 4). For a detailed account by two experts, see: Thomas H. Johnson, M. Chris Mason, 'Down the AfPak Rabbit Hole', *Foreign Policy*, 1 March 2010.

26. Communications with Taliban cadres in Peshawar and Quetta, summer 2012; interview with senior field commander in Wardak, October 2011.

27. Source in the Taliban structure in Pakistan, January 2013.

28. Interview with commander, Maywand, Kandahar Taliban 12, December 2014; Interview with advisor to Sirajuddin Haqqani, Taliban Leadership 13, January 2015. See also Javid Ahmad, 'Pakistan's Secret War Machine', *The National Interest*, May 7, 2018; Coll, *Directorate* S.

29. Interview with adviser, Pakistan, Adviser 2, July 2015; Interview with senior member of Zerbati Commission, Taliban Leadership 14, February 2015; Interview with Haqqani provincial cadre, Haqqani 4, February 2015.

30. Iranian adviser to Jundullah, Advisers 3, July 2015.

31. Interview with commander, Maywand, Kandahar Taliban 12, December 2014.

32. Source in the Taliban structure in Pakistan, January 2013, February 2013. See also Anand Gopal, 'Serious Leadership Rifts Emerge in Afghan Taliban', *CTC Sentinel*, November 2012, Vol 5, Issue 11; Huma Yusuf, 'Mullah Abdul Ghani Baradar: Are other Taliban leaders hiding in Karachi?', Christian Science Monitor, 16 February 2010; Zia ur Rehman, 'Exposing the Karachi-Afghanistan', Oslo: NOREF, December 2013.

33. Contacts with cadres of the Quetta Finance Commission, 2013–14.

34. Interview with fighter, Kandahar Taliban 1, August 2014; Interview with fighter, Kandahar Taliban 7, Zherai, August 2014.

35. Interview with former commander of Faruq Mahaz, Maywand, December 2014 (Kandahar Taliban 11).

36. Interview with former commander, Faruq Mahaz, Kandahar Taliban 10, Maruf, December 2014.

37. Interview with Kandahar elder 4, Panjwai, February 2015.

38. Interview with former member of the Rahbari Shura, September 2014 (Leadership 7).

39. Taliban commander in Nahr-i Seraj, May 2012.

40. Taliban commander in Nawzad, May 2012.

41. Yousufzai.

42. Interview with former commander, Baradar Mahaz, Ghazni Taliban 15, May 2015.

43. Interview with fighter, Paktia, Haqqani 3, February 2015.

44. Interview with former Taliban cadre, Kandahar, July 2015, Kandahar Taliban 18; Interview with former group commander of Mansur Mahaz, Ghazni Taliban 16, May 2015; Interview with former commander, Baradar Mahaz, Ghazni Taliban 15, May 2015; Interview with commander, Baghlan Taliban 17, May 2015; Interview with former commander, Baghlan Taliban 18, May 2015; Interview with Logar elder, Baraki Barak, Haqqani elder 1, February 2015; Interview with Haqqani elder 2, Mohamamd Agha, Logar, February 2015; Interview with cadre, Samangan province, Taliban OP55, March 2014.

45. Interview with former commander, Kandahar Taliban 21, May 2015.

46. Interview with former commander, Wardak Taliban 15, May 2015.

47. Interview with former fighter, Wardak Taliban 14, May 2015.

48. Interview with cadre, Kandahar Taliban 5, August 2014.

49. Interview with former group commander of Mansur Mahaz, Ghazni Taliban 16, May 2015; Interview with former fighter, Wardak Taliban 14, May 2015; Interview with former commander, Baghlan Taliban 18, May 2015; Interview with former commander, Taliban Kandahar 20, May 2015; Interview with Taliban commander, Ghazni Taliban 9, August 2014.

50. Interview with former commander, Dadullah Mahaz, Kandahar Taliban 22, July 2015; Interview with former commander, Kandahar Taliban 21, May 2015.

51. Interview with former fighter, Wardak Taliban 14, May 2015.

52. Interview with former Taliban commander, Mohammad Agha (Logar), Haqqani Taliban 11, March 2015; Martin, *An Intimate War,* pp. 200–1; Interview with commander, Wardak Taliban 2, Jaghatu, June 2014; Interview with commander, Sorkhrod, Nangarhar Taliban 9, March 2015; Interview with Uruzgan Taliban 1, Shahid Hassas, commander, March 2015.

53. Interview with former Taliban cadre, Kandahar, July 2015, Kandahar Taliban 18; Interview with former commander, Baghlan Taliban 16, May 2015; Interview with former commander, Baradar Mahaz, Ghazni Taliban 15, May 2015; Interview with former commander, Nawur, Ghazni Taliban 17, May 2015; Interview with former commander, Wardak Taliban 15, May 2015; Interview with commander, Baghlan Taliban 17, May 2015; Interview with former commander, Baghlan Taliban 18, May 2015; Interview with former senior member of Gardi Jangal Shura, Kandahar Taliban 19, July 2015; Interview with former commander, Kandahar Taliban 21, May 2015; Interview with former commander, Dadullah Mahaz, Kandahar Taliban 22, July 2015; Interview with former commander, Taliban Kandahar 20, May 2015.

54. Interview with former commander, Baghlan Taliban 16, May 2015; Interview with former commander, Baradar Mahaz, Ghazni Taliban 15, May 2015; Interview with former commander, Nawur, Ghazni Taliban 17, May 2015; Interview with former fighter, Wardak Taliban 14, May 2015; Interview with former commander, Wardak Taliban 15, May 2015; Interview with commander, Baghlan Taliban 17, May 2015; Interview with former commander, Taliban Kandahar 20, May 2015; Interview with former commander, Kandahar Taliban 21, May 2015.
55. Interview with former fighter, Wardak Taliban 14, May 2015.
56. Interview with commander, Kapisa Taliban 1, March 2015.
57. Interview with former commander, Baghlan Taliban 16, May 2015.
58. Interview with former commander, Nawur, Ghazni Taliban 17, May 2015.
59. Interview with commander, Kapisa Taliban 1, March 2015; Interview with former Taliban commander, Mohammad Agha (Logar), Haqqani Taliban 11, March 2015; Interview with commander, Sorkhrod, Nangarhar Taliban 9, March 2015.
60. Interview with former commander, Shindand, Herat Taliban 8, December 2014.
61. Interview with Ghazni Elder 4, Giro, July 2014.
62. Interview with commander, Baghlan Taliban 6, Baghlan Jadid, September 2014; Interview with commander, Baghlan Taliban 1, September 2014; Interview with commander. Dandi Ghori, Bagjlan Taliban 2, September 2014; Interview with commander, Baghlan-e Jadid, Baghlan Taliban 3, September 2014; Interview with commander, Baghlan Jadid, Baghlan Taliban 4, September 2014; Interview with commander, Burka, Baghlan, September 2014; Interview with cadre, Baghlan Jadid, Baghlan Taliban 7, July 2014; Interview with commander, Dandi Ghori, Ghazni Taliban 9, July 2014; Interview with commander, Baghlan Jadidi, Baghlan Taliban 10, July 2014; Interview with commander, Wardak (Chak), Taliban OP39, June 2014; Interview with commander, Wardak Taliban 2, Jaghatu, June 2014; Interview with group commander, Wardak Taliban 3, July 2014; Interview with commander, Wardak Taliban 5, July 2014; Interview with cadre, Baghlan Taliban 11, March 2015; Interview with Taliban cadre, Dandi Ghori, Baghlan Taliban 13, March 2015; Interview with Mahaz representative, Ghazni, December 2014, Ghazni Taliban 11; Interview with district governor, Ghazni Taliban 13, January 2015; Interview with commander, Jaghori, Ghazni Taliban 14, January 2015; Interview with group commander, Khost, Haqqani 2, January 2015; Interview with fighter, Paktia, Haqqani 3, February 2015; Interview with cadre, Paktia, Haqqani 4, February 2015; Interview with cadre, Paktia, Haqqani 5, February 2015; Interview with fighter, Paktika, Haqqani 6, February 2015; Interview with provincial cadre of the Haqqani networks, February 2015, Haqqani 8; Interview with commander, Logar (Mohammad Agha), Haqqani 9, February 2015; Interview with group commander, Cheshti Sharif, Herat Taliban 3, December 2014; Interview with group commander, Herat Taliban 5, December 2014; Interview with commander, Kandahar Taliban 9, Shorabak, August 2014; Interview with commander, Maywand, Kandahar Taliban 12, December 2014.
63. Interview with commander, Jaghatu, Eardak Taliban 9, July 2014; Interview with fighter, Kandahar Taliban 1, August 2014; Interview with group commander, Shindand, Herat Taliban 5, December 2014; Interview with group commander, Kandahar Taliban 2, August 2014; Interview with fighter, Kandahar Taliban 6,

Maruf, August 2014; Interview with fighter, Kandahar Taliban 7, Zherai, August 2014; Interview with fighter, Kandahar Taliban 8, Spin Boldak, August 2014; Interview with former commander, Arghandab, Kandahar Taliban 17, December 2014; Interview with commander, Zherai, Kandahar Taliban 14, December 2014; Interview with Toor-e Pagri commander, Bati Kot, Nangarhar Taliban 4, April 2015; Interview with dilghay commander, Behsud, Wardak Taliban 10, March 2015; Interview with Taliban cadre in Wardak, March 2015, Wardak Taliban 11; Interview with cadre, Wardak Taliban 12, March 2015.

64. Kandahar elder 1, Zhirai, November 2014.
65. Interview with Baradar Mahaz cadre, August 2014 (Kandahar Taliban 4).
66. Interview with commander, Dandi Ghori, Bagjlan Taliban 2, September 2014; Interview with commander, Baghlan Jadidi, Baghlan Taliban 10, July 2014; Interview with former Tora Bora Mahaz commander, Nangarhar Taliban 7, April 2015; Interview with Taliban cadre, Baghlan, May 2015, Baghlan Taliban 14; Interview with Taliban cadre, Dandi Ghori, Baghlan Taliban 13, March 2015; Interview with Mahaz representative, Ghazni, December 2014, Ghazni Taliban 11; Interview with cadre, Mansur Mahaz, Ghazni Taliban 12, January 2015; Interview with district governor, Ghazni Taliban 13, January 2015; Interview with commander, Jaghori, Ghazni Taliban 14, January 2015; Interview with provincial cadre of the Haqqani networks, February 2015, Haqqani 8; Interview with group commander, Cheshti Sharif, Herat Taliban 3, December 2014; Interview with group commander, Herat Taliban 5, December 2014; Interview with Toor-e Pagri commander, Bati Kot, Nangarhar Taliban 4, April 2015; Interview with Nangarhar Taliban 3, Bati Kot, April 2015; Interview with commander, Shindand, Herat Taliban 5, December 2014; Interview with commander, Bati Kot, Nangarhar Taliban 5, April 2015; Interview with Taliban cadre in Wardak, March 2015, Wardak Taliban 11; Interview with group commander, Shindand, Herat Taliban 5, December 2014.
67. Interview with commander, Jundullah Mahaz, Baghlan Taliban 11, March 2015; Burke, *The 9/11 Wars*, location 6097.
68. Interview with former commander, Zherai, Kandahar Taliban 15.
69. Interview with former Taliban commander, Mohammad Agha (Logar), Haqqani Taliban 11, March 2015; Interview with former fighter, Baghlan Taliban 15, May 2015; Interview with former commander, Baghlan Taliban 16, May 2015; Interview with former group commander of Mansur Mahaz, Ghazni Taliban 16, May 2015; Interview with former commander, Baradar Mahaz, Ghazni Taliban 15, May 2015; Interview with former commander, Nawur, Ghazni Taliban 17, May 2015; Interview with former commander, Kandahar Taliban 16, Spin Boldak, December 2014; Interview with former commander, Zherai, Kandahar Taliban 15; Interview with former fighter, Wardak Taliban 14, May 2015; Interview with former commander, Wardak Taliban 15, May 2015; Interview with former commander, Baghlan Taliban 18, May 2015; Interview with former commander, Taliban Kandahar 20, May 2015; Interview with former commander, Kandahar Taliban 21, May 2015; Interview with former commander, Dadullah Mahaz, Kandahar Taliban 22, July 2015; Interview with former commander, Arghandab, Kandahar Taliban 17, December 2014.

70. Interview with former Taliban cadre, Kandahar, July 2015, Kandahar Taliban 18; Interview with former fighter, Baghlan Taliban 15, May 2015; Interview with Taliban cadre, Baghlan, May 2015, Baghlan Taliban 14; Interview with cadre, Baghlan Taliban 11, March 2015; Interview with Taliban cadre, Dandi Ghori, Baghlan Taliban 13, March 2015; Interview with group commander, Sattar Mahaz, Faryab Taliban 6, December 2014; Interview with Taliban cadre, Almar, Faryab Taliban 1, December 2014; Interview with Mahaz representative, Ghazni, December 2014, Ghazni Taliban 11; Interview with commander, Jaghori, Ghazni Taliban 14, January 2015; Interview with former group commander of Mansur Mahaz, Ghazni Taliban 16, May 2015; Interview with former commander, Baradar Mahaz, Ghazni Taliban 15, May 2015; Interview with provincial cadre of the Haqqani networks, February 2015, Haqqani 8; Interview with group commander, Cheshti Sharif, Herat Taliban 3, December 2014; Interview with group commander, Herat Taliban 5, December 2014; Interview with former commander, Arghandab, Kandahar Taliban 17, December 2014; Interview with former commander, Zherai, Kandahar Taliban 15; Interview with Taliban cadre in Wardak, March 2015, Wardak Taliban 11; Interview with former commander, Wardak Taliban 15, May 2015; Interview with commander, Baghlan Taliban 17, May 2015; Interview with former commander, Kandahar Taliban 21, May 2015; Interview with former commander, Dadullah Mahaz, Kandahar Taliban 22, July 2015; Interview with former commander, Baghlan Taliban 18, May 2015.

71. Interview with commander, Kapisa Taliban 1, March 2015; Interview with former Taliban commander, Mohammad Agha (Logar), Haqqani Taliban 11, March 2015; Interview with commander, Sorkhrod, Nangarhar Taliban 9, March 2015; Interview with Uruzgan Taliban 1, Shahid Hassas, commander, March 2015; Interview with former commander, Shindand, Herat Taliban 8, December 2014.

72. Interview with former fighter, Baghlan Taliban 15, May 2015; Interview with former commander, Baghlan Taliban 16, May 2015; Interview with cadre, Faryab Taliban 4, December 2014; Interview with former group commander of Mansur Mahaz, Ghazni Taliban 16, May 2015; Interview with former commander, Baradar Mahaz, Ghazni Taliban 15, May 2015; Interview with former commander, Nawur, Ghazni Taliban 17, May 2015; Interview with former commander, Kandahar Taliban 16, Spin Boldak, December 2014; Interview with former commander, Arghandab, Kandahar Taliban 17, December 2014; Interview with former commander, Zherai, Kandahar Taliban 15; Interview with former fighter, Wardak Taliban 14, May 2015; Interview with former commander, Wardak Taliban 15, May 2015; Interview with former commander, Baghlan Taliban 18, May 2015; Interview with former commander, Kandahar Taliban 21, May 2015; Interview with former commander, Dadullah Mahaz, Kandahar Taliban 22, July 2015.

73. Interview with former Taliban cadre, Kandahar, July 2015, Kandahar Taliban 18; Interview with former commander, Taliban Kandahar 20, May 2015.

74. Interview with Afghan security official and with Taliban-sympathiser from Chahar Dara, Kunduz, October 2010.

75. *Xinhua*, 19 October 2010; according to a witness of the first meeting between Qari Zia and German officers from the nearby PRT, Zia's first question was whether the Americans now would erase his name from their list of commanders to be killed.

76. Interview with commander, Kapisa Taliban 1, March 2015.

77. Ibid.

78. Ibid.

79. Interview with Uruzgan Taliban 1, Shahid Hassas, commander, March 2015

80. Interview with commander, Kapisa Taliban 1, March 2015; Interview with former Taliban commander, Mohammad Agha (Logar), Haqqani Taliban 11, March 2015.

81. Interview with Elder OP2, Nad Ali, March 2012.

82. Interview with Elder OP15, Nad Ali, March 2012.

83. Interview with Elder OP22, Sangin, May 2012.

84. Interview with Elder Op17, Nad Ali, March 2012; Interview with Elder OP23, Nahr-i Seraj, June 2012.

85. Interview with commander, Kapisa Taliban 1, March 2015.

86. Interview with senior cadre of Ibrahim Mahaz, OP52, February 2013; Interview with former commander of Faruq Mahaz, Maywand, December 2014 (Kandahar Taliban 11); Martin, *An Intimate War*, p. 174.

87. Interview with cadre, Kandahar Taliban 5, August 2014; Interview with former member of the Rahbari Shura, September 2014 (Leadership 7); Source in the Taliban structure in Pakistan, March 2013; Interview with commander, Helmand, Taliban OP4, December 2011.

88. Source in the Taliban structure in Pakistan, September 2013.

89. Interview with commander, Jaghatu, OP57, January 2013; Interview with Dadullah Mahaz, July 2013, Kandahar Taliban 3, August 2014.

90. Interview with Dadullah Mahaz, July 2013, Kandahar Taliban 3, August 2014.

91. Interview with former member of Rahbari Shura, Taliban leadership 7, September 2014.

92. Interview with commander, Wardak Taliban 6, July 2014.

93. Interview with Uruzgan Taliban 1, Shahid Hassas, commander, March 2015

94. Interview with member of Commission in Quetta Shura, Leadership 1, September 2014; Interview with senior cadre of Quetta Shura, Taliban leadership 17, February 2015; Interview with senior member of Abdul Majid Mahaz, September 2014 (Leadership 2); Interview with member of political commission, Miran Shah Shura, September 2014 (Leadership 4); Interview with commander, Zherai, Kandahar Taliban 14, December 2014.

95. Interview with commander, Maywand, Kandahar Taliban 12, December 2014; Interview with commander, Zherai, Kandahar Taliban 14, December 2014.

96. Interview with former member of the Rahbari Shura, September 2014 (Leadership 7); Interview with senior cadre of Quetta Shura, Taliban leadership 17, February 2015.

97. Interview with senior cadre of Quetta Shura, Taliban leadership 17, February 2015.

98. Interview with Rahbari Shura member, August 2015, Taliban Leadership 40.

99. Interview with commander, Zherai, Kandahar Taliban 14, December 2014.

100. Interview with cadre, Ghor, Taliban Leadership 41, January 2014; Interview with cadre, Zakir Mahaz, Farah province, January 2014, Taliban OP120.

101. Interview with cadre, Zakir Mahaz in Badghis province, Taliban OP75, January 2014.

102. Interview with cadre, Zakir Mahaz, Nimruz province, Taliban OP121, January 2014; Interview with cadre, Abdul Matinullah Mahaz, Nimruz province, Taliban OP122, January 2014.

103. This is noted by several southern Taliban sources in interviews carried out in Helmand in the summer of 2012; Source in the Taliban structure in Pakistan, January 2013; Interview with member of Commission in Quetta Shura, Leadership 1, September 2014; Source in the Taliban structure in Pakistan, January 2013.

104. Communications with Taliban cadres in Peshawar and Quetta, summer 2012. For somewhat different but partly complementary accounts see Anand Gopal, 'Serious Leadership Rifts Emerge in Afghan Taliban', *CTC Sentinel*, 28 November 2012; Sami Yousufzai, 'Afghanistan: Will the Taliban Destroy Itself?', *The Daily Beast*, 17 December 2012; Anand Gopal, 'Qayyum Zakir: The Afghanistan Taliban's rising mastermind', *Christian Science Monitor*, 30 April 2010; Farzad Lameh, 'Taliban leadership disagreements, in-fighting grow', *Central Asia Online*, 16 June 2010; Interview with cadre, Ibrahim Mahaz, Kandahar province, Taliban OP123, July 2013; An interview with cadre, Abdul Majid Mahaz, Kandahar province, Taliban OP124, July 2013.

105. Communications with Taliban sources in Quetta and Peshawar, summer 2012; Interview with former commander, Taliban Kandahar 20, May 2015; Interview with former commander, Kandahar Taliban 21, May 2015; Interview with former commander, Daddullah Mahaz, Kandahar Taliban 22, July 2015; Interview with former commander of Faruq Mahaz, Maywand, December 2014 (Kandahar Taliban 11).

106. Interview with former member of the Rahbari Shura, September 2014 (Leadership 7).

107. Interviews with Taliban commanders in Helmand, 2011–12. See Farrell and Giustozzi.

108. An interview with cadre, Ibrahim Mahaz, Kandahar province, Taliban OP123, July 2013.

109. Communications with Taliban sources in Quetta and Peshawar, summer 2012; communication with UN official, Kabul, contacted autumn 2012.

110. Ron Moreau, 'New Leaders for the Taliban', *Newsweek*, 16 January 2011; communications with Taliban cadres in Peshawar and Quetta, summer 2012

111. Source in the Taliban structure in Pakistan, September 2012.

112. Source in the Taliban structure in Pakistan, January 2013.

113. Source in the Taliban structure in Pakistan, June 2013, Qari Baryal had one meeting with Mansur in Quetta

114. Interview with *Nizami massul* of Nahrin district, Baghlan, September 2012.

115. Interviews with various Taliban commanders/cadres of the Quetta Shura, autumn 2012; Interview with former commander, Taliban Kandahar 20, May 2015; Source in the Taliban structure in Pakistan, November 2012.

116. Interviews with two Taliban commanders/cadres linked to Mansur's faction in the Quetta Shura, October 2012; Interview with member of political commission in Miram Shah Shura, Taliban Leadership 4, September 2014; nterview with leader of local Taliban armed group, Helmand, October 2012.

117. Source in the Taliban structure in Pakistan, August 2012.

118. Source in the Taliban structure in Pakistan, January 2013.
119. Source in the Taliban structure in Pakistan, January 2013.
120. Source in the Quetta Shura, contacted in September 2013; Interview with former member of Rahbari Shura, Taliban leadership 7, September 2014.
121. Source in the Taliban structure in Pakistan, Sept 2013, Meeting on 6 September 2013 about the changes in the Quetta Shura.
122. Source in the Taliban structure in Pakistan, December 2013.
123. Interview with former commander, Taliban Kandahar 20, May 2015; Interview with former commander, Kandahar Taliban 21, May 2015; Interview with former commander, Dadullah Mahaz, Kandahar Taliban 22, July 2015.
124. Interview with commander, Kandahar Taliban 13, Zherai, December 2014; Interview with cadre, Kandahar Taliban 5, August 2014; Interview with former commander, Dadullah Mahaz, Kandahar Taliban 22, July 2015; Interview with a Dadullah *loy mahaz* group commander, December 2012.
125. Source in the Taliban structure in Pakistan, December 2013.
126. Source in the Taliban structure in Pakistan, November 2013.
127. Source in the Taliban structure in Pakistan, January 2014. See also: Ghanizada, 'Afghan Taliban leaders killed in Pakistan while seeking peace talks', *Khaama Press*, 11 January 2014; 'Who is killing Afghan Taliban in Pakistan?', *Sunday Times* (Islamabad), 26 January 2014; 'Taliban Commanders Being Targeted In Pakistan', *The Messenger*, 11 January 2014; 'Pakistan: Taliban Killings in Pakistani City May Be Part of Pattern', *Daily Pakistan Today*, 11 January 2014.
128. Interview with Taliban cadre, Baghlan, May 2015, Baghlan Taliban 14.
129. See Antonio Giustozzi and Silab Mangal, 'Violence, the Taliban and Afghanistan's 2014 elections', Washington: USIP, 2015.
130. Source in the Quetta Shura, contacted in May 2014; Interview with group commander, Kandahar Taliban 2, August 2014.
131. Interview with Baradar Mahaz cadre, August 2014 (Kandahar Taliban 4).
132. Interview with Baradar Mahaz cadre, August 2014 (Kandahar Taliban 4); Interview with cadre, Kandahar Taliban 5, August 2014; Interview with fighter, Kandahar Taliban 6, Maruf, August 2014.

## 5. THE TALIBAN'S TACTICAL ADAPTATION

1. Yousufzai, 'Taliban's Oral…'.
2. Interview with commander, Jaghatu, Eardak Taliban 9, July 2014; Interview with commander, Baghlan Jadid, Baghlan Taliban 4, September 2014.
3. Malkasian, *War Comes to Garmser*, p. 124.
4. Patrick Bishop, *3 Para*, London: Harper, 2007, p. 215.
5. Kick Flynn, *Trigger Time*, London: Orion books, 2011, p. 32; Stephen Grey, *Operation Snakebite*, London: Viking, 2009, p. 248.
6. James Fergusson, *A Million Bullets*, London: Bantam, 2008, p. 245.
7. Bill Ardolino, 'Aggressive Marine tactics thin enemy ranks, alter Taliban tactics', *The Long War Journal*, April 11, 2011; Malkasian, *War Comes to Garmser*, pp. 193, 195; Gopal, 'The Battle for Afghanistan', pp. 36, 39; Interview with group commander,

Herat Taliban 5, December 2014; Interview with cadre, Kandahar Taliban 5, August 2014;

8.    Interview with Dadullah Mahaz, July 2013., Kandahar Taliban 3, August 2014.

9.    Interview with commander, Wardak Taliban 7, Daimirdad, July 2014.

10.   Interview with commander, Musa Qala, Taliban OP136, May 2012.

11.   Interview with commander, Gard Sarai District, Taliban OP137, April 2012; Interview with Paktia Commander, Taliban OP10, Gard Serai, March 2012; Interview with Wardak commander Taliban OP 12, Sayed Abad, December 2011; Interview with Kandahar commander Taliban OP 14, Panjwai, December 2011; Interview with Commander, Ajristaan District, Ghazni, Taliban OP138, May 2012.

12.   Interview with commander, Gard Serai, Taliban OP94, April 2012.

13.   Ron Moreau, 'Dam Busters', *The Daily Beast*, Apr 17, 2008.

14.   Jerry Meyerle and Carter Malkasian, 'Insurgent tactics in southern Afghanistan, 2005–2008', CNA, 2009.

15.   Interviews with Taliban commanders, Helmand, Taliban OP18, 3 March 2012.

16.   David Haynes, Mercy Corps, reported a four-fold increase in the number of former Taliban combatants enrolling in the NGO's vocational training course (July 2012); one of the team's researchers travelling to the districts of Helmand also noticed lower numbers of Taliban in the field (May–June 2012).

17.   Interview with commander, Baghlan Taliban 1, September 2014.

18.   Interview with commander, Gard Serai, Taliban OP93, April 2012.

19.   Taliban commander in Nawzad, May 2012.

20.   Taliban commander in Nahr-i Seraj, May 2012.

21.   Taliban commander in Garmser, June 2012.

22.   Interview with Wardak commander Taliban OP 13, Sayed Abad, December 2011.

23.   Interviews with Taliban commanders, Helmand, Taliban OP18, 3 March 2012.

24.   Ibid.

25.   Ron Moreau, 'America's New Nightmare'.

26.   Jerry Meyerle and Carter Malkasian, 'Insurgent tactics in southern Afghanistan, 2005–2008', CNA, 2009.

27.   Interviews with Taliban commanders, Helmand, Taliban OP18, 3 March 2012.

28.   See: A. Giustozzi and A. Baczko, 'The Politics of the Taliban's Shadow Judiciary, 2003–2013', *Central Asian Affairs*, 1 – 2014, 199-224, and A. Giustozzi, 'The Taliban's military courts', *Small Wars and Insurgencies*, vol. 25, n. 2, 2014.

29.   Interview with Kandahar commander Taliban OP 14, Panjwai, December 2011.

30.   Interview with Taliban commander in Garmser, 2012, Taliban OP 161.

31.   On Helmand, see: Patrick Bishop, *3 Para*, London: Harper, 2007, p. 215. See also: Chris Wattie, *Contact Charlie*, Toronto: Key Porter Books, 2008, p. 214.

32.   Thomas H. Johnson, 'Taliban Adaptations and Innovations', in *Small Wars and Insurgencies*, Volume 24, 2013 - Issue 1.

33.   Interview with group commander, Cheshti Sharif, Herat Taliban 3, December 2014; Interview with group commander, Shindand, Herat Taliban 5, December 2014.

34.   Interview with group commander, Cheshti Sharif, Herat Taliban 3, December 2014; Interview with fighter, Kandahar Taliban 7, Zherai, August 2014.

35.   Interview with Taliban commander in Sangin, May 2012.

36.  Taliban commander in Garmser, Helmand, June 2012.

37.  Interview with commander, Marjah, Taliban OP87, May 2012.

38.  Interview with Shamsatoo Mahaz cadre, Hissarak, Nangarhar Taliban 6, April 2015.

39.  Interview with Shamsatoo Mahaz cadre, Hissarak, Nangarhar Taliban 6, April 2015. On the take-off of the IED campaign see also Alec D. Barker, 'Improvised Explosive Devices in Southern Afghanistan and Western Pakistan, 2002–2009', *Studies in Conflict & Terrorism*, 34:8, 2011, 600-620.

40.  Interview with member of political commission in Miran Shah Shura, Taliban Leadership 4, September 2014; Burke, 9/11 wars, location 6086.

41.  Tony Harnden, *Dead Men Risen*, London: Quercus, 2011, p. 205.

42.  Rayment, pp. 7, 61.

43.  Roy Gutman, 'Afghanistan war: How Taliban tactics are evolving', *The Christian Science Monitor*, 15 March 2010.

44.  Interview with Baradar Mahaz cadre, August 2014 (Kandahar Taliban 4).

45.  Taliban commander in Garmser, OP 161, June 2012.

46.  'Most bombs in Afghan war 'made from banned fertiliser', *AFP*, 12 July 2010

47.  Tom Vanden Brook, 'Report: Pakistan hindering efforts to curb Taliban IEDs', *USA Today*, 6/5/2012. See also: Alec D. Barker.

48.  'US to help Pakistan army counter IED blasts', *The Peninsula*, 21 October 2012; 'JIEDDO working to reverse trend for larger IEDs in Afghanistan', *Asd news*, 23 October 2012.

49.  Jon Boone, 'How Taliban's lethal IEDs keep troops guessing in Afghanistan', *The Guardian*, 7 March 2012.

50.  Rayment, 128.

51.  'New fears over Taliban bomb tactics, after blast penetrates mine-resistant vehicle', *AFP*, 11 July 2012; Rowan Scarborough, 'Taliban alters its deadly IED tactics', *The Washington Times*, 6 April 2011.

52.  Sami Yousafzai, 'Afghanistan: The Taliban's Dangerous New Munitions', *The Daily Beast*, 18 October 2012.

53.  Interview with senior member of Mine Commission, Miran Shah Shura, Taliban leadership 16, February 2015.

54.  Ibid.

55.  Ibid.

56.  Interview with cadre, Faryab Taliban 4, December 2014; Interview with cadre, Mansur Mahaz, Faryab Taliban 5, December 2014; Interview with group commander, Sattar Mahaz, Faryab Taliban 6, December 2014; Interview with commander, Andkhoy, Faryab Taliban 7, December 2014; Interview with Taliban cadre, Almar, Faryab Taliban 1, December 2014; Interview with cadre, Almar, Faryab Taliban 2, December 2014; Interview with cadre, Mansur Mahaz, Faryab Taliban 3, December 2014; Interview with commander of Abdullah Zekria, Herat Taliban 6, Shindand, December 2014; Interview with Taliban cadre in Wardak, March 2015, Wardak Taliban 11.

57.  Interview with Baradar Mahaz cadre, August 2014 (Kandahar Taliban 4).

58.  ISAF source, May 2011.

59.  Interview with senior member of Mine Commission, Miran Shah Shura, Taliban leadership 16, February 2015.

60. Interview with senior member of Mine Commission, Miran Shah Shura, Taliban leadership 16, February 2015.

61. Personal communication with ISAF officers, 2010.

62. Interviews with Taliban commanders in Panjwai and Zhari, summer 2011.

63. Interview with Commander, Gard Sarai District, Taliban OP137, April 2012; Interview with Helmand commander, Nad Ali, OP Taliban 4, December 2011.

64. Interview with adviser to Serajuddin Haqqani, Leadership 13, January 2015.

65. Interview with senior member of Mine Commission, Miran Shah Shura, Taliban leadership 16, February 2015.

66. Interview with fighter, Kandahar Taliban 8, Spin Boldak, August 2014; Interview with member of Safi Shura, Nangarhar Taliban 2, April 2015.

67. Rowan Scarborough, 'Taliban alters its deadly IED tactics', *The Washington Times*, 6 April 2011.

68. Joanna Wright and Jeremy Binnie.

69. Tom Vanden Brook, 'Report: Pakistan hindering efforts to curb Taliban IEDs', *USA TODAY*, 5 June 2012; Rowan Scarborough, 'U.S. troops winning war against IEDs of Taliban', *The Washington Times*, 24 May 2012.

70. Interview with former commander, Zherai, Kandahar Taliban 15, December 2014; Interview with former commander, Arghandab, Kandahar Taliban 17, December 2014.

71. Interview with Taliban cadre, Baghlan, May 2015, Baghlan Taliban 14; Interview with member of Quetta Political Commission, Taliban Leadership 1, September 2014; Interview with commander, Jundullah Mahaz, Baghlan Taliban 11, March 2015; Interview with Taliban cadre, Dandi Ghori, Baghlan Taliban 13, March 2015; Interview with district governor, Ghazni Taliban 13, January 2015; Interview with provincial cadre of the Haqqani network, February 2015, Haqqani 8; Interview with former commander, Arghandab, Kandahar Taliban 17, December 2014; Interview with member of Safi Shura, Nangarhar Taliban 2, April 2015; Interview with Toor-e Pagri commander, Bati Kot, Nangarhar Taliban 4, April 2015; Interview with commander, Bati Kot, Nangarhar Taliban 5, April 2015; Interview with Shamsatoo Mahaz cadre, Hissarak, Nangarhar Taliban 6, April 2015; Interview with cadre, Shirzad, Nangarhar Taliban 8, April 2015.

72. Interview with Baradar Mahaz cadre, August 2014 (Kandahar Taliban 4).

73. Interview with cadre, Mansur Mahaz, Faryab Taliban 3, December 2014; Interview with fighter, Paktia, Haqqani 3, February 2015; Interview with former commander, Kandahar Taliban 16, Spin Boldak, December 2014.

74. 'Al-Somood Interview of Almullah Akhthar Muhammad Mansur: The Taliban's Military Commander – Kandahar District', *Al-Somood*, July 2007; 'Al-Somood Interviews The Islamic Emirate Of Afghanistan Military Official For The Maidan Shahr District', *Al-Somood*, July 2010.

75. Interview with former commander, Zherai, Kandahar Taliban 15.

76. Interview with senior member of Abdul Majid Mahaz, Taliban leadership 2, September 2014; Interview with senior member of Matinullah Mahaz, Taliban leadership 3, August 2014; Interview with group commander, Shindand, Herat Taliban 5, December 2014; Interview with cadre, Kandahar Taliban 5, August 2014.

77. Interview with fighter, Kandahar Taliban 1, August 2014; Interview with former member of Rahbari Shura, Taliban leadership 7, September 2014; Interview with Dadullah Mahaz, July 2013, Kandahar Taliban 3, August 2014; Interview with fighter, Kandahar Taliban 6, Maruf, August 2014; Interview with fighter, Kandahar Taliban 8, Spin Boldak, August 2014.

78. Interview with fighter, Paktia, Haqqani 3, February 2015; Interview with Baradar Mahaz cadre, August 2014 (Kandahar Taliban 4).

79. Interview with fighter, Paktika, Haqqani 6, February 2015.

80. Interview with commander, Logar, Haqqani 7, February 2015.

81. Interview with Logar elder, Baraki Barak, Haqqani elder 1, February 2015.

82. Interview with senior member of Mine Commission, Miran Shah Shura, Taliban leadership 16, February 2015. Feb 2015

83. Interview with senior member of Zerbati Commission, Miran Shah Shura, Taliban Leadership 14.

84. See Andrew Fraser, 'Deadly Ends: Canada, NATO and Suicide as a Weapon of War in Modern Afghanistan', *Canadian Army Journal,* Vol. 12.2 (Summer 2009) pp. 50–61.

85. See: Antonio Giustozzi, 'The resilient oligopoly', Kabul: AREU, 2012, for the case of Atta Mohammed, the governor of Balkh province.

86. On the early days of suicide bombing in Afghanistan see: David B. Edwards, *Caravan of Martyrs: Sacrifice and Suicide Bombing in Afghanistan,* Oakland: University of California Press, 2017, Kindle edition, location 446ff.; Coll, p. 261.

87. Interview with deputy, Miran Shah Shura, Taliban leadership 15, February 2015; Interview with adviser to Serajuddin Haqqani, Leadership 13, January 2015.

88. *Al Somood* 1, January 2006.

89. Interview with deputy, Miran Shah Shura, Taliban leadership 15, February 2015.

90. Ibid.

91. Ibid.

92. Interview with senior member of Ijraya Shura, Taliban leadership 21, May 2015; Interview with Toor-e Pagri commander, Bati Kot, Nangarhar Taliban 4, April 2015; Interview with commander, Bati Kot, Nangarhar Taliban 5, April 2015.

93. Interview with member of Safi Shura, Nangarhar Taliban 2, April 2015; Interview with cadre, Shirzad, Nangarhar Taliban 8, April 2015; Interview with Shamsatoo Mahaz cadre, Hissarak, Nangarhar Taliban 6, April 2015.

94. Interview with deputy, Miran Shah Shura, Taliban leadership 15, February 2015.

95. Interview with district governor, Ghazni Taliban 13, January 2015; Interview with commander, Jaghori, Ghazni Taliban 14, January 2015.

96. Interview with group commander, Cheshti Sharif, Herat Taliban 3, December 2014.

97. Interview with member of Safi Shura, Nangarhar Taliban 2, April 2015; Interview with commander, Bati Kot, Nangarhar Taliban 5, April 2015.

98. Interview with senior member of Abdul Majid Mahaz, Taliban leadership 2, September 2014; Interview with former member of Rahbari Shura, Taliban leadership 7, September 2014; Interview with member of political commission in Miran Shah Shura, Taliban Leadership 4, September 2014; Interview with senior member of Matinullah Mahaz, Taliban leadership 3, August 2014; Interview with member of

Quetta Political Commission, Taliban Leadership 1, September 2014; Interview with Taliban cadre, Baghlan, May 2015, Baghlan Taliban 14; Interview with commander, Jundullah Mahaz, Baghlan Taliban 11, March 2015; Interview with Taliban cadre, Dandi Ghori, Baghlan Taliban 13, March 2015; Interview with cadre, Paktia, Haqqani 4, February 2015; Interview with Dadullah Mahaz, July 2013, Kandahar Taliban 3, August 2014; Interview with cadre, Kandahar Taliban 5, August 2014. About Baradar: Interview with former commander, Arghandab, Kandahar Taliban 17, December 2014.

99. Interview with deputy, Miran Shah Shura, Taliban leadership 15, February 2015.

100. Interview with deputy, Miran Shah Shura, Taliban leadership 15, February 2015.

101. Taliban sources in Quetta, September 2012.

102. Simon Robinson, 'The World's Worst Suicide Bombers?', *Time*, 28 July 2007; Sami Yousufzai and Ron Moreau, 'The Fallout from the AWK Murder', *The Daily Beast*, 14 July 2011; Dion Nissenbaum, 'Taliban attacks in Afghanistan show growing sophistication', *McClatchy Newspapers*, 15 July 2010; Brian Glyn Williams, 'Suicide bombings in Afghanistan', *Jane's Islamic Affairs Analyst,* September 2007; Brian Glyn Williams, 'Mullah Omar's missiles', Washington: Middle East Policy Council, May 2007.

103. '"New generation" of tech-savvy Taliban fighters', *AFP*, 26 July 2012.

104. Interview with cadre, Kandahar Taliban 5, August 2014.

105. Interview with cadre, Faryab Taliban 4, December 2014; Interview with cadre, Mansur Mahaz, Faryab Taliban 5, December 2014; Interview with group commander, Sattar Mahaz, Faryab Taliban 6, December 2014; Interview with commander, Andkhoy, Faryab Taliban 7, December 2014; Interview with cadre, Mansur Mahaz, Faryab Taliban 3, December 2014.

106. Interview with deputy, Miran Shah Shura, Taliban leadership 15, February 2015.

107. Interview with Faryab Elder 1, Almar, May 2015; Interview with Faryab Elder 2, Almar, May 2015; Interview with Faryab Elder 4, Khwaja Sabz Posh, May 2015; Interview with Faryab Elder 6, Qaysar, May 2015; Interview with Faryab Elder 7, Qaysar, May 2015; Interview with Faryab Elder 8, Jhwaja Sabz Posh, May 2015; Kandahar elder 1, Zhirai, November 2014; Interview with Kandahar elder 2, Daman, November 2014; Interview with former Taliban commander, Mohammad Agha (Logar), Haqqani Taliban 11, March 2015; Interview with Baghlan elder 8, Dandi Ghori, July 2014; Interview with Herat elder 1, Pashtun Zarghun, April 2015; Interview with Herat elder 3, member of Peace Committe, April 2015; Interview with Herat elder 2, Obeh, April 2015; Interview with Nangarhar elder 3, Bati Kot, March 2015; Interview with Wardak elder 4, Sayed Abad, July 2014.

108. Interview with Faryab Elder 3, Qaysar, May 2015; Interview with Herat elder 5, Shindand, April 2015.

109. Declan Walsh, 'Taliban assassins target the clerics faithful to Kabul', *The Observer*, 27 August 2006.

110. ISAF officer, contacted September 2011.

111. Interviews with Afghan notables from Jowzjan, 2010.

112. Julius Cavendish, 'Afghan Taliban hone hit-and-run tactics, assassination campaign', *Christian Science Monitor*, 10 June 2010.

113. Personal communication with UNHCR official, Kabul, 2010.

114. Interview with senior member of Intelligence department of the Peshawar Shura, Taliban leadership 42, July 2015.

115. Interview with Haqqani cadre, Kabul, December 2016.

116. Interview with member of Quetta Political Commission, Taliban Leadership 1, September 2014; Interview with former member of Rahbari Shura, Taliban leadership 7, September 2014.

117. Interview with former commander, Baghlan Taliban 16, May 2015.

118. Gopal, 'The Battle for Afghanistan', p. 37.

119. Interview with Herat elder 1, Pashtun Zarghun, April 2015; Interview with Herat elder 2, Pashtun Zarghun, April 2015; Interview with Herat elder 3, member of Peace Committee, April 2015; Interview with Herat elder 6, Chist-i Sharif, April 2015; Interview with Herat Elder 7, Chest-i Sharif, April 2015; Interview with Kandahar elder 3, Panjwai, February 2015; Interview with Kandahar elder 4, Panjwai, February 2015; Interview with Kandahar elder 5, Maiwand, February 2015; Interview with Kandahar elder 7, Daman, February 2015; Interview with Kandahar Elder 13, Zherai, February 2015; Interview with Nangarhar elder 9, Khogyani, March 2015; Interview with Nangarhar elder 10, Bati Kot, March 2015; Interview with Faryab Elder 1, Almar, May 2015; Interview with Nangarhar elder 3, Bati Kot, March 2015; Interview with Faryab Elder 3, Qaysar, May 2015; Interview with Faryab Elder 4, Almar, May 2015; Interview with Faryab Elder 6, Qaysar, May 2015; Interview with Faryab Elder 7, Qaysar, May 2015; Interview with Faryab Elder 8, Jhwaja Sabz Posh, May 2015; Interview with Ghazni elder 5, Andar, August 2014; Interview with Nangarhar elder 10, Bati Kot, March 2015; Interview with Logar elder, Baraki Barak, Haqqani elder 1, February 2015; Interview with Haqqani elder 2, Mohammad Agha, Logar, February 2015; Interview with Kandahar elder 2, Daman, November 2014; Interview with Kandahar elder 9, Panjwai, February 2015; Interview with Kandahar elder 14, Dand, February 2015; Interview with Nangarhar elder 3, Bati Kot, March 2015; Interview with Nangarhar elder 6, Shirzad, March 2015; Interview with Wardak elder 4, Sayed Abad, July 2014; Interview with Wardak elder 5, Jaghatu, July 2015; Interview with Wardak elder 6, Jaghatu, July 2015; Interview with Wardak elder 1, Jaghatu, July 2014; Interview with Wardak elder 7, Sayed Abad, July 2014; Interview with Wardak elder 3, July 2014.

120. Interview with Nangarhar elder 7, Achin, March 2015; Interview with Nangarhar elder 8, Shinwar, March 2015; Interview with Nangarhar elder 10, Bati Kot, March 2015; Interview with Wardak elder 2, Wardak, July 2014; Interview with Wardak elder 4, Sayed Abad, July 2014.

121. Malkasian, *War Comes to Garmser*, p. 212

122. Interview with Uruzgan Taliban 1, Shahid Hassas, commander, March 2015; Interview with former commander, Shindand, Herat Taliban 8, December 2014; Interview with former commander, Baghlan Taliban 16, May 2015; Interview with former fighter, Baghlan Taliban 15, May 2015; Interview with former group commander of Mansur Mahaz, Ghazni Taliban 16, May 2015; Interview with former commander, Nawur, Ghazni Taliban 17, May 2015; Interview with commander, Baghlan Taliban 17, May 2015; Interview with former commander, Baghlan Taliban

18, May 2015; Interview with former commander, Taliban Kandahar 20, May 2015; Interview with former commander, Kandahar Taliban 21, May 2015; Interview with former commander, Dadullah Mahaz, Kandahar Taliban 22, July 2015.

123. Interview Kandahar elder 9, Panjwai, February 2015.

124. Interview with former fighter, Wardak Taliban 14, May 2015.

125. See: http://www.understandingwar.org/green-on-blue/ for a graph illustrating the trend; also Ehsan Mehmood Khan, 'Anatomy of green-on-blue attacks', Islamabad: Pak Institute for Peace Studies, 2012.

126. Ian Traynor, 'Nato withdrawal from Afghanistan could be speeded up, says Rasmussen', *The Guardian*, 1 October 2012.

127. *Shahamat*, October 2012.

128. NATO source, September 2012.

129. Mujib Mashal, 'Shadow of the Infiltrator', *Time*, 15 October 2012.

130. Interviews carried out in Helmand, April–July 2012.

131. Interview with commander, Sangin, Taliban OP128, May 2012.

132. Interview with commander, Kajaki, Taliban OP94, May 2012.

133. Interview with commander, Sangin, Taliban OP130, June 2012.

134. Personal communication with British Army Officer, July 2012.

135. Ben Anderson, *No Worse Enemy*, Oxford: Oneworld, 2011, p. 43.

136. Ron Moreau, 'Dam Busters', *The Daily Beast*, 17 April 2008.

137. Interview with commander, Baghlan, Taliban OP134, October 2011; Interview with commander, Wardak Taliban 4, July 2014; Interview with group commander, Wardak Taliban 3, July 2014; Interview with Commander, Wardak Taliban 5, July 2014; Interview with commander, Wardak Taliban 6, July 2014; Interview with commander, Wardak Taliban 7, Daimirdad, July 2014; Interview with commander, Baghlan Jadid, Baghlan Taliban 4, September 2014; Interview with commander, Wardak Taliban 4, July 2014.

138. Interview with commander, Helmand, Taliban OP 21, September 2011.

139. Interview with fighter, Kandahar Taliban 1, August 2014; Interview with commander, Jaghatu, Wardak Taliban 9, July 2014; Interview with fighter, Kandahar Taliban 1, August 2014; Interview with fighter, Kandahar Taliban 7, Zherai, August 2014; Interview with fighter, Kandahar Taliban 8, Spin Boldak, August 2014; Interview with cadre, Baghlan Jadid, Baghlan Taliban 7, July 2014; Interview with commander, Dandi Ghori, Ghazni Taliban 9, July 2014; Interview with commander, Kajaki, Taliban OP135, June 2012.

140. Interview with commander, Baghlan Taliban 6, Baghlan Jadid, September 2014.

141. Interview with member of Miran Shah Military Commission, Taliban leadership 38, June 2015.

142. C.J. Chivers, 'The Weakness of Taliban Marksmanship', *New York Times*, 2 April 2010; C.J. Chivers, 'Afghan Marksmanship: Pointing, Not Aiming', *New York Times*, 9 April 2010; C.J. Chivers, 'Afghan Marksmen — Forget the Fables', *New York Times Blog*, 26 March 2010; C.J. Chivers, 'A Firsthand Look at Firefights in Marja', *New York Times Blog*, 19 April 2010. A rare example of accurate sniping is mentioned for Marjah in 2010 by C.J. Chivers, 'Putting Taliban Sniper Fire in Context', *New York Times Blog*, 20 April 2010.

143. Anderson, *No Worse Enemy*, pp. 126–31, 161–3; Bing West, *The Wrong War*, New York: Random House, 2011, pp. 85–7.

144. Terri Judd, 'Sharp rise in Army deaths from small arms fire prompts inquiry into Taliban snipers', *The Independent*, 21 June 2010.

145. One active in Khost is mentioned in an obituary in *Al Somud* n. 59 (Sheikh Al Hadith Awal Dar).

146. Posted by Administrator on 10 February 2010: http://www.militaryringexpress. com/blog/post/2246722; see also: 'OEA Team Threat Report: Civilian Shields Effective for Taliban', Kabul: ISAF, 23 April 2010; Afghanistan Taliban 'using human shields' – general; Thomas Harding, Taliban 'used civilians as human shields when British attacked', *The Telegraph*, 18 August 2008.

147. Interview with former commander, Kandahar Taliban 16, Spin Boldak, December 2014.

148. Julian Borger and Richard Norton-Taylor, 'British special forces seize Iranian rockets in Afghanistan', *The Guardian*, 9 March 2011; Stuart Tootal, *Danger Close*, London: Murray, 2009, p. 173.

149. Carlotta Gall and Eric Schmitt, 'Taliban Breached NATO Base In Deadly Clash', *The New York Times*, 15 July 2008.

150. See for example: David Kilcullen, *The Accidental Guerrilla*, Oxford: Oxford University Press, 2009, pp. 39-40.

151. Sean Rayment, *Into the Killing Zone*, London: Constable, 2008, p. 80.

152. Interview with member of Mashhad Military Commission, Taliban leadership 36, July 2015.

153. Interview with member of Peshawar Military Commission, Taliban leadership 37, July 2015.

154. Interview with member of Miran Shah Military Commission, Taliban leadership 38, June 2015; Interview with member of Quetta Military Commission, Taliban leadership 29, June 2015; Interview with member of Peshawar Military Commission, Taliban leadership 37, July 2015.

155. Interview with member of Mashhad Military Commission, Taliban leadership 36, July 2015.

156. Interview with member of Miran Shah Military Commission, Taliban leadership 38, June 2015; Interview with cadre, Paktia, Haqqani 4, February 2015; Interview with senior member of the Mashhad Logistics Commission, Taliban Leadership 33, July 2015.

157. Doug Beattie, *Task Force Helmand*, London: Simon & Schuster, 2009, p. 126; Matt Dupee, 'The Taliban acquisition of anti-aircraft platforms', *The Long War Journal*, 2 November 2010.

158. Individual ISAF officers have alternatively confirmed or denied the use of missiles by the Taliban (personal communications, 2008-10). See also Declan Walsh, 'Afghanistan war logs: US covered up fatal Taliban missile strike on Chinook', *The Guardian*, 25 July 2010. See also James Fergusson, *A Million Bullets*, London: Bantam, 2008, p. 191.

159. Personal communication with former ANSO official, Kabul, 2010; personal communication with foreign diplomat, Kabul, 2009; Declan Walsh, 'Afghanistan

war logs: US covered up fatal Taliban missile strike on Chinook', *The Guardian*, 25 July 2010; Habiborrahman Ibrahimi, 'Taliban claim new missiles downing aircraft', *Afghanistan Recovery Report*, Issue 408, 7 September 2011.

160.  Taliban sources in Quetta and Peshawar, contacted 2011–12.

161.  Source in the Taliban structure in Pakistan, March 2013; Interview with member of Peshawar Military Commission, Taliban leadership 37, July 2015.

162.  Interview with member of Miran Shah Military Commission, Taliban leadership 38, June 2015; Interview with member of Quetta Military Commission, Taliban leadership 29, June 2015; Interview with senior member of Zerbati Commission, Miran Shah Shura, Taliban Leadership 14; Interview with member of Peshawar Military Commission, Taliban leadership 37, July 2015; Interview with cadre, Paktia, Haqqani 4, February 2015; Interview with adviser, Pakistan, Adviser 2, July 2015.

163.  Interview with Iranian adviser to Jundullah, Advisers 3, July 2015.

164.  Interview with senior member of Zerbati Commission, Miran Shah Shura, Taliban Leadership 14.

165.  Interview with member of Miran Shah Military Commission, Taliban leadership 38, June 2015.

166.  Interview with senior member of Mine Commission, Miran Shah Shura, Taliban leadership 16, February 2015.

167.  Interview with member of Peshawar Military Commission, Taliban leadership 37, July 2015.

168.  Interview with Commander, Garmser District, Taliban OP139, June 2012.

169.  Interviews carried out in 2011–12 in seven districts of Helmand province.

170.  Interview with commander, Taliban OP140, October 2011.

171.  Interview with commander, Baghlan, Taliban OP134, Oct 2011.

172.  Taliban sources in Quetta and Peshawar, summer 2012.

173.  'Afghan Defence Ministry says over 600 army soldiers killed in two months', Text of report by privately-owned Noor TV, 27 August 2012. US DoD sources put the casualties of the Afghan security forces in 2012 at 33 per cent higher than in 2011.

174.  May Jeong, 'The Patient War: What awaits Trump in Afghanistan', *Harpers*, February 2017.

175.  Interview with Commander, Nahr-e Saraj, Taliban OP142, May 2012.

176.  Taliban commander in Garmser, May 2012.

177.  Rayment, 74, 253; interviews with Taliban commanders, Helmand, 2011.

178.  Rayment, 85; Interview with commander, Sangin, Taliban OP141, November 2014; Kim Hughes, *Painting the Sand*, London: Simon & Schuster, 2017, Kindle edition, Location 2520ff.

179.  Interview with commander, Sangin, Taliban OP128, May 2012.

180.  Taliban commander in Musa Qala, May 2012.

181.  Interview with Aadviser, Pakistan, Adviser 2, July 2015; Interview with Iranian adviser to Jundullah, Advisers 3, July 2015

182.  Interview with adviser, Pakistan, Adviser 2, July 2015.

183.  Iranian adviser to Jundullah, Advisers 3, July 2015.

## 6. ORGANISATIONAL ADAPTATION

1.  Interview with senior member of Abdul Majid Mahaz, September 2014 (Leadership 2).
2.  Communications with high-ranking cadres in both Peshawar and Quetta, summer 2012.
3.  Contact with Quetta Military Commission source, July 2015.
4.  Interview with commander, Kandahar Taliban 9, Shorabak, August 2014.
5.  Interview with cadre, Abdul Matin Mahaz, Nimruz province, Taliban OP122, January 2014.
6.  Interview with cadre, Mansur Mahaz, Helmand province, Taliban OP99, June 2013.
7.  Interview with Taliban field commander, Jaghatoo district, Wardak, September 2012.
8.  Interview with cadre, Janan Mahaz, Kandahar province, Taliban OP125, July 2013.
9.  Interview with cadre, Mansur Mahaz, Uruzgan province, Taliban OP78, May 2013.
10. Interview with cadre, Mansur Mahaz, Helmand province, Taliban OP99, June 2013.
11. Interview with Rahbari Shura member, August 2015, Taliban Leadership 40.
12. Interviews with two commanders in Helmand, March 2012.
13. Interview with former commander, Musa Qala, Helmand, Taliban OP26, September 2011.
14. Interview with member of Mashhad Military Commission, Taliban leadership 36, July 2015; Interview with member of Peshawar Military Commission, Taliban leadership 37, July 2015.
15. Interview with member of Peshawar Military Commission, Taliban leadership 37, July 2015.
16. Interviews with senior field commanders from different *loy mahaz*es, October 2012.
17. Interview with field commander in Helmand, December 2012; Interview with Taliban field commander from Babaji, Helmand, December 2011.
18. Interview with member of Quetta Military Commission, Taliban leadership 29, June 2015.
19. Interview with member of Quetta Military Commission, Taliban leadership 29, June 2015.
20. Interview with member of Peshawar Military Commission, Taliban leadership 37, July 2015.
21. Source in the Taliban structure in Pakistan, November 2012.
22. Source in the Taliban structure in Pakistan, September 2013.
23. Interview with Rahbari Shura member, August 2015, Taliban Leadership 40.
24. Interview with adviser to Serajuddin Haqqani, Leadership 10, January 2015.
25. Interview with member of Miran Shah Military Commission, Taliban leadership 38, June 2015; Source in the Taliban structure in Pakistan, March 2013.
26. Interview with member of Quetta Military Commission, Taliban leadership 29, June 2015.
27. Interview with member of Peshawar Military Commission, Taliban leadership 37, July 2015.
28. Interview with member of Peshawar Military Commission, Taliban leadership 37, July 2015.

29. Interview with member of Mashhad Military Commission, Taliban leadership 36, July 2015; Interview with adviser, Pakistan, Adviser 2, July 2015.

30. Interview with member of Miran Shah Military Commission, Taliban leadership 38, June 2015.

31. Interview with cadre, Kandahar Taliban 5, August 2014.

32. Interview with fighter, Kandahar Taliban 1, August 2014.

33. Interview with fighter, Kandahar Taliban 1, August 2014; Interview with group commander, Kandahar Taliban 2, August 2014; Interview with Baradar Mahaz cadre, August 2014 (Kandahar Taliban 4); Interview with fighter, Kandahar Taliban 6, Maruf, August 2014; Interview with fighter, Kandahar Taliban 7, Zherai, August 2014; Interview with fighter, Kandahar Taliban 8, Spin Boldak, August 2014; Interview with commander, Kandahar Taliban 9, Shorabak, August 2014; Interview with former commander, Arghandab, Kandahar Taliban 17, December 2014; Interview with group commander, Kandahar Taliban 2, August 2014; Interview with Kandahar Taliban 3, August 2014.

34. Interview with fighter, Kandahar Taliban 1, August 2014; Interview with fighter, Kandahar Taliban 6, Maruf, August 2014; Interview with commander, Kandahar Taliban 9, Shorabak, August 2014.

35. Interview with deputy, Taliban Leadership 23, May 2015.

36. Interview with member of Peshawar Military Commission, Taliban leadership 37, July 2015.

37. Interview with member of Miran Shah Military Commission, Taliban leadership 38, June 2015.

38. Interview with Adviser, Pakistan, Adviser 2, July 2015; Interview with member of Quetta Military Commission, Taliban leadership 29, June 2015; Interview with member of Mashhad Military Commission, Taliban leadership 36, July 2015; Interview with member of Peshawar Military Commission, Taliban leadership 37, July 2015; Source in the Taliban structure in Pakistan, May 2015; Source in the Taliban structure in Pakistan, December 2014.

39. Martin, *An Intimate War*, p. 173.

40. Interview with commander, Helmand, Taliban OP127, December 2011.

41. Interview with commander, Bati Kot, Nangarhar Taliban 5, April 2015; Interview with fighter, Kandahar Taliban 8, Spin Boldak, August 2014; Interview with group commander, Kandahar Taliban 2, August 2014.

42. Interview with commander, Helmand, Taliban OP127, December 2011.

43. Interviews with Taliban commanders and elders in Nuristan, 2011; Interviews with Taliban commanders in Helmand, summer–autumn 2011.

44. Interview with commander, Marjah, Taliban OP129, June 2012.

45. Interview with commander, Bati Kot, Nangarhar Taliban 5, April 2015.

46. Interview with commander, Sangin district, Taliban OP130, June 2012; Interview with commander, Wardak Taliban 8, Sayed Abad, July 2014; Interview with Commander, Kajaki District, Taliban OP91, June 2012; Interview with commander, Mosa Qala district, Taliban OP95, June 2012.

47. Interview with fighter, Kandahar Taliban 6, Maruf, August 2014.

48. Interview with commander, Nawzad District, Taliban OP 131, May 2012.

49.  Interview with commander, Nahar-i-Seraj District, Taliban OP132, June 2012; Interview with commander, Kajaki district, Taliban OP94, May 2012; Interview with cadre, Barg Matal district, Taliban OP132, January 2012; Interview with commander, Mosa qala. Taliban OP89, May 2012.

50.  Interview with commander, Marjah District, Taliban OP87, May 2012.

51.  Interview with commander, Nahre Saraj, Taliban OP133, July 2012.

52.  C. J. Chivers, 'In Eastern Afghanistan, at War With the Taliban's Shadowy Rule', *The New York Times*, 6 February 2011. See also: Ben Brandt, 'The Taliban's Conduct of Intelligence and Counterintelligence', *CTC Sentinel*, 1 June 2011.

53.  Sources within Janan Mahaz, contacted July 2013.

54.  Interview with senior member of Peshawar Shura Logistics commission, Taliban Leadership 31, June 2015; Interview with senior member of the Quetta Shura logistics commission, Taliban Leadership 30; Interview with senior member of the Miran Shura provincial logistics Commission, Taliban Leadership 28, June 2015; Interview with Rahbari Shura member, August 2015, Taliban Leadership 40.

55.  Interview with senior members of Peshawar Shura Logistics commission, Taliban Leadership 31, June 2015; Interview with cadre, Jaghatu, Taliban OP57, January 2013.

56.  Interview with senior member of the Quetta Shura logistics commission, Taliban Leadership 30, June 2015; Interview with senior member of the Miran Shura provincial logistics Commission, Taliban Leadership 28, June 2015.

57.  Interview with senior member of the Mashhad Logistics Commission, Taliban Leadership 33, July 2015.

58.  Interview with senior members of Peshawar Shura Logistics commission, Taliban Leadership 31, June 2015; Interview with senior member of the Quetta Shura logistics commission, Taliban Leadership 30, June 2015; Interview with senior member of the Mashhad Logistics Commission, Taliban Leadership 33, July 2015.

59.  Interview with senior members of Peshawar Shura Logistics commission, Taliban Leadership 31, June 2015; Interview with senior member of the Quetta Shura logistics commission, Taliban Leadership 30, June 2015; Interview with senior member of the Mashhad Logistics Commission, Taliban Leadership 33, July 2015.

60.  Interview with senior member of the Mashhad Logistics Commission, Taliban Leadership 33, July 2015; Interview with senior members of Peshawar Shura Logistics commission, Taliban Leadership 31, June 2015; Interview with senior member of the Quetta Shura logistics commission, Taliban Leadership 30, June 2015; Interview with senior member of the Miran Shura provincial logistics Commission, Taliban Leadership 28, June 2015.

61.  Interview with member of Miran Shah Military Commission, Taliban leadership 38, June 2015.

62.  Interview with senior members of Peshawar Shura Logistics commission, Taliban Leadership 31, June 2015; Interview with senior member of the Quetta Shura logistics commission, Taliban Leadership 30, June 2015; Interview with senior member of the Miran Shura provincial logistics Commission, Taliban Leadership 28, June 2015; Interview with senior member of the Mashhad Logistics Commission, Taliban Leadership 33, July 2015.

63.  Interview with senior members of Peshawar Shura Logistics commission, Taliban
     Leadership 31, June 2015; Interview with senior member of the Mashhad Logistics
     Commission, Taliban Leadership 33, July 2015.

64.  Interview with senior member of the Mashhad Logistics Commission, Taliban
     Leadership 33, July 2015.

65.  Interview with senior members of Peshawar Shura Logistics commission, Taliban
     Leadership 31, June 2015; Interview with senior member of the Quetta Shura
     Logistics Commission, Taliban Leadership 30, June 2015; Interview with senior
     member of the Miran Shura Provincial Logistics Commission, Taliban Leadership
     28, June 2015; Interview with senior member of the Mashhad Logistics Commission,
     Taliban Leadership 33, July 2015.

66.  Interview with senior members of Peshawar Shura Logistics commission, Taliban
     Leadership 31, June 2015; Interview with senior member of the Quetta Shura
     Logistics Commission, Taliban Leadership 30, June 2015; Interview with senior
     member of the Miran Shura Provincial Logistics Commission, Taliban Leadership
     28, June 2015; Interview with senior member of the Mashhad Logistics Commission,
     Taliban Leadership 33, July 2015.

67.  Interview with senior members of Peshawar Shura Logistics Commission, Taliban
     Leadership 31, June 2015; Interview with senior member of the Quetta Shura
     Logistics Commission, Taliban Leadership 30, June 2015; Interview with senior
     member of the Miran Shura Provincial Logistics Commission, Taliban Leadership
     28, June 2015.

68.  Interview with senior member of the Mashhad Logistics Commission, Taliban
     Leadership 33, July 2015..

69.  Interview with senior member of Peshawar Shura Logistics commission, Taliban
     Leadership 31, June 2015; Interview with senior member of the Quetta Shura
     Logistics Commission, Taliban Leadership 30, June 2015; Interview with senior
     member of the Miran Shura Provincial Logistics Commission, Taliban Leadership
     28, June 2015; Interview with senior member of the Mashhad Logistics Commission,
     Taliban Leadership 33, July 2015; Interview with senior member of Peshawar Military
     Commission, Taliban leadership 22, April 2015.

70.  Interview with senior member of the Quetta Shura logistics commission, Taliban
     Leadership 30, June 2015; Interview with senior member of the Miran Shura
     Provincial Logistics Commission, Taliban Leadership 28, June 2015; Interview with
     senior member of the Mashhad Logistics Commission, Taliban Leadership 33, July
     2015.

71.  Interview with cadre, Nimruz, Taliban OP36, January 2014; Interview with cadre,
     Dost Mohamamd Mahaz, Parwan province, Taliban OP61, February 2014; Interview
     with Taliban cadre, Baghlan, May 2015, Baghlan Taliban 14; Interview with cadre,
     Baghlan Taliban 11, March 2015; Interview with Taliban cadre, Dandi Ghori,
     Baghlan Taliban 13, March 2015; Interview with Mahaz representative, Ghazni,
     December 2014, Ghazni Taliban 11; Interview with cadre, Mansur Mahaz, Ghazni
     Taliban 12, January 2015; Interview with district governor, Ghazni Taliban 13,
     January 2015; Interview with cadre, Paktia, Haqqani 4, February 2015; Interview
     with provincial cadre of the Haqqani network, February 2015, Haqqani 8; Interview

with fighter, Kandahar Taliban 1, August 2014; Interview with Taliban cadre in Wardak, March 2015, Wardak Taliban 11; Interview with cadre, Wardak Taliban 12, March 2015.

72. Interview with Moulavi Omar Akbar, provincial representative of Mansur Mahaz in Sar-e-pul province, Taliban leadership 40, March 2014; Interview with cadre, Zakir Mahaz, Sar e pul province, Taliban OP54, March 2014; Interview with cadre, Atiqullah Mahaz, Kabul province, February 2014, Taliban OP58; Interview with cadre, Dost Mohammad Mahaz, Kabul province, Taliban OP60, February 2014; Interview with cadre, Zakir Mahaz, Kabul province, Taliban OP36, February 2014; Interview with cadre, Dost Mohammad Mahaz, Parwan province, Taliban OP61, February 2014; Interview with cadre, Parwan province, Taliban OP62, February 2014; Interview with cadre, Jundullah Mahaz, Parwan province, Taliban OP63, February 2014; Interview with cadre, Kapisa province, Taliban OP65, February 2014; Interview with cadre, Bamyan province, Taliban OP66, February 2014; Interview with Cadre, Panjshir province, Taliban OP67, February 2014; Interview with cadre, Abdul Matin Mahaz, Farah province, Taliban OP68, February 2014; Interview with cadre, Atiqullah Mahaz, Laghman province, Taliban OP34, January 2014.

73. Interview with commander, Jaghori, Ghazni Taliban 14, January 2015; Interview with cadre, Baghlan Taliban 11, March 2015.

74. Interview with Moulavi Yousaf Is-haqzai, representative of Zakir Mahaz in Badghis province, Taliban OP69, January 2014.

75. Interview with cadre, Sar pul province, Taliban OP70, March 2014.

76. Interview with cadre, Jowzjan province, Taliban OP72, March 2014; Interview with cadre, Sar pul province, Rahbari Shura, Taliban OP73, March 2014; Interview cadre, Mansur Mahaz, Ghor province, Taliban OP47, January 2014.

77. Interview with cadre, Abdul Raziq Mahaz, Farah province, Taliban OP 74, January 2014; Interview with cadre, Zakir Mahaz in Badghis province, Taliban OP75, January 2014.

78. Interview with commander, Baghlan Taliban 6, Baghlan Jadid, September 2014.

79. 'AFGHANISTAN: NGO alleges US "occupation" of Helmand clinics', *IRIN News*, 8 September 2009; 'NGO: ISAF Attack Afghan Hospitals, Violating 'All Established Rules'', *FNA*, 8 December 2012; Interview with commander, Baghlan Jadid, Baghlan Taliban 4, September 2014; Interview with commander, Dahan-e Ghori, Baghlan Taliban 8, July 2014; Interview with commander, Giro, Ghazni Taliban 2, August 2014; Interview with commander, Wardak Taliban 4, July 2014; Interview with commander, Wardak (Chak), Taliban OP39, June 2014; Interview with group commander, Wardak Taliban 3, July 2014; Interview with commander, Wardak Taliban 7, Daimirdad, July 2014.

80. Interview with senior member of Mashhad Recruitment Commission, Taliban Leadership 35, July 2015; Interview with senior member of Peshawar Shura Recruitment Commission, Taliban leadership 34, July 2015; Interview with senior member of Miran Shah Recruitment commission, Taliban Leadership 18, February 2015; Interview with senior member of Quetta Recruitment Commission, Taliban Leadership 24, March 2015; Interview with senior member of Mashhad Recruitment Commission, Taliban Leadership 35, July 2015.

81.  Interview with senior member of Peshawar Shura Recruitment Commission, Taliban leadership 34, July 2015.

82.  Interview with Commander, Dadullah Mahaz, Taliban OP81, October 2012; Interview with cadre, Dost Mohammad Mahaz, Kunar province, Taliban OP79, January 2014; Interview with cadre, Dost Mohammad Mahaz, Laghman province, Taliban OP80, January 2014; Interview with senior member of Mashhad Recruitment Commission, Taliban Leadership 35, July 2015.

83.  Interview with former Taliban commander, Mohammad Agha (Logar), Haqqani Taliban 11, March 2015.

84.  Interview with senior member of Quetta Recruitment Commission, Taliban Leadership 24, March 2015.

85.  Interview with Rahbari Shura member, August 2015, Taliban Leadership 40.

86.  Interview with senior member of Quetta Recruitment Commission, Taliban Leadership 24, March 2015.

87.  Interview with senior member of Miran Shah Recruitment commission, Taliban Leadership 18, February 2015.

88.  Ibid.

89.  Ibid.

90.  Interview with senior member of Peshawar Shura Recruitment Commission, Taliban leadership 34, July 2015.

91.  Interview with senior member of Mashhad Recruitment Commission, Taliban Leadership 35, July 2015.

92.  Ibid.

93.  Ibid.; Interview with senior member of Mashhad Office, Taliban Leadership 6, October 2014.

94.  Interview with senior member of Mashhad Recruitment Commission, Taliban Leadership 35, July 2015; Interview with senior member of Peshawar Shura Recruitment Commission, Taliban Leadership 34, July 2015; Interview with senior member of Miran Shah Recruitment commission, Taliban Leadership 18, February 2015.

95.  Interview with senior member of Quetta Recruitment Commission, Taliban Leadership 24, March 2015.

96.  Ibid.

97.  Interview with senior member of Miran Shah Recruitment commission, Taliban Leadership 18, February 2015.

98.  Interview with Rahbari Shura member, August 2015, Taliban Leadership 40.

99.  Interview with senior member of Miran Shah Recruitment commission, Taliban Leadership 18, February 2015.

100. Interview with senior member of Peshawar Shura Recruitment Commission, Taliban Leadership 34, July 2015.

101. Interview with senior member of Mashhad Recruitment Commission, Taliban Leadership 35, July 2015.

102. Interview with senior member of Matinullah Mahaz, Taliban Leadership 3, August 2014.

103. Interview with senior member of Abdul Majid Mahaz, Taliban Leadership 2, August 2014.

104. Interview with Rahbari Shura member, August 2015, Taliban Leadership 40.
105. Interview with senior member of Miran Shah Recruitment commission, Taliban Leadership 18, February 2015.
106. Interview with Commander, Badakhshan, Taliban OP82, January 2013; Interview with cadre, Wakhan, Taliban OP84, January 2013; Interview with commander, Baghlan, Dandi Ghori, Taliban OP83, October 2012; Interview with Taliban cadre, Naim Mahaz, Taliban OP22, January 2013.
107. Interview with Rahbari Shura member, August 2015, Taliban Leadership 40.
108. Interview with former commander of Faruq Mahaz, Maywand, December 2014 (Kandahar Taliban 11); Interview with commander, Kandahar Taliban 13, Zherai, December 2014; Interview with former commander, Faruq Mahaz, Kandahar Taliban 10, Maruf, December 2014.
109. Interview with commander, Baghlan Taliban 6, Baghlan Jadid, September 2014; Interview with commander, Baghlan-e Jadid, Baghlan Taliban 3, September 2014; Interview with commander, Baghlan Jadid, Baghlan Taliban 4, September 2014; Interview with commander, Baghlan Taliban 1, September 2014; Interview with commander. Dandi Ghori, Bagjlan Taliban 2, September 2014; Interview with Baghlan elder 8, Dandi Ghori, July 2014; Interview with Baghlan elder 10, Dandi Ghori, July 2014; Interview with commander, Dahan-e Ghori, Baghlan Taliban 8, July 2014; Interview with commander, Baghlan Jadidi, Baghlan Taliban 10, July 2014; Interview with Ghazni Elder 1, Rashidan, August 2014; Interview with commander, Giro, Ghazni Taliban 2, August 2014; Interview with Ghazni Taliban 5, August 2014; Interview with commander, Ghazni Taliban 8, August 2014; Interview with Taliban commander, Ghazni Taliban 9, August 2014; Interview with Commander, Ghazni (Andar), August 2014, Ghazni Taliban 10; Interview with Ghazni Elder 3, Qarabagh, August 2014; Interview with Ghazni elder 2, Khogyani, August 2014; Interview with commander, Ghazni Taliban 6, August 2014; Interview with commander, Ghazni Taliban 7, August 2014; Interview with Ghazni Elder 10, Khogyani, July 2014; Interview with Wardak elder 4, Sayed Abad, July 2014; Interview with Wardak elder 6, Jaghatu, July 2015; Interview with Wardak elder 7, Sayed Abad, July 2014.
110. Interview with commander, Ghazni Taliban 9, July 2014; Interview with commander, Baghlan Jadidi, Baghlan Taliban 10, July 2014; Interview with Wardak elder 1, Jaghatu, July 2014.
111. Interview with Wardak elder 6, Jaghatu, July 2015; Interview with commander, Wardak Taliban 6, July 2014; Interview with Wardak elder 3, July 2014.
112. Interview with commander, Dahan-e Ghori, Baghlan Taliban 8, July 2014.
113. Interview with former commander, Baghlan Taliban 16, May 2015; Interview with former fighter, Baghlan Taliban 15, May 2015.
114. Interview with former fighter, Baghlan Taliban 15, May 2015; Interview with former group commander of Mansur Mahaz, Ghazni Taliban 16, May 2015; Interview with former commander, Kandahar Taliban 16, Spin Boldak, December 2014; Interview with former commander, Arghandab, Kandahar Taliban 17, December 2014; Interview with former commander, Zherai, Kandahar Taliban 15; Interview with former commander, Baghlan Taliban 18, May 2015.

115. Interview with former commander, Taliban Kandahar 20, May 2015.

116. Interview with former commander, Baradar Mahaz, Ghazni Taliban 15, May 2015.

117. Interview with student proselytiser, Nangarhar Taliban 9, June 2015; Interview with student proselytiser, Zabul Taliban 1, June 2015; Interview with student proselytiser, Wardak Taliban 16, June 2015; Interview with adviser, Pakistan, Adviser 2, July 2015; Interview with Faryab Elder 3, Qaysar, May 2015.

118. Interview with Adviser, Pakistan, Adviser 2, July 2015.

119. Taliban sources in Quetta and Peshawar, contacted in July 2012.

120. Interview with Taliban cadre in Wardak, March 2015, Wardak Taliban 11; Interview with provincial cadre of the Haqqani network, February 2015, Haqqani 8.

121. Interview with district governor, Ghazni Taliban 13, January 2015.

122. Interview with commander, Nahr-i Seraj, Taliban OP 86, May 2012; Interview with commander, Marjah, Taliban OP 87, May 2012; Interview with Mahaz representative, Ghazni, December 2014, Ghazni Taliban 11; Interview with commander, Nahr-i Seraj, Taliban OP90, May 2012; Interview with commander, Kajaki, Taliban OP94, May 2012.

123. Interview with Taliban cadre, Baghlan, May 2015, Baghlan Taliban 14; Interview with cadre, Faryab Taliban 4, December 2014; Interview with cadre, Mansur Mahaz, Faryab Taliban 5, December 2014; Interview with commander, Andkhoy, Faryab Taliban 7, December 2014; Interview with Taliban cadre, Almar, Faryab Taliban 1, December 2014; Interview with cadre, Mansur Mahaz, Faryab Taliban 3, December 2014; Interview with fighter, Kandahar Taliban 1, August 2014; Interview with group commander, Kandahar Taliban 2, August 2014; Interview with fighter, Kandahar Taliban 6, Maruf, August 2014; Interview with fighter, Kandahar Taliban 7, Zherai, August 2014; Interview with fighter, Kandahar Taliban 8, Spin Boldak, August 2014; Interview with commander, Kandahar Taliban 9, Shorabak, August 2014; Interview with *dilghay* commander, Behsud, Wardak Taliban 10, March 2015.

124. Interview with commander, Jaghori, Ghazni Taliban 14, January 2015.

125. Interview with cadre, Almar, Faryab Taliban 2, December 2014.

126. Interview with Taliban cadre, Dandi Ghori, Baghlan Taliban 13, March 2015.

127. Interview with commander, Garmser, Taliban OP53, June 2012; Interview with commander, Kajaki, Taliban OP88, May 2012.

128. Interviews carried out in April–July 2012.

129. Interview with commander, Ghazni Taliban 4, August 2014; Interview with Ghazni Taliban 5, August 2014; Interview with Taliban commander, Ghazni Taliban 9, August 2014; Interview with commander, Ghazni Taliban 3, August 2014; Interview with Commander, Ghazni (Andar), August 2014, Ghazni Taliban 10; Interview with commander, Ghazni Taliban 6, August 2014; Interview with commander, Wardak Taliban 4, July 2014; Interview with commander, Wardak (Chak), Taliban OP39, June 2014; Interview with commander, Ghazni Taliban 8, August 2014; Interview with commander, Wardak Taliban 2, Jaghatu, June 2014; Interview with group commander, Wardak Taliban 3, July 2014; Interview with commander, Wardak Taliban 7, Daimirdad, July 2014; Interview with commander, Wardak Taliban 8, Sayed Abad, July 2014; Interview with commander, Wardak Taliban 6, July 2014; Interviews with Taliban commanders, Helmand, Taliban OP18, 3 March 2012.

130. Interview with commander, Musa Qala, Taliban OP89, May 2012.
131. Interviews with Taliban commanders, Helmand, Taliban OP18, 3 March 2012; Interview with commander, Kajaki, Taliban OP91, June 2012.
132. Interview with commander, Garmser, Taliban OP92, July 2012.
133. Interview with commander, Nawzad, Taliban OP93, June 2012.
134. Interview with Taliban OP2, Nad Ali, December 2011.
135. Interview with commander, Musa Qala, Taliban OP95, June 2012.
136. James Fergusson, *A Million Bullets*, London: Bantam, 2008, p. 196, 121.
137. Interview with member of Quetta Military Commission, Taliban leadership 29, June 2015.
138. Interview with member of Mashhad Military Commission, Taliban leadership 36, July 2015.
139. Interview with member of Peshawar Military Commission, Taliban leadership 37, July 2015.
140. Interview with adviser to Serajuddin Haqqani, Leadership 13, January 2015.
141. Ibid.
142. Interview with member of Miran Shah Military Commission, Taliban leadership 38, June 2015.
143. Interview with senior member of Intelligence department of the Peshawar Shura, Taliban leadership 42, July 2015; Interview with senior member of Intelligence department of the Quetta Shura, Taliban Leadership 43, July 2015.
144. Interview with senior member of Intelligence department of the Quetta Shura, Taliban Leadership 43, July 2015.
145. Interview with senior member of Intelligence department of the Peshawar Shura, Taliban leadership 42, July 2015.
146. Interview with senior member of Intelligence department of the Miran Shah Shura, Taliban Leadership 39, July 2015; Interview with senior member of Intelligence department of the Peshawar Shura, Taliban leadership 42, July 2015; Interview with senior member of Intelligence department of the Mashhad Shura, Taliban Leadership 44, July 2015.
147. Interview with senior member of Intelligence department of the Mashhad Shura, Taliban Leadership 44, July 2015.
148. Interview with senior member of intelligence department of the Mashhad Shura, Taliban Leadership 44, July 2015.
149. Interview with senior member of Intelligence department of the Miran Shah Shura, Taliban Leadership 39, July 2015; Interview with senior member of Intelligence department of the Peshawar Shura, Taliban leadership 42, July 2015; Interview with senior member of Intelligence department of the Quetta Shura, Taliban Leadership 43, July 2015; Interview with senior member of Intelligence department of the Mashhad Shura, Taliban Leadership 44, July 2015.
150. Interview with former commander, Musa Qala, Helmand, Taliban OP26, September 2011.
151. Borzou Daragahi, 'Afghan Taliban intelligence network embraces the new', *Los Angeles Times*, 13 April 2011.

152.  C. J. Chivers, 'In Eastern Afghanistan, at War With the Taliban's Shadowy Rule', *The New York Times*, 6 February 2011. See also: Ben Brandt, 'The Taliban's Conduct of Intelligence and Counterintelligence', *CTC Sentinel*, 1 June 2011.

153.  Interview with senior member of Intelligence department of the Peshawar Shura, Taliban leadership 42, July 2015.

154.  Interview with senior member of Intelligence department of the Quetta Shura, Taliban Leadership 43, July 2015.

155.  Interview with senior member of Intelligence department of the Miran Shah Shura, Taliban Leadership 39, July 2015; Interview with senior member of Intelligence department of the Peshawar Shura, Taliban leadership 42, July 2015; Interview with senior member of Intelligence department of the Quetta Shura, Taliban Leadership 43, July 2015; Interview with senior member of Intelligence department of the Mashhad Shura, Taliban Leadership 44, July 2015.

156.  Interview with senior member of Intelligence department of the Miran Shah Shura, Taliban Leadership 39, July 2015; Interview with senior member of Intelligence department of the Peshawar Shura, Taliban leadership 42, July 2015; Interview with senior member of Intelligence department of the Quetta Shura, Taliban Leadership 43, July 2015; Interview with senior member of Intelligence department of the Mashhad Shura, Taliban Leadership 44, July 2015.

157.  Interview with senior member of Intelligence department of the Miran Shah Shura, Taliban Leadership 39, July 2015; Interview with senior member of Intelligence department of the Peshawar Shura, Taliban leadership 42, July 2015; Interview with senior member of Intelligence department of the Quetta Shura, Taliban Leadership 43, July 2015; Interview with senior member of Intelligence department of the Mashhad Shura, Taliban Leadership 44, July 2015.

158.  Martin, *An Intimate War*, p. 130; Interview with former commander, Kandahar Taliban 16, Spin Boldak, December 2014.

159.  See on the *layha*: Kate Clark, 'The Layha: Calling the Taliban to Account', Kabul/ Berlin: Afghanistan Analysts Network, 2011; Thomas Johnson and Matt Dupee, 'Analysing the new Taliban Code of Conduct (Layeha): an assessment of changing perspectives and strategies of the Afghan Taliban', *Central Asian Survey*, vol. 31 issue 1, 2012, pp. 77–91.

160.  Nagamine; Clark, 'The Layha', p. 6.

161.  Article 15 of the 2006 *layha*. See Nagamine.

162.  Nagamine.

163.  Article 78 of the 2010 *layha*, Article 59 of the 2009 *layha*, italics added. Taken from Nagamine.

164.  Interview with former commander, Shindand, Herat Taliban 8, December 2014.

165.  Source in the Taliban structure in Pakistan, October 2012; Communication with Taliban cadre in Peshawar, August 2012.

166.  Taliban *layha*, 2010.

167.  See Clark, 'The Layha'.

168.  Sami Yousafzai and Urs Gehriger, 'The new Taliban codex', *Die Weltwoche*, 16 November 2006.

169.  Johnson and Dupee, 'Analyzing the Taliban code...'.

170.  Nagamine.

171.  Ibid.

172.  Interviews with two mawlavis, respectively members of the Taliban Ulema Council in Kandahar province and of the Ulema council of the Peshawar Shura, March 2015.

173.  Source in the Taliban structure in Pakistan, August 2013; Interview with commander, Maywand, Kandahar Taliban 12, December 2014.

174.  Interview with commander, Maywand, Kandahar Taliban 12, December 2014; Interview with former commander, Kandahar Taliban 16, Spin Boldak, December 2014; Interview with former commander, Arghandab, Kandahar Taliban 17, December 2014.

175.  Nagamine, Johnson and DuPee, 'Analysing the new Taliban Code...', p. 89, footnote 6.

176.  Clark, 'The Layha'.

177.  Interview with Taliban group commander in Wardak, October 2011.

178.  Thomas H. Johnson and Matthew C. Dupee, 'Analysing the New Taliban Code of Conduct (Layeha): An Assessment of Changing Perspectives and Strategies of the Afghan Taliban', *Central Asian Survey*, vol. 31 issue 1, 2012, pp. 77–91, 78.

179.  Mike Williams, 'How the British presence in Sangin restored trust in government', *The Guardian*, 20 September 2010: http://www.guardian.co.uk/commentisfree/2010/sep/20/british-forces-in-sangin, retrieved 14 March 2013.

180.  Interview with Taliban group commander in Wardak, October 2011.

181.  Taliban cadre in Peshawar, contacted October 2012.

182.  Interview with former commander, Musa Qala, Helmand, Taliban OP26, September 2011.

183.  Interview with former commander, Nawur, Ghazni Taliban 17, May 2015.

184.  Interview with former commander, Baghlan Taliban 16, May 2015.

185.  Interview with former commander, Baradar Mahaz, Ghazni Taliban 15, May 2015.

186.  Interviews with Taliban commanders and elders in Deh Rawood, autumn 2011.

187.  Interview with Baghlan elder 8, Dandi Ghori, July 2014; Interview with Wardak elder 7, Sayed Abad, July 2014; Interview with former commander, Baghlan Taliban 16, May 2015; Interview with former group commander of Mansur Mahaz, Ghazni Taliban 16, May 2015; Interview with former fighter, Wardak Taliban 14, May 2015; Interview with former commander, Wardak Taliban 15, May 2015; Interview with former commander, Dadullah Mahaz, Kandahar Taliban 22, July 2015.

188.  Interview with former commander, Taliban Kandahar 20, May 2015; Interview with former commander, Kandahar Taliban 21, May 2015.

189.  Graham Lee, *Fighting Season*, London: Gerald Duckworth & Co, 2012, p. 93.

190.  Interview with former fighter, Wardak Taliban 14, May 2015.

191.  Interview with Baghlan elder 1, Dandi Ghori, July 2014; Interview with Baghlan elder 2, Baghlan Jadid, July 2014; Interview with Baghlan elder 8, Dandi Ghori, July 2014; Interview with Baghlan elder 9, Burka, July 2014; Interview with Baghlan elder 10, Dandi Ghori, July 2014; Interview with Baghlan elder 3, Baghlan Jadid, July 2014; Interview with Baghlan elder 4, Baghlan Jadid, July 2014; Interview with Baghlan elder 5, Baghlan Jadid, July 2014; Interview with Baghlan elder 6, Dandi Ghori, July 2014; Interview with Baghlan Elder 7, July 2014; Interview with Ghazni Elder 1, Rashidan, August 2014; Interview with Ghazni Elder 3, Qarabagh, August

2014; Interview with Ghazni elder 2, Khogyani, August 2014; Interview with Ghazni elder 4, Qarabagh, August 2014; Interview with Ghazni elder 5, Andar, August 2014; Interview with Wardak elder 1, Jaghatu, July 2014; Interview with Faryab Elder 1, Almar, May 2015; Interview with Faryab Elder 2, Almar, May 2015; Interview with Faryab Elder 3, Qaysar, May 2015; Interview with Faryab Elder 4, Khwaja Sabz Posh, May 2015; Interview with Faryab Elder 6, Qaysar, May 2015; Interview with Faryab Elder 7, Qaysar, May 2015; Interview with Faryab Elder 8, Jhwaja Sabz Posh, May 2015; Interview with Faryab Elder 4, Almar, May 2015.

192. Interview with Baghlan elder 1, Dandi Ghori, July 2014; Interview with Baghlan elder 2, Baghlan Jadid, July 2014; Interview with Baghlan elder 8, Dandi Ghori, July 2014; Interview with Baghlan elder 9, Burka, July 2014; Interview with Baghlan elder 10, Dandi Ghori, July 2014; Interview with Baghlan elder 3, Baghlan Jadid, July 2014; Interview with Baghlan elder 4, Baghlan Jadid, July 2014; Interview with Baghlan elder 5, Baghlan Jadid, July 2014; Interview with Baghlan elder 6, Dandi Ghori, July 2014; Interview with Baghlan Elder 7, July 2014; Interview with Ghazni Elder 1, Rashidan, August 2014; Interview with Ghazni Elder 3, Qarabagh, August 2014; Interview with Ghazni elder 2, Khogyani, August 2014; Interview with Ghazni elder 4, Qarabagh, August 2014; Interview with Ghazni elder 5, Andar, August 2014; Interview with Herat elder 2, Obeh, April 2015; Interview with Faryab Elder 1, Almar, May 2015; Interview with Faryab Elder 2, Almar, May 2015; Interview with Faryab Elder 3, Qaysar, May 2015; Interview with Faryab Elder 4, Khwaja Sabz Posh, May 2015; Interview with Faryab Elder 4, Almar, May 2015; Interview with Faryab Elder 6, Qaysar, May 2015; Interview with Faryab Elder 7, Qaysar, May 2015; Interview with Faryab Elder 8, Jhwaja Sabz Posh, May 2015; Interview with Kandahar elder 5, Maiwand, February 2015; Interview with Nangarhar elder 6, Shirzad, March 2015; Interview with Nangarhar elder 9, Khogyani, March 2015; Interview with Nangarhar elder 10, Bati Kot, March 2015; Interview with Herat Elder 7, Chest-i Sharif, April 2015.

193. Interviews carried out in 2014 in nine provinces.

194. Interview with group commander, Cheshti Sharif, Herat Taliban 3, December 2014.

195. Interview with commander, Wardak Taliban 8, Sayed Abad, July 2014.

196. Interview with commander, Wardak Taliban 4, July 2014; Interview with commander, Wardak (Chak), Taliban OP39, June 2014; Interview with group commander, Wardak Taliban 3, July 2014; Interview with ommander, Wardak Taliban 5, July 2014; Interview with commander, Wardak Taliban 6, July 2014; Interview with commander, Wardak Taliban 7, Daimirdad, July 2014; Interview with commander, Wardak Taliban 8, Sayed Abad, July 2014; Interview with commander, Jaghatu, Eardak Taliban 9, July 2014.

197. Interview with Taliban judge in Badghis, Taliban OP23, autumn 2011. For the case of two commanders in Wardak, see: Gopal, 'The Battle for Afghanistan', p. 23.

198. Interview with Jundullah commander, OP115, October 2012; Interview with Satter Mahaz cadre, Baghlan, OP110, September 2012

199. A. Giustozzi, 'The Taliban's military courts', *Small Wars and Insurgencies*, vol. 25, n. 2, 2014.

200. Interview with elder in Sayedabad, Elder OP 11, autumn 2011.

201. Interview with former commander, Wardak Taliban 15, May 2015.

202. Giustozzi, 'The Taliban's military courts'.

203. Ibid.

204. Interview with a head of a Taliban Regional Judicial Committee, Paliban OP162, spring 2012.

205. Giustozzi, 'The Taliban's military courts'.

206. Ibid.

207. Ibid.

208. Ibid.

209. See: Giustozzi et al., 'The politics of justice'.

210. Gopal, 'The Battle for Afghanistan', p. 27

211. Interview with commander, Sorkhrod, Nangarhar Taliban 9, March 2015; Interview with Uruzgan Taliban 1, Shahid Hassas, commander, March 2015; Interview with cadre, Baghlan Jadid, Baghlan Taliban 7, July 2014; Interview with commander, Wardak (Chak), Taliban OP39, June 2014; Martin, *An Intimate War*, pp. 179–81.

212. Interview with elder in Pech, Elder OP25, winter 2011-12; Interview with elder in Watapur, Elder OP26, winter 2011–12.

213. Interview with former Taliban commander, Mohammad Agha (Logar), Haqqani Taliban 11, March 2015.

214. Interview with member of Mashhad Military Commission, Taliban leadership 36, July 2015.

215. Interview with member of Peshawar Military Commission, Taliban leadership 37, July 2015.

216. Interview with commander, Kapisa Taliban 1, March 2015; Interview with commander, Sorkhrod, Nangarhar Taliban 9, March 2015; Interview with Uruzgan Taliban 1, Shahid Hassas, commander, March 2015.

217. Interview with member of Mashhad Military Commission, Taliban leadership 36, July 2015.

218. Interview with Commander, Badakhshan, Taliban OP28, January 2013.

219. Source in the Military Commission of Quetta, contacted April 2015.

220. Interview with member of Quetta Military Commission, Taliban leadership 29, June 2015.

221. Interview with group commander, Dadullah Mahaz, Taliban OP50, December 2012.

222. Interview with commander, Sorkhrod, Nangarhar Taliban 9, March 2015.

223. Interview with Taliban cadre in Wardak, March 2015, Wardak Taliban 11.

224. Interview with cadre of Sattar Mahaz, Kunar, January 2014, Taliban OP38.

225. Interview with member of Miran Shah Military Commission, Taliban leadership 38, June 2015.

226. Interview with Qari Shir Afzal, provincial *nizami massoul* of Kunar Province, January 2014, Taliban OP32; Interview with Moulavi Miwand, provincial representative of Mansur Mahaz in Laghman Province, January 2014 Taliban OP33; Interview with Moulavi Amanullah, representative of Atiqullah Mahaz in Laghman Province, January 2014, Taliban OP34; Interview with Qari Ihsanullah Ihsan, representative of Ghor province from Ihsan Rahim Mahaz, January 2014, Taliban OP35; Interview with Mullah Latifullah, provincial representative of Zakir Mahaz

in Kabul Province, February 2014, Taliban OP36; Interview with Qari Asadulalh, provincial *mahaz* representative for Jundullah Mahaz in Parwan province, February 2014, Taliban OP37.

227. Interview with senior member of Abdul Raziq Mahaz, Taliban Leadership 5, October 2014.
228. Source in the Taliban structure in Pakistan, August 2013.
229. Interview with senior member of Matinullah Mahaz, Taliban Leadership 3, August 2014.
230. Interview with senior member of Abdul Majeed Mahaz, Leadership 2, August 2014.
231. Interview with Taliban cadre, Baghlan, May 2015, Baghlan Taliban 14; Interview with commander, Jundullah Mahaz, Baghlan Taliban 11, March 2015.
232. Interview with former group commander of Mansur Mahaz, Ghazni Taliban 16, May 2015; Interview with former commander, Nawur, Ghazni Taliban 17, May 2015; Interview with group commander, Khost, Haqqani 2, January 2015; Interview with fighter, Paktia, Haqqani 3, February 2015; Interview with cadre, Paktia, Haqqani 5, February 2015; Interview with commander, Logar, Haqqani 7, February 2015; Interview with commander, Logar (Mohammad Agha), Haqqani 9, February 2015; Interview with fighter, Paktika, Haqqani 6, February 2015; Interview with former commander, Wardak Taliban 15, May 2015.
233. Interview with Haqqani elder 2, Mohamamd Agha, Logar, February 2015; Interview with group commander, Khost, Haqqani 2, January 2015; Interview with fighter, Paktia, Haqqani 3, February 2015; Interview with commander, Logar, Haqqani 7, February 2015; Interview with Logar elder, Baraki Barak, Haqqani elder 1, February 2015; Interview with fighter, Paktika, Haqqani 6, February 2015; Interview with former Taliban commander, Mohammad Agha (Logar), Haqqani Taliban 11, March 2015.
234. Interview with Taliban cadre, Dandi Ghori, Baghlan Taliban 13, March 2015; Interview with cadre, Mansur Mahaz, Faryab Taliban 5, December 2014; Interview with group commander, Sattar Mahaz, Faryab Taliban 6, December 2014; Interview with commander, Andkhoy, Faryab Taliban 7, December 2014; Interview with Taliban cadre, Almar, Faryab Taliban 1, December 2014; Interview with Mahaz representative, Ghazni, December 2014, Ghazni Taliban 11; Interview with cadre, Mansur Mahaz, Ghazni Taliban 12, January 2015; Interview with district governor, Ghazni Taliban 13, January 2015; Interview with commander, Jaghori, Ghazni Taliban 14, January 2015; Interview with group commander, Cheshti Sharif, Herat Taliban 3, December 2014; Interview with group commander, Herat Taliban 5, December 2014; Interview with group commander, Shindand, Herat Taliban 5, December 2014; Interview with commander, Shindand, Herat Taliban 5, December 2014; Interview with group commander, Kandahar Taliban 2, August 2014; Interview with fighter, Kandahar Taliban 7, Zherai, August 2014; Interview with Nangarhar Taliban 3, Bati Kot, April 2015; Interview with cadre, Wardak Taliban 12, March 2015; Interview with Toor-e Pagri commander, Bati Kot, Nangarhar Taliban 4, April 2015; Interview with commander, Bati Kot, Nangarhar Taliban 5, April 2015; Interview with *dilghay* commander, Behsud, Wardak Taliban 10, March 2015; Interview with Baghlan elder 6, Dandi Ghori, July 2014; Interview with Baghlan

Elder 7, July 2014; Interview with Ghazni Elder 1, Rashidan, August 2014; Interview with Wardak elder 6, Jaghatu, July 2015; Interview with commander, Wardak (Chak), Taliban OP39, June 2014; Interview with Wardak elder 3, July 2014; Interview with former Tora Bora Mahaz commander, Nangarhar Taliban 7, April 2015; Interview with Taliban cadre, Baghlan, May 2015, Baghlan Taliban 14; Interview with commander, Jaghori, Ghazni Taliban 14, January 2015; Interview with Haqqani elder 2, Mohamamd Agha, Logar, February 2015; Interview with fighter, Kandahar Taliban 1, August 2014; Interview with fighter, Kandahar Taliban 6, Maruf, August 2014; Interview with former commander, Zherai, Kandahar Taliban 15; Interview with former commander, Baghlan Taliban 16, May 2015; Interview with former commander, Kandahar Taliban 21, May 2015; Interview with former commander, Dadullah Mahaz, Kandahar Taliban 22, July 2015; Interview with cadre of Mansur Mahaz in Sar-e-pul province, Taliban OP40, March 2014; Interview with cadre, Ghor, Taliban OP41, January 2014.

235. Interview with commander, Jundullah Mahaz, Baghlan Taliban 11, March 2015; Interview with former commander, Taliban Kandahar 20, May 2015; Interview with cadre of Zakir Mahaz in Kabul province, Taliban OP36, February 2014; Interview with commander, Wardak (Chak), Taliban OP39, June 2014; Commander, Wardak Taliban 5, July 2014.

236. Interview with former fighter, Wardak Taliban 14, May 2015.

237. Interview with Haqqani elder 2, Mohammad Agha, Logar, February 2015; Interview with Logar elder, Baraki Barak, Haqqani elder 1, February 2015.

238. Interview with district governor, Ghazni Taliban 13, January 2015.

239. Interview with fighter, Kandahar Taliban 8, Spin Boldak, August 2014.

240. Interview with cadre, Baghlan Taliban 11, March 2015.

241. Interview with commander, Jundullah Mahaz, Baghlan Taliban 11, March 2015; Interview with former commander of Mawlavi Kabir, Hissarak, Nangarhar Taliban 1, April 2015; Interview with commander, Bati Kot, Nangarhar Taliban 5, April 2015; Interview with commander, Jundullah Mahaz, Baghlan Taliban 11, March 2015; Interview with Taliban cadre, Dandi Ghori, Baghlan Taliban 13, March 2015; Interview with provincial cadre of the Haqqani network, February 2015, Haqqani 8; Interview with group commander, Kandahar Taliban 2, August 2014; Interview with Baghlan elder 2, Baghlan Jadid, July 2014.

242. Interview with commander, Wardak Taliban 6, July 2014; Interview with Haqqani elder 2, Mohammad Agha, Logar, February 2015; Interview with fighter, Paktia, Haqqani 3, February 2015.

243. Interview with group commander, Khost, Haqqani 2, January 2015; Interview with fighter, Paktia, Haqqani 3, February 2015; Interview with cadre, Paktia, Haqqani 5, February 2015; Interview with commander, Logar, Haqqani 7, February 2015; Interview with commander, Logar (Mohammad Agha), Haqqani 9, February 2015; Interview with fighter, Paktika, Haqqani 6, February 2015.

244. Interview with Baradar Mahaz cadre, August 2014 (Kandahar Taliban 4); Interview with cadre, Kandahar Taliban 5, August 2014.

245. Interview with cadre, Faryab Taliban 4, December 2014; Interview with fighter, Kandahar Taliban 1, August 2014; Interview with Toor-e Pagri commander, Bati

Kot, Nangarhar Taliban 4, April 2015; Interview with commander, Sorkhrod, Nangarhar Taliban 9, March 2015; Interview with group commander, Khost, Haqqani 2, January 2015; Interview with commander, Logar (Mohammad Agha), Haqqani 9, February 2015; Interview with former commander, Baradar Mahaz, Ghazni Taliban 15, May 2015.

246. Interview with commander, Sorkhrod, Nangarhar Taliban 9, March 2015.

247. Interview with provincial cadre of the Haqqani network, February 2015, Haqqani 8; Interview with Toor-e Pagri commander, Bati Kot, Nangarhar Taliban 4, April 2015; Interview with cadre, Baghlan Taliban 11, March 2015; Interview with Mahaz representative, Ghazni, December 2014, Ghazni Taliban 11; Interview with cadre, Mansur Mahaz, Ghazni Taliban 12, January 2015; Interview with Taliban cadre in Wardak, March 2015, Wardak Taliban 11; Interview with cadre, Wardak Taliban 12, March 2015; Interview with Logar elder, Baraki Barak, Haqqani elder 1, February 2015.

248. Interview with fighter, Kandahar Taliban 7, Zherai, August 2014.

249. 'Taliban Resistance Stiffens in Marjah', *CBS/AP*, 18 February 2010; Michael M. Phillips and Alan Cullison, 'Taliban Resistance Stalls New Rule in Marjah', *Wall Street Journal*, 20 February 2010; Richard A. Oppel, 'Violence Helps Taliban Undo Afghan Gains', *New York Times*, 3 April 2010.

250. Interview with fighter, Kandahar Taliban 6, Maruf, August 2014; Interview with fighter, Kandahar Taliban 8, Spin Boldak, August 2014; Interview with commander, Kandahar Taliban 9, Shorabak, August 2014; Interview with cadre, Sar-i pul, Taliban OP42, March 2014; Interview with cadre, Farah province, Taliban OP43, January 2014; Interview with commander, Maywand, Kandahar Taliban 12, December 2014; Interview with commander, Zherai, Kandahar Taliban 14, December 2014.

251. Interview with cadre, Mansur Mahaz, Badghis province, Taliban OP49, January 2014; Interview with cadre, Majid Mahaz, Paktika, Taliban OP44, February 2014; Interview with cadre, Sattar Mahaz, Kunar, Taliban OP45, January 2014; Interview with cadre, Naim Mahaz, Kunar province, Taliban OP46, January 2014; Interview with cadre, Naim Mahaz, Kunar province, Taliban OP46, January 2014; Interview with cadre, Mansur Mahaz, Kunar province, January 2014; Interview with cadre, Mansur Mahaz, Ghor province, Taliban OP47, January 2014; interview with cadre, Ghor province, Ihsan Rahim Mahaz, Taliban OP35, January 2014; Interview with cadre, Abdul Majid Mahaz, Ghor province, Taliban OP48, January 2014.

252. Taliban sources in Helmand, autumn 2011; Interview with group commander, Khost, Haqqani 2, January 2015.

253. Interview with Baghlan elder 1, Dandi Ghori, July 2014; Interview with Baghlan elder 2, Baghlan Jadid, July 2014; Interview with Baghlan elder 8, Dandi Ghori, July 2014; Interview with Baghlan elder 9, Burka, July 2014; Interview with Ghazni Elder 3, Qarabagh, August 2014; Interview with Ghazni elder 2, Khogyani, August 2014; Interview with Ghazni elder 4, Qarabagh, August 2014; Interview with Ghazni elder 5, Andar, August 2014; Interview with commander, Ghazni Taliban 6, August 2014; Interview with Ghazni Elder 6, Andar, July 2014; Interview with Ghazni elder 9, Rashidan, July 2014; Interview with Ghazni Elder 10, Khogyani, July 2014; Interview with Wardak elder 2, Wardak, July 2014; Interview with Haqqani elder 2, Mohammad

Agha, Logar, February 2015; Interview with cadre, Mansur Mahaz in Sar-e-pul province, Taliban OP40, January 2014.

254. Interview with former Taliban commander, Mohammad Agha (Logar), Haqqani Taliban 11, March 2015.

255. Interview with Taliban cadre, Dandi Ghori, Baghlan Taliban 13, March 2015; Interview with *mahaz* representative, Ghazni, December 2014, Ghazni Taliban 11; Interview with fighter, Paktika, Haqqani 6, February 2015; Interview with group commander, Khost, Haqqani 2, January 2015.

256. Interview with group commander, Khost, Haqqani 2, January 2015; Interview with fighter, Paktia, Haqqani 3, February 2015; Interview with commander, Logar, Haqqani 7, February 2015; Interview with provincial cadre of the Haqqani network, February 2015, Haqqani 8; Interview with commander, Logar (Mohammad Agha), Haqqani 9, February 2015; Interview with Taliban cadre in Wardak, March 2015, Wardak Taliban 11; Interview with commander, Logar, Haqqani 7, February 2015; Interview with Taliban cadre, Baghlan, May 2015, Baghlan Taliban 14; Interview with fighter, Paktia, Haqqani 3, February 2015.

257. Interview with commander, Jaghori, Ghazni Taliban 14, January 2015.

258. Interview with fighter, Paktia, Haqqani 3, February 2015; Interview with cadre, Paktia, Haqqani 4, February 2015.

259. Interview with Haqqani elder 2, Mohamamd Agha, Logar, February 2015; Interview with Logar elder, Baraki Barak, Haqqani elder 1, February 2015; Interview with Helmand elder 1, Sangin, April 2015; Interview with commander, Logar, Haqqani 7, February 2015.

260. Interview with Haqqani elder 2, Mohamamd Agha, Logar, February 2015.

261. Interview with Taliban cadre, Dandi Ghori, Baghlan Taliban 13, March 2015; Interview with *mahaz* representative, Ghazni, December 2014, Ghazni Taliban 11.

262. Source in the Taliban structure in Pakistan, June 2013; Source in the Taliban structure in Pakistan, July 2013.

263. Interview with former commander, Arghandab, Kandahar Taliban 17, December 2014; Interview with member of Political Commission in Quetta, Taliban Leadership 1, September 2014.

264. Interview with cadre, Samangan province, Taliban OP55, March 2014; Kick Flynn, *Trigger Time*, London: Orion Books, 2011, p. 116; Bishop, *3 Para*, p. 191; Interview with commander, Garmser, Taliban OP53, June 2012.

265. Interview with commander, Nad Ali, Taliban OP4, December 2011; Interview with former member of Rahbari Shura, Taliban leadership 7, September 2014; Interview with cadre, Zakir Mahaz, Sar e pul province, Taliban OP54, March 2014; Interview with Toor-e Pagri commander, Bati Kot, Nangarhar Taliban 4, April 2015; Interview with commander, Kapisa Taliban 1, March 2015; Personal communication with David Mansfield, September 2011; personal communication with Fabrizio Foschini (AAN), October 2012; 'Le Logar, province jadis tranquille aujourd'hui secouée par la rébellion', *Agence France Presse*, 16 October 2012; Interview with former commander, Arghandab, Kandahar Taliban 17, December 2014; Interview with former commander, Kandahar Taliban 16, Spin Boldak, December 2014; Interview with former commander, Zherai, Kandahar Taliban 15.

266.  Interview with commander, Sangin, Taliban OP56, June 2012; Interview with cadre, Baghlan Jadid, Baghlan Taliban 7, July 2014.
267.  Interview with senior member of Miran Shah Recruitment Commission, Taliban Leadership 18, February 2015.
268.  Interview with adviser, Pakistan, Adviser 2, July 2015.

## 7. THE TROUBLED COMEBACK OF THE QUETTA SHURA 2014

1.    Interview with Baradar Mahaz cadre, August 2014 (Kandahar Taliban 4).
2.    Interview with fighter, Kandahar Taliban 6, Maruf, August 2014.
3.    Interview with cadre, Zakir Mahaz, Helmand province (Kajaki), Helmand Taliban 1, December 2014; Interview with Baradar Mahaz cadre, August 2014 (Kandahar Taliban 4); Interview with commander, Kandahar Taliban 9, Shorabak, August 2014.
4.    Interview with senior cadre of Quetta Shura, Taliban leadership 17, February 2015.
5.    Interview with senior cadre of Quetta Shura, Taliban leadership 17, February 2015.
6.    Interview with senior member of political commission of the Miran Shah Shura, Taliban Leadership 4, September 2014; Interview with commission member, Quetta, Taliban leadership 1, September 2014.
7.    Interview with commander, Kandahar Taliban 13, Zherai, December 2014.
8.    Interview with senior member of Abdul Majid Mahaz, Taliban leadership 2, August 2014.
9.    Interview with member of Commission in Quetta Shura, Leadership 1, September 2014; Interview with senior cadre of Quetta Shura, Taliban leadership 17, February 2015; Interview with commander, Maywand, Kandahar Taliban 12, December 2014; Interview with commander, Zherai, Kandahar Taliban 14, December 2014.
10.   Source in the Taliban structure in Pakistan, August 2013.
11.   Source in the Taliban structure in Pakistan, September 2014
12.   Kandahar elder 1, Zhirai, November 2014.
13.   Interview with senior cadre of Quetta Shura, Taliban leadership 17, February 2015.
14.   Kandahar elder 1, Zhirai, November 2014.
15.   Source in the Taliban structure in Pakistan, November 2013.
16.   Interview with senior member of Hussain Rahimi Mahaz, Taliban leadership 11, January 2015.
17.   Source in the Taliban structure in Pakistan, November 2014.
18.   Interview with senior member of Intelligence department of the Quetta Shura, Taliban Leadership 43, July 2015.
19.   Interview with senior member of Peshawar Military Commission, Taliban leadership 22, April 2015.
20.   Source in the Taliban structure in Pakistan, November 2012.
21.   Source in the Taliban structure in Pakistan, September 2013.
22.   The issue was raised many times in interviews and in contacts in 2012–15.
23.   Taliban sources in Quetta, contacted August 2015.
24.   Taliban sources in Quetta, contacted August 2015.
25.   Source in the Taliban structure in Pakistan, June 2015.
26.   Taliban sources in Quetta, contacted August 2015.

27. Taliban sources in Quetta, contacted August 2015.
28. Taliban sources in Quetta, contacted October 2015.
29. Source in the Taliban structure in Pakistan, July 2015; Source in the Taliban structure in Pakistan, July 2015.
30. Source in the Taliban structure in Pakistan, October 2015.
31. Taliban sources in Quetta, contacted October 2015.
32. Source in the Taliban structure in Pakistan, November 2015; Source in the Taliban structure in Pakistan, December 2015.
33. Taliban sources in Quetta, contacted October 2015.
34. Interview with close collaborator of Mullah Mansur Dadullah, Taliban OP 143, November 2015.
35. Source in the Taliban structure in Pakistan, August 2015.
36. Ibid.
37. Ibid.
38. Ibid.
39. Ibid.
40. Source in the Taliban structure in Pakistan, October 2015.
41. Source in the Taliban structure in Pakistan, August 2015.
42. See on this: Gretchen Peters, *Seeds of Terror*; Mansfield, 'Understanding…'. Also on the evidence see: Burke, *9/11 wars*, Kindle edition Location 5848.
43. Source in the Taliban structure in Pakistan, February 2013; Interview with former member of Rahbari Shura, Taliban leadership 7, September 2014.
44. Taliban source within the Quetta Shura administration, contacted June 2015.
45. Interviews with finance commissions cadres in Quetta, Peshawar, Miran Shah and Mashhad, October 2015.
46. Interview with smuggler, Kandahar province, November 2015; Interview with smuggler, Nangarhar Province, October 2015; Interview with smuggler, Badakhshan province, November 2015; Interview with smuggler, Balkh Province, November 2015; Interview with smuggler, Parwan Province, November 2015.
47. Interview with smugger, Balkh Province, November 2015; Interview with smuggler, Nimruz Province, November 2015.
48. Interview with smuggler, Kandahar Province, November 2015; Interview with smuggler, Balkh province, November 2015; Interview with smuggler, Nangarhar Province, November 2015; Interview with smuggler, Badakhshan Province, November 2015; Interview with smugger, Balkh Province, November 2015.
49. Interview with smuggler, Badakhshan province, November 2015.
50. Source in the Taliban structure in Pakistan, September 2013.
51. Masadykov.
52. Taliban sources contacted in the Iran offices, summer 2013.
53. Interview with former cadre of Ghulam Yahya Akbari, Herat Taliban 1, December 2014.
54. Taliban sources contacted in the Iran offices, summer 2013.
55. Taliban sources contacted in Peshawar, May 2013.
56. Taliban sources contacted in the Mashhad Office, summer 2013.
57. Interview with Taliban trainee of the Pasdaran, Logar Province, September 2013.

58. Interview with commander of Pasdaran group in Takhar Province, September 2013.
59. Interview with senior member of Mashhad Office, Taliban Leadership 6, October 2014; Interview with close collaborator of Ali Reza Atah, Taliban leadership 12, January 2015; Interview with senior Taliban active in western Afghanistan, Leadership 5, October 2014.
60. Source in the Taliban structure in Pakistan, October 2012.
61. Taliban sources contacted in the Iran offices, summer 2013.
62. Taliban sources contacted in the Iran offices, summer 2013.
63. Interview with group commander, Cheshti Sharif, Herat Taliban 3, December 2014.
64. Source in the Taliban structure in Pakistan, October 2012.
65. Taliban sources contacted in the Iran offices, summer 2013; Source in the Taliban structure in Pakistan, August 2012.
66. Source in the Taliban structure in Pakistan, October 2012.
67. Taliban sources contacted in the Iran offices, summer 2013.
68. An interview with a provincial representative of Naim network in Oruzgan province, August 2013.
69. Taliban sources contacted in the Iran offices, summer 2013.
70. Interview with senior member of Mashhad Office, Taliban Leadership 6, October 2014; Interview with close collaborator of Ali Reza Atah, Taliban leadership 12, January 2015.
71. Interview with cadre, Zakir Mahaz, Helmand province (Kajaki), Helmand Taliban 1, December 2014.
72. Interview with senior Taliban active in western Afghanistan, Leadership 5, October 2014.
73. Interview with senior member of Mashhad Recruitment Commission, Taliban Leadership 35, July 2015; Interview with cadre, Zakir Mahaz, Helmand province (Kajaki), Helmand Taliban 1, December 2014.
74. Interview with commander of Abdullah Zekria, Herat Taliban 6, Shindand, December 2014.
75. Interview with senior Taliban active in western Afghanistan, Leadership 5, October 2014.
76. Interview with Rahbari Shura member, August 2015, Taliban Leadership 40; Interview with senior cadre of Quetta Shura, Taliban leadership 17, February 2015.
77. Source in the Taliban structure in Pakistan, June 2015.
78. Interview with member of Mashhad Military Commission, Taliban leadership 36, July 2015.
79. Ibid.
80. Source in the Taliban structure in Pakistan, June 2014; Interview with cadre, Zakir Mahaz, Helmand Province (Kajaki), Helmand Taliban 1, December 2014.
81. Source in the Taliban structure in Pakistan, August 2015.
82. Interview with former cadre of Ghulam Yahya Akbari, Herat Taliban 1, December 2014; Interview with commander of Amanullah Khan, Herat Taliban 2, December 2014; Interview with group commander, Cheshti Sharif, Herat Taliban 3, December 2014; Interview with group commander, Herat Taliban 5, December 2014; Interview with group commander, Shindand, Herat Taliban 5, December 2014.

83.   Interviews with Taliban cadre, Helmand, Taliban OP20, October 2014.

84.   Ibid.

85.   Ibid.

86.   Interview with senior member of the Mashhad Logistics Commission, Taliban Leadership 33, July 2015.

87.   Source in the Taliban structure in Pakistan, June 2015, (Meeting, 5 June 2015 in Tehran, Iran)

88.   Interview with senior Taliban active in western Afghanistan, Leadership 5, October 2014; Interview with member of Mashhad Military Commission, Taliban leadership 36, July 2015; Interview with senior Taliban active in western Afghanistan, Leadership 5, October 2014; Source in the Taliban structure in Pakistan, May 2015; Interview with group commander, Herat Taliban 5, December 2014.

89.   Interview with senior member of Mashhad office, Taliban Leadership 6, October 2014; Interview with senior Taliban active in western Afghanistan, Leadership 5, October 2014; Interview with commander of Abdullah Zekria, Herat Taliban 6, Shindand, December 2014.

90.   Interview with commander of Abdullah Zekria, Herat Taliban 6, Shindand, December 2014.

91.   Interview with senior Taliban active in western Afghanistan, Leadership 5, October 2014. October 2014.

92.   Interview with senior member of Mashhad office, Taliban Leadership 6, October 2014; Interview with senior Taliban active in western Afghanistan, Leadership 5, October 2014; Interview with senior member of Mashhad Office, Taliban Leadership 6, October 2014; Interview with commander of Abdullah Zekria, Herat Taliban 6, Shindand, December 2014.

93.   Interview with senior Taliban active in western Afghanistan, Leadership 5, October 2014; Interview with commander of Abdullah Zekria, Herat Taliban 6, Shindand, December 2014.

94.   Interview with commander of Abdullah Zekria, Herat Taliban 6, Shindand, December 2014.

95.   Interview with member of Mashhad Military Commission, Taliban leadership 36, July 2015.

96.   Interview with senior Taliban active in western Afghanistan, Leadership 5, October 2014.

97.   Interview with member of Mashhad Military Commission, Taliban leadership 36, July 2015.

98.   Interview with senior member of Mashhad office, Taliban Leadership 6, October 2014; Interview with commander of Abdullah Zekria, Herat Taliban 6, Shindand, December 2014; Interview with senior Taliban active in western Afghanistan, Leadership 5, October 2014.

99.   Interview with senior member of Mashhad Office, Taliban Leadership 6, October 2014.

100.  Interview with commander of Abdullah Zekria, Herat Taliban 6, Shindand, December 2014.

101.  Interview with senior member of Mashhad Office, Taliban Leadership 6, October 2014; Interview with senior Taliban active in western Afghanistan, Leadership 5, October 2014.

102.  Interview with senior Taliban active in western Afghanistan, Leadership 5, October 2014.

103.  Ibid.

104.  Interview with senior member of Mashhad Office, Taliban Leadership 6, October 2014.

105.  Ibid.

106.  Interview with commander of Abdullah Zekria, Herat Taliban 6, Shindand, December 2014.

107.  Interview with commander of Naim network, Helmand, Taliban OP 163, June 2013.

108.  Interview with former cadre of Ghulam Yahya Akbari, Herat Taliban 1, December 2014; Interview with commander of Amanullah Khan, Herat Taliban 2, December 2014; Interview with commander of Abdullah Zekria, Herat Taliban 6, Shindand, December 2014.

109.  Source in the Taliban structure in Pakistan, August 2015.

110.  Source in the Taliban structure in Pakistan, September 2015.

111.  Source in the Taliban structure in Pakistan, October 2015.

112.  Ibid.

113.  Ibid.; Borhan Osman, 'Toward Fragmentation? Mapping the post-Omar Taleban', Berlin: Afghanistan Analysts Network, 24 November 2015.

114.  Source in the Taliban structure in Pakistan, October 2015.

115.  Interview with close collaborator of Mullah Mansur Dadullah, Taliban OP 143, November 2015.

116.  Ibid.

117.  Source in the Taliban structure in Pakistan, October 2015.

118.  On this figure Taliban sources in Quetta and Rasool Shura members roughly agreed when contacted in early 2016.

119.  Interview with district governor of Rasool Shura, Zabul, Taliban OP 164, December 2016; Interview with group commander of the Rasool Shura, Zabul, Taliban OP 165, September 2016.

120.  Interview with member of Safi Shura, Nangarhar Taliban 2, April 2015; Interview with Nangarhar Taliban 3, Bati Kot, April 2015; Interview with senior member of Ijraya Shura, Taliban leadership 21, May 2015; Source in the Taliban structure in Pakistan, December 2013.

121.  Interview with senior member of Ijraya Shura, Taliban leadership 21, May 2015.

122.  Source in the Taliban structure in Pakistan, April 2016.

123.  Source in the Taliban structure in Pakistan, July 2013; Interview with cadre, Kapisa province, Taliban OP65, February 2014.

124.  Source in the Taliban structure in Pakistan, June 2013; Interview with senior member of Peshawar Military Commission, Taliban leadership 22, April 2015; Source in the Taliban structure in Pakistan, July 2013.

125.  Source in the Taliban structure in Pakistan, December 2013.

126. Source in the Taliban structure in Pakistan, August 2013.
127. Interview with senior member of Military commission, Peshawar, Taliban Leadership 22, May 2015.
128. Interview with deputy, Taliban Leadership 23, May 2015.
129. Interview with cadre, Baghlan Taliban 11, March 2015.
130. Interview with senior member of Abdul Majid Mahaz, Taliban leadership 2, September 2014.
131. Ibid.
132. Source in the Taliban structure in Pakistan, February 2015.
133. Interview with deputy, Peshawar Shura, Taliban leadership 23, May 2015.
134. Interview with senior member of Military commission, Peshawar, Taliban Leadership 22, May 2015.
135. Interview with deputy, Taliban Leadership 23, May 2015.
136. Ibid.; Interview with senior member of Military commission, Peshawar, Taliban Leadership 22, May 2015.
137. Interview with member of Peshawar Military Commission, Taliban leadership 37, July 2015; Source in the Taliban structure in Pakistan, June 2015.
138. Source in the Taliban structure in Pakistan, August 2015; Source in the Taliban structure in Pakistan, April 2016.
139. Interview with senior member of Intelligence department of the Peshawar Shura, Taliban leadership 42, July 2015.
140. Source in the Taliban structure in Pakistan, March 2015.
141. Interview with former Tora Bora Mahaz commander, Nangarhar Taliban 7, April 2015; Source in the Taliban structure in Pakistan, May 2015; Source in the Taliban structure in Pakistan, December 2015.
142. Interview with former commander Of Kabir, Hissarak, Nangarhar Taliban 1, April 2015.
143. Interview with Faryab Elder 1, Almar, May 2015; Interview with Faryab Elder 2, Almar, May 2015; Interview with Nangarhar Taliban 3, Bati Kot, April 2015. Interview with Faryab Elder 4, Khwaja Sabz Posh, May 2015; Interview with Faryab Elder 3, Qaysar, May 2015; Interview with Faryab Elder 4, Almar, May 2015; Interview with Faryab Elder 7, Qaysar, May 2015; Interview with Faryab Elder 8, Jhwaja Sabz Posh, May 2015.
144. Source in the Taliban structure in Pakistan, June 2015.
145. Sources in the Peshawar Shura, contacted in February, April and July 2016.
146. Interview with commander, Wardak Taliban 4, July 2014.
147. Interview with commander, Dahan-e Ghori, Baghlan Taliban 8, July 2014.
148. Interview with commander, Wardak (Chak), Taliban OP39, June 2014; Interview with commander, Wardak Taliban 8, Sayed Abad, July 2014; Interview with adviser to Serajuddin Haqqani, Leadership 10, January 2015.
149. Interview with commander, Ghazni Taliban 8, August 2014.
150. Interview with commander, Wardak Taliban 6, July 2014.
151. Interview with group commander, Shindand, Herat Taliban 5, December 2014.
152. Interview with fighter, Kandahar Taliban 1, August 2014.
153. Interview with group commander, Kandahar Taliban 2, August 2014.

154. Interview with fighter, Kandahar Taliban 6, Maruf, August 2014; Interview with fighter, Kandahar Taliban 7, Zherai, August 2014; Interview with fighter, Kandahar Taliban 8, Spin Boldak, August 2014; Interview with commander, Kandahar Taliban 9, Shorabak, August 2014; Interview with commander, Baghlan Jadid, Baghlan Taliban 4, September 2014; Interview with group commander, Herat Taliban 5, December 2014.
155. Interview with former commander, Nawur, Ghazni Taliban 17, May 2015.
156. Interview with Logar elder, Baraki Barak, Haqqani elder 1, February 2015.
157. Interview with fighter, Kandahar Taliban 7, Zherai, August 2014.
158. Interview with former commander, Arghandab, Kandahar Taliban 17, December 2014; Interview with former commander, Zherai, Kandahar Taliban 15, December 2014; Interview with former commander, Kandahar Taliban 16, Spin Boldak, December 2014.
159. Interview with former commander, Zherai, Kandahar Taliban 15, December 2014.
160. Interview with government official, Kandahar, May 2016.
161. Interview with Logar elder, Baraki Barak, Haqqani elder 1, February 2015; Interview with Haqqani elder 2, Mohamamd Agha, Logar, February 2015.
162. Interview with former fighter, Wardak Taliban 14, May 2015.
163. Interview with senior member of Intelligence department of the Peshawar Shura, Taliban leadership 42, July 2015.
164. Interview with senior member of Intelligence department of the Miran Shah Shura, Taliban Leadership 39, July 2015.
165. Interview with group commander, Cheshti Sharif, Herat Taliban 3, December 2014; Interview with fighter, Kandahar Taliban 7, Zherai, August 2014; Interview with fighter, Kandahar Taliban 8, Spin Boldak, August 2014; Interview with group commander, Herat Taliban 5, December 2014.
166. Interview with senior member of Peshawar Military Commission, Taliban leadership 22, April 2015.
167. Interview with senior member of Peshawar Military Commission, Taliban leadership 22, April 2015.
168. Interview with cadre, Paktia, Haqqani 4, February 2015.
169. Interview with senior member of Zerbati Commission, Miran Shah Shura, Taliban Leadership 14.
170. Interview with deputy, Miran Shah Shura, Taliban leadership 15, February 2015.
171. Interview with senior member of Zerbati Commission, Miran Shah Shura, Taliban Leadership 14.
172. Interview with fighter, Kandahar Taliban 1, August 2014.
173. Interview with commander, Baghlan Jadid, Baghlan Taliban 4, September 2014; Interview with fighter, Kandahar Taliban 7, Zherai, August 2014.
174. Source in the Taliban structure in Pakistan, September 2014.
175. Source in the Taliban structure in Pakistan, March 2015.
176. Interview with senior member of Peshawar Military Commission, Taliban leadership 22, April 2015.
177. Source in the Taliban structure in Pakistan, May 2015.
178. Source in the Taliban structure in Pakistan, June 2015.

179.  Source in the Taliban structure in Pakistan, April 2015; Interview with member of Miran Shah Military Commission, Taliban leadership 38, June 2015.

180.  Interview with member of Peshawar Military Commission, Taliban leadership 37, July 2015.

181.  Interview with senior cadre of Quetta Shura, Taliban leadership 17, February 2015; Interview with fighter, Kandahar Taliban 1, August 2014; Interview with group commander, Kandahar Taliban 2, August 2014; Interview with fighter, Kandahar Taliban 7, Zherai, August 2014; Interview with fighter, Kandahar Taliban 8, Spin Boldak, August 2014; Interview with commander, Kandahar Taliban 9, Shorabak, August 2014.

182.  Interview with fighter, Kandahar Taliban 6, Maruf, August 2014.

183.  Interview with member of Quetta Military Commission, Taliban Leadership 29, June 2015.

184.  Interview with Rahbari Shura member, August 2015, Taliban Leadership 40.

185.  Source in the Taliban structure in Pakistan, March 2015.

186.  Interview with senior member of Peshawar Military Commission, Taliban Leadership 22, April 2015.

187.  Source in the Taliban structure in Pakistan, June 2015.

188.  Interview with Taliban participant in the battle, August 2015; Abubakar Siddique, 'Taliban Victories in Helmand Province Prove Test for Afghan Government', *Terrorism Monitor*, XIV (12), 13 June 2016.

189.  Taliban sources in Quetta and Kunduz, contacted October 2015; Daniel Fisher and Christopher Mercado, 'Why Kunduz Fell', *Small Wars Journal*, 10 October 2016.

190.  Interview with adviser to Serajuddin Haqqani, Leadership 13, January 2015.

191.  Taliban source in Quetta, June 2015.

192.  Interview with member of political commission in Miran Shah Shura, Taliban Leadership 4, September 2014.

193.  Interview with member of political commission in Miran Shah Shura, Taliban Leadership 4, September 2014.

194.  Interview with member of Miran Shah Military Commission, Taliban leadership 38, June 2015; Interview with senior member of Zerbati Commission, Miran Shah Shura, Taliban leadership 14, January 2015; Interview with adviser to Serajuddin Haqqani, Leadership 10, January 2015; Interview with cadre, Paktia, Haqqani 4, February 2015.

195.  Interview with Toor-e Pagri commander, Bati Kot, Nangarhar Taliban 4, April 2015.

196.  Interviews with IS cadres in Nangarhar, 2015-16; contacts with Taliban cadres in Peshawar, 2015–16.

197.  Contacts with Taliban cadres in Peshawar and Miran Shahs, 2014–15.

198.  Interview with close collaborator of Mullah Mansur Dadullah, Taliban OP 143, November 2015.

199.  See: A. Giustozzi, *The Islamic State in Khorasan*, London: Hurst, 2018 for a full account of the expansion of IS in Afghanistan and its relationship with the Taliban.

200.  Interview with Faryab Elder 1, Almar, May 2015; Interview with Faryab Elder 4, Almar, May 2015; Interview with Faryab Elder 6, Qaysar, May 2015; Interview with Faryab Elder 7, Qaysar, May 2015; Interview with Baghlan elder 1, Dandi Ghori,

July 2014; Interview with Baghlan elder 8, Dandi Ghori, July 2014; Interview with Ghazni Elder 1, Rashidan, August 2014; Interview with Ghazni Elder 6, Andar, July 2014; Interview with Ghazni elder 9, Rashidan, July 2014; Interview with Ghazni Elder 10, Khogyani, July 2014; Interview with Herat elder 1, Pashtun Zarghun, April 2015; Interview with Herat elder 6, Chest-i Sharif, April 2015; Interview with Kandahar elder 4, Panjwai, February 2015; Interview with Wardak elder 2, Wardak, July 2014; Interview with Wardak elder 4, Sayed Abad, July 2014; Interview with Wardak elder 3, July 2014.

201. Interview with former commander, Arghandab, Kandahar Taliban 17, December 2014; Interview with former commander, Zherai, Kandahar Taliban 15, December 2014; Interview with former commander, Kandahar Taliban 16, Spin Boldak, December 2014.

202. Interview with former commander, Kandahar Taliban 16, Spin Boldak, December 2014; Interview with former commander, Zherai, Kandahar Taliban 15, December 2014.

203. Interview with former commander Of Kabir, Hissarak, Nangarhar Taliban 1, April 2015.

204. Interview with commander, Kandahar Taliban 13, Zherai, December 2014.

205. Interview with Ghazni Elder 3, Qarabagh, August 2014; Interview with Ghazni elder 2, Khogyani, August 2014; Interview with Wardak elder 5, Jaghatu, July 2015; Interview with Ghazni Elder 3, Qarabagh, August 2014.

206. Interview with Ghazni Elder 3, Qarabagh, August 2014.

207. See interview with Elder OP16, Sangin, April 2012; also interview with Elder OP4, Musa Qala, 8 March 2012.

208. Interview with Kandahar elder 3, Panjwai, February 2015; Interview with Baghlan elder 10, Dandi Ghori, July 2014; Interview with Baghlan elder 3, Baghlan Jadid, July 2014; Interview with Baghlan elder 6, Dandi Ghori, July 2014; Interview with Baghlan Elder 7, July 2014; Interview with Kandahar elder 5, Maiwand, February 2015; Interview with Baghlan elder 3, Baghlan Jadid, July 2014; Interview with Herat elder 3, member of Peace Committee, April 2015; Interview with Wardak elder 7, Sayed Abad, July 2014.

209. Interview with Baghlan elder 1, Dandi Ghori, July 2014.

210. Interview with Baghlan elder 8, Dandi Ghori, July 2014.

211. Interview with Kandahar elder 8, Dand, February 2015; Interview with Kandahar Elder 6, Zherai, February 2015.

212. Interview with former senior member of Gardi Jangal Shura, Kandahar Taliban 19, July 2015.

213. Interview with Baghlan elder 2, Baghlan Jadid, July 2014; Interview with Baghlan elder 3, Baghlan Jadid, July 2014; Interview with Baghlan elder 4, Baghlan Jadid, July 2014.

214. Interview with Baghlan elder 1, Dandi Ghori, July 2014.

215. Interview with commander, Burka, Baghlan, September 2014.

216. Interview with local researcher from Nahrin, Pul-e Khomri, June 2010.

217. Kandahar elder 1, Zhirai, November 2014.

218. Interview with Herat Elder 7, Chest-i Sharif, April 2015.

219. Interview with Kandahar elder 5, Maiwand, February 2015; Interview with Kandahar elder 3, Panjwai, February 2015.

220. Interview with Kandahar Elder 15, February 2015.

221. Interview with Herat elder 2, Pashtun Zarghun, April 2015; Interview with Nangarhar elder 8, Shinwar, March 2015; Interview with Faryab Elder 2, Almar, May 2015; Interview with Faryab Elder 3, Qaysar, May 2015; Interview with Faryab Elder 4, Almar, May 2015; Interview with Faryab Elder 8, Khwaja Sabz Posh, May 2015; Interview with Baghlan elder 9, Burka, July 2014; Interview with Baghlan elder 3, Baghlan Jadid, July 2014; Interview with Baghlan elder 4, Baghlan Jadid, July 2014; Interview with Herat elder 5, Shindand, April 2015; Interview with Herat Elder 7, Chest-i Sharif, April 2015; Interview with Nangarhar elder 3, Bati Kot, March 2015; Interview with Nangarhar elder 4, Spin Ghar, March 2015; Interview with Nangarhar elder 5, Khogyani, March 2015; Interview with Nangarhar elder 7, Achin, March 2015; Interview with Nangarhar elder 8, Shinwar, March 2015; Interview with Nangarhar elder 5, Khogyani, March 2015; Interview with Baghlan elder 4, Baghlan Jadid, July 2014.

222. Interview with Nangarhar elder 9, Khogyani, March 2015.

223. Interview with Ghazni elder 3, August 2014.

224. Interview with Adviser, Pakistan, Adviser 2, July 2015.

225. Iranian adviser to Jundullah, Advisers 3, July 2015.

226. Bill Roggio, 'US commander in Afghanistan downplays Taliban control of 10 percent of population', *The Long War Journal*, 23 September 2016.

227. Interview with senior member of Zerbati Commission, Miran Shah Shura, Taliban Leadership 14.

228. Source in the Taliban structure in Pakistan, August 2014.

229. Interview with commission member, Quetta, Taliban leadership 1, September 2014.

230. Interview with deputy, Peshawar Shura, Taliban leadership 23, May 2015.

231. Source in the Taliban structure in Pakistan, September 2015.

232. Source in the Taliban structure in Pakistan, October 2015.

## 8. CONCLUSION

1. Interview with the Dadullah Mahaz, July 2013, Kandahar Taliban 3, August 2014.

2. Interview with former fighter, Wardak Taliban 14, May 2015; Interview with former Taliban commander, Mohammad Agha (Logar), Haqqani Taliban 11, March 2015.

3. Interview with commander, Ghazni Taliban 8, August 2014; Martin, *An Intimate War*, p. 203.

4. Interview with Haji Akhtar Muhammad Safi, member of Safi Shura.

5. Interview with former group commander of the Mansur Mahaz, Ghazni Taliban 16, May 2015.

6. See also: Jack Fairweather, *The Good War: Why We Couldn't Win the War or the Peace in Afghanistan*, Kindle edition, locations 1591–1611, 1767ff; Anand Gopal, *No Good Men Among the Living: America, the Taliban, and the War through Afghan Eyes*, Kindle edition, locations 1814ff, 3141ff; 3202ff.

7. Interview with fighter, Kandahar Taliban 1, August 2014.

8.   Interview with former commander, Baghlan Taliban 16, May 2015; Interview with former fighter, Baghlan Taliban 15, May 2015; Interview with former group commander of Mansur Mahaz, Ghazni Taliban 16, May 2015; Interview with former commander, Baradar Mahaz, Ghazni Taliban 15, May 2015; Interview with former commander, Nawur, Ghazni Taliban 17, May 2015; Interview with former fighter, Wardak Taliban 14, May 2015; Interview with former commander, Wardak Taliban 15, May 2015; Interview with commander, Baghlan Taliban 17, May 2015; Interview with former commander, Baghlan Taliban 18, May 2015; Interview with former commander, Taliban Kandahar 20, May 2015; Interview with former commander, Kandahar Taliban 21, May 2015; Interview with former commander, Dadullah Mahaz, Kandahar Taliban 22, July 2015; Gopal, 'The Battle for Afghanistan'; Interview with commander, Kapisa Taliban 1, March 2015; Interview with commander, Sorkhrod, Nangarhar Taliban 9, March 2015; Interview with Uruzgan Taliban 1, Shahid Hassas, commander, March 2015; Interview with former commander, Shindand, Herat Taliban 8, December 2014; Interview with fighter, Paktia, Haqqani 3, February 2015; Interview with fighter, Paktika, Haqqani 6, February 2015; Interview with commander, Logar (Mohammad Agha), Haqqani 9, February 2015; Interview with former Taliban commander, Mohammad Agha (Logar), Haqqani Taliban 11, March 2015; Interview with cadre, Wardak, Taliban OP31, June 2013.

9.   Interview with Baghlan elder 9, Burka, July 2014.

10.  Commander, Wardak Taliban 5, July 2014.

11.  Interview with Baghlan elder 1, Dandi Ghori, July 2014.

12.  Interview with fighter, Paktia, Haqqani 3, February 2015.

13.  Interview with Helmand elder 1, Sangin, April 2015.

14.  Interview with former Taliban cadre, Kandahar, July 2015, Kandahar Taliban 18.

15.  Interview with commander, Logar (Mohammad Agha), Haqqani 9, February 2015; Interview with fighter, Paktika, Haqqani 6, February 2015; Interview with commander, Logar, Haqqani 7, February 2015; Interview with cadre, Paktia, Haqqani 5, February 2015; Interview with fighter, Paktia, Haqqani 3, February 2015; Interview with group commander, Khost, Haqqani 2, January 2015.

16.  Interview with commander, Baghlan Taliban 6, Baghlan Jadid, September 2014.

17.  Interview with commander, Baghlan Taliban 1, September 2014.

18.  Interview with Taliban electoral commissioner in Baghlan, 2014.

19.  Sarah Ladbury in collaboration with Cooperation for Peace and Unity (CPAU), Independent Report For The Department Of International Development (DFID), Testing Hypotheses On Radicalisation In Afghanistan, 'Why do men join the Taliban and Hizb-i Islami? How much do local communities support them?', Report, 14 August 2009, Kabul, p. 17.

20.  Interview with Nangarhar Taliban 3, Bati Kot, April 2015.

21.  Interview with former fighter, Baghlan Taliban 15, May 2015; Interview with former commander, Faruq Mahaz, Kandahar Taliban 10, Maruf, December 2014; Interview with former commander, Kandahar Taliban 16, Spin Boldak, December 2014; Interview with former commander of Faruq Mahaz, Maywand, December 2014 (Kandahar Taliban 11); Interview with former commander, Baradar Mahaz, Ghazni

Taliban 15, May 2015; Interview with former group commander of the Mansur Mahaz, Ghazni Taliban 16, May 2015.

22.　Interview with commander, Kandahar Taliban 13, Zherai, December 2014.

23.　Interview with former commander, Faruq Mahaz, Kandahar Taliban 10, Maruf, December 2014.

24.　Interview with former commander, Arghandab, Kandahar Taliban 17, December 2014.

25.　Interview with former commander, Faruq Mahaz, Maywand, December 2014 (Kandahar Taliban 11).

26.　Interview with former Taliban cadre, Kandahar, July 2015, Kandahar Taliban 18; Interview with former Taliban member, Helmand, July 2015, Helmand Taliban 2; Interview with former commander, Zherai, Kandahar Taliban 15; Interview with former commander, Nawur, Ghazni Taliban 17, May 2015; Interview with former commander, Baradar Mahaz, Ghazni Taliban 15, May 2015; Interview with former commander, Arghandab, Kandahar Taliban 17, December 2014; Interview with former commander, Nawur, Ghazni Taliban 17, May 2015; Interview with former commander, Wardak Taliban 15, May 2015; Interview with former commander, Baghlan Taliban 18, May 2015; Interview with former commander, Kandahar Taliban 21, May 2015; Interview with former commander, Daddullah Mahaz, Kandahar Taliban 22, July 2015; Interview with former fighter, Baghlan Taliban 15, May 2015.

27.　Interview with former commander, Kandahar Taliban 16, Spin Boldak, December 2014; Interview with former commander, Zherai, Kandahar Taliban 15.

28.　Interview with former commander of the Faruq Mahaz, Maywand, December 2014 (Kandahar Taliban 11).

29.　Interview with Commander, Ghazni (Andar), August 2014, Ghazni Taliban 10.

30.　Interview with former senior member of Gardi Jangal Shura, Kandahar Taliban 19, July 2015.

31.　'Independent review of Afghanistan 1393 national budget', Kabul: EPD, 2014.

32.　Interview with deputy, Quetta, Taliban Leadership 14, July 2015.

33.　Source in the Peshawar Shura administration, November 2013.

34.　See also: Peters, *Seeds of Terror*, p. 118

35.　Interviews with Taliban commander, Helmand, Taliban OP19, September 2011.

36.　Peters, *Seeds of Terror*, p. 126.

37.　Source in the Taliban structure in Pakistan, February 2013.

38.　Source in the Taliban structure in Pakistan, June 2015; Interviews with Taliban cadre, Helmand, Taliban OP20, October 2014.

39.　Interviews with Taliban commanders, Helmand, Taliban OP18, 3 March 2012.

40.　Interviews with Taliban commanders, Sayedabad, 2012.

41.　Source within the Quetta Shura, November 2016.

42.　Thomas A. Baylis, *Governing By Committee: Collegial Leadership in Advanced Societies*, New York: SUNY Press, 1989, p. 7.

43.　Baylis, p. 5.

# INDEX

INDEX

INDEX